British Liberalism and the United States

British Liberalism and the United States

Political and Social Thought in the Late Victorian Age

Murney Gerlach
Director
The Rhode Island Historical Society
USA

First published 2001 by
PALGRAVE
Houndmills, Basingstoke, Hampshire RG21 6XS and
175 Fifth Avenue, New York, N. Y. 10010
Companies and representatives throughout the world

PALGRAVE is the new global academic imprint of
St. Martin's Press LLC Scholarly and Reference Division and
Palgrave Publishers Ltd (formerly Macmillan Press Ltd).

ISBN 0–333–79009–X

This book is printed on paper suitable for recycling and
made from fully managed and sustained forest sources.

A catalogue record for this book is available
from the British Library.

Library of Congress Cataloging-in-Publication Data
Gerlach, Murney, 1950–
    British liberalism and the United States : political and
    social thought in the late Victorian age / Murney Gerlach.
        p. cm.
    Includes bibliographical references and index.
    ISBN 0–333–79009–X
    1. Liberalism—Great Britain—History—19th century.
    2. Great Britain—Politics and government—1837–1901.
    3. Liberalism—United States—History—19th century.
    4. United States—Politics and government—1865–1900.
    5. Great Britain—Relations—United States. 6. United
    States—Relations—Great Britain. I. Title.
    JC574.2.G7 G47 2001
    320.51'0941'09034—dc21
                                                        2001021872

10   9   8   7   6   5   4   3   2   1
10   09 08 07 06 05 04 03 02 01

Printed and bound in Great Britain by
Antony Rowe Ltd, Chippenham, Wiltshire

The England and the America of the present are probably the two strongest nations in the world. But there can hardly be a doubt as between the America and the England of the future, that the daughter, at some no very distant time, will, whether fairer or less fair, be unquestionably yet stronger than the mother.

O matre forti filia fortior

And for the political students all over the world it will beyond anything curious as well as useful to examine with what diversities, as well as what resemblances, of apparatus the two greater branches of a race born to command have been minded, or induced, or constrained, to work out, in their sea severed seats, their political destinies according to their respective laws.

William E. Gladstone, 'Kin Beyond Sea,'
North American Review, vol. cxxvii
(Sept.-Oct. 1878), p. 181

Contents

List of Abbreviations   x

Acknowledgements   xii

Preface   xiv

1 The Formation of American Relationships and Interests   1
   Introduction   1
   The American Civil War   5
   Fenianism, the *Alabama* claims, and the Geneva Treaty,
      1865–74   11
   British Liberals and their early American interests   13
   Charles Dilke: an American trip in 1866   17
   John Morley: an American trip and early interests   21
   James Bryce: early American impressions   26
   Conclusion   29
   Notes   30

2 Liberalism and the United States: Expanding
   American Activities, 1874–1880   38
   Introduction   38
   Lord Rosebery: America discovered   40
   William E. Gladstone and 'Kin Beyond Sea'   48
   Young Radicals and the United States: Dilke,
      Morley, and Chamberlain   57
   Conclusion   63
   Notes   64

3 The Liberal Ascendancy, Ireland, and Henry
   George, 1880–1886   71
   Introduction   71
   British foreign policy towards the United States,
      1880–85   73
   American protectionism and tariffs   76
   Anglo-American accord   78
   Irish-Americans, Fenians, and violence   81
   Henry George and land reform   94
   The American Constitution, federalism, and Home Rule   101

Conclusion 108
Notes 110

4 Gladstonian Liberalism, Home Rule, and American
Politics and Society, 1886–1892 121
Introduction 121
American federalism reconsidered 124
American protectionism and tariffs reconsidered 133
American currency and bimetallism 139
Anglo-American copyright 142
Gladstone: American activities and political issues 145
Conclusion 152
Notes 153

5 Liberal Ministries, Ideas, and Andrew Carnegie,
1892–1895 163
Introduction 163
American foreign policies 165
Irish Home Rule: American federal and constitutional
experiences 170
Silver, bimetallism, and currency issues 176
Liberal attitudes towards American labor, society,
and democracy 185
Andrew Carnegie: a transatlantic liberal 197
Conclusion 201
Notes 201

6 Venezuela, Silver, and Rapprochement, 1895–1898 211
Introduction 211
Anglo-Americans and international arbitration 213
Silver and bimetallism: final reconsiderations 217
Liberalism and informal diplomacy over Venezuela 219
The Venezuelan Settlement and Anglo-American
arbitration 227
Silver and the Presidential election of 1896 235
Studies of democracy 238
Silver and bimetallism defeated, 1896–97 241
Conclusion 244
Notes 246

Conclusion   257

Appendices
  I Biographical and American Notes   265
 II Dinner Engagements of William
      Hoppin and Henry White, 1870s–1890s   272
III Letter from Gresham to Rosebery, 1895   275

Bibliography   276

Index   305

List of Abbreviations

Abbreviations used for private papers:

BP	Bryce Papers
Car.P	Carnegie Papers
Ch.P	Chamberlain Papers
DP	Dilke Papers
God.P	Godkin Papers
GP	Gladstone Papers
HP	Harcourt Papers
LP	Lowell Papers
NP	Norton Papers
RP	Rosebery Papers
WP	Henry White Papers

Abbreviations used for printed works:

AHR	*American Historical Review*
AM	*Atlantic Monthly*
CHR	*Canadian Historical Review*
CM	*Cornhill Magazine*
CR	*Contemporary Review*
Econ.HR	*Economic History Review*
EHR	*English Historical Review*
FR	*Fortnightly Review*
HJ	*Historical Journal*
IHRB	*Institute of Historical Research Bulletin*
JAS	*Journal of American Studies*
JBS	*Journal of British Studies*
JHI	*Journal of the History of Ideas*
MM	*Macmillan's Magazine*
MVHR	*Mississippi Valley Historical Review*
NAR	*North American Review*
Nat.R	*National Review*
NC	*Nineteenth Century*
Ne.R	*New Review*
PHR	*Pacific Historical Review*
PMG	*Pall Mall Gazette*

PP	*Parliamentary Papers*
PR	*Progressive Review*
RR	*Review of Reviews*
TRHS	*Transactions of the Royal Historical Society*
YC	*Youth's Companion*

Acknowledgements

I must thank many individuals and note the great help that many libraries and research repositories have given me in the course of the work on this book. I must comment in particular on the debt of gratitude that I have to a number of specific individuals, libraries, and research entities for their kind permission to cite from private manuscript and paper holdings. I wish to thank especially the staffs of the Bodleian Library, Oxford; the British Library; the Library of Congress; and the Brown University libraries, among many others.

From repositories in the United Kingdom, I would like to thank the Hon. Mrs. Crispin Gascoigne for permission to cite from the Harcourt Papers; Special Collections at the main Library of the University of Birmingham to cite from the Chamberlain Papers; the Public Record Office to quote from various Crown copyright materials, including Cabinet Papers and Foreign Office Papers; the British Library of Political & Economical Science for the rights to make references to the T. H. Farrer Papers; The Trustees of the National Library of Scotland to cite from the Rosebery Papers; Gillian Ingall, for permission to cite from the Bryce Papers in the Bodleian Library; and the British Library for regular and periodic permission to cite from papers in its various collections, especially the papers of William E. Gladstone.

From repositories in the United States I would like to thank the Houghton Library at Harvard University for permission to quote from a number of holdings and papers; the Library of Congress, especially to cite from the Thomas Bayard, Andrew Carnegie, John Hay, Whitelaw Reid, and Theodore Roosevelt collections; the New York Public Library for permission to quote from the Andrew Carnegie Autograph Collection, Henry George Papers, William Ewart Gladstone Papers, Albert Shaw Papers, and Samuel Ward Papers; the Massachusetts Historical Society to cite from the Dana Family Papers, Winthrop Family Papers, Edward Atkinson Papers, Grenville H. Norcross Autograph Collection; the Huntington Library to quote from the George Smalley Manuscripts; the Moncure Conway Papers, Rare Book and Manuscript Library, Columbia University; and the Boston Public Library/Rare Books Department, Courtesy of the Trustees, to publish and quote from the Kate Field Papers.

My gratitude too exists to my family, friends and colleagues who have stood by me and helped with their professional and moral support as I worked on this book over a long period of time. My study of Anglo-American relations in the nineteenth century started in the 1970s, when I worked on an MA thesis looking at the relationship of the London *Times* with American news. That interest carried over into my doctoral work at Oxford University in the late 1970s and early 1980s, under the tutelage and support of the late Herbert Nicholas and Colin Matthew, and also my former supervisor Kenneth O. Morgan, The Queen's College, Oxford. This work is based fundamentally on the dissertation, which I now have had a chance to revisit and bring to light, little work having been advanced over the period of two decades on this rich and fascinating period of history, though many monographs and reinterpretations have been produced on British political and social thought, especially British liberalism. Thus to many I owe much, and for reading drafts of this book recently: Floyd Parsons (especially for his most careful and considered review of the complete manuscript), Peter Stansky, Eugenio Biagini, Kenneth O. Morgan, and for reviewing and commenting on earlier versions, Colin Matthew, G. H. Le May, A. E. Campbell, and my father Lee Gerlach. I am also very grateful for the support, friendship, and advice of many over the years who have helped me, especially Duncan MacLeod, David J. Weber, Author E. Hughes, Perry Curtis, Joyce O. Appleby, James O. Gump, Iris Engstrand, Kenneth Wilburn, Bruce Hoffman, Dorothy Gerlach, my late mother Katherine Gerlach, and Vartan Gregorian. I have gained much from the writings of James Bryce and his American interests by Hugh Tulloch, and from the insights on Victorian politics of Angus Hawkins and Eugenio Biagini. I must thank also the Board and the staff of the Rhode Island Historical Society, for the chance to make a new home in the Society as its director, and to sit in the former bedroom, now my office, of the late Senator Nelson Aldrich; to Al Klyberg and James K. Mahoney, in particular, for their friendship and encouragement of this project while carrying on with my regular duties. I wish too to thank Carol Holscher, my secretary at the Society, for her constant assistance, and Anne Rafique for her meticulous and close reading and editing of the manuscript. Most of all, to my wife Shirl, and four children, whose hours I interrupted and family plans I skewed over the years, to Chris, Brendan, Julia, and Greg, I owe and thank the most. To be a part of my family has been the most wonderful reward in life.

Dr. Murney Gerlach

Aldrich House
The Rhode Island Historical Society
Providence, Rhode Island

January, 2001

Preface

During the period following the American Civil War, the United States turned inward, conscious of the need to rebuild after several years of horrendous destruction. There was a vast wave of exuberance in the tremendous American potential for self-development. American growth during the Gilded Age has few, if any, parallels in modern history. Between 1860 and 1900, American population more than doubled, industrial output soared, and new commercial and territorial empires were acquired throughout the world. Thus, by the dawn of the twentieth century, she became an imperial power, in many respects, as great a power as the older nation states of Europe: France, Spain, Germany, and Great Britain. Old World acquiescence to the greatness of the United States came haltingly throughout the nineteenth century; in the end it finally was granted. The British had a special interest in her progress in that America was her offspring, shared her heritage, customs, and language. The habitual jealousy between the two Anglo-Saxon countries persisted, but in the long run progress for the one has largely meant progress for the other. Gladstone's realization – *O matre forti filia fortior* – that the daughter was so much more powerful than the mother came relatively early compared with that of other late Victorian statesmen.[1] By the start of the twentieth century few voices would hesitate at the truth that lay behind evocations to the effect that Britain and America would be equal partners in the grand Anglo-Saxon future.

This study is concerned mainly with the political and social ideas of the leading Liberal politicians in the late Victorian age, but it also discusses these topics in association with the thoughts of American politicians and individuals active in the context of Anglo-American relations between the end of the American Civil War and the start of the twentieth century. The study's limits fundamentally revolve around an analysis of the dominant themes at the hiatus of the Liberal age in the politics of Great Britain in the late Victorian Age. It is an attempt to examine the relationships of these politicians with the United States during a period of placid Anglo-American diplomatic relations, bounded by two periods of intense activity – the settlement of the *Alabama* claims in the Geneva Treaty in 1871–72, and the settlement of the Venezuelan boundary dispute in 1896–97. Yet this was a period, according to the historian H. C. Allen, when there was 'the ripening of cordiality and laying the groundwork for actual international coopera-tion.'[2]

The extensive and variable connections that existed between influen-tial Victorian Liberals and the United States as well as what they imag-ined, observed, and understood about the country are traced. Visits to America, friendships and correspondence with Americans, and pro-nouncements upon American developments reveal both favorable and critical views of the country. The central characters are William E. Gladstone, Lord Rosebery, John Morley, Sir William V. Harcourt and James Bryce, but other Liberals, some Conservatives and Liberal-Unionists, and various Americans come into focus at important stages of this study. I turn my attention towards a series of problems which can perhaps best be stated in the form of questions. How attentively did Liberal leaders follow developments in the United States? Which American issues were most seriously examined, and why? Did Liberal leaders form sympathies for the people and institutions of the United States similar to those which James Bryce, an astute student of American politics and the author of the seminal examination of America in our period, *The American Commonwealth*, so clearly held? And finally, did American friendships, methods of government, or modes of behavior have any influence on the actions and political philosophies of Liberal leaders? How did the United States impact upon British Liberalism in the late Victorian age?

In responding to these questions, my debt to other historians becomes evident. More than forty years ago, the late Henry Pelling described the changing, and even completely reversing, shifts of British political opinion towards the United States. From 1900, the increasingly socialistically oriented British 'left' viewed with some aversion aspects of American democratic experiences, whereas in 1867 the same radical wing – even the same men in many cases – had acclaimed the republic's triumph in the Civil War as a major stimulus for progressive reform in Britain.[3] Hugh Tulloch, in *James Bryce's American Commonwealth: The Anglo-American Background* and in an article, 'Changing British Attitudes towards the United States in the 1880s,'[4] discussed the nuances and shifts in British Liberal opinion towards America. He focused attention on Liberal academics in addition to Bryce, notably Edward A. Freeman, Lord Acton, A. V. Dicey and Goldwin Smith. Such issues as the merits of the American Constitution were 'unobtrusive but active element[s] in the political discourse of Britain in the 1880s and with particular reference to the Irish question.'[5] In addition, Edmund Ions succeeded in reaffirming Bryce's wide range of American connections.[6] The late Robert Kelley, an American historian of intellectual movements, traced the similarities between the political ideologies and progressive outlooks of transatlantic liberal personalities, including Gladstone and President Grover Cleveland.[7] And Jon Roper discussed British and American critics of democracy, primarily concentrating on the early and mid-nineteenth century, including figures such as Matthew Arnold, John Stuart Mill, Thomas Carlyle, John Ruskin, and William Morris.[8] Finally, a long overdue re-evaluation of the importance of Great Britain to American foreign policy in the second half of the nineteenth century appeared about twenty years ago in a work by Charles Campbell.[9] It becomes overwhelmingly evident on the basis of work by a number of historians that British Liberals had real and vigorous connections with the United States.

In the past decade or so there have been a number of excellent studies of British Liberalism, analyses of the rise and fall of government and party from the 1850s through the 1890s. Works by Jonathan Parry, Eugenio Biagini, Angus Hawkins, Alan Sykes, Terry Jenkins, and Michael Bentley have examined the Liberal, and also the Conservative, age of the late nineteenth century.[10] *The Gladstone Diaries*, edited by the late Colin Matthew, have illuminated for many the details of the dominating Liberal figure of the age. The general notion that the impact of the United States on British reformers was intermittent and partial at best needs closer examination.[11] As Eugenio Biagini has commented recently, 'it was the United States that was most admired by British democrats.' He also found that working-class radical and plebeian groups demonstrated 'interest, even euphoria, over the progress and events towards the North and President Lincoln's legacy at the time of the American Civil War.'[12]

It also becomes apparent that there are certain limitations to my predecessors' evaluations of the Liberal–American relationship. Thus, for instance, in Roy Jenkins' seminal and beautifully written study of Gladstone, there are very few remarks upon Gladstone's American interests, his agonizing over his position regarding the South during the Civil War or his warm acquaintance with the industrialist Andrew Carnegie.[13] More recently, Gladstone's American interests have been recognized;[14] but in these various cases, my debt to other historians grows conspicuously for these recognized lapses in the social and political aspects of Anglo-American relations in the late Victorian age.

Several myths have been inadvertently perpetuated about Anglo-American history in the late Victorian age. The view that British Liberals and radicals in the 1880s and 1890s turned against the virtues of American democracy, which Conservatives praised, disguises both the increasingly wide variety of American interests and the opinions of British statesmen. A continuing fascination of historians with James Bryce has tended to obscure the important transatlantic roles of other leading Liberals. By the end of the nineteenth century, Gladstone, Morley, Rosebery, and Harcourt, among others, had established reputations on both sides of the Atlantic for their pronouncements upon the United States. Kelley has described the transatlantic community in the age of Gladstone, but he says nothing about the direct associations of actual personalities and the influences these may have had on British and American history. In a book review, John Sproat laments 'the dearth of specific materials' concerning relations among British and American reformers during the Gilded Age.[15] Yet contrary to his view, there exists a wide variety of materials. Finally, while European influences upon the mind of American Progressives have been weighed importantly, little has been said about the impact of American ideas on either the British political mind or life.[16] Such influences became much more pervasive in the 1900s, as has been so well demonstrated by Daniel T. Rodgers in *Atlantic Crossings. Social Politics in a Progressive Age*, but they certainly were not insignificant in the period between the 1860s and 1890s.[17]

Influence, obviously, can be both positive and negative. It is a primary purpose of this study to shed greater light on the relationship between British Liberalism and the United States: to arrive at a more balanced understanding of the rich social and political themes in transatlantic history. To produce such a synthesis, it is patently necessary to build upon the pioneering historical work of others. On the other hand, access to a plethora of sources, both primary and secondary, on both sides of the Atlantic, has enabled this study to take on a character independent from any which has preceded it. From the point of view of British history, the United States is viewed as a minor theme, but one which nonetheless surfaces significantly at times in debates on major internal and external issues: Irish Home Rule, free trade versus fair trade, isolationist or aggressive foreign policies, bimetallism, and currency reforms. From the point of view of American history, British Liberalism often had noticeable, even sizeable, impacts upon American reformers, political leaders, and events, and stood out as a model for reform-minded American leaders.

This study is necessarily selective. While it essentially moves forward in a chronological fashion, it pauses at times to examine more fully certain key events or ideas. Since events and ideas intermingle to spark the Liberals, and liberalism's relationship with the United States, they are discussed within the context of each other rather than in separate sections covering connections and themes.

There is one final qualification upon this study. In the sense that British historians have described the actual events, trends, and ideas which constitute British history and American historians have done likewise for their respective topics, it is necessary to reconstruct the history between the two countries as a separate historical manifestation with elements of British and American history but also as a single unique tapestry and compound. This study falls under the mantles of diplomatic, intellectual, political, and social history. My paramount aim is to establish the nature of transatlantic links, their frequency as well as their character, for only then is it possible to estimate the real impact that individuals and their ideas from one side of the Atlantic may have had on their compatriots on the other side.

Notes

1. 'Kin Beyond Sea,' *North American Review*, vol. cxxvii (Sept.–Oct. 1878), p. 181.
2. *Great Britain and the United States. A History of Anglo-American Relations (1783–1952)* (London, 1954), p. 519.
3. *American and the British Left: From Bright to Bevan* (New York, 1957).
4. James Bryce's *American Commonwealth: The Anglo-American Background* (Woodbridge, 1988) and 'Changing British Attitudes towards the United States in the 1880s,' *Historical Journal*, vol. xx (1977), pp. 825–40.
5. *James Bryce's American Commonwealth*, p. 128.
6. *James Bryce and American Democracy, 1870–1922* (London, 1968).
7. *The Transatlantic Persuasion: The Liberal-Democratic Mind in the Age of Gladstone* (New York, 1969).
8. *Democracy and its Critics: Anglo-American Democratic Thought in the Nineteenth Century* (London, 1989).
9. *The Transformation of American Foreign Relations, 1865–1900* (New York, 1976).
10. Jonathan Parry, *The Rise and Fall of Liberal Government in Victorian Britain* (New Haven, CT, 1993); Eugenio F. Biagini, *Liberty, Retrenchment and Reform. Popular Liberalism in the Age of Gladstone, 1860–1880* (Cambridge, 1992); Alan Sykes, *The Rise and Fall of British Liberalism 1776–1988* (London, 1997); T. A. Jenkins, *The Liberal Ascendancy, 1830–1886* (London, 1994); Angus Hawkins, *British Party Politics, 1852–1886* (London, 1988); and Michael Bentley, *The Climax of Liberal Politics. British Liberalism in Theory and Practice 1868–1918* (London, 1987).
11. Kenneth O. Morgan, 'The Future at Work: Anglo-American Progressivism 1890–1917,' in H. C. Allen and Roger Thompson (eds), *Contrast and*

Connection: Bicentennial Essays in Anglo-American History (London, 1976), p. 251.

12. *Liberty, Retrenchment and Reform,* p. 69.
13. Roy Jenkins, *Gladstone. A Biography* (New York, 1995) and Richard Shannon, *Gladstone. Volume One. 1809–1865* (Chapel Hill, NC, 1992) and *Gladstone: The Heroic Minister, 1865–1898* (London, 1999).
14. Peter J. Parish, 'Gladstone and America,' in P. J. Waller (ed.), *Politics and Social Change in Modern Britain* (London, 1998).
15. Review of Richard Titlow's *American Import Merit: Origins of the United States. Civil Service and the Influence of the British Model* (Washington, 1979) in the *American Historical Review,* vol. lxxxv, no. i (Feb. 1980), p. 225.
16. M. B. Stokes, 'The Origin of the Progressive Mind in the United States: the social thoughts of twelve progressive publicists in the period up to 1910' (Oxford Univ. DPhil thesis, 1977).
17. (Cambridge, MA: 1998). See especially chapter 2, 'The Atlantic World', pp. 33–75.

1
The Formation of American Relationships and Interests

Introduction

In February 1874, William Ewart Gladstone resigned from the premiership following an election earlier in the month in which the Conservatives led by Benjamin Disraeli had won a clear parliamentary majority of 52. The Liberal government of 1868–74 had been a memorable one. The party, inspired by its leader and the general reform impulse set in motion by the act of 1867, responded with the passage of a series of well-known measures, including Forster's Education Bill, Cardwell's army reforms, Bruce's Licensing Bill, reform of the civil service and judicature, and the Irish Land Act. The leaders and the party had worked together in a surprisingly harmonious fashion to produce an ' "era of liberation" in reform politics.'[1] There were no obvious reasons why the Liberals would not return to similarly constructive policies after a period of rest and re-evaluation of individual, party and national responsibilities. In fact, their retirement from office was for a long six years. Their policies would never be so productive or their party so cohesive throughout the remainder of the nineteenth century as during Gladstone's first ministry.

Certain other Liberals emerged as leaders of their party in Parliament and the country during the late Victorian age. Unquestionably, Gladstone, already the Grand Old Man, was the dominating figure of British Liberalism while he was alive. Whether in command of the government or in retirement, his deeply intense, moralistic, perverse, but always compelling personality inspired major national movements and dictated the fortunes of other Liberal leaders. His passion for overriding, single moral causes constantly threatened throughout his life to call him forth into the political arena – hence, in part, his campaigns

1

for franchise reform, anti-Beaconsfieldism, and Home Rule for Ireland. Unlike other Liberal leaders between the 1870s and 1890s, he had had a long and distinguished political career by the 1870s, marked by Scottish, Tory, and Peelite influences. His ability to form and maintain Liberal governments from 1868 to 1872, 1880 to 1885, briefly in 1886, and from 1892 to 1894, proved the power of his personality and his influence over an increasingly fragmented party. His high church beliefs were devout, his knowledge of past and present history wide as well as eclectic, and his work habits puritanical. His ideas and age isolated him more and more from personal friends but his extraordinary stamina and obdurate pursuit of high principles earned him a world-wide respect.

There were alongside Gladstone other Liberals – young men in the early 1870s – whose contributions paled in comparison, but who nevertheless greatly aided Liberalism and the Liberal party during the rest of the century. A future Prime Minister, Archibald Primrose, the fifth Earl of Rosebery, stood out prominently within a body of peers who seemingly worked hard to demonstrate their intransigence and reactionary outlook. A youthful wanderlust took Rosebery on extensive journeys around the world as a young man and made him, despite his dilettantism, an authority on foreign affairs. Rosebery's marriage into the great banking family of the Rothschilds and his contributions to Gladstone's Midlothian campaigns in 1879 and 1880 certainly aided his fortunes. By the mid-1880s, he had become a strong contender for the future leadership of the party. In 1885, Reginald Brett, the future Viscount Esher, declared to Rosebery that 'Morley (and Chamberlain) consider *you* a possible and dangerous competitor in the race for Power with the Democracy.'[2] In 1886 he became Foreign Secretary under Gladstone. Though he never published so extensively in Liberal journals as Gladstone, Morley, or Chamberlain, he earned a similar reputation for being a mouthpiece for Liberalism through his oratory and support for popular causes (Scottish rights, London reforms, and imperial federation). He also demonstrated some ability, at least until the mid-1890s, to abstain from the bitter party feuds: his membership of the Lords helped in that respect. In March 1894 he succeeded Gladstone as Liberal Prime Minister.

There were other younger Liberals who became active and strong voices within the context of Gladstonian Liberalism in the 1870s. One, John Morley, became an MP in 1883 and subsequently held a series of important offices in Liberal ministries well into the twentieth century. In 1886 and between 1892 and 1895 he was Chief Secretary for Ireland, and stood closely with Gladstone in the belief that Home Rule for

Ireland was the paramount issue facing Great Britain in the late 1880s and early 1890s. Morley was an 'intellectual in politics,' and constantly fought to protect the rights of individuals and make sense out of a confused and contradictory late Victorian world. The task was insurmountable and often led to fits of despondency and depression. Thus, his friendships with energetic, enthusiastic, and practical men (Joseph Chamberlain and Scottish-American Andrew Carnegie) became of vital importance to his political outlook. Between 1867 and 1882, Morley was the indefatigable editor of the *Fortnightly Review* in which he nurtured strong programmes of a rationalist, nonconformist Liberalism, and extolled the virtues of John Stuart Mill. Throughout the remainder of his life, he continued to write for journals and in addition authored numerous works on great Liberal minds, such as Richard Cobden, James Stuart Mill, and Gladstone.

The other future major Liberal leader not as yet an MP in the early 1870s was Joseph Chamberlain. A thoroughly practical man, a Unitarian provincial outsider from Birmingham and untutored in some of the refinements of an Oxford education, he was driven by a deep conscience to improve working and living conditions. He had an uncanny skill for organization and an immense capacity for work; obstinately, he never acknowledged defeat or gave up a struggle. In the late 1860s and early 1870s, as mayor for Birmingham, he led an energetic campaign for municipal and educational reform that precipitated him into national prominence. Along with Morley, his 'partner' in the 1870s, he formulated and popularized radical schemes for the rejuvenation of the Liberal party. Chamberlain and Gladstone, in time, became bitter antagonists but the younger man supported the older throughout the 1870s as the radicals' 'best card' believing that 'he can't continue in public life for very much longer.'[3] In the second Gladstone ministry, Chamberlain was President of the Board of Trade, and in the third, briefly, President of the Local Government Board. His Unauthorized Programme dominated the 1885 general election. But in 1886, Chamberlain eventually broke with Gladstone on Home Rule for Ireland and started the Liberal Unionist party. Thereafter, Chamberlain increasingly mixed with Conservatives and former Whigs. In 1895, he joined the Salisbury ministry as Colonial Secretary and thus confirmed the change of party affiliation. Yet Chamberlain's positions between 1874 and 1895 were always essentially democratic, deeply humanitarian and progressive; thus, he is viewed as much more a part and parcel of the history of British Liberalism than that of Conservatism – at least before 1895.

William Vernon Harcourt was also one of the most important Liberal leaders in the late Victorian age, while Charles Dilke and James Bryce were other prominent Liberals but with varying political fortunes. Harcourt and Dilke were both elected to Parliament in 1868 and at early ages established themselves as experts on international affairs, particularly those concerning the United States. Harcourt became the Whewell Professor of International Law at Cambridge and held this post for several years. A man of immense ability and acumen, he never quite inspired a popular backing as did Gladstone, Chamberlain, and Rosebery. He was always slightly austere with a wounding sarcasm. While friendly with both radicals and Whigs, he allied himself fairly regularly with the Gladstonian section of the party, and his political fortunes steadily ripened. From 1880 to 1885, he was Home Secretary; in 1886 he became Chancellor of the Exchequer as he did again from 1892 to 1895. Between 1896 and 1898 he acted as leader of the party.

On the other hand, after a meteoric rise to prominence, Dilke's political fortunes plummeted even more rapidly. In 1885, he was President of the Local Government Board and had been an MP for Chelsea for almost twenty years. In 1887, he was ruined by the Crawford divorce scandal and no longer a member of Parliament. In the 1890s he edged his way back into a measure of party prominence, after winning an election for the Forest of Dean constituency in 1892, but never fully recovered from the divorce affair. James Bryce was not elected to the Commons until 1880. A lawyer, classical scholar, Alpinist, traveller and author, he held several positions in Liberal ministries in the nineteenth century, but he was most celebrated for his political astuteness and international understandings. He became the unquestioned British authority upon the politics, law, and social structure of the United States. There were other Liberals in addition to Dilke, Harcourt, and Bryce who were of significance – Lord Hartington (leader of the Liberals from 1874 to 1880), Earl Granville, Hugh Childers, and Lord Spencer.

There were also many devout Liberals not in Parliament – businessmen, journalists, men of letters, and even scientists – who made large contributions to late Victorian liberalism.[4] However, in the end the intricacies of Liberal party politics between 1886 and 1898 were so fraught with feuds, factions, and realignments that it is impossible to establish the specific contribution of these others to Liberalism. Certainly though, Gladstone, Rosebery, Harcourt, Chamberlain, and Morley stood out as the most conspicuous, active and enduring leaders of the Liberal party and Liberalism, while Dilke and Bryce were as prominent at particular times. It is they who will provide the core of this study, focusing as it does on Gladstonian Liberalism before William Ewart Gladstone's death in 1898.

The American Civil War

The United States burst into the mainstream of British political life between 1860 and 1874 as the result of a series of strained developments in Anglo-American relations. The American Civil War, the *Alabama* claims, Irish-American Fenianism, and the Geneva Arbitration Treaty all generally focused British attention upon the United States. In addition, there were British movements for franchise and educational reform in the late 1860s, which attracted comparisons between British and American institutions.

The end of the Civil War also reopened normal channels of transatlantic exchange, and Englishmen and Americans were quick to visit each other's countries. These were also years when the future leaders of the Liberal party were formulating their primary political and foreign interests. In 1861, only Gladstone was middle-aged. Harcourt was 34, Chamberlain was 25, Morley and Bryce 23, Dilke 18, and Rosebery but 14. Since the United States played such an important role in British political life between 1861 and 1874, it was natural that it also deeply influenced the Liberal leaders. Their American interests and associations formulated before the 1870s in turn influenced their relationship with the United States in the late Victorian age, and hence need to be underlined.

The Civil War which raged from 1861 until 1865 attracted enormous British attention.[5] The military heroism of Generals Grant, Sherman, Jackson, and Lee; the epic conflicts at Bull Run, Shiloh, and Gettysburg; and the attempts of President Lincoln and Jefferson Davis to gain British support excited both Conservatives and Liberals. Whether it was believed the Confederacy had the right to national self-determination, whether slavery should be abolished, or whether the loss of the Confederacy would mean the loss of Lancashire's vital cotton supplies, were major considerations in determining whether the British supported the North or the South. By and large, British Liberals became the staunchest students of the war for two primary reasons. First, their party was responsible for the conduct of British-American policy (Palmerston's Whig-Liberal ministry was in power from June 1859 until October 1865). Second, the outcome was often seen as a vital test of the success or failure of democratic principles of progress and liberty to which many Liberals so earnestly subscribed. John Stuart Mill believed the war 'was destined to be a turning point, for good or evil, of the course of human affairs for an indefinite duration.'[6] John Morley declared in 1875 that it had been 'the greatest popular issue in our time.'[7] Liberals of the upper classes led by Palmerston and Lord John Russell usually supported the South, while the radical, middle-class and 'university' Liberals spurred on by John Bright, W. E. Forester, John Stuart Mill, and Richard Cobden, were inspired by great moral causes to favor the North.[8] The Liberal leaders basically aligned themselves according to this classification, but as historian Peter J. Parish has recently noted, the Civil War was confusing to the British and 'clearly it provided no simple, reliable litmus-paper test for separating the forces of progress and reaction, liberalism and conservatism.'[9]

The Civil War postures of William Ewart Gladstone caused him great anguish throughout the remainder of his life. Although he supported the North near the end of the war and made various pro-Union pronouncements throughout, it is quite clear that in 1862 he championed the cause of the Confederacy. His declaration on 7 October at Newcastle that the Confederates had 'made a nation'[10] was not a careless statement or, as he reminisced in 1896, 'only a mistake ... of incredible grossness,'[11] but the product of thought, study, and personal philosophy. There were other instances of Gladstone's support for the South in 1862, both in official and private correspondences. In September 1862, he had written to Arthur Gordon that 'it has long been (I think) clear that Secession is virtually an established fact & that Jeff. Davis & his comrades have made a nation.'[12]

Gladstone viewed the Civil War as an issue of self-determination, not slavery which he certainly opposed, and his pro-Southern statements were completely consistent with his calls for Greek and Italian nationalistic movements and independence. As noted, it was very easy to have been confused over the issues of the war. Earl Granville and the young Lord Hartington, members of the same circles of Liberal aristocratic friendships as Gladstone, had much difficulty in assessing American developments. Granville declared in 1862:

> I doubt whether any European Government really understands American politics, or the objects of the North and of the South, and of the different states once released from the hope of preserving the Great Union; or the views of the different important parties in The Republic.[13]

Hartington made a journey to the United States in 1862, traveled in both Southern and Northern States, and met Lincoln, General

McClellan, and William Seward in the North and Jefferson Davis and others in the South. He arrived at unmistakably pro-Southern positions; a development that supports the frequently referred to hypothesis that British aristocrats and the Southern 'cavaliers' were naturally tempermental partners. To his father, he wrote in 1862:

> I am afraid I am becoming very Southern in my opinions. The people here are so much more in earnest about the thing than the North seem to be, that it is almost impossible not to go a good way with them, though one may think they were wrong at first. I hope Freddy [his brother] won't groan much over my rebel sympathies, but I can't help them.[14]

In another letter he admitted that 'notwithstanding my confusion, I am decidedly very Southern in the main.'[15] But whereas Granville had made little study of American events and Hartington was only a young highly impressionable man at the time, Gladstone could not as easily make claims to ignorance or superficial analysis.

Gladstone had always been a keen student of the United States. In 1852 a large proportion of his reading had been on American affairs[16] and in the 1860s he read more than ever on similar topics. For instance, in 1862, he read J. Stirling's *Letters from the Slave States* (1857), Frederick Olmsted's *Journeys and Explorations in the Cotton Kingdom* (1861), J. R. Gilmore's popular novel *Among the Pines* (1862), J. E. Cairnes' *The Slave Power; its character, career, and probable designs: being an attempt to explain the real issues involved in the American contests* (1862), and many articles and speeches.[17] These he studied along with the vast number of official papers upon the United States, many of which passed over his desk as a Cabinet minister when in office. In addition, he had friendly contacts with the American Minister in London, Charles Francis Adams, and with various other prominent American visitors in London, such as Cyrus Field, the developer of the transatlantic cable, Senator Walker, Confederate agent James Spence, and Charles Sumner, the renowned abolitionist Senator from Massachusetts. From 1865 until his death, Gladstone had made claims, as will be seen, that he had always stood by the United States during the Civil War. This is not borne out by the facts. Informed familiarity, associations, and self-fulfilling philosophies made him pro-Confederate during 1862.

A group of younger Liberal figures had various backgrounds but they mainly supported the North for the larger part of the war. Morley made a speech in support of the North as early as December 1861 in Blackburn Hall;[18] the final victory of the Union 'quickened his faith in democracy and his efforts for reform.'[19] Bryce, who was similarly a member of the 'university' liberals, broadly endorsed the North.[20] Dilke's first vote in the Cambridge Union in 1862 was in favor of a motion 'That the cause of the Northern States is the cause of humanity and progress, and that the widespread sympathy with the Confederates is the result of ignorance and misrepresentation.'[21] He maintained an avid interest in the United States throughout the war. In 1864 he even contemplated writing an essay on 'the future of the Anglo-Saxon race both in the United States and Australasia.'[22] The idea was evidently the germ for his later works on Anglo-Saxon developments. Chamberlain was influenced by pro-Northern attitudes active in the Lancashire business world and inspired by John Bright.[23] In the first instance, the aristocratic Rosebery sided with the South and evinced youthful glee at the thought of an exciting major conflict. 'The secession of South Carolina seems to me an event so wonderful' and 'I suppose the Yankees hope for something great from the clever Mr. Lincoln.'[24] It seems that Rosebery became an advocate of the North, but on what grounds, or with how much conviction, is open to question. In 1865, he was not yet matriculated at Oxford and had not formed the serious American interests and friendships which he developed in the 1870s.

More than any of his younger contemporaries, Harcourt worked his way independently through the complexities, prejudices, and rhetoric about the Civil War to form clear and influential views. It was on the basis of a series of letters published in *The Times* under the assumed name of 'Historicus' that Harcourt demonstrated a legal expertise which later resulted in his appointment to the Whewell chair of international law at Cambridge. The letters were usually closely argued studies of Anglo-American legal issues.[25] Harcourt's biographer claimed that 'Historicus' 'clarified the discussion and cleared the path to reasonable decisions.'[26] John Delane, the editor of *The Times*, Lord Russell, Foreign Minister Lord Clarendon, and even Disraeli showed great respect for his arguments and solicited advice on American issues.[27] Americans also valued the contributions of 'Historicus.' Charles Francis Adams wrote to him that 'I trust I need not say how much we in America have valued your own labors'[28] and the Massachusetts judicial scholar Richard Henry Dana Jr emphasized:

> The Government & people of the U. States owe you a debt of gratitude for your convincing & fearless exposition of many principles of

international law which have borne in our favor in this our life & death struggle. We know your purpose has not been to aid one side or the other, but, with a judicial mind, to quiet excitement, clear the atmosphere, & correct the public mind, but this course, so ably pursued has been of incalculable benefit to us, &, I assure you, is appreciated.[29]

Such British and American opinion certainly supports the view that Harcourt had a much more marked impact on Anglo-American relations in the 1860s than is usually assumed. On the vital question as to whether or not the South had 'made a nation,' he affirmed, though in this instance with hindsight, that the South 'committed, it is true, the greatest of political faults, that of attempting a revolution which could not possibly be successful.'[30] Throughout the war, his articles usually endorsed the North and opposed any recognition of the belligerent status of the South. Harcourt and Gladstone, in contradistinction to other Liberals in this study, took active public positions on the Civil War.[31] Those stances haunted them long after the surrender at Appomatox Courthouse on 9 April 1865.

Gladstone's address in 1862 was constantly cited by Americans as a bitter source of Anglo-American enmity. Charles Lester, author of a vicious tirade upon England, made a particularly bold attack upon Gladstone's Southern views.[32] While Gladstone typically was quick to apologize fully ('I took too much upon myself in expressing such an opinion'),[33] he admitted in 1870 that such hostile American views to a distant speech made him 'very fearful of giving opinions with regard to the proper course for foreign nations to pursue in junctures, of which, after all, I think they have better means of forming a judgement than foreigners can possess.'[34] But nothing more exasperated Gladstone than the United States government which turned to argue for payment of indirect claims because of the Confederate raids on Northern shipping. In the second chapter of their case to the Geneva Tribunal of 1871, Americans argued that 'an unfriendly course' had been pursued 'by Great Britain toward the United States from the outset to the close of the insurrection of 1861–65.' The accusation was directly focused on Gladstone and other former Cabinet members.[35] The Prime Minister quickly wrote an expression of his warm sympathies towards the United States, but his Cabinet colleagues prevailed upon him not to send it because it would most likely inflame not appease American sensibilities. He finally sent the letter on 28 November, over six months after he had written it.[36] Gladstone's genuinely sympathetic feelings towards the United States, despite his 1862 pro-Southern stance, were often discussed by Americans. His relationship with the United States was based upon reverence for the principles upon which the United States was founded, great admiration for the founding fathers of American democracy, a belief in the virtues of the Anglo-Saxon race, and animated by philosophies of Christian charity and international harmony. For a variety of reasons, it also became an aim of Gladstone's to generate more favorable opinion from Americans of his attitudes towards the United States. This became increasingly clear in the 1870s and 1880s.[37]

Harcourt was attacked in the 1860s too as being too pro-American and was also urged to outline his views towards the United States. It was a remarkable quality of Harcourt's letters in *The Times* upon a series of Anglo-American legal developments that they were notably un-biased. He argued equally from American and British precedents. He declared for American positions on some issues and for British on others.[38] In January 1868, Harcourt was finally forced publicly to defend his series of Anglo-American articles. His defense was impassioned and persuasive.

You sneer at my pretensions to 'have done all I can to be polite and agreeable to Americans.' You are unjust in this. I never said I had been 'polite and agreeable' to Americans. I said I had done what I could to 'maintain the friendship of England and America.'...I argued for America when it was proposed, contrary to the precedents and the principles of the law of nations, to recognize the independence of the Southern States. I argued for America when it was sought to violate or restrict the belligerent right of blockade. I argued for America when the English Government were attacked for stopping the Confederate Rams. I argued for America and against the English Government in favour of excluding the *Alabama* from ports of the realm. I argued for America in these cases because I thought she had the right on her side, though the public voice of a large and influential class in England was against her. I argued for England and against America in the case of the *Trent*, in the case of the *Alabama* claims and above all on the question of the recognition of belligerency, because I knew her to be in the wrong... That I have been unfair to America is a charge which I know the opinion of America will not sustain. I may have been mistaken. God knows it is likely enough. But in endeavouring to elucidate questions which concern the peace of two kindred nations which I equally admire – which

I could almost say I equally love – I have to do the best to my ability, and with some labour and industry, delivered what I believe to be right. I have been the partisan of no Government and the advocate of neither nation. I have sought peace where it alone can be found – in the paths of law, of justice and of truth. Pray excuse this egotism, but it is the nature of any man to protest against injustice.[39]

Harcourt clearly deserves a position alongside the great Liberal voices of Bright, Cobden, and Mill for advocating reason and patience on the part of British statesmen during the Civil War. That epic had molded the great interests of the future Liberal leaders in the United States. Notwithstanding the variety of their opinions or the detail in which they studied events, Harcourt's declaration to Lord John Russell, that 'I have always thought that American affairs acted as a singularly true touchstone of English Liberalism,'[40] itself held true. In fact, the years immediately following the Civil War found the leaders, especially the younger, eager to explore and study the large New World democratic republic which had triumphed over the Confederacy in devastating times.

Fenianism, the *Alabama* claims, and the Geneva Treaty, 1865–74

Between 1865 and 1874 – the end of the Civil War to the end of Gladstone's first ministry – Anglo-American relations returned to a relatively peaceful state of normality. At the same time, these were critical periods in the history of both countries, and to a lesser extent of Anglo-American relations. In the United States, the problem of Reconstruction and reincorporation of the South into the nation was immense. The Republican Presidents Andrew Johnson (1865–9) and Ulysses Grant (1869–73) both struggled with questionable success amid turbulent political rivalries. The Radical Republicans came within a vote of impeaching Johnson, while Grant's administration was found guilty of corruption. In Great Britain, franchise extension in 1867 helped precipitate the country on a series of further administrative, educational, and political reforms. Gladstone's first ministry from 1868 to 1874 was unquestionably his greatest, and American issues were not unimportant during its course. These essentially fall into broad types of classification: first, Anglo-American diplomatic issues; second, American parallels to British domestic events; and finally, private American contacts and associations.

Irish-American Fenianism, the *Alabama* claims, and the Geneva Treaty of 1872 were the three most acutely shared problems for British and American statesmen. Gladstone as the Liberal Prime Minister and Granville as Foreign Secretary had leading roles to play in formulating British policy towards the United States, but such newly elected Liberals as Harcourt and Dilke also took a close interest.

Irish-American Fenian raids into Canada from 1867 to 1871, and sporadic Fenian inspired uprisings in Ireland itself, made Fenianism a critical problem to Canada, Great Britain, and the United States. The Irish historian F. S. L. Lyons emphasizes that the British response 'helped to bring the whole problem of the Fenian movement nearer to the mainstream of British politics.'[41] Gladstone and Granville, in particular, sought conciliatory solutions: both were very wary of the incendiary nature of Irish nationalistic claims. They exchanged typical comments on Fenianism in 1869. Gladstone cautioned 'My own opinion of the American Fenians is so bad, that I should incline to act upon the safe side, as it is called.'[42] Granville outlined to his chief later in the year:

> If I were an autocrat I would release all the Fenians not withstanding the bluster of their friends, but as you are not in that position, and have a very difficult task before you, you had better do nothing for them at present.[43]

Harcourt and Dilke also cautioned against dealing too severely with the Fenians. Historicus's articles often dealt with the problems of establishing proper naturalization laws and alien guidelines,[44] while Dilke spoke 'against Fenianism in spite of [his] intense sympathy for it.'[45] Dilke had had the added benefit of first-hand observation of Fenianism which he had gained on a trip to the United States and Canada in 1866 and 1867, to which we will return. Fenianism partially died out of its own accord in the early 1870s, but Irish-American problems again became one of the main American related interests of the Liberal leaders in the turbulent 1880s and 1890s.

The extent to which the British should pay for damages caused to Northern shipping by British-built Confederate-operated raiders like the *Alabama* was the second major Anglo-American diplomatic issue of the period. It was similar to that of Fenianism in that it was drawn out throughout the 1860s because of the nature of American politics. President Grant's Republican administration desired to earn as many laurels as possible in foreign policy, in part in order to draw attention away from adverse publicity brought about by the corrupt 'Whiskey

Ring' and a faltering Reconstruction policy in the South. By promoting Anglophobia, the Republican administration could gain votes, especially those of the Irish. In England, the Liberal government continued to pursue conciliatory policies.[46] However, when in 1871 the famous abolitionist, Senator Charles Sumner, demanded British payment for indirect as well as direct damages caused by the raiders, the British press and public erupted with hostility to the United States. While Gladstone also was provoked by the extreme nature of Sumner's demands, he sought first to calm his Cabinet. Finally, after rancorous transatlantic debate, negotiators decided to convene a neutrally supervised conference in Geneva with representatives from five countries.

The year 1872 was a presidential one in the United States and the Geneva Conference became a heated political issue. However, the good sense of the American Minister Charles Francis Adams and Chief Justice Sir Alexander Cockburn, the two nominees to the Conference, helped to save the day for an agreement. In Great Britain, the formerly pro-Northern Liberals such as Bright, Forster, the Duke of Argyll, and the writer Thomas Hughes, spoke continually for accord. They even boldly suggested a treaty for international arbitration.[47] On the eve of a supposed failure, the tribunal's decision was widely announced. The British paid £3 200 000 for damages, and the indirect claims were dropped.

The decision mollified most parties. As Adrian Cook, the historian of the *Alabama* claims, has put it in discussing the dropping of those claims: 'For the first time since the War of 1812, a sizable body of American opinion admitted that Britain was right and the United States wrong.'[48] More importantly, all serious Anglo-American differences had been dispelled; hostile American criticism of England clearly subsided. Gladstone more than anyone else was responsible for the successful outcome, 'because it was his courageous authorization of major concessions that made them possible.'[49] The Liberals' fortunes had become tied even more closely to those of the United States. Liberal leaders had helped to positively stem the volatile Anglo-American tide of differences which percolated between 1868 and 1872.

British Liberals and their early American interests

Other American concerns arose in the 1860s which had nothing to do with Anglo-American foreign relations or diplomacy, but presented themselves in the course of discussing purely British political issues. The debate on the extension of the franchise in 1867 was the most striking example of how a domestic issue fostered numerous discussions of American parallels. Henry Pelling reiterates that 'Although this was purely an issue of British internal politics, America figured prominently throughout the controversy, and in the mouths of partisans on both sides was virtually a synonym for democracy.'[50]

Gladstone, for one, responded earnestly to Disraeli's attempt to associate the Liberal party with 'mobs' and 'corruption' in the United States: to Americanize the Liberal party.[51] The controversy spread rapidly into newspapers, periodicals, and books. In 1867 the 'university' Liberals produced seminal works on reform politics with the publication of collective works, *Essays on Reform* and *Questions for a Reformed Parliament*. These essays generally 'expressed sympathy with the ideal of democratic government.'[52] Those by Leslie Stephen, Lord Houghton, and Goldwin Smith, who had all visited America by 1867, often praised aspects of democratic institutions in the United States.[53]

Other British debates also focused on parallels and developments in the United States, especially those on education, temperance, immigration, and free trade. The Liberal MP, Jesse Collings, made a notable trip across the Atlantic to study American education; his report played an important role in the drafting of the Education Bill of 1870.[54] Neal Dow, the leading American temperance reformer, had close links with British compatriots.[55] Irish emigration to the United States fostered myriad transatlantic Irish associations, whether familial, ideological, political, or economical.[56] The burgeoning American protectionist movement alarmed most Englishmen, who were so committed to mid-Victorian trends of free trade. Debates on religion also had their American aspects. Thus that firm believer in church disestablishment, Joseph Chamberlain, wrote to the brother of Ralph Waldo Emerson for information on religious education.[57] In brief, there was a renewed interest in the United States from 1867 to 1874 as a product of related developments in Great Britain.

Finally, there was a great burst of direct associations between Englishmen and Americans – following the end of the disruptive Civil War – from 1865 and 1874. Transatlantic associations were pushed on by the same enterprising spirit which historians Ronald Robinson and J. Gallagher identified as the basis of the British drive for overseas empires: a desire to proliferate 'private relations with enterprising individuals and classes within foreign and colonial societies.'[58] In the 1860s and 1870s, Great Britain and especially London became the Mecca which all pre-eminent Americans sought to visit. There, they sought to mingle within prominent literary, political, and social circles;

to join such select London clubs as the St James, Cosmopolitan, Athenaeum, Reform, and Travellers'; and to acquire invitations to the grand functions at the homes of the titled nobility. It was only a matter of time before the younger Liberal leaders gained valuable American acquaintances in Britain. This was facilitated by the fact that several Liberal politicians, John Bright, Lord Houghton, the Duke of Argyll, Thomas Hughes, and the man of letters Leslie Stephens were frequent hosts of American friends in London.[59]

At the same time, British politicians turned themselves to journey to the United States with equally fervent motives. Travel to America came to have as important a value for young aspiring British statesmen as travel to Europe. With the resumption of friendly relations with America following 1865, and with the increasing ease and quickness of the previously rough Atlantic trip,[60] Liberal leaders joined the current. Visits to America did not always ensure that ignorance or images of the United States would give way to intelligent, well-constructed views, but then they were usually immeasurably helpful in upgrading the quality of British knowledge of the United States. It was a fact known to most Liberals that there was not enough knowledge of the United States in political circles. Thomas Hughes, Herbert Spencer, and John Morley thus helped to found an organization on 25 January 1871 named the Anglo-American Association to combat 'The lamentable ignorance of contemporary American history, which exists in England, even amongst otherwise well-instructed politicians.'[61] This body died soon thereafter, but the desire to encourage knowledge and direct associations with the United States on the part of those who had such backgrounds did not. The editor of *Macmillan's Magazine*, Alexander Macmillan, professed to Gladstone in 1867 right after taking his first visit to the United States, 'I spent eight pleasant weeks among that *great people*, and am strongly impressed with the conviction that young men aiming to be statesmen in England would derive great benefit from a long visit to the United States, and mixing freely with all classes.'[62] Several years later, Francis Lawley, a former Liberal MP for Beverley and a *Times* correspondent in America during the war, exhorted the young Rosebery to make his American trip 'as prolonged as possible as I think it [America] the most instructive country in the world for a politician; far more so than this grave of the buried past from which I am now writing [Rome].'[63] Gladstone and Harcourt never made the voyage to the United States, but many other Liberal figures did so and many went several times.

While there were general educational reasons for visiting the United States, British public figures went for specific purposes as well. In fact, historian Allan Nevins argues convincingly that British visits to the United States gained a new seriousness and purposefulness after 1870.[64] In 1873, the agricultural laborers' leader Joseph Arch (a future Liberal MP) went to investigate the possibilities for immigration of farm workers. Edward Watkin and Hugh Childers also spent a considerable amount of time in North America on railway business, while the future Liberal MP, the freethinker Charles Bradlaugh, conducted three popular lecture tours in 1873, 1874, and 1875. Other reasons included marriage and professional responsibilities.

The Irish leader Charles Parnell went to pursue a prospective wife in 1871 while the Conservative Randolph Churchill visited his wife's country for the first and only time in 1876. Lyon Playfair, an important Liberal and friend of Gladstone's, married an American in 1878 and thereafter usually took a yearly visit to the Eastern seaboard. Goldwin Smith also married, a Canadian, and in the 1870s settled permanently in Toronto. Henry Hyndman, the Marxist leader of the Social Democratic Federation and member of the staff of the *Pall Mall Gazette* between 1871 and 1880; the Irish journalist, author, and politician Justin McCarthy; and the future Conservative MP Louis Jennings, all had professional motives for making the United States their home in the 1870s. Jennings even edited the *New York Times* between 1868 and 1876 and played a major role in exposing the corruption of Boss Tweed in New York.

The list of visits could be extended much further. What is important about them is that they were taken for specific reasons as well as a general purpose to travel, and that those who took them increasingly turned themselves to studying the United States. They not only wrote influential books and articles, or encouraged others to journey to America, but also gave private views of American events in proliferating correspondence with politicians and correspondents back in England. For example, Goldwin Smith supplied his Liberal friends with various impressions of the United States when he returned to England and in letters. In 1871, he reported to Gladstone that the Prime Minister's 'Apology for the escape of the *Alabama* seems to me to be accepted in the best spirit.'[65] In 1871, he wrote to Dilke that an article in the *New York Times* on 'American opinion of Sir Charles Dilke' should be understood as being motivated by the anti-Liberal sympathies of the editor, Louis Jennings, who 'systematically attacks all English Liberals: Gladstone and Bright as well as yourself.'[66] He informed Harcourt in 1866 of American presidential politics and the uncertain state of Fenianism.[67] Those British politicians who had visited and knew the United States kept up a steady stream of comments to their former and past colleagues, as well as friends. By the 1890s, the stream had turned into a flood.

There was then between 1865 and 1874 a proliferation of associations between British and Americans in all forms, of British comments upon America, and of an enhanced belief in the importance of the United States to politicians. From amid these transatlantic currents, the contacts developed by Dilke, Morley, Bryce, and Rosebery emerged as some of the most important established by British politicians with the United States in the late-nineteenth century. Dilke made his first trip to the United States in 1866, Morley in 1867, Bryce in 1870, and Rosebery in 1873; each trip left deep impressions of American politics and society. American friendships immediately assumed places of prominence in the lives of each. Moreover, the four young Liberals became publicists for more informed British views of America, sought to stimulate British political contacts with Americans, and were powerful voices calling for close Anglo-American relations.

Charles Dilke: an American trip in 1866

Charles Dilke first journeyed to America in the summer of 1866 with a specific aim in mind. In the course of studying radicalism, he had become fascinated by the American Perfectionist movement of the 1830s.[68] His trip was ostensibly to further investigate such communistic experiments in America with the end product to have been a book. However, once there, he developed an appetite for traveling everywhere and seeing everything, and the initial project fell by the wayside.[69] Grander ideas filled his mind, as he admitted after the tour.

> The idea which in all the length of my travels has been at once my fellow and my guide – a key wherewith to unlock the hidden things of strange new lands – is a conception, however imperfect, of the grandeur of our race, already girdling the earth, which it is destined, perhaps, eventually to overspread.[70]

Throughout his American travels, Dilke became increasingly enamoured with the greatness of the country, and of its unlimited potential. For him, American success came to represent magnificent achievements of Great Britain and the Anglo-Saxon race. 'Through America, England is speaking to the world.'[71] In the words of one of his biographers, 'Dilke, indeed, was as naturally disposed to be pro-American as it is possible to imagine.'[72]

Dilke traveled in the South, East, and the West as well as Canada. From where he landed in Norfolk, Virginia, he proceeded to trace a circuit which took him from Washington DC, New York, Boston, Quebec, Cincinnati, Kansas City, Denver, Salt Lake City, and finally San Francisco. All along the way, he mingled with various classes of Americans – cowboys, policemen, politicians, and men of letters. He met many of the prominent men in Cambridge, Massachusetts, New York, and Washington DC; those in politics tended to be Republicans. From New York, he wrote that his father must be 'astonished at the number of people I have mentioned having met: ... I have kept a list of names – that I must have made over 100 acquaintances in New York alone.' While these were not close friends as Dilke acknowledged, he had 'had the great advantage of talking intimately with this number of people, & of hearing their opinions upon all subjects.'[73] He observed Fenian conventions. He attended debates in the House and the Senate, and commencement ceremonies at Harvard, and he visited camp fires in the Rocky Mountains, and Chinese restaurants in Chinatown in San Francisco. His observations on the United States were profuse and were captured in a series of letters to his father and family.[74] Upon his return to England, he reorganized these and added further comments, thus producing a two-volume work on his trip around the world, *Greater Britain: A Record of Travel in English-Speaking Countries during 1866–1867*. The book was an instantaneous success and went through many editions in various languages.

Greater Britain is largely a recapitulation of youthful experiences of world adventure, and the author makes no great pretence at exposing the strengths and weakness of Anglo-Saxon institutions.[75] Nonetheless, the young author made a series of critical evaluations about the United States: political parties, protectionism, religion, education, condition of cities, and national character. While these were generally adulatory, others were decidedly cool with grave apprehensions about the future.

Dilke's faith in the viability of democratic and republican institutions was confirmed by American party politics, and he readily endorsed the philosophy of the Republican party.[76] Lincoln's party was the party of radicalism and centralization, and that which most likely would be able to change the Constitution. Direct election of presidents and continued franchise reforms were two specific methods that would bring about needed constitutional change and preserve the country from states' rights and strict constructionist Democrats. Dilke isolated for particular condemnation the manner in which American party organizations were displayed in Britain as 'so dictatorial, so despotic' and chosen 'by caucuses and conventions composed of the idlest and most worthless of its population.'[77] Such British representations Dilke called some of 'the grossest mis-statements...made to us in England.' The caucus and convention systems were in practical terms fair and systematic means for selecting the best men: only in New York were they, perhaps, less successful. But, that was owing to the Irish, a foreign influence. Dilke exhorted even 'no "side issues" should be allowed to disguise the fact that the Democratic is the party of New York, the Republican the party of America.'[78] Perhaps, there was no better indication of the vitality of republican institutions than what he found in the notoriously dangerous and debauched streets of San Francisco.

Now-a-days the citizens [of San Francisco] are remarkable, even among Americans, for their love of law and order. Their city, though still subject to a yearly deluge from the outpourings of all the over-crowded slums in Europe, is, as the New Yorker said, the best policed in all America. In politics, too, it is remarked that party organizations have no power in this State from the moment that they attempt to nominate corrupt or time-serving men. The people break loose from their caucuses and conventions, and vote in a body for their honest enemies rather than for corrupt friends. They have the advantage of singular ability, for there is not an average man in California.[79]

Even in San Francisco, Dilke concluded, democracy had emerged triumphant. From such observations Dilke believed that republican forms of government were the most durable and could and would triumph everywhere that Anglo-Saxons established society.[80] That in the final analysis is the singular theme of *Greater Britain*: that 'an Anglo-Saxon people even in those climates [South America] would gradually become the dominant race.'[81]

During his American trip, Dilke collected a vast range of statistics upon American education, religion, and emigration. While he found much to praise in the free school system of Harvard and the University of Michigan,[82] he discovered, surprisingly, that 'the religious prospects [were] not bright.'[83] The Anglican Church and a movement towards Supernaturalism were gaining strength, but other faiths were in decline, and even less devout. In San Francisco and Chicago, 'there is much external show in the shape of church attendance; in neither does religion strike its root deeply into the hearts of citizens, except so far as it is alien and imported.'[84] There was an over-multiplication of faiths, less faith in the various denominations. In the end, Dilke's belief in the separation of church and state, and his opposition to denominational education were reinforced by such observations.

One American development aroused Dilke's anger more than any other – the growing protectionist trade policies. By the late 1860s, in an effort to build up her war-torn economy, the United States had instituted mild protectionism. In 1869 duties of 47 percent were levied upon specific articles entering the United States. Britain, on the other hand, was the apostle of free trade, and for Liberals like Dilke, raised on Cobdenite principles, adherence to free trade and liberalism went hand in hand. It is no wonder that with regard to American protectionism Dilke exclaimed: 'The greatest of all democratic stumbling-blocks is said to be Protection.'[85] From the plains of Missouri, he wrote to Henry Peto: 'Protection! Protection! Protection! ... Oh, my dear Peto, your economical mind would be driven wild by these things as mine was till I got used to it.'[86] But while Dilke's confrontations with American protectionist arguments did nothing to alter his own support for free trade, he came to 'see how much there is to be said for the wrong side.'[87] He set out these American arguments so clearly in *Greater Britain* that some readers mistakenly were shocked into thinking that Dilke himself had become a protectionist. The young Liberal could find no reasonable economic arguments for protectionism – to pay higher prices on goods and taxes on imports – but there was some sound political evidence in its favor. In other words, protectionism helped to consolidate national unity that could lead to greater ultimate wealth. The problems with such American policies, though, as Dilke inferred, were that competition for bounties and duties among the various industrial classes would eventually lead to some being supported at the expense of others; inequities and corruption would probably ensue. Furthermore, a 'Free Trade system lends itself better to ... wider modern sympathies than does Protectionism'[88] insofar as keeping open avenues of exchange and amity. In the end, Dilke's American trip impressed him tremendously with the endless examples of the fruits of American institutions. Except for those of protectionism, the Democratic party, and religion, he found few blemishes upon the American body politic.

The best evidence that the American trip etched deep an impression upon Dilke is attested to by his actions upon his return to England. Not only did he take a year off to write *Greater Britain*, but he also made frequent American references in the course of his political life. Thus, for example, in Chelsea in November 1867 he praised the machinery of government both in Virginia and Australasia.[89]

Moreover, on another occasion, he had lavish words for a new favorite topic, the unity of the Anglo-Saxon race. 'Our true alliance ... is not with the Latin peoples, but with men who speak our tongue, with our brothers in America.'[90] In 1869, Dilke gave evidence concerning the United States to a select committee hearing on municipal elections.[91] In an article on 'Free Schools' in 1873, he discussed American school systems.

> In Connecticut 10,000 children, and 30,000 in New York, were brought into the schools for the first time by the adoption of a free-school system, and that in a single year, while average attendance of children was increased by fourteen days out of a hundred and thirty. This increase in regularity of attendance disproves the argument against free schools, which is stated in words, 'the poor only value that for which they pay.'[92]

Oliver Wendell Holmes of Cambridge, Massachusetts dealt with Dilke's queries and Goldwin Smith reported on the American reception of his views.[93] Most interestingly, Miss Kate Fields, the London correspondent of the *New York Tribune*, became one of Dilke's closest friends. Through Miss Fields, Dilke had a constant vehicle for reports on American news, and what was more, a firm supporter of his Republican pronouncements. Their meetings in the late 1860s and early 1870s were frequent, whether at the House of Commons or elsewhere throughout the country. Dilke addressed her affectionately as 'dear Cuffy.'[94] In the winter of 1873–74, she wrote a series of letters, 'Notes from the United States,' which Dilke published in his periodical, the *Athenaeum*.[95] By the fall of the Liberal government in 1874, Dilke had established important views of the United States and significant relationships with Americans which heightened his affinities with republicanism and radical democracy.

John Morley: an American trip and early interests

A reading of John Morley's *Autobiography* highlights an apparent lack of interest in the United States during the author's first visit in 1867. Morley most clearly remembered the overall hospitality of the Americans, especially that of Charles Sumner, a young clerk, and author named Walt Whitman, and newspaper editors like Gordon Bennett and Edwin L. Godkin of the *New York Nation*. There is little attention given to specific American events or interests.[96] This is misleading. Quite to the contrary, Morley conceived his visit in 1867 as of great personal and political importance. He declared to a frequent American contributor to the *Fortnightly Review*, the London-based preacher Moncure Conway, that 'My trip is to ascertain as much as I can of the country, in every aspect; with an eye upon the defects of my own country.'[97]

With the proprietor of *Macmillan's Magazine*, Alexander Macmillan, Morley made special arrangements which underlay the importance of the trip to him: to write a book on the United States. In October 1867, he had approached the editor who responded by approving the scheme, and Macmillan also agreed to finance Morley's travels. Morley told him that his trip was 'less rash than it may seem – for the project has been maturing in my mind for two years past.' His book would be an 'inquiry into the dominant social ideas of the U.S. with half an eye upon the renovation of our own ideas.'[98] Morley was hardly less excited than Dilke about the prospects of visiting the United States as soon as it was possible.

On 25 November, Morley arrived in New York. He made careful plans for an extensive tour: Boston, Albany, Niagara, Chicago, Cincinnati, Philadelphia, Washington (where he would stay until he had 'catechised all the men in the place'), Charleston, Augusta, and New Orleans.[99] However, his plans were dashed when suddenly he fell ill and had to shorten his trip abruptly. The only cities in which he spent any amount of time were New York and Washington DC. Any idea of writing a book disappeared and he left America having made hardly any studies of her characteristics. As Morley recorded:

> I was wise enough in 1868 to leave the country without venturing, with such meteoric short notice, in spite of many urgent demands, on a single original idea as to the institutions of the American Union, their durability, or the sort of pattern they were destined to supply for democracy in Europe.[100]

However, back in London Morley made arrangements to improve the quality of the American articles for the *Fortnightly Review*, which he edited at the time. For himself, he regularly read such American papers as *The Nation* and kept up with developments in the United States.[101] He found it necessary to remind his writers of the need for American perspectives. Thus, he exhorted Conway 'to tell us something about the American situation without reference to English matters, of wh. lately we've had enough.'[102] For contributions of American articles, Morley turned to several prominent Americans and Englishmen who had extensive knowledge of the United States. Moncure Conway was the most frequent contributor in the 1860s; but in the mid-1870s, he relinquished his position to the experienced former editor of the *Chicago Tribune*, future Mugwump, and Liberal-Republican Horace White. Morley's good friend Charles Norton wrote an article on emigration; the future Irish MP Justin McCarthy one upon American prohibition; and the British journalist Edward Dicey (brother of A. V. Dicey) also on politics.[103] Morley preferred to rely upon this string of broadly liberal-minded men, sympathetic to notions of Anglo-American cordiality, to spell out the *Fortnightly*'s American stories and analyses. In only one case did Morley himself evidence his personal American views.

Throughout Morley's political career, Ireland consumed his attention as no other issue and his visit to America in 1867 had profoundly surprised him insofar as the extreme Anglophobia of the Irish was concerned. He referred to his own disappointment with the American Irish shortly after his return to Britain in a speech.

> Why, the first spectacle I saw was a procession of some thousands of Irishmen, who had once, most of them, been fellow subjects of our own, marching in military array, to hear, to applaud, and to sympathise with, speeches against the nation which had driven them forth. I can assure you who have never seen an organisation of this sort against your country, that the sight is one of the most painful and bitter that can afflict a man who loves his country and its fair name among the nations of the earth.[104]

Morley blamed the British, not the Americans, for the 'low character' of the Irish-Americans. This view was spelled out clearly in a review of a book, *The Irish in America*, by the Irish MP John Maguire.

> Englishmen, at any rate, have no right to point to the moral of the corruption and inefficiency of democratic government by the outrageous scandals of the New York municipality. The Irish who in that city and elsewhere do their best to spoil the great republican experiment are the direct products not of the American republican, but of the English oligarchic system. There is nothing more heroic about the Americans than the fortitude and resolution with which they encounter their annual floods of Irish who we send over, as a rule, without a shilling in their pockets, or two civilized and orderly ideas in their heads.[105]

While Maguire and Morley did not regard British institutions as faultless, the social and political culture of New York was very disturbing. Morley's concern for the Irish elements in British–American relations would increasingly grow more important to him in the 1880s and 1890s.

Morley's presence in London between 1868 and 1874 brought him into frequent contact with Americans. He not only had associations with the contributors to the *Fortnightly*, like Conway and White, but met such visitors as Edward Pierce, the biographer of Charles Sumner.[106] But one American, Charles Norton, became one of his closest friends during the period and their friendship underlined the intellectual accord between two leading British and American Liberals.

Charles E. Norton was a respected member of the Harvard intellectual elite with substantial contacts in the Anglo-American journalistic and political worlds. He was particularly close with the Irishman and editor of *The Nation*, Edwin L. Godkin, with whom he shared many views on American issues. Both supported General Grant for the Republican party's candidate for the presidential election of 1868, but by the early 1870s turned to form the splinter or break away movement known as the Liberal-Republicans. Norton spent most of 1868, 1869, 1872, and 1873 in England, and carefully studied the political and social conditions in Britain, which he found fascinating. Before long, he had declared himself to be thoroughly in agreement with the Liberals and in opposition to the Conservatives.

> I have tried in vain all winter [1869] to find a convinced Tory, – man who read history, had travelled, & preserved his faith in Toryism as the system by which the world should be regulated. But there seems to be no such character. The Conservatives have nobody of distinct political principles; they are simply well off & desirous to remain so, conservative by position & by birth.[107]

On the other hand, Norton found profound intellectual agreement with various Liberal intellectuals and politicians such as: the positivist Frederic Harrison; MP from Elgin Boroughs, Grant Duff; Fellow at Christ Church and cousin of William Harcourt, Vernon-Harcourt; and Morley. As with most of his British friends, Norton found the social conditions of Britain to be abominably bleak, represented by what he saw as a wide gulf between the higher and lower classes. The condition of agricultural and factory laborers was deplorable; that of the lower class ('tramps, the thieves, the vagabonds') still worse. A spirit of revolution abounded in Britain.

> The best Englishmen are the most dissatisfied, & the clearest thinkers scarcely see a hope short of revolution. The very roots of

political and religious belief are disturbed, – & outside of the comparatively small circle of those whose circumstance, – that is outside the Tory aristocracy & the Tory high church, there is no faith left sufficiently vigorous to be operative in the formation of active convictions. The actual condition of English thought is extraordinary; nothing is settled; the old dykes are breaking down, & everybody is asking: What is this coming to?[108]

Norton admired Gladstone's leadership, because it was just and honorable, despite the fact that it lacked 'an ardent devotion to freedom and humanity.'[109] There was no comparison, according to the American, between the humane and thoughtful actions of the Liberal government, and the humiliating demagoguery of Charles Sumner and Hamilton Fish.

Events, philosophies, and circumstances coalesced to produce the Morley–Norton friendship. Shortly after Norton's arrival in England in 1868, he selected an article by John Morley as 'the best and frankest illustration I have seen in print of a very common condition of opinion.'[110] Moreover, Norton spent a large part of the autumn of 1868 in Bromley in Kent, only five miles away from Frederic Harrison. The latter, one of the leading liberal intellectuals under the influence of the French positivist philosopher Auguste Comte, was Morley's closest friend. It was inevitable that Norton should meet Morley through his acquaintance with Harrison. In January 1869, Harrison did arrange a dinner at the Reform Club for the other members of his small Comtist circle (Richard Congreave, Professor Beesley, Henry Crompton, and Morley) to meet Norton.

The United States was one of the prime topics of discussion during the evening of conversation. There was obviously much intellectual rapport between Norton, Morley, and the other Comtists.[111] Norton reported to Godkin that 'We talked of political systems, of America & of England, their development & prospects, – and of little else, – all evening. I was greatly interested in the talk.' Further, he added that though he found himself at odds with some of the hard Comtists like Congreave, Morley and Harrison were the friendliest and 'the least doctrinaire of the party.'[112]

In fact, the arguments that Norton put forth against some of the members were clear outlines of the very weaknesses that Morley himself was beginning to find in Comtist positions. Norton attacked the group at the Reform Club. He argued that the 'best way to secure the ideal community is to secure first the best & largest development of the individual.'

Conversely, the Positivists wanted to construct a system, agnostic and humanitarian in spirit, but which called for the sacrifice of the individual for the good of the system. Norton found the Positivist arguments 'cold & hard in their view of poverty & distress which prevails around them.'[113] These views were almost akin to Morley's. In the late 1860s and early 1870s, Morley underwent a conversion from Comte to 'Millite' principles, despite the pleading of his former friends, like Harrison. Individualism now became a central concern for Morley. As D. A. Hamer has outlined:

> The individual remained the starting-point and basis for Morley's social and political thinking. He insisted that there was the greatest chance of social progress if the freedom and self-respect of each individual were strengthened and he were left alone as much as possible.[114]

In Norton, Morley found an intellectual soul-mate with whom he could share his innermost thoughts, and between 1869 and 1874 they often met. One such encounter was warmly described by the American.

> A long and interesting visit from Morley occupied the morning. Much talk on the deepest matters of concern. In belief and opinion I agree with him more nearly than with most men. He is eminently sincere, and clear-minded, and has nothing of the narrow hard-and-fastness of the professed Comtists. He is altogether a worthy disciple of Mill.
>
> Religion, Utilitarianism, the modern view of Morals, political opinion in England, and the United States, were some of the subjects on which we talked.[115]

On many occasions between 1869 and 1873 the two men exchanged frank, often lengthy letters.[116] Morley's knowledge of the United States most certainly increased both in quantity and quality as a result of Norton's friendship and the relationship illustrated the intellectual agreement between a leading British Liberal and a prominent American Liberal-Republican. By 1874, Morley had been sufficiently influenced by his American trip, journalistic activities, and American friendships to be considered an Anglo-American man.

James Bryce: early American impressions

James Bryce's first American trip in the summer of 1870 inaugurated a relationship with the United States that would become a passionate and consuming interest for the next fifty years. His journey was largely the result of the proddings of his university friends, Goldwin Smith, Leslie Stephen, and Edward and Albert Dicey. The latter, in fact, became his travelling companion for a good part of his 1870 journey.[117] Bryce ventured north into Canada and as far west as Illinois, but surprisingly not to Washington DC. Thus, he missed the opportunity to mix and mingle with leading American politicians. Both the first visits of Dilke and Rosebery were more extensive than Bryce's. However, that should not obscure the fact that Bryce reached some early acute understandings about the United States.

American politics, society, and education attracted Bryce's deepest interest. In the study of these he was influenced by his own legal background, by education at Oxford, and by serving on the Taunton Commission, a Royal Commission to examine the condition of English and Welsh schools. In America, he made his best friends with a group of Republican intellectuals and journalists, who easily introduced him to American journalism, Harvard law school, and the Eastern intellectual aristocracy. The Brahmins – Oliver Wendell Holmes Jr, future Supreme Court justice; James Russell Lowell, future American Minister at the Court of St James; Charles W. Eliot, the President of Harvard University; and the New York journalist Edwin Godkin – were all to become lifelong friends. 'Bryce felt an unusual affinity with these people. In many respects, they were the exact counterpart of the liberals he liked and admired at home. In some ways they were even more radical in their opinions, and certainly more open-minded.'[118] Excited by his American experiences, Bryce was hardly back in England before he turned to begin a series of articles on American society, education, law, and politics.[119]

On the whole, Bryce was inspired by the merits of American institutions. For him, there were many obvious similarities between the United States and Great Britain.

> There is no great difference in the law of the two nations, and still less in their religion; the two social instincts, sympathies, and prejudices of the people are substantially the same; both alike are possessed by a belief in the principle of laissez-faire; dislike State interference, even when the State is their own creation; have little taste for uniformity of method, or logical consistency of principle, and great confidence in the possibility of putting everything straight by the action of vigorous individuals.[120]

Furthermore, Bryce thought that the British could 'profit much better by her [American] example in the way either of imitation or avoidance than we can by theirs.'[121] American politics was perhaps the most difficult American topic for an Englishman to understand, but Bryce was fortunate in his opportunities. In New York, his friends enabled him to attend a Democratic convention and to hear eminent speakers including the future Presidential candidate Samuel J. Tilden. Bryce considered the outrages committed by the Irish-influenced Boss Tweed to be disgraceful. New York was 'beyond all comparison the worst governed city in the States, probably one of the worst, that is to say, most corruptly, governed in the civilized world.' But, on the other hand, Bryce acknowledged that New York was 'quite exceptional in America' and its conditions unique.[122] In words reminiscent of those Morley used to describe the influx of coarse Irish elements into America and New York, Bryce stated:

> It is, so to speak, a foul, stagnant pond, into which all the drains and polluted streams of Europe and America have been discharging themselves, the rascaldom of all the eastern half of the States as well as the ignorance and wretchedness of Ireland and our own cities.[123]

Unfortunately, though, New York was not the only American city with problems in Bryce's view. In a city such as Chicago which Bryce greatly praised, the 'class of professional politicians has of late years weakened it.'[124] From the beginning, Bryce found disturbing conditions in the large American cities.

Bryce heaped lavish praise upon the qualities of the average American citizen, society, and customs. The Englishman affirmed 'that the tone of the great mass of individual American citizens is infinitely higher than that of the class to which they entrust their public business.'[125] He found American society infinitely freer and more open than the English. American free and mixed schools, happier marriages, Boston's measure to relieve the growth of pauperism (not as great a malady as it was in England), and legal education were all developments which Bryce described and praised in some detail.[126] Again, his opinions were arrived at on the basis of good efforts by friends such as Oliver W. Holmes Jr, who directed him around Harvard, and the Superintendent of public schools in Chicago. Before too long, Bryce believed the exceptional qualities of the average American citizen and admirable conditions within society would justify the American conception of the nation's great future. American resources were after all unlimited. Politics were corrupt, but that, Bryce hoped, was only an aberration, capable of redemption.[127]

Though Bryce's American interests had been fully excited, his relationship with the United States was not as active during the 1870s as may be assumed. While he wrote several perceptive American articles, as has been mentioned, he declined to contribute regularly to *The Nation*. His time was fully occupied. He could only promise Godkin 'now and then, when anything of special interest turns up [upon continental politics], to send you a stray article.'[128] Although he corresponded with Oliver Wendell Holmes Jr and Charles Eliot,[129] his American correspondence also did not blossom until the 1880s. In London, Bryce worked as a barrister and mingled with Liberals and associated himself with liberal causes. When not committed to business, Bryce spent a good amount of time in the 1870s traveling about Europe and climbing Alpine peaks. Bryce's American interests had been aroused prior to 1874, but his direct relationship with the country and its people was no more extensive than that of such other young Liberal leaders as Morley, Dilke, and Rosebery.[130]

Conclusion

In general, the United States influenced the main exponents of British Liberalism – especially Gladstone, Harcourt, Morley, Dilke, and Bryce – between 1860 and 1874 in a variety of respects. First, the country was involved in framing varied diplomatic responses over the Civil War, Fenianism, and the *Alabama* claims settlement. Liberals, whether in office or in private, worked hard to conciliate Anglo-American animosities and build transatlantic understanding. Secondly, America struck the Liberal mind as providing a series of examples of parallels to its own concerns, such as the franchise or educational reform. In most of these cases, America was usually viewed from a distance and wore the guise either of a host of threatening, unworthy, and alarming images, or of the best example of the vitality and success of democratic institutions. Emotion and prejudice underlay Liberal reactions to many American developments, as it would have with any Englishman. Thirdly, the United States offered a host of specific topics to study. While Liberals had studied the glorious battles of the Civil War with acute attention, they only occasionally observed the various major developments of the late 1860s and early 1870s. The attempted impeachment of President Andrew Johnson, Reconstruction, and the condition of the blacks gained some British and Liberal attention, but mainly by those like Dilke, and later in the 1870s by the Scottish Liberal George Campbell, MP, and Rosebery who spent time in the South.[131]

Notes

1. D. A. Hamer, *Liberal Politics in the Age of Gladstone and Rosebery. A Study of Leadership and Policy* (Oxford, 1972), p. 37. More recent interpretations of Liberalism in the 1860s–1880s have emphasized the divisive and contentious dimensions of liberalism, and the battles with the Whigs or Gladstone's own role in stubbornly contributing to the lack of coherence in the Liberal party. See J. P. Parry, *Democracy and Religion: Gladstone and the Liberal Party, 1865–1875* (Cambridge, 1986), his article, 'Religion and the Collapse of Gladstone's First Government, 1870–1874,' *Historical Journal*, vol. 25 (1982), pp. 71–101, and his *The Rise and Fall of Liberal Government in Victorian Britain* (New Haven, CT, 1993), especially pp. 247–73; and T. A. Jenkins, 'The Rise and Fall of Gladstonian Liberalism,' in *The Liberal Ascendancy, 1830–1886* (London, 1994).
2. R. Brett to Rosebery, 20 Jan. 1885, cited in H. C. G. Matthew, *The Liberal Imperialists. The Ideas and Politics of a Post-Gladstonian Elite* (Oxford, 1972), p. 11.
3. Brit. Mus., Addit. MSS 43885 (Dilke Papers): Chamberlain to Dilke, 10 Oct. 1876, f. 49.
4. See Appendix I for the Liberal leaders who figure in this study. Liberalism refers to the politics, practices, and personalities of the British Liberal party, while liberalism refers to the attitudes of open-mindedness, belief in individual freedom, and an ideology associated with reform movements. Dimensions and discussions of liberalism and Liberalism are treated more thoroughly in E. Biagini, 'The Dilemmas of Liberalism,' in M. Pugh, (ed.), *A Companion to Modern European History, 1871–1945* (London, 1997) and in his *Liberty, Retrenchment and Reform: Popular Liberalism in the Age of Gladstone, 1860–1880* (Cambridge, 1992). Liberalism is viewed as an extension of popular reform movements dating from the advent of Chartism, and as this study shows had a transatlantic context.
5. The standard work upon Anglo-American relations during the Civil War is E. D. Adams, *Great Britain and the American Civil War*, 2 vols (New York, 1925). Other helpful works include Peter J. Parish, *The American Civil War* (London, 1975) and W. D. Jones, 'The British Conservatives and the American Civil War', in *American Historical Review*, lviii (April 1953), pp. 527–43.
6. J. S. Mill, *Autobiography* (New York, 1873), p. 266. See also, J. S. Mill, 'The Contest in America,' *Fraser's Magazine* (Feb. 1862).
7. Morley, 'The Liberal Eclipse,' *FR*, vol. xvii, n.s. (Feb. 1875), p. 297.
8. Liberal positions towards the United States during the war are best treated in 'Gladstone and America,' *Gladstone*, ed. Peter J. Jagger (London, 1998), pp. 85–103; the works by E. D. Adams and Peter J. Parish; C. Collyer, 'Gladstone and the American Civil War,' *Proceedings of the Leeds Philosophical Society*, vol. vi (1951), pp. 583–94; A. Whitridge, 'British Liberals and the American Civil War,' *History Today*, vol. xii (1962), pp. 688–95; C. Harvie, *The Lights of Liberalism. University Liberals and the Challenge of Democracy 1860–86* (London, 1976), pp. 97–115; and the standard biographies of the Liberal leaders.
9. 'Gladstone and America,' p. 86.

10. The complete text of Gladstone's speech reads: 'We know quite well that the people of the Northern States have not yet drunk of the cup – they are still trying to hold it far from their lips – which all the rest of the world see they nevertheless must drink of. We may have our own opinions about slavery; we may be for or against the South; but there is no doubt that Jefferson Davis and other leaders of the South have made an army; they are making, it appears, a navy; and they have made, what is more difficult than either, they have made a nation' (*The Times*, 9 Oct. 1862).

11. Cited in E. J. Feuchtwanger, *Gladstone* (London, 1975), p. 115. Roy Jenkins in his recent biography of Gladstone discusses more fully Gladstone's 1896 reminiscences of his career: 'This declaration [that Jefferson Davis had made a nation] most unwarrantable to be made by a minister of the crown with no authority other than his own, was not due to any feeling of partisanship for the South or hostility to the North. Many who wished well to the Northern cause despaired of its success…The friends of the North in England were beginning to advise that it should give way, for the avoidance of further bloodshed and greater calamity…My offence was indeed only a mistake, but one of incredible grossness, and with such consequences of offence and alarm attached to it, that my failing to perceive them justly exposed me to very severe blame' (*Gladstone*, pp. 238–39). Jenkins also cited another passage: 'And strange to say, *post hoc* though perhaps not *propter hoc*, the United States have been that country in the world in which the most signal marks of public honour have been paid me, and which my name has been the most popular, the only parallels being Italy, Greece, and the Balkan Peninsula' (J. Brooke and M. Sorenson, eds, *The Prime Ministers' Papers: W. E. Gladstone*, 4 vols (London, 1971–81) i, pp. 133–34 and 250).

12. Cited in H. C. G. Matthew, *The Gladstone Diaries*, vol. v (Oxford, 1978), p. xliii. Matthew underlines that Gladstone's speech was both 'premediated and popular' and that his 'view was not as heretical in liberal and northern circles as was subsequently made out.' Gladstone to Gordon, 22 Sept. 1862, GP, 44533, f. 25.

13. Granville to Lord Russell, 27 Sept. 1862, cited in E. Fitzmaurice, *The Life of Granville George Leveson Gower Second Earl Granville K.G. 1815–1891*, 2 vols (London, 1905), i, p. 443.

14. Cited in B. Holland, *The Life of Spencer Compton, Eighth Duke of Devonshire*, 2 vols (London, 1911), i, p. 48.

15. Ibid., i, p. 53. For Hartington's American journey, see pp. 39–54.

16. M. R. D. Foot and H. C. G. Matthew, *The Gladstone Diaries*, vol. iii (Oxford, 1974), p. lii.

17. Matthew, *The Gladstone Diaries*, vol. vi (Oxford, 1978), pp. 90–164, *passim*.

18. F. W. Hirst, *Early Life & Letters of John Morley*, 2 vols (London, 1927), i, p. 42.

19. F. W. Knickerbocker, *Free Minds: John Morley and His Friends* (Cambridge, MA 1943), p. 126.

20. Ions, *James Bryce and American Democracy 1870–1922* (London, 1968), pp. 30–1.

21. S. Gwynn and G. Tuckwell, *The Life of the Rt. Hon, Sir Charles W. Dilke, Bart., M.P.*, 2 vols (London, 1917), i, p. 30.

22. Ibid., i, p. 56.

23. J. L. Garvin, *The Life of Joseph Chamberlain*, 3 vols (London, 1932–34), i, pp. 59–61 and 86. Also see Peter J. Marsh, *Joseph Chamberlain: Entrepreneur in Politics* (New Haven, CT, 1994), pp. 508 and 516.

24. National Library of Scotland, MSS 10071 (Rosebery Papers): Rosebery to George, Easter 1861, f. 3.

25. *The Times* republished many of the letters in *Letters by 'Historicus' on Some Questions of International Law* (London, 1863) and *American Neutrality* (London, 1865). A complete record of Harcourt's (Historicus's) articles written for *The Times* and other journals in the 1860s can be found in the Bodleian Library, Oxford MSS (William Vernon Harcourt Papers), Boxes 247–49.

26. A. G. Gardiner, *The Life of Sir William Harcourt*, 2 vols (London, 1923), i, p. 129.

27. Ibid., i, pp. 125–48 and 162–9. For letters between Harcourt and leading British figures on American topics between 1862 and 1873, see HP, Boxes 199–203.

28. HP, Box 201, C. F. Adams to Harcourt, 3 May 1865, f. 32.

29. Ibid., Box 200, R. H. Dana Jr to Harcourt, 26 Nov. 1863, ff. 118–19. See ibid., 6 July 1863, ff. 83–4.

30. Gardiner, *Life of Harcourt*, i, p. 129.

31. The most vociferous of all Liberals were those for the North: John Bright, Richard Cobden, William Forster, the Duke of Argyll, and Lord Houghton. See, for instance, *Speeches of John Bright, M.P. on the American Question* (London, 1865).

32. *The Glory and Shame of England*, 2 vols (New York, edn 1866), ii, pp. 175–87. Lester had historically involved himself in mischievous episodes related to prominent figures. In 1854, he tried to blackmail President Pierce. M. Gerlach, 'The Times of London: Editorial Policy and the American News, 1850–1861' (San Diego State Univ. MA thesis, 1976), pp. 107–13.

33. Brit. Mus., Addit. MSS 44413 (Gladstone Papers): Gladstone to Lester, 8 Aug. 1867, f. 66.

34. J. Morley, *The Life of William Ewart Gladstone*, 3 vols (London, 1903), ii, p. 344.

35. *The Case of the United States to be Laid Before the Tribunal of Arbitration to be Convened at Geneva* (Washington, DC, 1871), pp. 87–100.

36. The letter was printed in *Harper's New Monthly Magazine*, vol. liv (Dec. 1876), pp. 105–9, and is also included in Matthew, *The Gladstone Diaries. Vol. VIII. 1871–1874* (Oxford, 1982), pp. 243–50. For Liberal leaders' discussions on the letter, see A. Ramm, *The Political Correspondence of Mr. Gladstone and Lord Granville 1868–1876*, 2 vols (London, 1952), ii, pp. 313, 348, 350, 364–5 and 443.

37. For the outcome of Gladstone's letter of 28 Nov. 1872 and additional efforts by Gladstone to generate friendly American opinion, see ibid., Chapter II, pp. 58–70.

38. Gardiner, *Life of Harcourt*, i, pp. 195–207.

39. *PMG*, 25 Jan. 1868, cited in Gardiner, *Life of Harcourt*, i, pp. 198–9.

40. Harcourt to Russell, Nov. 1865, cited in Gardiner, *Life of Harcourt*, i, p. 169. See Harcourt's sane and moderating stand during the Anglo-American crisis over Venezuela – similar to his role from 1863–72. See Chapter VI, pp. 219–27.

41. *Ireland Since the Famine* (London, 1971), p. 127. For further treatments of British reactions to American Fenians see: W. D'Arcy, *The Fenian Movement in the United States, 1858–1886* (Washington, DC, 1947); B. Jenkins, *Fenians and Anglo-American Relations during the Reconstruction* (Ithaca, NY, 1969); and L. O'Brien, *Fenian Fever: An Anglo-American Dilemma* (New York, 1971).
42. A. Ramm, *Correspondence of Gladstone and Granville*, i, p. 63.
43. Ibid., i, p. 67.
44. See *The Times*, 27 May 1867 ('The Fenian Convicts'); 10 Jan. 1868 ('British Citizenship'); 6 Feb. 1868 ('The Status of Aliens'); and 12 Feb. 1868 ('The Law of Aliens').
45. DP, 43901, Dilke to?, ff. 134–5.
46. For instance, see A. Ramm, *Correspondence of Gladstone and Granville*, i, pp. 208–12. For other discussions of British conciliatory actions over the *Alabama* damages, see R. Jenkins, *Gladstone. A Biography* (London, 1995), pp. 356–60, and R. Shannon, *Gladstone: Heroic Minister, 1865–1898* (London, 1999), pp. 74–5, 108–9, and 113–14.
47. For Liberal participation in the *Alabama* claims negotiations, see A. Cook, *The Alabama Claims. American Politics and Anglo-American Relations, 1865–1872* (Ithaca, NY, 1975); M. M. Robson, 'The *Alabama* Claims and the Anglo-American Reconciliation, 1865–71,' *CHR*, vol. xlii (1961), pp. 1–22; and M. M. Bullen, 'British Policy towards Settlement with America, 1865–1872' (Univ. of London PhD thesis, 1955).
48. Cook, *The Alabama Claims*, p. 244.
49. C. S. Campbell, *From Revolution to Rapprochement: The United States and Britain, 1783–1906* (New York, 1974), p. 13. For the additional efforts of Gladstone, see Matthew, *The Gladstone Diaries. Vol. VIII. 1871–1874*, *passim*.
50. *America and the British Left from Bright to Bevan* (New York, 1957), p. 10. Pelling's chapter on 'America and the British Reform Struggle, 1865–7' discusses the whole debate in a most interesting light (pp. 7–29).
51. Hansard, 3rd series, vol. clxxxiii, 27 Apr. 1866, 119.
52. C. Harvie, *Lights of Liberalism*, p. 11.
53. *Essays on Reform* (1867): Houghton, 'On the Admission of the Working Classes as Part of our Social System; and on their Recognition for all Purposes as Part of the Nation,' pp. 45–66; Stephen, 'On the Choice of Representatives by Popular Constituencies,' pp. 85–126; and Smith, 'The Experience of the American Commonwealth,' pp. 217–38.
54. *An Outline of the American Schools System: with Remarks on the Establishment of the Common Schools in England* (Birmingham, 1868).
55. See Chapter 5, p. 196.
56. Two interesting studies are A. Schrier, *Ireland and the American Emigration 1850–1900* (Minneapolis, MN, 1958) and H. L. Malchow, *Population Pressures: Emigration and Government in Late 19th Century Britain* (Palo Alto, CA, 1979).
57. Garvin, *Life of Chamberlain*, i, p. 90.
58. R. Robinson and J, Gallagher, *Africa and the Victorians: The Official Mind of Imperialism* (London, 1961), p. 3.
59. The most conspicuous Americans among Liberal circles in Britain in the late 1860s were the diplomat John Lothrop Motley; journalists Kate Field and

George Washburn Smalley; men of letters Henry W. Longfellow, James R. Lowell, Charles E. Norton, and Oliver W. Holmes, Jr, and politicians William Lloyd Garrison and Charles Sumner. See, in particular, G. W. Curtis (ed.), *The Corrrespondence of John Lothrop Motley*, 2 vols (London, 1889), ii, pp. 259–319.

60. The Atlantic crossing by 1875 took approximately eight days. See P. S. Bagwell and G. E. Mingay, *Britain and America, 1850–1939: A Study of Economic Change* (London, 1970), p. 117.

61. R. H. Heindel, *The American Impact on Great Britain, 1898–1914: A Study of the United States in World History* (Philadelphia, 1940), p. 38. Thomas Hughes wrote his friend James Lowell about the organization: 'I have been busy in establishing an Anglo-American Committee here to cultivate a more intimate knowledge of your politics & specially of all questions at issue between us, & I think it is likely to prove a useful & influential organization.' Houghton Library, Cambridge, MA (Lowell Papers): bMS Am 765, New Years Eve, 1870 (442).

62. 26 Nov. 1867, cited in G. Macmillan, *Letters of Alexander Macmillan* (London, 1908), p. 234.

63. RP, 10073, Lawley to Rosebery, 19 Nov. 1873, f. 241.

64. *America Through British Eyes* (New York, 1948), pp. 305–41.

65. GP, 44303, Smith to Gladstone, 14 May 1871, f. 190.

66. DP, 43909, Smith to Dilke, 31 Nov. 1871, ff. 227.

67. HP, Box 201, Smith to Harcourt, 27 Nov. 1866, ff. 149–50 and 10 Dec. 1866, ff. 152–3.

68. The Perfectionists, who for a time successfully carried on their ideas in New York in the Oneida community, believed that if man freed himself from his selfishness, he could achieve a perfect state on earth.

69. Gwynn and Tuckwell, *Life of Dilke*, i, p. 59. For Dilke's life also see David Nicholls, The Lost Prime Minister: A Life of Sir Charles Dilke (London, 1995).

70. C. Dilke, *Greater Britain: A Record of Travel in English-Speaking Countries during 1866 and 1867*, 2 vols (London, 1868), i, p. vii.

71. Ibid., and p. viii.

72. R. Jenkins, *Sir Charles Dilke. A Victorian Tragedy* (London, 1958), p. 35.

73. DP, Dilke to his father, 11 July 1866, f. 119.

74. Ibid., 43900, ff. 100–210.

75. Dilke's reflections upon the United States are contained in *Great Britain,* i, pp. 1–318.

76. Dilke wrote to his father: 'The Senate have allowed the infamous tariff-bill to fall to the ground. This fact has done much to destroy my copperhead sympathies, & to lead me back to my first love – the Republican party; at the same time I think the president has – on the whole – taken up a wiser position than that of the *extreme* radicals, ...' DP, 43900, 20 July 1866, f. 124.

77. Dilke, *Greater Britain*, i, p. 291.

78. Ibid., i, p. 295.

79. Ibid., i, p. 244.

80. Richard Rapson declares: 'The British visitors may have regarded the manner in which the Americans conducted their government as comic, colorful, confusing, disgraceful, or fascinating; but they did not regard it as

especially significant. American politics, to them, resembled some rough-house but harmless game played for thrills, but not for serious stakes.' *Britons View America: Travel Commentary, 1860-1935* (Seattle, WA, 1970), p. 126. Rapson seriously underestimates the importance with which British Liberals viewed American institutions and politics. American protectionism, bimetallism, Irish-American intrigues, and Anglo-Saxon racism could hardly be taken lightly. Curiously, Rapson says little about Dilke's and nothing about, Rosebery's and Chamberlain's published trips to America.

81. DP, 43900, Dilke to his father, 16 Oct. 1866, f. 210.
82. Ibid., Dilke to his father, 16 Aug. 1866, f. 144. Michigan was 'the only university in the world *completely democratic* in character & government.'
83. Dilke, *Greater Britain*, i, p. 317.
84. Ibid., i, p. 314.
85. Ibid., ii, p. 59.
86. DP, 43909, 22 Aug. 1866, f. 81.
87. Ibid.
88. *Greater Britain*, ii, p. 68.
89. Gwynn and Tuckwell, *Life of Dilke*, i, pp. 74–5.
90. Ibid., i, p. 104.
91. PP, *Report of the Select Committee on Parliamentary and Municipal Elections* (1868–69), VIII (352), pp. 402–16.
92. FR, vol. xiv, n.s. (Dec. 1873), pp. 793–4.
93. DP, 43909, Holmes to Dilke, 14 Oct. 1877, f. 85 and Smith to Dilke, 31 Nov. 1971, ff. 226–7.
94. Boston Public Library, MS KF nos. 125–235, vol. ii (Kate Field Collection): Dilke to Field letters, 1871–74, nos. 152–64 are the most intimate of the series of letters.
95. L. Whiting, *Kate Field, A Record* (New York, 1899), p. 321. Also see pp. 282–4 on the relationship between Field and Dilke.
96. John Morley, *Recollections*, 2 vols (London, 1917), i, p. 52 and ii, pp. 104–6.
97. Butler Library, Columbia University, New York (Conway Papers): M. Conway to Morley, 6 Nov. 1867.
98. Brit. Mus., Addit. MSS 55055 (Macmillan Co. Papers): Morley to A. Macmillan, 3 Nov. 1867, f. 6.
99. Ibid., Morley to A. Macmillan, 28 Nov. 1867, f. 8.
100. Morley, *Recollections*, ii, p. 106.
101. Houghton Library, Cambridge, MA, bMS Am 1083 (Godkin Papers): Norton to Godkin, 13 Jan. 1869 (734).
102. Conway Papers, Morley to M. Conway, 13 Feb. 1867.
103. FR, C. Norton, 'On Emigration,' vol. vi (Aug. 1869), pp. 189–99; E. Dicey, 'The Republican Defeat in the United States,' vol. xvi (Dec. 1874), pp. 824–35; and J. McCarthy, 'Prohibitory Legislation in the United States,' vol. x (Aug. 1871), pp. 166–79.
104. Hirst, *Early Life of Morley*, i, pp. 122–3.
105. Morley, FR, vol. iii (Feb. 1868), p. 221.
106. Houghton Library, Cambridge, MA, bMS Am 1088 (Norton Papers): Morley to Norton, 31 July 1869 (4858).
107. God.P, Norton to Godkin, 8 June 1869 (737).

108. LP, bMS Am 765, Norton to Lowell, 30 Aug. 1868 (587). The same views are expressed in a letter to Godkin, God. P, 20 Aug. 1868 (726).

109. God.P, Norton to Godkin, 9 Oct. 1868 (729).

110. LP, bMS Am 765, Norton to Lowell, 30 Aug. 1868 (587).

111. Harrison wrote Norton a fascinating letter in 1871 which spelled out both Harrison's admiration for most Americans' understanding of republicanism and of his frequent communications with Americans. 'I have been very much struck to find how far better & more fairly the "Commune" is judged by Americans than by Englishmen. The root spirit of Republicanism, which an Englishman can only realise in imagination, but which an American feels as the postulate of every practical idea, and again that more true sense of nationality & patriotism which Americans have, not as with us for rather – not any longer – corrupted by feelings of race domination – & degenerating into a sort of domineering Imperialism – these two elements, the Republicanism, & the Patriotism of American public life have enabled Americans to see the strong side of the Commune better than Englishmen. I have received quite a crowd of communications from Americans on this subject – both in the U.S. & in Europe.' NP, 30 Aug. 1871 (3054). For general relationships between British and American Comtists, see Christopher Kent, *Brains and Numbers: Elitism, Comtism, and Democracy in Mid-Victorian England* (Toronto, 1978), especially pp. 37–8.

112. God.P, Norton to Godkin, 13 Jan. 1869 (734).

113. Ibid.

114. *John Morley: Liberal Intellectual in Politics* (Oxford, 1968), p. 49.

115. S. Norton and M. A. Howe (eds), *Letters of Charles Eliot Norton*, 2 vols (Boston, 1913), i, p. 432.

116. NP, Morley to Norton, 18 Jan. 1869–20 Feb. 1873 (4851–70). Charles Norton's close personal and intellectual relations with British liberals are admirably discussed recently in James Turner's *The Liberal Education of Charles Eliot Norton* (Baltimore, 1999).

117. Bryce's journal of his 1870 trip is the best source for his first American impressions. Bodleian Library, Oxford (Bryce Papers): USA 41. Ions, also, describes in some detail Bryce's 1870 trip: *Bryce and American Democracy*, pp. 39–80. See also, 'Bryce as Traveller,' in Tulloch, *James Bryce's American Commonwealth: the Anglo-American Background* (Woodbridge, 1988), pp. 54–61.

118. Ions, *Bryce and American Democracy*, p. 45 and Tulloch, *James Bryce's American Commonwealth*, passim.

119. 'American Experience in the Relief of the Poor,' *MM* vol. xxv (Nov. 1871), pp. 54–65; 'The Legal Profession in America,' *MM* vol. xxv (Jan. 1872), pp. 206–17; 'American Judges,' *MM*, vol. xxv (Mar. 1872), pp. 422–32; and 'On Some Peculiarities of Society in America,' *CM* vol. xxvi (Dec. 1872), pp. 704–16.

120. Bryce, 'American Experience in the Relief of the Poor,' p. 55.

121. Ibid.

122. Ibid., p. 59. Bryce reported his dismay at New York to his Oxford friend, Edward A. Freeman. 'They [Boss Tweed] are the biggest set of rogues and scoundrels in existence; a gang of robbers in New York city, mostly Irish, have gained complete control of the Irish and "rowdy" vote in that city: ... The worst feature to us is the indifference with which the corruption,

even the gross corruption of the New York judges seem to be viewed; and the way in which the votes of members of the state legislatures are openly sold.' BP, 9, Bryce to E. Freeman, 26 Sept. 1870, f. 164.

123. 'American Experience in the Relief of the Poor,' p. 59.
124. 'The Legal Profession in America', p. 212. Also, see BP, USA 41 (1870 Diary), pp. 65–71.
125. 'American Judges,' p. 432.
126. See note 119.
127. 'American Judges,' *passim*. Bryce's further notions of American democracy, as well as discussions of the relationship between Bryce's *American Commonwealth and Democracy in America* by Alexis de Tocqueville are treated by Stefan Collini, Donald Winch, and John Burrow, *That Noble Science of Politics: A Study in Nineteenth-Century Intellectual History* (Cambridge, 1983), pp. 239–43 and also John Burrows, *Whigs and Liberals: Continuity and Change in English Political Thought* (Oxford, 1988), pp. 44–6.
128. God.P, Bryce to Godkin, 4 Feb. 1871 (75).
129. Harvard Law Library, Cambridge, MA, (Holmes Jr Papers): Holmes Jr to Bryce, Box 38 F. 8 and Bryce to Holmes, Box 38 F. 12, and BP, USA 2, Bryce to Eliot.
130. Rosebery's 1873 American trip is discussed in Chapter 2, pp. 40–5.
131. G. Campbell, *White and Black. The Outcome of a Visit to the United States* (London, 1879) and Dilke, *Greater Britain*, 4th edn (London, 1869), pp. 3–27. For British and Scottish views of Reconstruction, see C. A. Bolt, 'British Attitudes to Reconstruction in the United States, 1863–77' (London Univ. College, PhD thesis, 1966–67) and H. M. Finnie, 'Scottish Attitudes to American Reconstruction, 1865–1877' (Univ. of Edinburgh PhD thesis, 1974).

2
Liberalism and the United States: Expanding American Activities, 1874–1880

Introduction

During the period of Disraeli's (later Earl of) Beaconsfield ministry of 1874–80, each prominent Liberal had his own distinct remedy for the ills of the party. They seldom worked together, except Chamberlain, Morley, and Dilke for the radical cause, and moved in and out of national political life almost at will. As D. A. Hamer explains: 'There were numerous different "schools of thought" and ideas as to where and by what means "progress" should now be sought, but Liberalism now no longer possessed a coherent and unifying, because generally accepted, ideological base.'[1] Yet there was one redeeming factor which marked the interrelationships between leading Liberals in what Vincent calls 'the community of sentiments'[2] during the opposition years of the 1870s. Ideological differences did not yet lead them to engage in personal and party feuds. Their relationships were fairly amicable, no matter how dissatisfied occasional private opinions showed them to be of their fellow Liberals' actions and ideas. This particularly characterized the relationships between the principal figures in this study: Gladstone, Chamberlain, Rosebery, Morley, and Harcourt.

British political debate during the Conservative ascendancy was dominated by foreign and imperial issues, notably the Turkish atrocities in Bulgaria, the 1878 Eastern crisis, the war in Afghanistan, and the Zulu War in South Africa. Liberals participated in the debates, but only slowly developed unified opposition policies. Not even the Eastern question served 'as a viable issue to bring the Liberals out of their political slump.'[3]

On the other hand, the Eastern question did inspire Gladstone's re-entry into active politics and silenced all who thought he would relinquish the reins of his party's leadership. Gladstone's re-entry also helped to raise a more coherent Liberal policy in opposition to Beaconsfield 'imperialism.' From 1878 to 1880, the Liberals did increasingly unify over the Conservatives' wars in Afghanistan and South Africa. When the Liberals turned to fight the election of 1880, they did so with exceptional energy and party organization. Gladstone's moving campaign perorations in Scotland – his first Midlothian addresses – symbolized the new breath of life in the Liberal party. The speeches focused primarily on foreign policies: on policies of self-determination, non-intervention, and enlightened international morality. In the 1880 election, the Liberals thoroughly trounced the Conservatives. They not only won an outright majority but could hope to count on additional support from a body of Irish Home Rulers.

Throughout these six years, Liberal leaders were much freed to pursue their private interests. Gladstone sought quiet in his studies at Hawarden after he unofficially resigned the leadership of the party in the Commons in February 1874 (officially a year later). More and more, he left the running of parliamentary affairs to others in the belief that 'there is much to be done with the pen, all bearing on high and sacred ends.'[4] His views were taken directly to the public to a greater extent than ever: either in speeches like those on Turkish atrocities or those during the Midlothian campaign. He also turned to write numerous articles for Liberal periodicals, especially the *Nineteenth Century* and the *North American Review.*

Chamberlain, Morley, Dilke, and Bryce also published their views in similar journals while all the leaders except Morley and Rosebery made frequent speeches in the 1870s. With Chamberlain's election to Parliament as a member for Birmingham in 1874, all save Morley and Bryce had entered Liberal parliamentary politics. Nonetheless, in his editorial capacity and through his friendships, Morley particularly maintained as active a role in such national debates as anyone possibly could though not a member of Parliament. At the same time, there was a great deal of opportunity for foreign travel. All the primary Liberal leaders except Harcourt traveled extensively in Europe. In addition, Rosebery and Dilke traveled around the world and the former made three visits to the United States. Bryce spent many months scaling mountains around the world. In short, writing and traveling were as primary occupations for Liberal leaders as their official party and parliamentary responsibilities.

After Gladstone's retirement in 1874, Harcourt and Granville were left as the Liberal experts on American diplomatic issues to raise questions or advocate policies in parliamentary debate. Before 1874 they had shown acute interest and none more so than the eloquent 'Historicus.' However, during the Beaconsfield ministry there were few 'Historicus' letters. None of these dwelt on American problems and by 1876 they had ground to a complete halt. While there were British–American diplomatic incidents in these years, the policies of the statesmen prevented the issues from reaching platforms of debate. The American Secretary of State, Hamilton Fish, and the British Foreign Secretaries, Derby and then Lord Salisbury, maintained inflexible positions towards each other's countries throughout the 1870s. Fish delayed from 1872 until 1876 appointing a commissioner to the Halifax Tribunal to settle problems stemming from the Geneva Tribunal. Derby would not consider demands for Britain to pay damages to American fishermen after the Fortune Bay incident in 1878. Such diplomatic maneuvering only concealed and further removed American diplomatic issues from parliamentary and national attention. It is noteworthy to discover that on only three occasions in the period of 1874 to 1880 did Liberals do more than merely request information on specific American items, and then their observations were limited to one issue. In 1876 Granville pressed for a loose interpretation of the existing extradition understanding with the United States to allow Americans to 'try [men] for a second offence.'[5] Granville raised the question again six months later.[6] There has rarely been a period in the history of parliamentary debates during which such little attention was given to American diplomatic issues by politicians as between 1874 and 1880. This has led at least one historian to conclude that 'After the end of Reconstruction, and with the settlement of the *Alabama* claims question arising from the Civil War, British interest in American domestic politics declined.'[7] However, closer examination of the facts leads to a different conclusion. Liberal leaders maintained, and in some important instances extended, their private interests in the United States in the 1870s. Three areas of the Liberal leader–American relationship stood out: first, Rosebery's extensive American preoccupations; second, Gladstone's distinct private American activities; and finally, Morley's and Chamberlain's attention to American developments as the result of their political and journalistic activities.[8]

Lord Rosebery: America discovered

Lord Rosebery made three visits to the United States between 1873 and 1876; these led to some of his closest friendships and to a series of experiences that made him knowledgeable on American society and politics. More so than with Dilke, Bryce, and Morley who had had similar opportunity for American travel, Rosebery's associations were with a group of politicians and socialites from New York and Washington, DC – not the Cambridge-based liberal and intellectual-minded Republicans. Many were Democrats. When Rosebery returned to England, he often reciprocated American hospitality he had received, by entertaining visitors in London, or at his estates at Mentmore or the Durdans. Marriage also played a key role. With Rosebery's marriage in 1878 to Hannah Rothschild of the wealthy European banking family, the Rosebery households became the foci of prominent literary, political, and social gatherings. Throughout the 1870s, Rosebery acted as a benefactor of Anglo-American contacts. The noted novelist Henry James, the colorful socialite Sam Ward, and the controversial author-journalist William Hurlbert all were part of the intimate Rosebery coterie in Britain. Before Rosebery became deeply involved in British politics, he pursued his American relationship with keen resolution.

Rosebery's first American trip lasted from 30 September 1873 when he landed in New York, until his departure from the same city on 17 December. The majority of his time was spent in New York, Boston, and Washington DC, but his circuit took him to Ottawa, Quebec, and Montreal in Canada, as well as west to Provo in Utah and Chicago.[9] His close friend and former secretary to Gladstone, Francis Lawley, provided him with advice and a batch of introductions. These were primarily to a series of prominent bankers, journalists, and social figures in New York, notably William Stewart, Samuel Ward, William Hurlbert, William Duncan, and August Belmont.[10] Two became a couple of Rosebery's closest friends. William Hurlbert and Samuel Ward were Rosebery's primary American friends in the 1870s. Hurlbert was a brilliant journalist but erratic individual, who between 1876 and 1883 edited the *New York World*. Thereafter, he spent the majority of his life in Great Britain and Europe. He became deeply interested in British politics, especially British–Irish relations, and authored two books: *Ireland under Coercion: The Diary of An American* and *England under Coercion*.[11] The 1890s were troubled years for him; because of a legal suit he was ostracized from society and eventually forced to leave England. His opposition to Irish Home Rule did not endear him to many of his earlier Gladstonian Liberal friends, including Rosebery.[12] However, in the 1870s, Rosebery and Hurlbert were still good friends.

On the other hand, Sam Ward and Rosebery remained in the closest of relations until the former's death in 1884. Ward was a socially cultivated

Democrat with few equals in his inside knowledge of politics on the East coast. One of his biographers had this to say about him.

> They called Sam Ward, the 'King of the Lobby,' and he was. Henry Adams, surveying the Washington scene, found 'few figures on the Paris stage more interesting and dramatic than old Sam Ward, who knew more of life than all the departments of government put together, including the Senate and the Smithsonian.' He enjoyed prerogatives accorded to few government leaders; ... [13]

Sam Ward opened innumerable doors into the American political and social worlds for Rosebery. Ward's excitement at meeting Rosebery in 1873 was profound. To Lawley, he wrote about the 'great & unexpected happiness your introduction of our dear Rosebery shed upon my wayward & shadowy life.'[14] Thomas Bayard, a future Secretary of State, Minister in London, and friend of Rosebery's, described the earl as 'a charming fellow and quite possibly the future Prime Minister of England.'[15]

Ward, Hurlbert, and Rosebery formed the 'Mendacious Club.' Ward was the 'president,' Hurlbert the 'liar,' and Rosebery the 'sycophant.' They met whenever possible, either in the United States or Great Britain, to discuss social and political events. It was Ward, primarily, who was responsible for introducing Rosebery to a string of politicians with whom the Englishman shared dinners, long talks, and walks during his first American trip. Some of his most important American acquaintances in the 1870s were Thomas Bayard; the former Attorney-General and future Secretary of State, William Evarts; the prominent Republican and friend of President Grant, Senator Roscoe Conkling; the future Secretary of State James Blaine; Secretary of State Hamilton Fish; and two future Presidents, James Garfield and Chester Arthur.[16] When Ward went to England in 1879 and again in the 1880s, Rosebery returned the favors and introduced the American into British society. Ward had his own rooms at each of Rosebery's homes and spent long periods of time with the Roseberys. The American socialite and 'politico' and the aristocratic young statesman were the most intimate of companions and friends, from 1873 to 1884.[17]

During his first trip to America in 1873, Rosebery had exceptional opportunities for observing the operations of American society and politics. He visited Congress, departments of government, port authorities, police stations, local schools, charitable institutions, and many other bodies. Rosebery was afforded as good an opportunity as Bryce and Dilke (in many respects better), to form early knowledgeable views of the United States. Unfortunately, his evaluations of America in 1873 were so uncritically favorable that they are slightly disappointing. In his enthusiasm for everything American, there were few critical remarks upon specific weaknesses, or, for that matter, strengths of American developments. Rosebery himself was the first to admit of his partiality and for his reasons for such a position.

> It is easy to taunt and to deride, to point to a small vulgarism here and a petty venality there, and then to denounce the whole state as one stinking mass of corruption. The blotches exist indeed but they are the blemishes of the growing youth which are the virile promise of a coming beard and a splendid manhood.[18]

Thus, Rosebery leaves only a string of adulatory, general, not particularly precise reflections upon a series of American themes and events.

Among the American aspects that captured some of Rosebery's attention were religion, the standard of living, industrial manufactures, political conventions, and geography. Wherever he turned, Rosebery found that the United States was at least the equal of nations in Europe, often the latter's superior. On religion, he declared 'I cannot pretend to say if the Americans are a religious people (as the cant phrase goes): but I have certainly never seen a nation so given to building and attending churches.'[19] On the standard of living, he observed: 'Almost everyone has the means of living with some comfort, there is therefore less envy, less desire to disturb the order of things than in those old states.'[20] Nor did the young earl bemoan the lack of tradition or ancient customs in America. Rather, he praised their industry and inventions: 'They [Americans] cherish and beautify the industrial objects which form their pride and their means of support.'[21] More surprisingly, Rosebery, unlike Morley and Bryce, found nothing disturbing about a mass Democratic political demonstration in New York. He lavished great praise on the orderly conduct and decorum of the 'monster procession of American citizens.' He even went so far as to call the torchlight procession 'both a great moral spectacle and a great political lesson.' In fact, that event did much to persuade Rosebery that American civilization had advanced farther than that in Europe.

> It was not the mere numbers though they were impressive enough; it was rather the sign of a civilisation which could not as yet be found in Europe. There was, apparently, perfect sobriety: in my

country there would certainly have been no such aggregation of human beings without much drunkenness. There was perfect order without the intervention of the police: in my country there would have been tumult, disorder and a great force of constabulatory...

...Instead of rushing about as is the way elsewhere in times of political excitement to make political centres of themselves, they were satisfied to merge their own individuality in the great mass. There was no anxiety to assert a fitful personality by the delivery of speeches.[22]

Such laudatory observations of the United States were commonplace views of his.

Before Rosebery left the United States, he made one attempt to summarize its strengths, weaknesses, and novelty. His five basic topics had little to do with institutional imbalances or perceptive comparisons with Europe, but rather derived from external, geographical, or ethnic factors:

1. Size – no republic has ever been carried on on so large a scale.
2. Difference of races immigrating.
3. Difference of races as affected by variety of climates.
4. Differences of the interests of the various regions.
5. Increase of luxury and expenditure.[23]

Some of Rosebery's American infatuation was certainly the by-product of his relationships with Sam Ward and William Hurlbert, who as free-living, enthusiastic Democrats ignited in the young peer an almost blind adulation for American progress.

With a typically American fervor, Rosebery assumed the mantle of philanthropist in the spirit of a Carnegie or Rockefeller. After a visit to St Vincent's Home for Boys in New York, he took it upon himself to support and educate at $136 a year a poor boot black. It was a charitable act that did not go unnoticed by Americans. A small Catholic journal, the *Elizabeth Daily Journal*, paid a glowing tribute to Rosebery: 'If they have any more Roseberys over there, let us by all means have them.'[24] When Rosebery finally turned to leave the shores of America, he did so with great reluctance. He left, in his own words, 'greatly pleased with America.'[25]

And so my dream is over. I suppose I have been there but can I be sure – At any rate I am back in England – miserably smoky and narrow as ever. Is it a dream that I have been in a country where all are born equal before the law? Where every man has the means of obtaining the dearest object of the Anglo-saxon's heart, a plot of land of his own on which to live and die? Where each son of the soil carries in his wallet not the staff of a field marshal, for field marshals are abhorrent to the spirit of the country, but a possible passport to the White House, to the Bench of the Supreme Court, to every eminent position without exception that the State can afford. Where none as in heaven is before or after another, where none can afford to shut himself up in the shallow exclusiveness of wealth, lest he be left fixed though not a star, where every Citizen is a conductor of the electric spark of political power.[26]

Rosebery's second American visit in the winter of 1874–75 was vastly different from his first. Eager to see other parts of the United States than the metropolitan Eastern seaboard, Rosebery set off for an extensive tour of the Southern states. From Philadelphia, his wanderings took him to Annapolis, Baltimore, Savannah, New Orleans, and then even on to Cuba where he visited Trinidad, Havana, and Crefugios.[27] On this circuit, he collected facts, evidently studied certain problems, and arrived at a distinct interest in certain Southern developments. In one instance, he summarized a fairly lengthy part of Dilke's argument in *Greater Britain*: on what grounds Americans opted for their protectionist trade system. In another case, he reflected on how far Catholicism had grown in America while in Cuba he could hardly find a church open at Christmas.[28] But two topics emerged for serious study – the condition of the blacks and Confederate Civil War history.

Rosebery was keenly fascinated by the condition of the blacks in Cuba and the Southern states. While he acknowledged that the South had accepted what was then a thing of the past, Rosebery himself found it difficult to accept the blacks as part of an advancing progressive civilization. 'The negroes are very puzzling in their habits.'[29] On another instance, he reflected: 'The Southern whites claim to being compelled to carry revolvers as a protection against the negroes who carry knives or razors, which latter they prefer.'[30] Southern whites, Rosebery concluded, still oriented their lives very much around sheer survival. In Cuba, Rosebery was horrified at the vice and depravity. 'If anyone would know how low and degrading vice may be made let him go to Havana. The brothels have an open porte cochere [sic]. I never was so sickened in my life at any sight.'[31] These vices were not only those of the lower classes. Those of the aristocracy were 'incredible.'

Then there was a series of adventures with cockroaches, scorpions, and rats that in the end, no doubt, fostered Rosebery's general antipathy to Latin America.[32] Like most Victorian Englishmen, he saw the blacks as an inferior race and looked upon American expansion in Central and South America as a benevolent and civilizing movement, one that fulfilled the destiny of Anglo-Saxon institutions.

The second topic which stimulated Rosebery's interests was the Confederate stance during the Civil War. Rosebery had some excellent opportunities for delving into the past conflicts. He met former Confederate President Jefferson Davis, as well as such generals as Dick Taylor and Beauregard. From Jefferson Davis, there was apparently little to learn, for during their meeting the former remained inanimate and quiet. Not surprisingly, Davis declared 'the United States Government was the basest and simplest tyranny now existing.'[33] But with Generals Taylor and Beauregard, Rosebery held long talks about the Mexican War as well as the Battle of Bull Run and military strategy.[34] In the end, his second trip to America provided Rosebery with a series of experiences of another section of the country. While he had been tested by the physical and social conditions, his enthusiasm for the United States did not diminish, but only increased.

One curious incident occurred in 1875 after Rosebery returned from his North American visit in 1874–75. His interest in Cuba probably went a long way towards explaining why in December 1875, Francis Lawley approached him for his participation in an adventurous but somewhat risky investment scheme. The project, which was allegedly supported by Charles Sumner and an American banker, called for the establishment of a national bank on the island of Santo Domingo. It was a project in the best capitalist and imperialistic traditions and Rosebery would be its first president. The capital would be privately subscribed and Rosebery's name would not be mentioned. His salary would be at least £2500 a year, and his 'indirect advantage will be that the Bank will have cotton & sugar & tobacco plantations & that it will own 80 square miles of the most magnificent mahogany trees in the world.'[35] Evidently, Rosebery did not accept the offer, for there was no other mention of the scheme in subsequent correspondence between Lawley and Rosebery. The young Liberal's reasons are not known, but perhaps his unpleasant memories of cockroaches and brothels had persuaded him that Caribbean islands were not the best places for sensitive investments.

Far less is known about Rosebery's third visit to America than about the first two. He ventured to few new places and the purpose of the 1876 journey was most likely to renew his friendships with Ward and

Hurlbert. Rosebery also apparently visited the International Exhibition in Philadelphia. It was one of the major attractions for Englishmen in America in 1876.[36] After his return to England, Rosebery assumed the role of champion for closer Anglo-American associations.

Rosebery was frequently prevailed upon by members of the aristocracy for letters of introduction to Americans. In the same manner in which Leslie Stephen or Matthew Arnold had provided such services for many young Liberals, Rosebery himself provided them for others in the 1870s and 1880s. Thus, for instance, Rosebery wrote such a letter for Captain Byng, who had been an Etonian schoolmate of his; for Lord Ronald Gower, the son of the Duke of Sutherland; for the Earl of Dunraven; and for Captain George A. Percy, the nephew of the Duke of Northumberland.[37] The letter for Captain Percy was typical. It also evinces the typically playful and intimate tone in which he always wrote to his 'dear Sam.'

When I am asked by the rising youth of this country to give them an introduction to the principal poetical, theological and political celebrities of America, I invariably surprise them by giving them one simple note with your image and superscription upon it. When I am asked the reason of my giving only one letter, I reply that under your sombrero may be found an epitome of all the poetry, theology and politics of America, – nay, if it were not something of a bull I should say a great deal more. But, besides that, there are some sparks of geology, philosophy, facetiae, gastronomy, and philoprogenitiveness. Besides that, you have studied in its native wilds that savage and relentless animal, the mother-in-law. You have, moreover, moulded the millionaire, cauterized the courtesan and probed the prig. Hail! Representative of this highest Culture! Allow me to present at your feet Captain George Algernon Percy of the Grenadier Guards, – nephew of the Duke of Northumberland. If you can instruct him in the way he should go, you will have gratified his contemporary at Eton and your affectionate disciple,

A. R. Sycophant, M. C.[38]

Rosebery not only sought to ensure that Englishmen had ample opportunities for seeing the United States, but also promoted friendly Anglo-American relations, by acting as host to Americans in Britain. General Dick Taylor visited him in 1875; William Hurlbert in 1878; Thomas Bayard in 1879; and finally, and most importantly, Samuel

Ward in 1879. Ward reported on the unsparing hospitality the Roseberys heaped upon him. 'They made a great deal more of me than I expected or deserved and I was quite dazed by the overwhelming kindness I met at every corner. I paid three visits to Dalmeny where its charming mistress adopted me as her uncle & half a dozen to Mentmore.'[39] Other Americans were to follow suit in the 1880s, notably the novelist Henry James, the journalist George Smalley, and the industrialist Andrew Carnegie. Rosebery was a prime inspiration for Anglo-American contacts in the 1870s and 1880s.[40]

In many respects, the United States was one of Rosebery's most important interests in the 1870s, especially before he entered actively into Liberal politics. Whenever he had an opportunity, he journeyed to America and his friendships with Hurlbert, perhaps Bayard, and certainly Ward were all close. His American experiences had given him a wide range of practical knowledge of the country. While he demonstrated a traveler's mentality towards many American developments, it seems certain that his perceptions gained acumen as the decade progressed. Long talks with Ward certainly helped. He received the *Congressional Globe* from the United States and followed important events, such as a controversial trial – the Beecher-Tilton affair.[41] No other Liberal leader demonstrated such a youthful infatuation with the United States as Rosebery.

William E. Gladstone and 'Kin Beyond Sea'

Between 1874 and 1880, Gladstone demonstrated a keen sensitivity to any mention of his former pro-Southern sympathies. While American opinion warmed to Gladstone and largely forgot these ill-timed remarks, Gladstone was still haunted by his past.[42] One issue particularly bothered the former Prime Minister in the 1870s. The second chapter of the American case which was presented to the Geneva Tribunal had focused on the unfriendly attitudes of Gladstone in 1862.[43] With a strong determination, Gladstone finally prevailed over other members of his Cabinet and sent his long explanatory letter of 28 November 1872 to the American Minister, General Schenck. Gladstone did not receive a final response from Secretary of State Fish until 1876. The delay only seemed to Gladstone to signal American official hostility to his case.

In February 1873, General Schenck answered all of Gladstone's anxieties and accepted his explanations most warmly. Schenck assured him that 'all contention is now happily at an end' and 'we will not use so much as a single word that will revive it.' He concluded in the clearest manner.

> I am quite satisfied, not only by your general disclaimer, but by the proofs of expressed opinion & feeling of which you make citation, that you had never any conscious hostility towards the Government of the United [*sic*] nor a desire to see their Union broken up.[44]

Schenck promised to pass on the contents of the letter to his superiors in Washington, who would no doubt accept them as 'a grateful & voluntary manifestation of personal good will.'[45] Such strong assurances should have resolved the problem for Gladstone, yet he wanted further assurance of his innocence from higher American officials. He desired this because 'it was under their authority that the Case of the U. States was framed & published, & on that authority still rest the personal charges agst. me contained in it.'[46]

A breakdown in communications now occurred between Gladstone, Schenck, and the American Secretary of State, Hamilton Fish, which only seemed to confirm to Gladstone that Fish still harbored ill feelings. In July 1875, Gladstone remonstrated to Fish through Schenck that 'something remains due to me.'[47] An explanation of the delay finally came. Fish had written Schenck a letter marked 'private' on the matter as early as 1873 but Schenck felt that he had first to check with Fish before sending the contents on to Gladstone. That process curiously took over two and a half years. Not until late in November 1875 did Gladstone receive a copy of Fish's earlier letter: a view which he had awaited anxiously for almost five years.[48]

The American Secretary did not give in to Gladstone's protests fully or easily. While Fish indicated deep respect for the former Prime Minister as a statesman and acknowledged that Gladstone had not been as anti-Northern as Lord Russell, he insisted that, by virtue of his eminence, Gladstone's remarks had helped considerably to align British opinion against the Union. Fish accepted some of his apologies and even saw 'a spirit of justice (in many instances)' in Gladstone's speeches but stood firmly in the belief that he had been wrong. Fish wrote that he was 'obliged to look at the question as it was at *the time* & I cannot but think that, unconsciously at least, he fell in with the expressions of those around him who were hostile & unfriendly.'[49] Gladstone was not satisfied. He had only one more course open to him by which he might prove that Americans had forgiven him; as always, that lay in the arena of public opinion.

On 1 January 1876, America's centennial year, Gladstone wrote to Fish, asking permission to publish both his and the Secretary of State's letters in an American newspaper. Gladstone's motives and sentiments for doing so were clearly stated. They were to persist as central themes in Gladstone's American relationship throughout the remainder of his life.

> My motive admits of a very simple explanation. I constantly receive from America assurances of good will, from a multitude of various quarters, for which I am very grateful: and I am desirous to place before [and] among the people of the United States as may feel any interest in the matter, the evidences contained in that letter of what have been at all times my feelings towards their country...
>
> My sentiments of respecting the relations of our two countries make me very anxious that in the small degree in which my name may be associated with them it should carry with it no suggestion except those of peace and good will.[50]

Fish reluctantly gave his approval to the publication of the letters, yet only after several modifications had been made. Lord Russell's hostility could not be specifically referred to and no suggestion could be made to the effect that Fish's views were other than private. Fish's sensitivity in the matter was obviously heightened by the fact that 1876 was an election year. Grant's administration was suffering severe criticism. In December 1876, *Harper's New Monthly Magazine* printed Gladstone's letter.[51] It is difficult to measure the character of the American reception of the Gladstone–Fish letters, for they attracted little American public notice. On the other hand, Gladstone was evidently satisfied. The editor, H. M. Alden, was overjoyed by Gladstone's willingness to publish in his journal, paid him twenty pounds sterling and sought further contributions.[52]

The details of this incident underline how assiduously Gladstone attempted to eradicate any memory of his pro-Southern and anti-American remarks.[53] His article 'Kin Beyond Sea' in 1878 as well as his article in *Harper's Magazine* must be seen as public articulations to the American people. Gladstone was very conscious of emphasizing the warm feelings he held for the United States.[54] When Gladstone was on the verge of assuming office in 1880, he was involved in yet another scheme publishing former British attitudes towards the Confederacy. In October 1879 he wrote to the American Secretary of State William Evarts to discover the sources behind an article that had just been published in the *North American Review*. It touched on

Disraeli's affiliations with the Confederates. Gladstone wished to unearth any 'further evidence of Mr. Disraeli's dealings with the Confederacy, or expressions of sympathy with it.'[55] Evarts' response was cautious. He told Gladstone that he would first have to look into the issue before he could give Gladstone 'publicity to those [letters] – which you express an interest.'[56]

With the formation of Gladstone's second ministry in April 1880, his attention turned to other matters; perhaps Evarts refused to allow Gladstone the access he desired. No further mention can be found regarding Gladstone's apparent plan to expose Disraeli's Confederate leanings. While Gladstone continued to address with a sense of guilt the negative American opinion because of his pro-Southern declarations),[57] Americans themselves, through invitations to visit the United States, letters of a flattering kind, and the sending of articles, clippings, books, and comments, were responsible for encouraging Gladstone's genuine interest in the United States. In time Gladstone came to hold a particularly warm spot in the hearts of the American people and his person stood very much for Anglo-American harmony and understanding.

After Gladstone retired from the Liberal leadership in 1874, some of his American acquaintances – Reverdy Johnson (the former American Minister), Cyrus Field, and Richard Henry Dana Jr – sent him consoling letters.[58] Johnson also enclosed a newspaper clipping from the *New York Tribune* which by and large described the rising American public reverence for Gladstone during the 1870s. The Liberal leader who had formerly 'attacked the Union' had become the model statesman.

> The fashion that Mr. Gladstone has set, the *manner* of his political course, is perhaps nearly as important to England as the special measures which he has accomplished. He has inculcated and impressed upon the imaginations of young men a new idea of the profession of the statesman. The new statesman is to be a man of pure life and of moral enthusiasm, profoundly in sympathy with all the best endeavors of men and society, profoundly anxious to be not of temporary but of permanent service to his country. And not to his country alone, but to mankind. Fashions change, we know. A new man may set a new fashion. But it will be long, we imagine, before so great and so illustrious an example will occupy the attention of Englishmen.[59]

In addition to such warm compliments, specific honors also were showered upon Gladstone. None could have been more satisfying than that of the American Academy of Arts and Sciences which elected Gladstone a 'foreign honorary member' to replace the recently departed father of liberalism, John Stuart Mill.[60] In a sea of American praise, specific currents can be pointed out in their correspondences to the Liberal leader.

Numerous attempts were made to persuade Gladstone to visit the United States. Such invitations were also extended to such British heroes, in American eyes, as John Bright, but by no means in such large numbers, or from such far-ranging quarters as those which reached the Grand Old Man. These entreaties were most urgent in the years when Gladstone was out of office, as from 1874 to 1880.

Cyrus Field emphasized that 'nothing so rapidly restores exhausted energies as a sea voyage & a perfect change of scene'[61] and the jurist Dana Jr noted 'that you will have here a reception which no European, unconnected like Lafayette with our history, has ever had.' Dana cajoled Gladstone at length.

> Here is a new world, under new conditions, which will greatly interest you as a social philosopher, & publicist, and a person interested in the future of your race, – of humanity. Here is scenery you have never beheld or much read about, and a new experience of living, social, political & economical alike. In Europe, you see each race working in its old, deep rut. Here, you will see an amalgamation of races and religions, more or less carried out, – at least – in close cooperation. In short, all will be new, and, I cannot doubt interesting.[62]

Field's home would be Gladstone's, 'our Railways are very luxuriously fitted up,' and 'All our best people would welcome you heartily.'[63] And the invitations did come from the best people. The President of Harvard, Charles Eliot, asked Gladstone to 'deliver a course of ten lectures … on national revenue, the development of national resources, the incidence of taxes, the relations of capital and labor,' or any other such subject.[64] The Secretary of State under President Hayes, William Evarts, and Bishop Potter of New York also extended felicitations.[65] Though Gladstone never traveled to the United States, these invitations no doubt were warmly received. They seem to have encouraged Gladstone to the view that Americans regarded him favorably.

Another form that Gladstone's relationship with the United States took was in terms of the ever increasing surge of books, articles, and miscellany which he received concerning the United States. Reverdy Johnson sent clippings relating to American opinion of Gladstone's resignation in

1874 and of Congressional action on the Geneva Award,[66] while Cyrus Field sent two volumes of *Picturesque America* and his brother's work describing a journey around the world.[67] The literary scholar at Yale, Ellis Yarnell, wrote about the American reception of Gladstone's article on 'Ritualism' in 1874 and the relevance of the article 'as far as America is concerned.'[68] Elihu Burritt, the Sanskrit scholar, forwarded him a work of his own on an introduction to Sanskrit,[69] and the editor of the *North American Review*, Allen Thorndike Rice, passed on a series of works and articles to help in the preparation of his article 'Kin Beyond Sea': *Burton's Thirty Years in the United States Senate*, de Tocqueville's masterful analysis of America, copies of the *North American Review*, and facts on American debts, armed forces, and amnesty.[70] Gladstone read and studied most of these works, and many more. More so than almost any of his parliamentary colleagues, Gladstone was able to keep track of American history and events through a steady flow of gratis printed matter from prominent Americans.

One communiqué from an American even led Gladstone to make public remarks which affected the livelihood of his correspondent. On 9 January 1877, Eugene Schuyler, the American consul general in Constantinople, sent Gladstone a French translation of his report on the Bulgarian massacres before English copies were generally available.[71] Gladstone thanked him greatly for his services and he was inspired even more in championing the cause of the Bulgarians. In fact, Schuyler's original report upon the Bulgarian atrocities from the site of the crimes, subsequently published in the *Daily News* on 29 August 1876, did much to spark the whole Gladstonian interest in the crisis. It provided the critical evidence which Gladstone used to such stunning effect in his pamphlet, *The Bulgarian Horrors and the Question of the East*.[72] At Blackheath and again at Taunton, Gladstone publicly praised Schuyler's name.[73] His audiences evidently responded enthusiastically, but not so the American government. Over a period they had become upset by Schuyler's exposure of sensitive information, and to none other than the former British Prime Minister. The American government severely reprimanded Schuyler, forbade him to send further reports to Gladstone, and in 1878 removed him from his position.[74] Gladstone had again, though quite unintentionally, helped cause an international incident that had irritated the American government, specifically Secretary of State Fish.

Another incident in the mid-1870s also demonstrated Gladstone's sincere respect for, and in this case strong friendship with, an American. When President Grant nominated as American minister to Britain Richard Henry Dana, the prominent American jurist and author who had been acquainted with Gladstone as far back as the 1850s, British Liberals privately and publicly rejoiced at the choice.[75] Both Gladstone and Harcourt were in touch with Dana. Both had deep respect for Dana's literary and intellectual talents. Thus, Gladstone had been 'struck by the very clear light in which he had argued the Papal question in 1875.'[76]

However, Gladstone's and other Liberals' happy anticipation of Dana as Minister was short lived. The Senate, led by a group of bitter Democrats, vigorously rejected the nomination in an effort to take advantage of President Grant in an election year. Liberal condemnation of the Senate's action was almost universal and the jobbery of American politics stood forth in their eyes. The former American Minister, John Lothrop Motley, reported the British political reaction to Dana.

> Not only men like the Duke of Argyll, Mr. Gladstone & other distinguished personages who are your personal friends but all the influential portion of that society with which you would have been brought into immediate & close relations – political, literary & social – feel how much has now been lost to both countries which so strongly gave the assent which the Senate has withheld.[77]

Gladstone had followed Dana's prospects with eagerness, and the American's rejection because of a body of Democrats did not endear American politics to the GOM. The issue probably puzzled Gladstone and may have helped to inspire a more serious study of American politics in 1877–78.

Gladstone turned to write his first article specifically upon American politics in 1878 and did so as a result of a variety of developments. But it was primarily the efforts of a persistent American journalist that led to the article. Many editors and journalists had sought contributions from Gladstone; they would increasingly petition him for favors in the 1880s and 1890s. It was Allen Thorndike Rice, a former undergraduate of Christ Church in Oxford and in 1877 the newly appointed editor of the *North American Review*, who finally reached Gladstone. In February 1877, 'in an attempt to infuse new life into the venerable periodical, and to sustain it as the leader of American thought,' Rice solicited a contribution from Gladstone. He believed that 'contributions from Europeans – especially Englishmen – would vastly increase both the interest and the power of the work.'[78] However, not until early May, when Rice visited Gladstone at Hawarden did the elder Liberal leader consent to such a contribution. Throughout the summer he worked on the article, often studying information on the United States from Rice. It was published in the September/October issue.

'Kin Beyond Sea' was an overwhelming commendation of the United States. While Gladstone's purpose was to view British institutions as favorably as American ones, he endorsed American progress to such an extent that the remarks about England seemed muffled to contemporaries. He emphasized that the United States 'will probably become what we are now, the head servant in the great household of the world, the employer of all employed, because her service will be the most, and ablest.' He added, 'But while we have been advancing with this portentious rapidity, America is passing us by in a canter.'[79] The study of each other's institutions was important for political students in England and America, and Gladstone made his contribution.[80] There were various common tendencies between the two countries – a preference for the practical to the abstract, tolerance of opinion, freedom of thought, high value on liberty, high premiums upon self-help, distrust of centralization, cherishing of municipal, local, and parochial liberties, and 'publicity as the vital air of politics.'[81]

> But as the British Constitution is the most subtle organism which has proceeded from the womb and the long gestation of progressive history, so the American Constitution is, so far as I can see, the most wonderful work ever struck off at a given time by the brain and purpose of man.[82]

When it came time to discuss specific American developments, Gladstone offered what he called a 'few, faint, and superficial' notices. He had 'not had the opportunities necessary for the careful and searching scrutiny' which he would have liked. The manner in which 'the American people should permit themselves continually to be disturbed by the business of the presidential elections' and the periodic 'clean sweep of the entire civil service'[83] earned a degree of censure from Gladstone. He also pointed out instances of 'occasional phenomena of local corruption,' 'the mysterious manipulation of votes for the presidency,' and 'the very curious influences which are shaping the politics of the negroes and of the South,'[84] as being worthy topics for discussion. However, Gladstone, preferred not to enter the lists. Rather, he returned to praise the unrivaled success with which the United States had fought a civil war, returned to a peace-time economy and society, and more remarkably still continually reduced her debt.

> In twelve years she has reduced her debt by £158,000,000 or at the rate of £13,000,000 for every year. In each twelve months she has done what we did in eight years; her self-command, self-denial, and

wise fore-thought for the future have been, to say the least, eight-fold ours.[85]

After a short discussion of the federal system of government, with some specific comments upon the independent nature of the office of the American presidency from either ministerial or popular influence, Gladstone devoted the bulk of the article to an analysis of the historic development of the English parliamentary system of government. Americans and Englishmen alike responded to Gladstone's article. The editor A. T. Rice was sure that the article would 'not soon be forgotten ... that there is here ... a loud clamor to hear your voice again.' Rice paid Gladstone £40 and sought other contributions on questions of the day: the negro question, a comparison between the American and British liberation of slaves, or another subject of his choice.[86] Cyrus Field commented that the article had 'created a very marked and favorable impression on our people.'[87] Englishmen were much more divided in opinion. Granville pointed out that 'The States have immense advantages in the extent and fertility of the soil, their inexhaustible mineral wealth, and their free institutions, but is it clear that they will always remain united?'[88] Hartington protested vigorously to Granville upon Gladstone's sympathies. 'What is the good of telling people that the Americans are going to beat us, and that he [Gladstone] rather likes it?'[89] Even the Liberal *Pall Mall Gazette* and the *Daily News* were startled by the prediction of Gladstone regarding America's future domination of world trade,[90] while *The Times* admonished Gladstone more strongly.[91] Gladstone's article had stimulated an outburst of Anglo-American attention to the two countries' relative political and economic strengths and weaknesses, almost in the same manner that his pamphlet on Bulgarian atrocities had greatly stirred another international controversy.

In the late 1870s, it had become clear to various Englishmen and Americans that Gladstone was deeply interested and involved in the United States. Moreover, he himself sought forums to express his favorable views towards America. Both in trying to absolve his former pro-Southern remarks and his 'Kin Beyond Sea' article, he had practical reasons for speaking out. He declared such in a letter in February 1879: 'I had a practical object in view. It was to act on the opinion of this country in favour of those financial & administrative measures which would form your best preparation for possible foul weather.'[92] During the 1880s, Gladstone turned often to express himself on American issues. These invariably had the double motives of addressing both the

British and American publics independently, and as a unified Anglo-Saxon community.

Young Radicals and the United States: Dilke, Morley, and Chamberlain

Between 1876 and 1880, three young leaders of the radical element of the Liberal Party – Chamberlain, Dilke, and Morley – were almost inseparable. Morley's and Chamberlain's partnership stood at its height, while Chamberlain stayed at Dilke's home in Sloane Street whenever in London. Dilke, Morley, and Chamberlain often dined, discussed, and wrote to each other; and in the course of their various journalistic and political activities, Chamberlain and Morley, in particular, turned to study American developments. At times, they were even as lavishly friendly towards America and her institutions as Rosebery and Gladstone.

Dilke and Morley had traveled to the United States and made close American friends by the mid-1870s. Kate Field and Charles Norton were associated respectively with Dilke and Morley, but these friendships evaporated in the 1870s. Dilke returned to America at the end of 1875 as part of a trip around the world, desperately trying to alleviate his deep sorrow over the death of his first wife. He visited Kate Field in New York and journeyed as far west as California. Unfortunately, he left hardly any notes upon the visit.[93] When Dilke returned to London in January 1876, he saw less and less of Miss Field. This development was partly motivated by Field's increased duties in the United States and partly by Dilke's apparent desire in 1875–76 to avoid people in society for a period of time.[94] At the same time, Morley's close intimacy with Norton also waned, though they corresponded on several occasions after 1874. But even by 1880, that channel of communication had come to an end. No attempt was made to reopen their association until another twenty years had elapsed. There is no evidence that there was any disagreement; rather, it seems to have been the result of two exceptionally busy men who did not have the time to devote hours to maintaining a distant transatlantic association by letters. While Dilke rarely found the United States a vital interest in the later 1870s, Morley discovered that his journalistic and literary responsibilities necessitated close attention to the United States.

In the pages of the *Fortnightly Review*, Morley ensured that the United States was thoroughly covered by American and British authorities. He regularly chose contributors who had high literary talents and who, not surprisingly, praised liberalism in politics. Two such individuals were Horace White and Edward Atkinson. In the 1870s, they wrote articles for Morley's review on a wide range of topics.[95] Both men were free traders, advocates of civil service reform, sound money men, and exponents of national and international moral relations. White was the editor of the *Chicago Tribune* from 1865 to 1874 and eventually succeeded E. L. Godkin as editor of the *New York Evening Post* in 1899 after years of work for the same newspaper. He was a foremost economic expert. Atkinson also was a prominent economist, and an industrialist who pioneered in improving architecture regulations. In England and especially in the tenets of British Liberalism, both men found inspiration for their American campaigns.[96] White's high regard for Great Britain never really changed from the time of his first visit in 1875.

> The new republic has, if anything, veered toward monarchy, while the old monarchy has manifestly drifted to republicanism.
> Of course when a country has settled all its great questions it will busy itself with its little ones. England has representative government, free trade, a sound currency, and light taxation. She has paid the *Alabama* claims, punished the Ashantees, and deposed the Guikwar of Baroda. Peace reigns in all her borders, and a good degree of contentment pervades all classes – higher, at all events, than her neighbours can boast, higher indeed than the United States can claim at the present time.[97]

Throughout the course of writing for Morley, White in particular urged constructive Anglo-American views which tended to honor Great Britain as much as or more than the United States. There were also excellent American articles by British authorities on the United States. The Liberal MP from Kirkcudbright, George Campbell, published his views of 'Black and White in the Southern States' in Morley's journal. The Liberal Henry Fawcett described the parallel rise of socialism in Germany and the United States (American socialism owing much to German influence), while the Conservative MP Louis Jennings wrote disparagingly upon the state of American politics in the election year of 1876.[98] One article upon Roman Catholicism in the United States by Francis Abbott,[99] Morley thought of such merit that he sent a copy of it to Gladstone, commenting that 'The Celtic half of it seems especially important.'[100] Not only was Morley called upon to guide the

Fortnightly's American positions, which he did on the basis of an essentially Liberal-Republican view,[101] but also himself wrote upon the United States.

In 1875, Morley began a new regular column in the *Fortnightly* which he entitled 'Home and Foreign Affairs.' In it the main domestic and foreign news was outlined. Initially, Morley wrote the 'Home Affairs' and the Belgian economist and scholar Laveleye consented to write the 'Foreign Affairs' section.[102] However, by March 1876, Morley resolved that the situation was untenable, and that Laveleye was 'so poor' that his contributions 'must come to a stop.'[103] The Belgian's comments upon American and French politics were particularly unsatisfactory to the editor. Accordingly, it appears Morley took over the authorship of both home and foreign sections.

Other literary responsibilities also inspired Morley's American studies. In 1876, Alexander Macmillan, who had first encouraged Morley to visit the United States, selected him to edit the 'English Men of Letters' series. This consisted of approximately twenty popular biographies of the most important British authors, from Chaucer to Wordsworth. Morley became responsible for assigning the subjects to various authors and for supervising the publication of the manuscripts. In the course of his own work on Edmund Burke and the editing chores of others, he studied American history and literature. As with Gladstone, Morley found much to praise in Burke's heroic efforts to bring about British understanding with the American colonies in the 1760s and 1770s.[104] Independent of any exact influence, Morley thought books should be written about American authors: Nathaniel Hawthorne, author of *The Scarlet Letter*; the poet and short-story writer, Edgar Allen Poe; and the traveler Washington Irving. After correspondence with his friend Norton, the field was narrowed to Hawthorne and Irving, and Morley sought the services of James Russell Lowell, author of the popular *Bigelow Papers* and, for a period, an editor of the *North American Review*. On Morley's behalf, Norton invited the Brahmin poet, Oliver Wendel Holmes, to take part. Both Lowell and Holmes declined.[105] A year later, Morley was still looking for an American contributor to treat either Hawthorne or Irving. In the end, he turned to the gifted expatriate novelist living in London, Henry James. They had met once at one of Lord Houghton's famous breakfasts,[106] but it was still surprising that Morley asked James, for the former had written in 1877 very critically of one of James' works, *French Poets and Novelists*.[107] James also had no initial inclination to write for Morley,[108] yet by October 1879 he had sent Morley the final proofs of a work on Hawthorne. The reasons for the final successful outcome are unclear, but the editor's praise for James' work was not. 'It will certainly be one of the most attractive of the whole Series.'[109]

Finally one further literary pursuit brought Morley into study of the United States. In 1877, in the midst of everything else, Morley began a biography of the Gladstonian Liberal hero, Richard Cobden. As the champion of free trade, a pacifist, and a man with strong political principles, and as an issue-oriented politician, Cobden fascinated Morley. Cobden had been greatly influenced by his American associations (especially those occasioned by his trips in 1835 and 1858). He had been known as 'the member for America.' Morley gave ample treatment to Cobden's major themes as well as to his strong pro-Northern stances during the Civil War and his friendship with Charles Sumner.[110]

The year 1876 was a propitious one insofar as the United States was concerned. Not only was it the American centennial but it was also a year which saw one of the most controversial presidential elections in American history. Republican Hayes, after the fierce bargaining of party caucuses, won the contest though he had lost the popular vote. British public interest in this strange passage in American political life soared.[111] No Liberal leader was more fascinated by this contest than Morley. To Charles Norton he wrote that 'We are all of us greatly interested at this moment in the doings' in America.[112] To Chamberlain, he maintained that he 'followed the matter pretty precisely.'[113] The main basis of his study was a regular reading of the *New York Tribune*, though he also turned frequently to the *New York Nation*. Morley took sides in the election. He was afraid that if the Democrats under Tilden won they would endorse 'a silent accomplice in a system of terrorism of the Blacks by the Whites.'[114] When Republican Hayes won despite the irregular electoral procedures, Morley was relieved.[115]

Throughout 1877, American political corruption received regular attention in British circles. When former President Grant arrived in London, British energy focused sharply upon him. No Liberal was more unstinting in his attack upon Grant's character and achievements than Morley.

He entered upon his high station after an experience which had elevated the popular sentiment on the other side of the Atlantic far above its ordinary level; but he quickly brought it down again to its accustomed depression. His tastes and habits showed no sign of elevation of character, and without being himself open to censure, he was deplorably careless of the standard of public duty among his associates.[116]

Other American prominent party politicians joined Grant in London in the summer of 1877, notably the former Democratic presidential candidate, Samuel Tilden, and the close Republican friend of Grant, Senator Roscoe Conkling. Whether Morley met either Conkling or Tilden, or even Grant, is uncertain. Some Liberals such as Harcourt, Granville, and Argyll did meet Grant, and probably the other Americans. What is certain is that neither Conkling nor Tilden was particularly well-received by the British political elite. Even the First Secretary of the American Legation, William Hoppin, described the two Americans' mediocre talents and poor reception. Tilden was 'a toothless, mumbling sort of personnage' and Conkling a politician filled with egotism, gestures, and vague illusory statements.[117] Grant, Tilden, and Conkling – whether Democrat or Republican – represented to Liberals like Morley, all that was corrupt, ignorant, and detestable in American politics. However, Morley remained loyal to the party of Lincoln, which included such virtuous liberal-minded Republican contributors to the *Fortnightly* as Charles Norton, Horace White, and Edward Atkinson. Through Morley, British Liberals spoke out against American politics in 1876–77.

Morley was suddenly joined by his close friend, the democratic Chamberlain, in a defense of American caucuses. Their controversial public stance grew out of a body of radical Liberal activities, centered in the West Midlands, and aimed at developing a nationwide Liberal political organization. On 31 May 1877, the National Liberal Federation was inaugurated in Birmingham under the leadership of Chamberlain. It called for municipal wards to elect a committee which then sent delegates to a Central Committee, numbering about six hundred members. A group of eleven 'Councils of Ten' was then selected out of the Central Committee which in fact controlled the Federations' activities. When the Liberal Federations gained successes in local elections, the result was an outpouring of accusations by Conservatives about the dangers of Liberal party organization. *The Times*, the former Liberal Home Secretary Robert Lowe, and Disraeli all denounced the Liberal organizations as corrupt, 'Americanized,' and managed by political bosses.[118] It was oddly coincidental that this happened in the aftermath of the 1876 presidential election and around the time of the London visits of Grant, Tilden, and Conkling. The discussion of the real characteristics of the federations became 'so cluttered up with

American parallels, … and with controversies about particular constituencies and policies, that they were never argued to any sort of conclusion.'[119] Chamberlain, Morley, and Gladstone all expressed themselves on political organizations at this time, in large part to distinguish between the American and British systems. 'Kin Beyond Sea' – a lavish praise of American institutions – was Gladstone's contribution to the debate. Chamberlain's views were just as controversial and almost as favorable to the United States.

The newly elected MP for Birmingham first publicly replied to the dire consequence of 'caucus politics' associated with the Federation in a letter to *The Times* on 1 August 1878. He argued that American and British politics were different, because the elected representatives in the former were 'dependent for [their] tenure on the success of the party to which [they] belong[ed].'[120] Such a spoils system did not exist in England. Chamberlain, however, preferred to evade any larger discussion of British–American parallels. Not until Morley asked him for an article on the Liberal organizations late in September did Chamberlain directly tackle the American question. The *Fortnightly*'s editor wanted to place his review's position in front of the British public, in part to correct references just published in the rival Liberal *Nineteenth Century*.[121] Morley wrote to Chamberlain that 'the subject has excited and will excite new interest in the country.[122] In preparing his article, Chamberlain decided to attack his critics even though he saw little prospect of converting them to his viewpoint. He undertook 'to claim the caucus as a really democratic institution' whether in the United States or Great Britain.

> The case of our opponents rests on 3 assumptions – 1. That the system of local & national Government in America is corrupt & degraded; 2nd That this is due to the Caucus; 3rd that the Bir[mingham] system is the same as the American Caucus and will lead to the same alleged results.[123]

Chamberlain disputed all these assumptions. For ten days he worked intensely on the article, and his efforts brought success. When Morley received the proofs, he exclaimed: 'the part about America is as good and strong as it can be.'[124]

Chamberlain's article did not contain his first reflective comments on American politics in the 1870s. In an earlier contribution to the *Fortnightly*, Chamberlain had praised the development of free schools in the United States as an aspect of the separation of church and state.

'The United States of America afford the best illustration in such a matter, because there, and there alone, has a free system been thoroughly and extensively carried out amongst a population having many similarities to our own.'[125] Relying upon reports from various states – New York, Michigan, New Jersey, Rhode Island, and others – as well as citations from Horace Greeley (Republican candidate for the presidency in 1872), Chamberlain demonstrated that Americans had better attendance, better mixtures of classes, and many benefits from universal use of free schools.[126] In his article on the caucus, Chamberlain also warmly endorsed many characteristics of American social and political institutions. He emphasized the good he saw in the American political system, its differences from the British system, and asserted that the British caucus would have a different history from that of the American caucus. In short, Chamberlain endorsed the caucus system just as enthusiastically for the United States as for Great Britain.

The aim of the caucus is essentially democratic: it is to provide for the full and efficient representation of the will of the majority, and for its definite expression in the government of the people. ...
America is the land of new ideas, and all of these have obtained a hearing, while many have been adopted. Public opinion on the questions of Slavery, Education, and Temperance has undergone the greatest change, and the Government of the country has readily moulded itself to the new conceptions of public right and duty which have from time to time found favour with the community. In truth, ... the caucus protects individuality and secures independence against tyranny.[127]

The American views in Chamberlain's 'The Caucus' were as friendly and flattering to America as those of Gladstone in 'Kin Beyond Sea.'[128] Both articles were published in the fall of the same year. Both disturbed large sections of British Conservative opinion of American institutions.[129] Both helped a great deal to confirm to British and American onlookers that British Liberals were pro-Americans; Gladstone's position never grew less warm towards the United States. In time, Chamberlain's was to do so.[130]

Conclusion

Throughout the Conservative ministry of 1874–80, the United States had emerged as an increasingly important side-interest of the majority of the leading Liberals. Gladstone, Rosebery, Morley, and Chamberlain each developed new personal American ties – in some cases fairly extensive American preoccupations. Rosebery's three visits; Gladstone's concern with his image and popularity; Morley's literary and journalistic pursuits; and Chamberlain's study of schools and caucuses – all were much more than passing concerns. The undisputed leader of the Liberals, Gladstone, demonstrated a desire to make startling predictions about the future of the United States. Luckily or astutely, his prediction of 1878 to the effect that the United States would assume the leadership of the Western world was more accurate than that on the Confederacy in 1862. But then Morley, Chamberlain, and the youthful Rosebery all had made similar projections concerning American society, industry, and institutions.

During the 1870s, Liberals often leaned more positively toward the politics and personalities of the Republican party, especially those of the Liberal-Republican group. Morley's and Bryce's early American friendships were with Liberal-Republicans.[131] Morley supported the Republican Hayes over the Democrat Tilden in the presidential contest of 1876. Gladstone and Harcourt were among the many Liberals who were distressed over the Democratic connivance in Richard Dana's rejection as the American Minister to Great Britain. Chamberlain apparently also sided with Republicans in the early 1880s.[132] At the same time, neither the Republican former President Grant or Senator Roscoe Conkling, nor the Democratic Tilden – all in London in the late 1870s – impressed Liberals. In large measure because of his close friendships with Samuel Ward and William Hurlbert, only Rosebery among British Liberals had extensive associations and respect for Democrats. Certainly, there was no clear picture of Liberals and Democrats generating particular ties or mutual understanding in the 1870s. The Liberal leaders' American interests and associations were a mixture of chance occurrence and private intermingling with a wide variety of Americans, more often literary and journalistic personalities than politicians. Their American interests were genuine but casual and irregular. They were almost unanimous in the deep respect for the United States, despite their reservation about the policies of Reconstruction, and their concern over political corruption, caucuses, and the curiously determined Presidential election of 1876.

Notes

1. *Liberal Politics in the Age of Gladstone and Rosebery. A Study in Leadership and Policy* (Oxford, 1972), pp. 40–1. Also see, T. A. Jenkins, 'Gladstone, the Whigs, and the Leadership of the Liberal Party, 1879–1880,' *Historical*

Journal, vol. 27 (1984), pp. 337–60 and *Gladstone, Whiggery and the Liberal Party, 1874–1886* (Oxford, 1988).

2. J. Vincent, *The Formation of the British Liberal Party 1857–68* (London, 1972), p. 31.

3. J. P. Rossi, *The Transformation of the British Liberal Party: A Study of the Tactics of the Liberal Opposition, 1874–1880* (Philadelphia, 1978), p. 127.

4. J. Morley, *The Life of William Ewart Gladstone*, 3 vols (London, 1903), ii, p. 523.

5. Hansard, 3rd series, ccxxx, 24 July 1876, 1776. See ibid., ccxxxi, 3 Aug 1876, 371–414.

6. Ibid., ccxxxii, 13 Feb. 1877, 249–50.

7. C. Bolt, *Victorian Attitudes to Race* (London, 1971), p. 73.

8. Other Liberal leaders who traveled in the United States and left accounts in the 1870s were: Joseph Arch (1874), Lord Brassey (1876), Charles Bradlaugh (1873–75), William Caine (1875–76), Hugh Childers (1874–77), William Forster (1874), George Campbell (1878), L. Courtney (1873), John Leng (1876), Lyon Playfair (1877–80), Henry Vivian (1877), E. Watkins (1878), and H. J. Wilson (1876).

9. For a complete itinerary, see A. R. C. Grant and C. Combe (eds), *Lord Rosebery's North American Journal – 1873* (London, 1967), p. 22.

10. RP, 10073, F. Lawley to Rosebery, 18 Aug. 1873, ff. 217–22, cited in Grant and Combe (eds), *Rosebery's 1873 Journal*, pp. 139–41.

11. *Ireland*, 2 vols (London, 1888) and *England* (London, 1893).

12. In 1886, Rosebery no longer had 'so frequent an intercourse' with Hurlbert. RP, 10085, J. Moore to Rosebery, 18 Mar. 1886, f. 117. See Morley's views of Hurlbert: GP, 44255, Morley to Gladstone, 28 Aug. 1888, ff. 266–7.

13. RP, 10074, 23 Dec. 1873, f. 4; cited in Grant and Combe (eds), *Rosebery's 1873 Journal*, p. 143.

14. Ibid.

15. Library of Congress, Washington DC (Bayard Papers): Box 179, S. Ward to T. Bayard, 1 Dec. 1873.

16. Grant and Combe (eds), *Rosebery's 1873 Journal, passim*.

17. When Rosebery left the United States in December 1873, he wrote a poem idolizing Sam Ward. See Thomas, *Sam Ward*, pp. 390–1.

18. Grant and Combe (eds), *Rosebery's 1873 Journal*, p. 138.

19. Marquess of Crewe, *Lord Rosebery*, 2 vols (London, 1931), i, p. 76. I have been unable to track down the original sources of Crewe's citations of Rosebery's American observations other than those in his 1873 journal.

20. Ibid., p. 73.

21. Ibid., p. 76.

22. Ibid., p. 78.

23. Ibid., p. 79.

24. 24 Dec. 1873; cited in Grant and Combe (eds), *Rosebery's 1873 Journal*, p. 146.

25. Crewe, *Rosebery*, i, p. 77.

26. Grant and Combe (eds), *Rosebery's 1873 Journal*, p. 138.

27. See Rosebery's unpublished short journal of his 1874–75 visit (RP, 10192).

28. Ibid., *passim*.

29. Ibid., p. 16.

30. Ibid., p. 15.
31. Ibid., p. 12.
32. Ibid., pp. 7–8 and 12–15.
33. Ibid., p. 21.
34. Ibid., pp. 19–20.
35. RP, 10074, F. Lawley to Rosebery, 9 Dec. 1875, ff. 168–71.
36. Charles Parnell, Randolph Churchill, and H. J. Wilson were some of the most prominent English visitors to the exhibition. Crewe discusses Rosebery's third visit, in *Rosebery*, i, pp. 81–2.
37. New York Public Library, New York (Ward Papers): Box 1 (1874–1879 folders). Most of the letters from Rosebery to Ward introducing Englishmen are included in M. Elliott's *Uncle Sam Ward and His Circle* (New York, 1938), pp. 580–600.
38. Ward Papers, Rosebery to Ward, 8 Mar. 1879, Box 1 (1879 folder), cited in Elliott, *Uncle Sam Ward*, p. 596.
39. Houghton Library, Cambridge, MA (Longfellow Papers): bMS Am 1340.2 (5820) Ward to Longfellow, 29 Feb. 1880 (342).
40. See Chapter 3, pp. 74–5.
41. Ward Papers, Rosebery to Ward: 16 Feb. 1874, Box 1 (1874 folder); 2 Aug. 1874, Box 1 (1874 folder); and 31 Aug. 1875, Box 1 (1875 folder).
42. For another discussion of Gladstone's sensitivity to the American experience and issues of the 1870s, see H. Tulloch, *James Bryce's American Commonwealth: the Anglo-American Background* (Woodbridge, 1988), pp. 68–79 and H. C. G. Matthew, *Gladstone. 1809–1874* (Oxford, 1986), pp. 186–8.
43. *The Case of the United States to be Laid Before the Tribunal of Arbitration to be Convened at Geneva* (Washington, DC, 1871), pp. 87–100.
44. GP, 44437, Schenck to Gladstone, Feb. 1873, f. 153.
45. Ibid., f. 154.
46. Ibid., 44442, Gladstone to Schenck, 20 Feb. 1874, f. 324.
47. Ibid., 44447, Gladstone to Schenck, 27 July 1875, f. 319.
48. Gladstone had been appraised of the nature of the impasse in a letter from Schenck on 14 Oct. 1875. Ibid., 44448, ff. 88–90.
49. Ibid., 44448, H. Fish to Schenck, 18 May 1875, f. 234.
50. Ibid., 44449, Gladstone to Schenck, 1 Jan. 1876, f. 4. See ibid., Gladstone to H. Fish, 26 June 1876, ff. 99–100.
51. No. 319 (Dec. 1876), pp. 105–9. For Fish's letter, see GP, 44451, H. Fish to Gladstone, 2 Aug. 1876, ff. 1–4.
52. GP, 44451, H. M. Alden to Gladstone, 5 Sept. 1876, ff. 118–19.
53. As H. C. G. Matthew has affirmed, Gladstone's 'letter to Schenck was his version of that defence and marked the start of that assiduous cultivation of American liberal opinion which was to be so marked a characteristic of his life.' *Gladstone. 1809–1874*, p. 188.
54. O. F. Aldis, 'Louis Napoleon and the Southern Confederacy,' vol. cxxix (Oct. 1879), pp. 342–60.
55. GP, 44461, Smalley to Gladstone, 3 Nov. 1879, f. 117.
56. Ibid., W. Evarts to Gladstone, 14 Nov. 1879, f. 146.
57. Many instances could be cited of Gladstone's refutations of published claims that he supported the South. For one such, see H. Clews, 'Great Britain and the Confederacy,' *NAR*, vol. cxlix (Aug. 1889), pp. 215–22.

58. GP, 44442, Johnson to Gladstone, 20 Feb. 1874, f. 310; 44443: C. Field to Gladstone, 10 Mar. 1874, ff. 74–5; and R. Dana Jr to Gladstone, 12 Apr. 1874, ff. 144–5.
59. Ibid., 44443, Johnson enclosure to Gladstone, 1874, f. 52.
60. Ibid., 44442, American Academy of Arts and Sciences to Gladstone, 28 Jan. 1874, f. 117.
61. Ibid., 44443, C. Field to Gladstone, 10 Mar. 1874, f. 74.
62. Ibid., R. Dana Jr to Gladstone, 12 Apr. 1874, ff. 144–5.
63. Ibid., 44454, C. Field to Gladstone, 27 Apr. 1877, f. 72 and 44457, C. Field to Gladstone, 7 June 1878, f. 32.
64. Ibid., 44457, C. Eliot to Gladstone, 27 July 1878, f. 156.
65. Ibid., 44455, Evarts to Gladstone, 27 Dec. 1877, ff. 348–9 and 44445, Potter to Gladstone, 1 Dec. 1874, ff. 132–3.
66. Ibid., 44443, Johnson to Gladstone, 12 May 1874, ff. 231–3.
67. Ibid., 44452, C. Field to Gladstone, 24 Nov. 1876, f. 160.
68. Ibid., 44444, Yarnell to Gladstone, 1 Oct. 1874, f. 282.
69. Ibid., 44452, Burritt to Gladstone, 6 Oct. 1876, ff. 35–6.
70. Ibid., 44457: A. T. Rice to Gladstone, 3 June 1878, ff. 9–10; 15 June 1878, ff. 44–5; and 12 July 1878, ff. 114–15.
71. Gladstone's associations with Schuyler are discussed in R. J. Jensen, 'Eugene Schuyler and the Balkan Crisis,' *Diplomatic History*, vol. v, no. i (Winter 1981), pp. 30–3. Also see Schuyler references in R. T. Shannon, *Gladstone and the Bulgarian Agitation 1876*, 2nd edn (London, 1975) and A. P. Saab, *Reluctant Icon: Gladstone, Bulgaria, and the Working Classes, 1856–1878* (Cambridge, MA, 1991).
72. (Sept. 1876), especially pp. 33–4.
73. Speech at Blackheath, 9 Sept. 1876; cited in *Historical Pamphlets: A–GL* (Bodleian Library, Oxford, 1876), p. 12 and speech at Taunton; cited in GP, 44453, Gladstone to Schuyler, 30 Jan. 1877, f. 62.
74. Ibid., Schuyler to Gladstone, 9 Mar. 1877, ff. 181–2.
75. Massachusetts Historical Society, Boston (Dana Jr Papers): Smalley to Dana Jr, 8 Mar. 1876 and Lord Coleridge to Dana Jr, 11 Mar. 1876, Box (1874–76). *Daily News*, 8 Mar. 1876.
76. Dana Jr Papers, Mrs Cavendish to Dana Jr, 4 Jan. 1875, Box (1874–76). For the Dana Jr–Harcourt relationship, see Harcourt to Dana Jr, 1 Aug. 1875, Box (1874–76), and for Dana Jr's son's visits with Liberals in 1875–76, see R. H. Dana, *Hospitable England in the Seventies: The Diary of a Young American 1875–1876* (Boston, 1921), especially pp. 1–145.
77. Dana Jr Papers, J. Motley to Dana Jr, 29 Apr. 1876, Box (1874–76). Lord Coleridge wrote to his friend Dana on the 'savage indignation' he felt towards the 'conduct of your own countrymen' and he was 'absolutely incredulous that such a thing were possible in the Senate.' Ibid., 17 Apr. 1876.
78. GP, 44453, Rice to Gladstone, 28 Feb. 1877, f. 154.
79. (Sept.–Oct. 1878), pp. 180–1.
80. Ibid., pp. 181–2. The fact that Gladstone was examining the American Constitution at the time is indicated by other references. See, for instance, 'Last Words on the County Franchise,' *NC*, vol. iii (Jan. 1878), pp. 205–6.
81. 'Kin Beyond Sea,' pp. 182–3.
82. Ibid., p. 185. This sentence became extremely famous, cited often by leading Anglo-Americans. See the cover to Carnegie's *Triumphant Democracy*

(London, 1886) and G. Bancroft's, *History of the Formation of the Constitution of the United States of America* (New York, 1882), p. 441.

83. 'Kin Beyond Sea,' p. 186.
84. Ibid., p. 187.
85. Ibid., p. 188.
86. GP, 44459, A. T. Rice to Gladstone, 6 Jan. 1879, ff. 23–4.
87. Ibid., C. Field to Gladstone, 6 Jan. 1879, f. 20.
88. Granville to Gladstone, 30 Oct. 1878, cited in E. Fitzmaurice, *Life of Granville George Leveson Gower, Second Lord Granville K.G.*, *1815–1891*, 2 vols (London, 1905), ii, p. 180.
89. 20 Sept. 1878, cited in B. Holland, *The Life of Spencer Compton, Eighth Duke of Devonshire*, 2 vols (London, 1911), i, p. 213.
90. *PMG*, 20 Sept. 1878 and the *Daily News*, 18 Sept. 1878.
91. *The Times*, 19 Sept. 1878.
92. Massachusetts Historical Society, Boston (Norcross Papers): Gladstone to S. Massett, 20 Feb. 1879, autographs. For another clarion call to Anglo-American understanding by Gladstone, see *Harper's New Monthly Magazine*, vol. liv (Dec. 1876), p. 105. ('My desire at all periods of my public life has been to promote and not to impede good understanding and warm attachment between our two countries.')
93. Dilke published later editions of *Greater Britain*, in which he made some new references to the changes he discovered in the United States in 1876. See 8th edn (1885), for example pp. 66, 85, 97, 104–5, and 171–4.
94. R. Jenkins, *Sir Charles Dilke. A Victorian Tragedy*, pp. 89–93 and 106–9. By 1876, Dilke started to mingle regularly in various social circles, but these did not include Kate Field.
95. H. White, 'An American's Impressions of England,' vol. xviii (Sept. 1875), pp. 291–305; 'The Financial Crisis in America,' vol. xix (June 1876), pp. 810–29; 'The American Centenary,' vol. xix (Oct. 1876), pp. 496–516; and 'Parliamentary Government in America,' vol. xxvi (Oct. 1879), pp. 505–17. E. Atkinson, 'An American View of American Competition,' vol. xxv (Mar. 1879), pp. 383–96 and 'The Railroads of the United States. Their Effects on Farming and Production in that Country and in Great Britain,' vol. xxviii (July 1880), pp. 83–104.
96. J. Logsdon, *Horace White, Nineteenth Century Liberal* (Westport, CT, 1971), especially pp. 269–77 and H. F. Williamson, *Edward Atkinson. The Biography of an American Liberal 1827–1905*, 2nd edn (New York, 1972), especially pp. 26–8, 37, and 75–8.
97. White, 'An American's Impressions of England,' pp. 291 and 296.
98. Campbell, vol. xxv. (Mar. 1879), pp. 449–68 and (Apr. 1879), pp. 588–607; Fawcett, 'The Recent Development of Socialism in Germany and the United States,' vol. xxiv (Nov. 1878), pp. 605–15; and Jennings, 'Unsettled Problems of American Politics,' vol. xx (Aug. 1876), pp. 198–213.
99. 'The Catholic Peril in America,' vol. xix (Mar. 1876), pp. 385–405.
100. GP, 44255, Morley to Gladstone, 28 Feb. 1876, f. 1.
101. Liberal-Republicans revolted from the Republican party in 1872 because of President Grant's opposition to political reform and the growth of political corruption within his administration.
102. University of Birmingham, Birmingham (Chamberlain Papers): Morley to Chamberlain, 29 Aug. 1875, JC 5/54/50.

103. Ibid., Morley to Chamberlain, 31 Mar. 1876, JC 5/54/90.
104. Morley, *Burke* (London, 1879), pp. 78–86.
105. LP, bMS Am 1094, Morley to Lowell, 7 Nov. 1877 (346) and NP, Morley to Norton, 10 Oct. and 9 Nov. 1877 (4872–3).
106. Houghton Library, Cambridge, MA (James Papers): bMS 1094, Morley to James, 9 Oct. 1878 (362)
107. L. Edel, *Henry James. The Conquest of London (1870–1881)* (Philadelphia, 1962), p. 299.
108. James Papers, bMS Am 1094, Morley to James, 9 Oct. 1878 (362).
109. Ibid., Morley to James, 13 Oct. 1879 (363).
110. Morley, *The Life of Cobden*, 2 vols (London, 1881), i, pp. 30–4 and ii, pp. 200, 220–4, and 370–419. In the 1880s, Morley examined Ralph Waldo Emerson's life and works in some detail. See 'Emerson,' *Critical Miscellanies*, 3 vols (London, 1886), i, pp. 293–347.
111. An American Republican, 'The Election for the Presidency,' *MM*, vol. xxxv (Dec. 1876), pp. 245–55; E. D. J. Wilson, 'The Political Crisis in the United States,' *NC*, vol. i (Apr. 1877), pp. 198–221; and G. Smith, 'A Word More About the Presidential Election,' *MM*, vol. xxxv (Mar. 1877), pp. 375–85.
112. NP, 7 Dec. 1876 (4871).
113. Ch.P, 28 Nov. 1876, JC 5/54/135.
114. *FR*, vol. xxi (Jan. 1877), p. 146.
115. Ibid., (Apr. 1877), pp. 598–9.
116. Ibid., vol. xxii (June 1877), p. 146. For other British attacks on 'Grantism' see *FR*, vol. xxi (Apr. 1877), pp. 597–8; E. Wilson, 'The Political Crisis in the United States,' p. 212; and most interestingly M. Arnold, *General Grant: An Estimate* (Boston, 1887), p. 4.
117. Houghton Library, Cambridge, MA (Hoppin Diaries): MS Am 986, vol. ii (1877), 29 July and 8 Aug. 1877, pp. 50 and 53. For further references on the extraordinary nature of Hoppin's diaries, see Appendix II.
118. *The Times*, 12 June 1877; R. Lowe, 'A New Reform Bill,' *FR*, vol. xxii (Oct. 1877), p. 446; and *The Times*, 31 July 1878. Moreover, the Liberals had not been helped by E. L. Godkin's prediction of corruption in Birmingham. See *The Nation*, vol. xxvii (5 Sept. 1878), p. 141 and H. Pelling, *America and the British Left From Bright to Bevan* (New York, 1957), pp. 34–40.
119. H. J. Hanham, *Elections and Party Management, Politics in the Time of Disraeli and Gladstone*, 2nd edn (London, 1978), p. 141. Also, see Pelling, *America and the British Left*, p. 34.
120. *The Times*, 1 Aug. 1878. For Chamberlain's activities and the Birmingham caucus, see J. Garvin, *The Life of Joseph Chamberlain* (London, 1932–34) 3 vols i, pp. 252–81.
121. W. F. Rae, 'Political Clubs and Party Organization,' vol. iii (May 1878), pp. 908–33.
122. Ch.P, 28 Sept. 1878, JC 5/54/219.
123. Ch.P, Chamberlain to Morley, 1 Oct. 1878, JC 5/54/223.
124. Ibid., Morley to Chamberlain, 20 Oct. 1878, JC 5/54/229.
125. 'Free Schools,' vol. xxi (Jan. 1877), p. 56.
126. Ibid., pp. 54–72, *passim*.
127. 'The Caucus,' *FR*, vol. xxiv (Nov. 1878), pp. 724–5.
128. Compare Chamberlain's endorsement ('America is foremost among the nations of the world in respect to the widespread intelligence of its citizens,

the rapid development of its resources, the general respect for law and order, and the universal acceptance of the principles of liberty and freedom,' p. 724) with Gladstone's, p. 55.

129. Pelling, *America and the British Left*, pp. 42–44. Chamberlain remained extremely sensitive to critics who wrote that his Birmingham organization would develop corrupt American practices. See Bodleian Library, Oxford (Goldwin Smith Papers, microfilm): Chamberlain to Smith, 14 Jan. 1882 (Reel 3), in response to Smith, 'The Machinery of Elective Government,' *NC*, vol. xi (Jan. 1882), 126–48.

130. Evidence also can be found on Chamberlain's hostility to American politics during the 1870s. See his speech on 'The Royal Family' at Birmingham, 17 Oct. 1874, in C. W. Boyd (ed.), *Mr. Chamberlain's Speeches*, 2 vols (London, 1914), i, p. 50, and speech on 'The Dignity of Municipal Reform,' 9 Nov. 1876, ibid., i, p. 73.

131. H. Tulloch, 'The Anglo-American Background of James Bryce's *American Commonwealth*,' Cambridge University PhD thesis, 1974) p. 294.

132. R. Kelley, *The Transatlantic Persuasion: the Liberal-Democratic Mind in the Age of Gladstone* (New York, 1969), p. 343.

3
The Liberal Ascendancy, Ireland, and Henry George, 1880–1886

Introduction

In April 1880, the Liberals swept to power on the basis of a campaign against Beaconsfieldism. From that time until 20 July 1886, the Liberal leaders controlled the affairs of government, except for approximately six months between Gladstone's second and third ministries from June 1885 to February 1886. Initially the Liberals had few specific programs in mind for domestic and social reforms. Moreover, a series of crises descended upon them and made it extremely difficult to govern. A rebellion in the Transvaal in 1880–81, Charles Bradlaugh's refusal to take the oath of office, turmoil in Egypt, General Gordon's death in Khartoum in 1885, and above all the problems of Ireland were but some of the more divisive issues. Gladstone's inability to control the machinery of parliamentary government, and Liberal party politics, further eroded Liberal unity.[1] Many Liberals were frustrated in their attempts to introduce specific measures for such reforms as that of land, education, municipal government, or Scottish, Welsh, and Irish devolution.

> Liberals such as Harcourt and Dilke who put a great deal of hard work into the preparation of Bills naturally became intensely frustrated; and the party in the House of Commons grew increasingly uneasy at the wholesale jettisoning every year of entire legislative programmes which contained measures that had been previously described by government spokesmen as of great urgency.[2]

In 1884, Liberal leaders came together long enough to pass the Third Reform Act, which extended the vote to county householders, but they also demonstrated a measure of discipline in passing Irish land reform (1881–82) and several electoral reforms (1883–85). But their celebrations were of short duration when the Liberal party fell from office in 1885. More importantly, Gladstone largely ignored *The Radical Programme* which Chamberlain and Morley drew up in the same year. Instead Gladstone turned to Home Rule for Ireland, and called upon all Liberals to unite in a single unswerving advocacy of his policy. Practical policies and personal relationships clashed. Friendships that had once been fast quickly fell apart. By June 1886, Morley was no longer Chamberlain's daily confidant; Dilke had made himself a political liability because of the Crawford divorce scandal; and Hartington had left the party. On 8 June, Chamberlain and Hartington led the Liberal Unionists into opposition to Gladstone's Home Rule Bill and defeated the measure 343 to 311. The Liberal party was split. It remained out of power for the next twenty years except for the short troubled period 1892 to 1895. While 1880 to 1886 had brought Liberal leaders into positions of power, their differences and a series of almost insoluble crises made the period in retrospect a bleak episode in the history of the Liberal party.

There were many prominent issues in Great Britain during the Liberal ascendancy. The United States, unlike during Gladstone's first ministry, was not one of them. Nonetheless, Liberal leaders had to formulate positions upon both official and unofficial American developments. The presidencies of the Republicans, Garfield and Chester Arthur (1881–85), and of the Democrat Grover Cleveland (1885–89) considered British relations, especially foreign policy, as of primary importance.[3] If for no other reason, British leaders had to carefully weigh their own policies towards the United States.

In addition, the growing intimate transatlantic friendships between Liberals and prominent Americans turned the former towards America. In many respects, British and American leaders were faced by similar developments in their respective countries: the direction of empire, excesses of democracy, foreign trade policies, the division of traditional political parties, and even political assassination. Thus, for instance, in the summer of 1881, President Garfield was killed by an angry office seeker, while in May 1882, the Chief Secretary for Ireland, Lord Frederick Cavendish, was stabbed to death in Phoenix Park, Dublin. In 1884, the American presidential election revolved around issues of political and urban reform, while in Britain franchise reform debates focused on similar problems. In short, there were a variety of reasons why the United States impinged itself upon the British Liberal leaders in a wide variety of forms from 1880 to 1886. For our purposes, these can be classified into four broad groupings: first, a series of American diplomatic issues; second, a host of Irish-American sponsored activities in the British Isles; third, the radical propositions of the American land reformer Henry George; and last, a plethora of references to the American experience that took active parts in the debate over Home Rule for Ireland. In the 1880s, the United States was no longer essentially the focus of interested casual study, but the target of serious critical evaluations by Liberal leaders. Their American understandings markedly affected their attempts to find solutions for British political and economic problems.

British foreign policy towards the United States, 1880–85

In the 1880s, successive American administrations pursued moderately expansionist commercial and territorial policies. The United States extended itself into Samoa, Hawaii, Central and South America, and the Far East. At the same time, American industrial output soared as protectionist trade policies protected home markets. The volume of American imports leaped from $466 million in 1879 to $767 million in 1882. Customs revenues increased from $137 million to $220 million over the same period, and railway expansion and steel production were prodigious.[4] The Liberal leaders, especially the Prime Minister, Gladstone, and the Foreign Secretary, Granville, generally acquiesced to the rapidly expanding greatness of the United States from 1880 to 1886. The six principles of foreign policy which Gladstone popularized during the Midlothian campaign were directed towards European affairs, but in practice they held equally for the United States.[5] Gladstone had not been in office long before he harkened back to the laurels of British policy over the Geneva settlement in his first ministry. In June 1880, the Prime Minister told the Commons:

> ... although we may think the sentence was harsh in its extent, and unjust in its basis, we regard the fine imposed on this country as dust in the balance compared with the moral value of the example set when these two great nations of England and America – which are among the most fiery and most jealous in the world with regard to anything that touches national honour – went in peace and concord before a judicial tribunal to dispose of these painful differences rather than to resort to the arbitrament of the sword.[6]

During the Liberal ascendancy, the leaders continued their conciliatory but firm policies towards American developments. Notable among these were the Fortune Bay incident, plans for an American isthmian canal in Panama, Irish-American revolutionary activities, extradition, international copyright, and American support of trade protectionism and international bimetallism.[7] The fact that the years 1880 to 1886 were harmonious for Anglo-American relations should not be looked upon as inevitable. The bluster of particular American statesmanship and the Anglophobia of the Irish-Americans easily could have precipitated Anglo-American relations nearer a breaking point had it not been for policies of reconciliation towards America by the Liberal ministry in Britain.[8]

The Fortune Bay incident still remained unsolved when the Liberals came to power. In the late 1870s, both Salisbury and the American Secretary of State Evarts had maintained equally stubborn positions. In Salisbury's case, he had refused to pay indemnities to American fishermen because of the damage done to them by Canadians. The Liberal government immediately presented the whole problem for close study and various reports demonstrated Britain's culpability in the matter. None was more revealing than the criticism of the Disraeli government's policies by the new First Lord of the Admiralty, Lord Northbrook. 'I do not think I ever read the history of an important and difficult transaction with greater regret as regards the manner in which it has been conducted on behalf of the British Government.'[9]

The two governments were not long in coming to a settlement, despite a few initial disagreements. In June 1881, the British Minister in America gave the new Secretary of State James Blaine a cheque for £15 000. What was as important as the settlement itself, was the manner in which it was achieved. Informal meetings and close friendships between British and American diplomats were much more apparent in the 1880s than in the 1870s. The American Minister in London from 1880 to 1885, James Russell Lowell, was most important.[10] A literate, cultured Liberal-Republican, and an Anglophile, he worked exceedingly closely with many Liberals, especially Granville.[11] Lowell's conciliatory qualities as a diplomat were clearly evidenced during the Fortune Bay negotiations. The First Secretary to the American Legation, William Hoppin, recorded Lowell's pro-British attitudes over Fortune Bay.

Monday   February 21, 1881

We have had some excitement at the Legation for two days past on account of the sudden determination of Mr. Evarts to show spunk in the Fishery business. Mr. Lowell is disposed to treat the matter with Lord Granville more mildly than our chief appears to wish.

Sunday   March 6, 1881

Mr. Lowell has been very much tried, indeed, questioning his own conduct during the negotiations as if he had done or omitted something to bring about this unfortunate termination. He is perhaps not an astute diplomatist, but he has higher & better qualities & has certainly been honest & industrious through the whole.[12]

Lowell demonstrated similar great friendliness to the Liberal administration throughout his tenure in London and Granville's own estimation of Lowell in March 1881 could hardly have been higher. 'Nobody can be more straightforward than Lowell. He's not only the most agreeable American, but one of the most agreeable men I have ever met.'[13] From 1880 to 1885, Lowell's ability to work amiably and closely with his friends Granville, Harcourt, and to a lesser extent Gladstone greatly facilitated the successful solutions to difficult Anglo-American diplomatic issues. This was particularly true over Irish-American problems where Lowell was earnestly in favor of pacification of Irish tempers and for radical Irish Home Rule.[14]

In general, the Gladstone ministry did not oppose American territorial expansion in the first half of the 1880s, with one notable exception. In 1881, the newly elected President Garfield appointed James Blaine as his Secretary of State and left him in almost exclusive charge of American foreign policy. Blaine's appointment was ominous for the Liberal government. His avid protectionism and frequent animosity to England made him in the 1880s one of the least favorable American politicians in the eyes of Liberal leaders. Historian Charles Campbell described Blaine's character succinctly.

His distrust of Europe did not serve the national interest. He was excessively political, notably in his penchant for cultivating the Irish at Great Britain's expense. He was inclined to use his power to do favors for his friends; this failing led to widespread suspicion of corruption (which, however, has never been proved). Restless, impatient, and impulsive, he was deficient in the prudence and steady persistence essential to good diplomacy.[15]

These characteristics were much in evidence over Blaine's declaration that the United States would assume full control of building a canal across the Panamanian isthmus. He rested his proclamation upon the Monroe Doctrine. This amounted to an abrogation of the Clayton-Bulwer Treaty of 1850 which had left Britain and the United States as joint custodians over future canal projects. Many prominent Americans gave Blaine their full support. Andrew Carnegie believed 'You are exactly right about the Clayton Treaty. America is going to control everything on this continent – that's settled.'[16]

Blaine's aggressive expansionist drives in Panama disturbed the Liberals. Gladstone and Granville both thought his declarations to be not only preposterous but also prejudicial to good Anglo-American relations. Edward Hamilton, Gladstone's private secretary, recorded that Blaine's moves 'excited Mr. G's wrath.'[17] Granville remonstrated that Blaine fired 'off this dangerous rocket without any care as to where it may fall.'[18] Gladstone saw the issue as not unrelated to British policy over the Suez canal, where Liberals had inherited Salisbury's commitments to control of that water. The Prime Minister affirmed that 'the claims of the U.S. are in themselves, apparently, extravagant, and they would not have a shadow of excuse but for the proceedings of the late Govt as to the Suez Canal.'[19] In the end, the Liberal government was saved the difficulty of finding a solution to Blaine's declaration. In the summer of 1881, President Garfield was killed by an assassin, and Blaine was replaced by Frederick Frelinghuysen and the American isthmian claims were dropped.

American protectionism and tariffs

A different kind of American aggression also disturbed Liberal leaders in 1881. Because of the increasing decline of industrial and agricultural prosperity both in Europe and the United States in the late 1870s, the latter had turned to a more strict protectionist trade policy.[20] While President Chester Arthur even attempted to reduce tariffs, Congress overrode his wishes and introduced the 'Mongrel Tariff' which kept the rates fairly high.[21] In Britain, there suddenly emerged a body of people who advocated that the British also adopt protectionist tariffs to aid home industry and agriculture. Furthermore, they feared that Britain would be flooded by American products, while theirs would not be able to compete with the American markets. In 1881, a Yorkshireman, W. Farrer Ecroyd founded the Fair Trade League which popularized the proposal that the British adopt American practices and impose duties on foreign goods. Liberal leaders turned to argue against protectionism and American-type tariffs.

Gladstone, Sir Lyon Playfair, Charles Dilke, and Chamberlain framed some of the most persuasive early arguments against American protectionism. In October 1881, in an important speech in Leeds, Gladstone concentrated on the United States. He noted that 'The case the people feel most is the case of America.'[22] He argued that the British were foolish for believing that taxing three million pounds of manufactured goods America sent Britain would compensate British producers who sent between thirty and forty million pounds of manufactured goods to America.[23] In another speech a day later, he emphasized that protectionism had hurt not helped America. Between 1850 and 1880, the American percentage of worked shipping had fallen from 15 to only 6 percent. In light of such adverse effects upon the United States, Gladstone went so far as to alter his famous 1878 prognostication about American superiority in 'Kin Beyond Sea.'

I gave sad offence to many – many of those who tell you that they are ruined already. They were extremely annoyed and offended on account of this, which was not a positive prediction, but an intimation of a probability ... And as long as America follows the doctrine of Protection, or as long as America follows the doctrines now known as those of Fair Trade, you are perfectly safe, and you need not allow, any of you, even your slightest slumbers to be disturbed by the fear that America will take from you your commercial primacy.[24]

In April 1882, Sir Lyon Playfair, who was intimately knowledgeable of the United States because of the yearly visits to his American wife's family in the Boston area, published a detailed study of the impact of American tariffs upon British industries. His arguments contradicted the 'fair traders,' who 'always point to the United States as the great illustration of the prosperity which is assumed to be the consequence of a protective system.'[25] Natural American advantages – cheap land, abundant raw materials, and untold mineral wealth – were more important for American prosperity than rates to protect woolen, cotton, and the iron and copper industries. Protection had decidedly harmful effects, most notably in raising the price of labor. 'All admit that the tariff is full of crudities and ought to be revised. But the protectionists are afraid to touch a single brick in the edifice lest the whole should fall.'[26] Playfair went one step further when he argued that American protection helped Britain.

The protective duties of America remove from us the most formidable competition in the markets of the world by raising its prices of production. They protect England in all neutral markets, and enable us to send even into the United States 25,000,000 l. of manufactured goods, while they return to us less than three millions.[27]

Playfair agreed completely with Gladstone. Unless the United States abandoned her protectionist trade policies, she would not assume her foremost position as 'the great manufacturing country of the world.'[28] Sir Charles Dilke also pronounced 'I am convinced that protection has had a most grievous effect upon the political and social condition of the modern world.'[29]

Even more interestingly, Joseph Chamberlain, the President of the Cobden Club meeting on 13 June 1885, argued that Britain prospered while the United States struggled because of free trade. In America, employment in the woolen industries had declined by 34 000 since 1882, woolen wages had dropped by 25 to 30 percent, and woolen exports were down from £72 000 in 1879 to £28 000 in 1884. On the other hand, British woolen fabric exports to the United States had reached 'the gigantic amount of over £3,100,000' by 1885. While Chamberlain became the foremost advocate of protectionist trade policies in the first decade of the twentieth century, in 1885 he was a keen enthusiast for Cobdenite principles.

> The general conclusion I want you to bear in mind is this – that although we cannot show any great change of opinion in foreign countries with regard to the extension of Free Trade, yet at least we can find in their experience conclusive evidence and proof of the soundness of Mr. Cobden's doctrines, and a great cause for congratulation to this country. At all events, the depression which has prevailed here as elsewhere throughout the world has not been intensified and accentuated by all kinds of artificial restrictions and by unjust and injurious tariffs.[30]

By the end of 1885, British industry and agriculture had started to recover some of its prosperity of the early 1870s. But between the depressions of 1877–79 and 1884–85 (especially in the cotton industry),[31] Liberal leaders had been very alive to the threats to their home markets by American protectionist tariff policies. They were unanimous in their condemnation of this form of American commercial agressiveness.[32]

Anglo-American accord

Despite some Liberal irritation at American protectionism and the simmering Irish-American troubles, more about which will be said shortly, they participated eagerly in the fall and winter of 1881–82 in a vigorous redefinition of Anglo-American friendship. In many ways, it was the most conspicuous such call since 1871–72, or perhaps since 1860.[33] This was due to some developments already touched upon, some that have not. Friendly personal relationships had been established with the new American Minister Lowell, and the Anglophobe Blaine was no longer in office. The Fortune Bay incident was fast on its way to a solution. However, just as important was President Garfield's assassination, a shock to the British as well as to Americans. Between being shot on 2 June 1881 and his death two months later, the British unanimously warmed to the plight of the leader of the United States. British papers ran daily bulletins on the president's condition, and thoroughly discussed American politics.

Gladstone led Britain in representing the country's bereavement for Garfield. 'We have seen him die with unparalleled suffering as a Christian and as a hero. That is recorded in the heart of this nation; it is like a new and perpetual pledge of amity and affection between the two countries.'[34] The *Pall Mall Gazette*, run by Morley, echoed similar views.

> Twelve months ago not one Englishman in a thousand had heard of his name. To-day there will scarcely be one Englishman in a thousand who will not read the telegram from Long Branch [site of Garfield's death] with regret as real and as deep as if the dead had been the ruler of our own … The communion of sorrow unites the ocean-sundered members of the English race to-day, and Americans and English are more closely united in sentiment than they have ever been since the fatal folly of an obstinate Monarch drove our kin beyond the sea into revolt against their Fatherland.[35]

Six days later, the *Pall Mall Gazette* went a step further. In an article 'England and America,' it advocated that England and America 'already one in spirit, should be united more closely in a political sense.'[36] Interestingly enough, it was probably William T. Stead, Morley's successor as editor, who wrote the article. Stead wrote to Lowell about the article.

> I am not without hope that an Anglo-American bond, is among the probabilities of the future & that the nexus between the various families of the English race, will be a permanent tribunal or Court of Conciliation & of Arbitration to which all disputes insoluble by diplomacy will be relegated for prompt & pacific settlement.[37]

While Anglo-American calls to common heritage and race had existed well before 1860,[38] and there had been arbitration talk during the Geneva settlement of 1871–72, the *Pall Mall Gazette*'s strong call for a permanent tribunal marked in many ways the start of the Anglo-American arbitration movement in Great Britain. By the 1890s, the movement gained large followings and achieved much success. Moreover, Stead's own journal, the *Review of Reviews*, would become one of the most conspicuous voices for Anglo-American harmony. Garfield's death had helped to give rise to a surge of calls for Anglo-American understanding.

In the fall of 1881, other evidence came from the United States that Britain and her former colonies were at the start of a new era of friendship. Two Liberal travelers in America, James Bryce and the Oxonian Edward Freeman, both reported changed American attitudes to the British. After journeying from the East Coast to Los Angeles, Bryce reported in a long and full letter to Gladstone all manner of American views. Much of the letter was devoted to Irish-American journalistic opinion which was violently anti-British but which did not 'seem adequately to represent' American opinion. Since Bryce had first visited the United States in 1870, there had been a remarkable shift in American opinion.

> The settlement of the *Alabama* question brought about (as you doubtless know) a great change of sentiment towards Britain; the last two months have completed the work then begun, and produced a livelier good will toward our nation and Government than has ever existed before. I was in the United States in 1870, when the *Alabama* claims were still unsettled, and am greatly struck by the difference between the language used then and now. The effusiveness of the present moment may not be maintained; for Americans are a somewhat changeable as well as sentimental people. But the good effects cannot wholly pass away. A sense of brotherhood between England and America exists at the moment here such as one would eleven years ago have wholly despaired of ever seeing.[39]

In the middle of delivering a series of lectures in the United States, Edward Freeman stopped to send some impressions to his countryman Bryce. 'Gladstone seems very popular on this side ... They clearly like when I tell them that in 1880 the two branches of the English people each put its best man at its head.'[40] In the fall of 1881, there was also a vast outpouring of American patriotism over the centenary of the British surrender at Yorktown. One orator, a prominent Bostonian lawyer, Robert C. Winthrop, sent Gladstone a copy of one of his speeches. It deeply moved Gladstone and also spurred him, in the words of his secretary Edward Hamilton, to '[pour] out his heart about the U.S.'[41] Nor was Gladstone to be outdone by Stead, Bryce, or Freeman in the eloquence of his prose on the closeness of Anglo-American relations.

Nothing can be happier than the relative positions of our respective countries. You have before you a stupendous destiny, and labour equal to your struggle. The unexampled task, which we have undertaken, is beyond ours [*sic*], but there is a most arduous and most elevated vocation in the mere effort to fulfill it, provided we have self-command and equity enough to direct our course upon the lines of justice. Our paths ought no more to clash, than two parallel lines in space; and natural ties are I hope rapidly bringing it about that each nation will have the second place in the affections of the other.[42]

On the last day of 1881, Edward Hamilton recorded the main accomplishments of the Liberals' first full year in office. 'Nothing has gone right for the Government in internal affairs; it has been a perpetual series of troubles – a perfect sea of them.' But in 'oversea' matters, Europe was calm, India, and South Africa settled. Moreover, 'we have drawn closer together the ties between this country and the United States.'[43] One of the first achievements of the Liberal ministry from 1880 to 1885 was to continue to cement Anglo-American relations, resuming a trend that they had established between 1868 and 1874.

Irish-Americans, Fenians, and violence

The Irish-Americans provided the greatest single threat to Anglo-American relations during the period of the Liberal government. Financial and moral support came from the American brethren of the distressed Irish, but so did the advocacy of revolutionary policies of murder, dynamite bombings, and other outrages. The Liberal leaders were faced with the most difficult task of solving the larger Irish question in a manner favourable to Englishmen and Irishmen, but also to Americans.[44]

The Irish question emerged afresh in the late 1870s as the result of the depressed condition of agriculture and trade. It was further spurred on by a series of bitter battles between landlords, usually absentee, and Irish tenant farmers. In 1877, there were evictions of 463 families and

236 reported outrages; in 1880, these figures had risen to 2000 evictions and 2590 outrages.[45] The Liberal government moved to redress Irish grievances and in 1881 passed both Forster's Coercion measure and a Land Act. The first inflamed the Irishmen, while the second did little immediately to help the actual impoverished conditions of peasants. The Irish leaders and their destitute followers turned elsewhere, mainly to the United States.

Many Irish emigrated to the United States in this period. In fact, the figures are staggering for the early 1880s. From 30058 in 1879, they jumped significantly to 83018 in 1880. They continued to maintain their highest late Victorian levels through 1883.[46] Irish Nationalist leaders also turned to the United States. Michael Davitt, the land reformer, sometime Nationalist MP, and friend of Henry George, 'found it easier to gain converts to his proposals in America than he had found it at home.'[47] Davitt like many other Irishmen was greatly inspired by Irish-Americans and the image of the United States.

> The Irish in the United States were steadily climbing upward socially and politically. They were being inoculated with practical ideas and schooled in domestic thought and action. American party organizations were training them for an active participation in public life, and in proportion as they lifted themselves up from the states of mere laborers to that of business peasants and of professional callings did they find the opportunities and means of taking an active part in the government of cities and States. These experiences and advantages reacted upon opinion in Ireland, through the increasing numbers of visitors, letters, and newspapers crossing the Atlantic, and in this manner cultivated the growth of more practical thought and purpose in our political movements at home.[48]

Another Irish Nationalist who was chairman of their parliamentary party, Charles Stewart Parnell, was greatly assisted by the American Irish. His trip to America in 1880 was of immense importance. He traveled over 16000 miles in North America and spoke in almost sixty cities.[49] Parnell continually exhorted his audiences that American and British-Irish had joint responsibilities for the condition of Ireland. 'None of us, whether we can be in America or in Ireland, or wherever we may be, will be satisfied until we have destroyed the last link which keeps Ireland bound to England.'[50] Parnell's pleas to Americans were far more than haphazard calls to gatherings of Irishmen. On 2 February 1880, Parnell addressed the House of Representatives. It was an honor rarely afforded even the most distinguished visitors to the United States. Parnell again emphasized the important role that America played in the Irish question.

> The public opinion of the people of America will be of the utmost importance in enabling us to obtain a just and suitable settlement of the Irish question. I have seen since I have been in this country so many tokens of the good wishes of the American people towards Ireland, I feel at a loss to express my sense of the enormous advantage and service which is daily being done to the cause of my country...For my part, I, who boast of American blood, feeling proud of the importance which has been universally attached on all sides to American opinion with regard to this matter, I feel proud in saying and believing that the time is very near at hand when you will be able to say that you have, in the way I have mentioned, and in no other way, been a most important factor in bringing about a solution of the Irish land question.[51]

Thus Irishmen, whether immigrants or parliamentary leaders, continuously focused their attention on the United States in the 1880s.

Americans responded with enormous financial and moral aid. Davitt, who had established the Irish Land League in 1879, helped form an American Land League in 1880. By June 1881, the latter league had over 1200 branches while one of the woman's groups was run by Parnell's sister, Fanny.[52] The Irish-American Patrick Ford was a primary medium for rallying moral and financial support for land reform in Ireland. His newspaper, the *Irish World*, was looked upon by all British classes as a major voice of the American Irish.[53] Between November 1879 and 30 June 1880, Americans provided £66 000 out of £69 000 raised for Irish relief, or 95 percent of the total. Similar American aid reached the Irish well into 1882. By October 1882, the American sum totaled £250 000.[54] Most of the money was used by the Land League but some also went to the Irish Nationalist MPs to alleviate actual distress. Thus, for instance, £10 000 went for the purchase of 'new seed-potatoes for the poorest of the Western peasantry.'[55] Other prominent Americans took up the Irish cause in the 1880s. The revolutionary leader Jeremiah O'Donovan Rossa, former leader of the Clan na Gael and founder of the United Irishmen, and the land reformer and politician Henry George were but two of the most active. In short, the American involvement in the Irish question in the 1880s was undeniable to all parties in Great Britain.

Initially, the Liberal government was little concerned with the Irish-American involvement in the Irish question. Gladstone, Foreign Secretary Granville, and Home Secretary Harcourt tried to moderate possible tensions between the American and British governments over periodic imprisonments of Irish-Americans under the Coercion Act. When John Devoy was released from a British prison, Harcourt exhorted the Commons in January 1881 that the longer Devoy and his comrades remained 'beyond the seas, whether on the other-side of the Atlantic or the Straits of Dover, the less notice we take of them the better.' Further, he added, 'We have got rid of John Devoy out of a convict prison and the U.S. have acquired him as an American citizen. And as we have got very much the best of the bargain I think we had better leave the matter as it stands.'[56] Gladstone also minimized the Irish-American presence in the Irish question. His stance was certainly influenced by constant reminders that Irish Anglophobia represented only a very small portion of American opinion. Bryce reported on Parnell's 'bad impression' in America and that 'the opinion of the native American people is altogether with your Government!'[57] Moreover, the American Minister James Lowell forwarded copies of Godkin's *Nation* and assured him that 'the *American* press [was] moderate in tone on the Irish question' and that he, privately, agreed 'heartily with … your notion of the case.'[58] Despite these assurances, it became increasingly apparent that there were real and dangerous Irish-American activities in the British Isles, which demanded specific policies from the Liberal leaders.

By the beginning of 1882, the Irish question had entered a new phase. The reconstruction of the Land League and Parnell's imprisonment in Kilmainham jail marked a 'shift of emphasis from agrarianism to constitutionalism.'[59] In 1882, the Irish National League was founded which directed its aims towards home rule for Ireland. At the same time, violence suddenly erupted throughout the British Isles. From January to October 1881, there were 46 individual attacks, 9 murders, 5 cases of manslaughter, and 32 of firing at persons in Ireland. They increased between mid-October 1881 and the end of April 1882 (the period of Parnell's imprisonment) to 75 attacks, 14 murders, and 61 firings.[60] On 6 May 1882, there occurred the stunning murder in Phoenix Park, Dublin, of the newly appointed Irish Secretary, the brother to Hartington, Lord Frederick Cavendish. In addition, a 'dynamite war' burst out with great force in most of the major cities in the British Isles.[61] It was directed largely by two American groups: O'Donovan Rossa's 'Skirmishers' and the United Irishmen of the secret society, Clan na Gael.

The war began on 14 January 1881 and did not end until the summer of 1887, but the worst years were from 1882 to 1885. In that period, the two American groups exploded bombs in such cities as Liverpool, Glasgow, Manchester, Birmingham, and London. In 1883, there were attacks upon Whitehall, the offices of *The Times*, and the London underground. In 1884 they extended to the London railway stations, Scotland Yard, and London Bridge. In 1885, the Clan na Gael bombing campaign reached the Tower of London and the House of Commons.[62] But how the Liberal leaders were to respond to the violent attacks, much worse than the Fenian-sponsored activities of the 1860s, was a problem of great complexity in that most of these were planned and sponsored by Americans.

Harcourt more than any other leader stirred himself and his colleagues to a stiff counteraction of the dangerous actions of Irish-Americans. As early as June 1881, he pressed Gladstone for 'a good hearing at the Cabinet today on the subject of the Assassination Literature in the United States.'[63] Throughout the period 1881 to 1885, following the Cabinet's approval on 13 June,[64] Harcourt collected samples of the Irish-American incitements to outrages in the British Isles from the *United Irishman* and the *Irish World*. These were circulated amongst the Cabinet and were a prime basis for a series of official remonstrances to the American government. Liberal leaders were clearly threatened by the violent language of the Irish-American press.

The announcement, published exclusively in the 'Mercury', that the Skirmishing Council of the United Irishmen had recorded a verdict of wilful murder and sentence of death against the Honourable Wm. Ewart Gladstone, Prime Minister of England, was cabled to London, and created the most intense excitement in official and other circles in the English capital.[65]

We have always warned the Land Leaguers in America that a constitutional agitation against England, without some physical force at the back of it, would be sure to be beaten by England; and we asked the Land League clubs when that time would come not to break up or dissolve, but to turn themselves into physical force or skirmishing clubs. The time is now come, for them to do that.[66]

Now men of the Irish race! Help your brothers at home to the fight; help them to dynamite – dynamite, fire and hell-fire in the heart of London, and in the heart of other English cities, and the tyrants and hypocrites of the world will very soon be obliged to withdraw their

English and Scotch cutthroats from Ireland, for the purpose of affording them protection in England. *That's our game.*[67]

While an official British remonstrance was addressed to the United States on 24 June, it had no effect on either the government or Irish-Americans. The American government were extremely hesitant to incur the wrath of the large block of Irish voters by reprimanding them. As the bombings predicted in the Irish-American press were executed in 1882, the Liberal government was forced into a difficult situation. William Forster, Chief Secretary for Ireland until he resigned in 1882 in response to the government's weak Irish policy, reminded the Commons on 9 February: 'I am obliged to bring in the United States, for a very good reason, because if it were not for some persons in the United States this agitation would not exist.'[68]

Harcourt was faced with a number of problems, and none of more paramount importance than that reliable and detailed information be collected. To Howard Vincent, the Director of the Criminal Division of Scotland Yard, the Home Secretary emphasized as early as 1881 that he was 'much disturbed at the absolute want of information in which we seem to be with regard to Fenian organization in London. All other objects should be postponed in our efforts to get some light into these dark places.'[69] To Gladstone, Harcourt sent E. P. Dewess's book *The Molly Maguires* and John Bagenal's *The American Irish*. The Prime Minister was especially impressed by the former: 'It throws more light on the case of Ireland than almost anything I have ever read.'[70] Not long thereafter, Morley, evidently in response to Gladstone, published extracts from Dewess's work in the *Pall Mall Gazette.*[71] However, Gladstone proved very difficult for Harcourt; the former was not convinced that there were real dangers of Fenianism in Britain. Harcourt complained about Gladstone's 'inveterate optimism' to the Lord Lieutenant for Ireland, Lord Spencer, who himself also wanted a policy of stronger retaliation against revolutionary actions.[72] Harcourt believed that the British were justified in pursuing harsh remedies – imprisonment, trials, and death sentences – as long as firm official remonstrances to the United States went largely unheeded. 'Fenianism is a permanent conspiracy against English rule which will last far beyond the time of my life & must be met by a permanent organization to detect & to control it.'[73] Gladstone disagreed. He thought that Harcourt overreacted, and wanted more cautious remedies. 'I do not admit that Irish considerations bear upon the specific question now under discussion between you & me; or that Fenian plots, at which he

[Spencer] has dealt a deadly blow, are a permanent institution of the country.'[74] Despite Gladstone's hesitations, Harcourt moved boldly ahead with Spencer's help in 1883 to establish a vast counter-terrorist system, which extended into Ireland, Scotland, France, Canada, and also the United States.

Harcourt's surveillance, information, and apprehension system called for close coordination between Cabinet members, police, detectives, and spies and was a complex organization.[75] Some of the most notable members were Sir Robert Anderson, who conducted the anti-Fenian police activities from Dublin Castle from 1883 to 1887; Edward Jenkinson, who was responsible for dealing with security in Ireland from 1882 to 1886; and Howard Vincent, a future Conservative MP who was Director of Scotland Yard and handled London security from 1878 until 1884. With each of these men, Harcourt kept in the closest touch.[76] In addition, spies like Baron LeCaron were used in America to secure inside information on the meetings of the Irish-American secret societies; consuls in many cities like New York, Chicago, and Philadelphia were kept busy forwarding many reports to the Home and Foreign Offices; and diplomats such as Henry Rose were pressed into service to make special reports.[77] While histories of British policy towards Ireland have often undervalued the Irish-American problem in the 1880s,[78] the evidence is strong that Liberal leaders saw that issue as critically important from 1882 to 1885.

On 3 March 1883, Harcourt circulated a Cabinet memorandum outlining the broadening nature of the Fenian conspiracy in Great Britain. One of the new leaders of the bombings and outrages was reported to be the former Irish Nationalist MP, Alexander Sullivan. Further, the Home Secretary professed: 'It may be concluded that dynamite is now the policy of the whole Fenian organization numbering hundreds or thousands of men – in fact the whole body of disaffected Irish Party both in America & in England.' He stressed in grave apprehension: 'The importance of this fact cannot be overestimated and we shall have to reckon with it. It makes in my judgement the nature of the Irish question far worse than it has ever yet been.'[79] By June, Harcourt was somewhat more optimistic, yet even his optimism was clouded with frustration.

All the information that reaches me is that the neck of the business is broken so far as evidence is concerned in Ireland and Gt. Britain. But the perpetual reserve of secure crime in America and the sally-port they have there prevent our eradicating the roots of the mischief, and I do not feel as if things were ever really safe so long as these horrid ruffians can come safely to and fro.[80]

Harcourt was not alone in his pessimism over the dangers of Fenianism. Morley discussed the dangers of Fenianism in articles on Ireland.[81] Other Liberal leaders – Gladstone, Granville, and Spencer – all were more and more forced to respond to a large number of diplomatic negotiations between America and Britain over Irish-Americans. They fall into four broad classifications of British response: arrest and trial of criminals, extradition, protection against assassination, and prevention of the publication of American press incitements to outrages.

The arrest and trial of the dynamiters presented significant problems for both the British Foreign Office and Home Office, as well as the Lord Chief Justice. The crux of the problem was that it was most difficult to determine who was really an American citizen. Any Irishman could argue he was an American if he had been across the Atlantic or had family members in the United States. Many Irishmen sought American citizenship to gain immunity for their actions. The sending of information and checking on sources was time consuming. It was also difficult for the British to speed up trials and the official position was to treat Irish-Americans no differently than Englishmen.[82] At first, Britain had carried out some particularly notorious arrests. Henry George, the land-reformer and at the time a correspondent for Patrick Ford's *Irish World*, was arrested in Ireland. James Lowell's and William Hoppin's protests to Granville were met with a quick release from jail and official and unofficial apologies.[83] However, by 1883 as the result of Harcourt's expanded intelligence and police operations, there were fewer improper arrests. Most trials increasingly led to harsh sentences. A typical case was that of Patrick O'Donnell, arrested, tried, and executed for his part in an 1883 bombing act. O'Donnell sought immunity as an American. When that failed, he tried to delay the sentence by introducing a hoard of American evidence to prove his innocence. Both President Arthur and the House of Representatives took up O'Donnell's case. Lowell was asked to make official protestations against British procedures.[84] Liberal leaders, however, refused to bend to American diplomatic pressure. Earl Selborne, the Lord Chancellor, fully concurred with Harcourt that the punishment should not be delayed. 'I entirely share your opinion, that O'Donnell was properly tried, and properly convicted, and that, unless criminal justice is to be entirely paralyzed in this country, no ground has been shewn, either for reprieve or for respite, in this case!'[85] Harcourt's hard position on Irish-American crimes was pronounced!

> As long as the money flows in from America we shall have no peace and I fear it will come in more than ever after the O'Donnell execution. The conduct of the Govt. of the U.S. in the matter has been detestable. I gave them as civil an answer as was consistent with an absolute refusal. But it will have a very bad effect on the American Irish to know that the Govt. of America has interested itself in favour of these villainies, and I fear a good deal of political mischief will be made out of it on the other side of the Atlantic.[86]

Generally, Harcourt, Selborne, Lord Chief Justice Coleridge, and Granville maintained a free hand in trying Irish-Americans. The British legal and police remedies met with fluctuating periods of success. But by the end of 1883, the 'dynamiters' were more and more contained and punished.[87]

A second problem revolved about the attempts of the British and American governments to work out a new extradition treaty; they were still bound by the Webster-Ashburton Treaty of 1842. Harcourt was Britain's expert on this, as he had concerned himself with extradition as far back as the 1860s during the earlier Fenian episodes.[88] Fundamentally, he was concerned that Britain retain the ability to enforce the law. During the Liberal ministry, negotiations were left up to Granville and Lowell. Their private talks were amicable, especially in the summer of 1884, but in the end unproductive.[89] The government was certainly aware that allowing murderers and dynamiters to be extradited from British jails would be a dangerous stance to take publicly.[90] A new Anglo-American extradition treaty did not evolve until July 1889,[91] when Irish-American agitation had ground to a halt in Britain.

The threatened assassination of British officials greatly worried the British government. After Lord Cavendish's murder in November 1882, threats of murder and assassination which daily appeared in the *Irish World*, the *United Irishman*, and other such journals could no longer be taken lightly. When Lord Coleridge was invited to deliver a series of lectures in America in the summer of 1883, there was real concern that he would have to cancel his trip because of threats on his life. Only after a period of frantic negotiations between British and American officials did Coleridge embark. Lowell promised that 'There can be no doubt either of their will or their [US] power to protect one who may be looked on as a national guest.'[92] The State Department assigned a bodyguard to protect Coleridge throughout the duration of the Chief

Justice's trip. His activities were curtailed in only one instance: threats from the Canadian Irish prevented him from visiting Canada.

Irish-American assassination threats continued to be taken seriously throughout the 1880s. The Prince of Wales, Gladstone, and Harcourt were among leading Englishmen who were specifically threatened. When Joseph Chamberlain journeyed to the United States in the winter of 1887–88, he also was assigned a bodyguard, and Pinkerton detectives accompanied him everywhere.[93] Fortunately, none of the threats materialized.

The fourth major problem concerning British responses to the United States over Irish-Americans was constituted by the manner in which the official British protestations over Fenian incitements to violence were presented and received by the American government. The Liberal ministry made such protestations on 24 June 1881, 15 June 1882, 17 March 1883, and 12 May 1883.[94] In March 1884, the issue again arose. Harcourt attracted the Cabinet's attention to the fact that the United States government had taken no positive action to repress the publication of the Irish-American's incendiary publications. Harcourt presented his views in a memorandum – 'Mr. Gladstone on Irish-American outrages and English secret service money.' He was supported, among others, by Lord Spencer and Edward Jenkinson, all of whom were 'convinced that we are any day on the eve of organised attempts at murder & outrages. And that the danger was never so great or so universal as it is at the present moment.'[95] Of particular consequence was the fact that the journalist Patrick Ford had established an Emergency Fund to avenge the death of the convict O'Donnell. Spencer had bitter words for the American government's intransigent positions. 'How monstrous is the position of the U.S. Govt. as to the Dynamite ruffians. They are in the U.S. territory to create engines of destruction; to destroy lives & property in England.'[96] When Granville officially protested once again to Secretary of State Frelinghuysen on 13 March 1884,[97] it was not until the end of November that the British had a reply. Both the Republican administration's delay and arguments infuriated the Liberal ministry. Frelinghuysen argued that the British did not legislate against the very crimes that they, the Americans, were being asked to provide legislation against. Nor had the British helped to protect Americans from the violent activities of the Molly Maguires, especially in the 1860s. In summarizing his arguments, the Secretary turned to logic to underscore the unanimity of the American position.

I do not see that there is similarity between the crime threatened and the crime committed. Threatening to commit a crime is by the law of England no evidence that the one making the threat committed the crime, but only evidence of intent and malice after he is by other proof connected with the crime. The publications and the crimes alluded to might be coincident, but still not dependent. *Post hoc* is not *propter hoc*. So far as I am informed, the people of the United States do not leave the President and the Cabinet to stand alone in denying the charge against this nation.[98]

The inflexible position of President Arthur's Republican administration towards the British Liberal government's serious problems of internal law and order certainly did not endear the Republican party to the Liberals. Harcourt's and Granville's frustration, in particular, stood out when a new wave of terror struck Britain in January and February 1885. There were bombings at the Tower of London, Westminster, and the House of Commons. In Rossa's *United Irishman* on 11 February, a certain Shaun O'Neill offered a 'reward of $10,000 for the body of the Prince of Wales, dead or alive!'[99] An important American event suddenly intervened. It gave the Liberal government an opportunity, which they had been unable to create themselves. It also brought about another significant reaffirmation of Anglo-American friendship, at least comparable to that of the winter of 1881–82.

In the presidential election of November 1884, the reform-minded Democratic Governor of New York, Grover Cleveland, defeated the old Anglophobe Republican, James Blaine. The contest was bitterly fought, close, and filled with personal slurs and invective aimed at capturing the Irish-American vote. The Republican party was severely split by Blaine's attitudes; the prominent 'Mugwumps' E. L. Godkin, Carl Schurz, and Horace White all defected to Cleveland. Blaine, evidently in an effort to gain Gladstone's unofficial personal sympathy, sent a copy of his *Twenty Years in Congress* and information about the American Irish to the Prime Minister in the fall of 1884.[100] However, it is not surprising considering Blaine's Anglophobe statements and the Republican party's stubborn refusal to help deter Irish-American acts of violence that Liberals most warmly supported Cleveland. Morley described the weakened condition of the Republican party[101] and Bryce commented to Godkin on Blaine's narrow defeat: 'It is depressing to think that corruption should have come so near to sitting in the chair at Washington.'[102] In addition, the Liberal MP for Hythe, Edward Watkin, forwarded a letter to Harcourt from an American friend, J. S. Moore (a prominent Democrat), who asserted

that Mr. Cleveland will inaugurate a new era of honest and efficient government and that he will sit upon the Irish ranter. Our two countries cannot remain at peace if assassination & revolution are to go on hatching in the U.S. without rebuke from the Government in power at Washington.[103]

Cleveland's victory was not only a triumph of generally liberal and democratic ideals – international peace, low tariffs, sound money, civil service reform, and other such causes – but it represented a triumph by the Republican 'Mugwumps' over the violent Irish factions in the United States. It is not surprising that Liberal leaders demonstrated an inclination to shift their earlier allegiances from the Republican party to those of Cleveland's Democrat–'Mugwump' alliance.[104]

Important private information assured Liberal leaders that the new Democratic administration would adopt a more friendly policy over Irish-American affairs with the Gladstonian government. J. S. Moore's long letter to Edward Watkin was circulated to various Cabinet leaders, including Lord Spencer and Harcourt. Moore emphasized the changed nature of the Democratic party, that the party was no longer ruled by the divisive Irish element. Many Irish leaders had turned to support the Republican Blaine because of his outspoken anti-British posture, and those who still remained within the Democratic party had lost much of their influence by early 1885. 'The feeling of the Democratic leaders (especially as we gained the victory) is to let the Irish element understand, that the Democratic party henceforth is their master, & "not their glove." '[105] Furthermore, Moore assured Liberals that the new Democratic administration would willingly settle the Irish-American difficulties.

> … Democratic leaders frequently … [and] naturally discussed this last outrage in London [bombing of the House of Commons], … And your wish and demand for Justice, will find a better and more fertile soil under Cleveland than you now dream of. I know the sentiments of Mr. Bayard on this subject. All I can say to you is, that his sentiments may well rejoice you. Mr. Gladstone is indeed the head of your Government.[106]

Bayard, the new Secretary of State, was most friendly towards British Liberals. His counterpart, the Foreign Secretary, was Rosebery with whom he had maintained occasional amicable intercourse since their first meetings early in the 1870s. In March 1884, Bayard wrote Rosebery:

> My interest in the affairs of my own country is scarcely greater than I feel in yours – and its safety and welfare. For it does seem to me

without vain glory or assumption, that to what these *two* countries contain of conscience, courage and capacity are committed the best hopes of civilization and human progress.[107]

Finally, there were signs that the Senate and various states were willing to legislate against Irish-American conspiracies and fulminating literature. Bills were introduced making possession of dynamite a felony. The signs from America were distinctly favorable.

Liberal leaders worked hard to consolidate an agreement with the new Democratic government on Irish-Americans early in 1885. Harcourt reprinted extracts of the *United Irishman* and circulated them to British and American leaders. Thus, he sent twenty copies of three different reprinted series to the British Ambassador in Washington, Sir Julian Pauncefote. They were to be given 'privately to any persons' who might aid the British case. 'I find among the best informed people in America that there is a great deal of ignorance and incredulity as to the existence of these abominations. I am myself taking measures privately to have them made known in the U.S.'[108] Effort was also spent on the exact wording of an official British remonstration concerning Irish-American assassination literature. Gladstone told Granville that the despatch was 'able' but that it needed further softening; 'at one or two points', he suggested, 'there is a little more of the "controversial spirit" than the introduction leads one to expect – might it not be slightly softened in tone here & there without spoiling the arguments.'[109] While Bayard responded indirectly and directly in a much more friendly manner than had his predecessor Frelinghuysen, he was reluctant to move too hastily. He wished to see the outcome of anti-dynamite legislation proposed in the Senate and various states.[110] Furthermore, he was obviously preoccupied with setting up the Department of State. Liberal leaders did not question this hesitation. Cleveland's Inaugural Address had made it patently clear that the two Anglo-Saxon governments were committed to the same principles: 'Peace, commerce, and honest friendship with all nations; entangling alliances with none.'[111]

After a series of disturbing years of Anglo-American relations with respect to Irish-Americans, the Liberal government's joy over the Cleveland administration's friendly pronouncements was profound.

Her Majesty's Government have learnt with the highest satisfaction of the friendly language employed by the President of the United States in his recent message on the subject of the necessity for the enlargement of the Laws of the United States 'to meet other emergencies which have arisen' and to punish overt reparations for the commission of criminal acts whether such acts are intended to be committed in the United States or in a Foreign Country with which the United States is at peace. This declaration confirmed as it has been by a remarkable assent throughout the Public Press of the United States and by the action of both branches of the Legislature in that Country, gives Her Majesty's Govt. entire confidence that the recommendation of the President of the United States to take up 'the prompt and thorough treatment of this question as one which intimately concerns the national honour' will lead to a practical and satisfactory remedy for the evils which you have been frequently instructed under the notice of the Govt. of the United States as arising out of the public and unpunished incitement to murder and outrage published in the United States. This state of things renders it fortunately unnecessary to reply in a controversial spirit to the despatch of Mr. F. of the 24th of Nov. last.[112]

Yet, ironically, when circumstances finally favored the Liberals' attempts to establish further Anglo-American agreements with President Cleveland, their political fortunes turned against them. In June 1885, Gladstone resigned and Salisbury came into office to form his first ministry. While the Liberals earned a short reprieve and again assumed command in the first half of 1886, this did not constitute a fair opportunity for consolidating relations with Cleveland's administration. What might have been a very substantial four years (1885–89) for cementing the Anglo-American relationship, promoted by two administrations with similar aims and principles, must in the end be only a matter of conjecture. What does seem certain is that Gladstonian Liberals and Cleveland Democrats were similarly inclined towards common political agendas and to respect and associate with each other. Both groups fervently desired an end to Irish-American terrorism.

Henry George and land reform

The American aspects of the Irish question in British politics can hardly be understood without some attention to the appeal of the famous American land reformer Henry George. Between 1882 and 1885, after the Land League had been wound up and Parnell concentrated thereafter on Home Rule, Henry George, Michael Davitt, Henry Hyndman (the Social Democrat), and several others carried the flag for land reform in the British Isles. No American, likely no Englishman, contributed so much to exposing the destitution, plights, and inequalities of the Irishmen as did Henry George. His seminal work, *Progress and Poverty*, published in America in 1879 and in Britain in 1881, swept both the United States and Great Britain in the early 1880s. Over 100 000 copies were sold in England in the 1880s alone. Moreover, George gave over a hundred lectures to English, Scottish, and Irish audiences during four lecture tours in the 1880s. He wrote many other important works upon the land question which adopted his particular analyses and remedies to the Irish situation, notably *The Irish Land Question* (1881) and *Social Problems* (1884).[113]

George's British popularity and his frequent expositions of Anglo-American parallel developments introduced many American analogies into the debate of British politics and society. 'Henry George, not Karl Marx, was the true catalyst of Britain's insurgent proletariat.'[114] In time, George's land-tax proposals became major planks in both the Liberal and Labour political platforms. There can be no doubt about his impact upon Radicals, Socialists, Fabians, and Labour in the 1880s but his influence upon British Liberalism, and especially Gladstonian Liberals, in the same decade was less clear cut.

George constantly linked parallel developments in Great Britain with those in America. It cannot be doubted that his views cast him distinctly into the radical wing of British politics.[115] He argued that the great cause of inequality in wealth arose because of unequal ownership of land between lower and upper classes. In order to get rid of poverty, it was necessary to get rid of the private ownership of land. '*We must make land common property.*'[116] Land should thus be nationalized and turned over to the people. Moreover, the landowners should not receive any compensation: 'The landowners have no rightful claim either to the land or to compensation for its resumption by the people, and, further than that, we see that no such rightful claim can ever be created.'[117] These ideas reverberated throughout the British Isles, they inspired the creation of Land Nationalization Associations, and Land Reform Associations, and they engendered both vehement support and opposition from individuals and groups of all kinds.[118]

The Liberal leaders accepted George's views with varying degrees of criticism; many Liberal parliamentarians had been first exposed to *Progress and Poverty* because George sent them personal copies of the book. The Duke of Argyll, Henry Fawcett, Leonard Courtney, Henry Labouchere, the former MP Thomas Hughes, the philosopher Herbert Spencer, and Gladstone all received copies.[119] Gladstone thanked

George for the 'interesting work' and reiterated that 'There is no question which requires a more careful examination than the land question.'[120] But thereafter, there is no evidence that Gladstone ever
seriously considered George's schemes of nationalization without compensation. It is doubtful that George ever met Gladstone, although
he did meet Chamberlain, Bryce, Dilke, and probably Morley and
Rosebery. In February 1891, Gladstone made it perfectly clear that he
had very little regard for George's land tax proposals at a time when
these had gained some degree of support from within the Liberal party.

> There are persons who view the proposals of Mr. George as propos-
> als of a very enlightened character, and who very much resent the
> use of hard words respecting them ... I will say that, as far as my
> examination or knowledge of his proposals goes, I find it extremely
> difficult, and indeed for myself, altogether impossible, to exclude
> them or extricate them, from the category of those plans to which
> hard words are no doubt commonly applied.[121]

It is obvious why Gladstone rejected George's ideas. In common with
Conservatives, Whigs, and land-holding Liberals, Gladstone saw George
as a dangerous visionary threatening to destroy the virtues and morals
of late Victorian society. While the Duke of Argyll and Gladstone differed over land reform, Argyll resigning from the Liberal party on the
1881 Land Act, they reached common ground on their characterization
of George in 1884:

> There has seldom been such a curious example as the immoral
> teachings of Mr. Henry George. Here we have a man who probably
> sincerely thinks he is a Christian, and who sets up as a philosopher,
> but who is not the least shocked by consequences which abolish the
> Decalogue, and deny the primary obligations both of public and of
> private honour.[122]

The future Conservative Prime Minister Arthur Balfour took a similar
stance. At the Industrial Remuneration Conference in Glasgow in
1885, he argued that George's remedies were strikingly illogical and
impractical. If, as George suggested, the rents of the landowners were
evenly distributed among the community at large, Balfour figured that
each individual would receive the paltry dole of £2.1.3s. 'Surely in all
the melancholy history of human delusions there never was a contrast
more melancholy than that to be observed between the grandeur of

the ends which this scheme is to attain, the audacious novelty of its proposed means, and the misery or pettiness of its inevitable results.'[123] Most Gladstonian Liberal leaders such as Harcourt, Bryce, Dilke, and Rosebery also were wholly uninfluenced by George's ideas. Bryce met George in the 1880s, but Harcourt refused to see him in 1882.[124]

On the other hand, two Liberal leaders, Morley and Chamberlain, were for a short period profoundly interested in George's notions. On 21 April 1882, one Walter Wren gave a dinner party at the Reform Club for Chamberlain, John Bright, and Henry George. The latter left two different accounts of the evening. Both pointed out the ideological similarities and differences between the American radical and the Birmingham radical. As Chamberlain had read George's articles for the *Irish World* and because Bright pushed the conversation in that direction, the main dinner talk was on Ireland and not specifically land reform. George recalled in 1883: 'I do not think my views upon the land question were ever once alluded to either by me or anyone else.'[125] George's estimation of Chamberlain surprisingly was not all that favorable: that Chamberlain was an opportunist, conservative, and not a genuine reformer.

> He impressed me as a very able man who had carried into politics keen business sense and power of combination but nothing of a reformer. My judgement of him was that he was an ambitious man who would go as far towards Democracy as was popular but no further, and that if he did not get his locks shorn by the fascination of aristocratic society might play an important part in English politics in the years to come.[126]

But after the evening was over, there were apparently no further personal associations between George and Chamberlain. While George had contributed an article to Morley's *Fortnightly Review* in April 1881, personal contacts between Morley and George were minimal if any. It was only through a close study of George's ideas – for a short period – that Morley and Chamberlain ever associated with the American land-reformer.

In 1882 and 1883, both Morley and Chamberlain were among a body of Liberal leaders who thought that land reform was most likely to bring a speedy settlement to the Irish question. As early as 1873, Chamberlain had called for 'free land' as part of a larger program of emancipation including 'free religion' and 'free education.' In 1882,

Morley also had come to the conclusion that the land issue was 'the next great business' and the unifying means of the Liberal party.[127] At the same time, Morley realized that land reform might not be enough. In 1881, he had suggested that a land bill 'will do much, but to reach the heart of the matter it will be necessary to go a great deal further than economic changes.'[128] It was not surprising that Morley used the columns of his *Pall Mall Gazette* for some of the first full analyses of *Progress and Poverty* by a major British periodical.[129] Morley's enthusiastic interest in George's views bubbled forth to his comrade Chamberlain on Christmas Eve in 1882.

> The workmen are full of the ideas of Henry George. They are reading his book by thousands of copies. In London 'Nationalisation of the Land' is the one subject that would furnish a base for agitation. Why? Not because the workmen want farms, but because they are beginning to suspect that the reason why they are crammed into lodgings (the average London workman and his entire family live in two rooms) and why if they want a little house of their own they must go to a distant suburb and pay 8/s a week and rates, is that the landlord and the land grabber screw a rack rent out of their necessities. They feel, too, at last, that it is the immigrants from the country who lower their wages and compete for room in the town – and this immigration arises from the land system.[130]

Chamberlain did not need a lot of encouragement. Together, both Liberals decided to undertake a common study of the various details of the major proponents of land reform. This meant hard study of John Stuart Mill, Alfred Wallace, and Henry George.[131] Chamberlain made very extensive notes upon George's and Wallace's schemes. Moreover, he sent them to Morley and suggested that they be published in the *Pall Mall Gazette*. On 24 and 29 January 1883, Morley printed Chamberlain's 'Short Notes on Land Nationalization.' They were Chamberlain's most extensive views upon George, views which he never substantially revised.

Chamberlain found a little to endorse in Wallace, but hardly anything in George. While Chamberlain and Morley both accepted most of the various social criticisms of the two land reformers, they found their remedies totally unrealistic. In the first instance, Chamberlain believed that the pictures painted by both Wallace and George of the depravity of the working classes were 'overdrawn.' 'The condition of the working classes has naturally improved; thrift and temperance are both more common; the hours of labour are less, wages are higher; education is becoming general.'[132] He also disputed both land reformers' contentions that the wealth had gone solely into the pockets of the landowners. On the contrary, profits from the land had been shared by all classes. While Chamberlain shared George's concern for the condition of the working classes – although he did not see it as such a dire situation as George – he categorically rejected George's remedies. Wallace's remedy of confiscation of rent was radical and unthinkable, while George's nationalization of land without compensation for the landlords was ridiculous and totally unpracticable.

> Mr. George's scheme proposes to secure the same object by still more violent methods. Mr. George asserts the right of the nation to confiscate all landed property, but as a compromise he would be satisfied with levying all taxation on land up to the full value of the rent, leaving the landlords in possession as mere collectors for the State ...
> Mr. George's assertion is that in some unexplained way all the increased wealth of the nation which now goes to a few will be transferred proportionately to all, or, in other words, that the 600 millions of increased income which has arisen during the last twenty years would, if landlordism had been abolished, have been divided among the whole population of 35 millions equally; but all this seems to proceed on the assumption that rent now devours the whole interest. The figures, however, show conclusively that this is not the case.[133]

That Chamberlain totally rejected George's schemes for land reform was again underlined in an article in the *Fortnightly Review* in February. 'If something be not done quickly to meet the growing necessities of the case, we may live to see theories as wild and methods as unjust as those suggested by the American economist adopted as the creed of no inconsiderable portion of the electorate.'[134] Rather, Chamberlain supported remedies which were incorporated in the Land Act of 1881. While that act had not given tenants equal wealth, it had in Chamberlain's view given 'the tenant practically perpetuity of tenure, and the property in his improvements.'[135]

It has been contended that George influenced Chamberlain to a great extent.[136] Undoubtedly, Chamberlain agreed with some of George's diagnosis of Irish social conditions. He also accepted that land reform was the first priority for Ireland.[137] Both men 'contended that poverty was the cause, not the result, of social ills' and 'attacked the landlord with righteous indignation.'[138] There were similarities in the views and actions of both reformers, but the influence was minimal. Indirectly, the agitation of both men helped the other. But George wanted a social revolution, while Chamberlain, a large property owner himself, merely adopted land reform as 'the key to the unravelling of a very complex social situation.'[139] It was also a means by which the Irish question could be solved without moving towards schemes of home rule, increasingly the focus of Gladstonian Liberal efforts. In 1885, Chamberlain rejected George even more swiftly than he had in 1883. His *Radical Programme* called for a land tax of four shillings in the pound, but he rejected George's and Wallace's remedies as 'not only drastic, but alarming, in their scope and magnitude.'[140] Both Chamberlain and his secretary responded fiercely to charges that Chamberlain had adopted George's methods and schemes. In 1885, Chamberlain declared:

> I have never used the language attributed to me, in reference to Mr. George. It is well known that I think him mistaken, and I don't agree with his conclusions, but I have no reason to doubt his perfect sincerity and honesty of intention.[141]

Chamberlain's and Morley's early excitement over George's ideas should not be taken as long-term influence. Throughout the 1880s, Chamberlain stuck firmly to his own land reform schemes, denounced George-style remedies, and plied a different path than George. Chamberlain wanted to increase the number of land owners, while George wanted a socialist revolution and the extinguishing of private ownership.

As a postscript, it should be stated that in the late 1880s, George's influence started to extend noticeably into the mainstream of British politics. During George's 1888 and 1889 British trips, he mingled closely with radical Liberals, as well as Scottish and Irish nationalists. He saw a great deal of William Saunders, Liberal MP and journalist; debated with the Liverpool Liberal Samuel Smith at the National Liberal Club on 4 June 1889; was inducted as a temporary member of the National Liberal Club; and received a more cordial reception from the Liberal press than on any of his earlier trips.[142] Welsh radicals like the young David Lloyd George were enthusiastic. Various Radicals even tried to persuade him to take up residence in England and stand for a Scottish constituency. Moreover, the Liberal party decided to adopt land reform as a plank in their political platform.[143] On the other hand, the Liberal leaders probably concerned themselves very little with George's ideas after 1890. Gladstonian Liberals – Rosebery, Harcourt, Morley, and

Bryce, including Gladstone – were all preoccupied with the issue of Home Rule for Ireland. Chamberlain had abandoned one party for associations with another, which was decidedly more hostile to George than even his old friends. In the 1890s, Labour and Radical groups adopted George's programs, but Gladstonian Liberals rarely countenanced such wild theories as appropriation of all land without compensation.

The American Constitution, federalism, and Home Rule

The Irish question had been dominated by certain issues from 1880 to 1885 – the Land League and agrarian agitation, Irish-American revolutionary activities, and the call for land reform from George and Chamberlain. In 1885 and 1886, it took on different characteristics. After his release from Kilmainham prison, Parnell and many of his Nationalist colleagues turned to the development of forms of self-government for Ireland. The movement slowly gathered momentum. Various Liberal leaders had often toyed with the idea of Home Rule for Ireland. In 1877, Morley admitted: 'Is it possible that by conceding some sort of Home Rule, we might be developing in the Irish a new sort of sense of responsibility?'[144] Bryce recalled how, in 1882, he and some of his fellow Liberals 'began to ask whether Home Rule might not be as much an English and Scottish question as an Irish question.'[145] In the winter of 1885, Home Rule became a much more public issue because of the Hawarden kite incident and Gladstone's conversion, though Gladstone like Bryce had previously gradually moved towards Home Rule. On 8 April 1886, Gladstone introduced his first Home Rule Bill, which was to precipitate such remarkable debate over the next years.

Throughout this period, the American experience impinged on the discussion of ways to reach self-government for Ireland. 'The intelligentsia took hold of the Irish question as a paramount test case of liberal principles in action, and discussed it in terms of the higher ideal ends of the party or as a considerable weapon in the party game. In the test case, the American analogies poured forth as in 1867.'[146] There were many ways in which Liberal leaders approached the American example. The Constitution, the Senate, the Supreme Court, clôture, federalism and democracy all received increased scrutiny and usually praise.[147] Nor were Gladstonians the only worshipers of American practices. Liberal Unionists found many conservative virtues in the American Constitution. In fact, one major alternative plan to Home Rule, Chamberlain's federal scheme, was based largely upon American and Canadian experience.

In the proposals for Home Rule between 1880 and 1886, frequent reference was made to the United States.[148] The manner in which the Constitution provided for the reservation of certain powers and preserved others for American states increasingly appealed to the British as a practical answer to the Irish question. A peer, Lord Blandford, suggested in 1882 that 'it is in studying the constitution of the American Republic that we shall find the most valuable example of successful effort to preserve the national feeling of people while at the same time conceding to them the most extended form of local administration.'[149] Many important Liberals also promoted the American example. The free-thinker MP, Henry Labouchere, who was particularly close to Chamberlain, Morley, and Herbert Gladstone in the mid-1880s, had an overriding aim to 'capture the G.O.M. for Home Rule.'[150] In his newspaper, *Truth*, he made frequent calls for 'separate assemblies for England, Scotland and Ireland, modeled upon the United States' constitution, with a superior imperial parliament.'[151] The Scottish Liberal, George Campbell, made his extensive trip to the American Southern States in 1878–79 to study the black question and also Home Rule. He reached very favorable opinions on American federalism, especially as it worked in 'the individual States.'

> I was the more anxious to see the character of this Home Rule, because I am entirely convinced that the work of the British Parliament is more and more overpassing the working power of the machinery; that things are rapidly coming to a serious block, if not a dead-lock, and that something must be done ... I wanted to know, then, if such things are better done in America ... I am bound to say that the result of very careful inquiry has been to convince me that the Americans have a very great advantage over us. It seemed to me that the State Legislatures are most useful institutions and that, through them, a very large amount of work is done, to the great benefit and satisfaction of their citizens, very much which with us is left undone altogether being there got through without hitch or difficulty.[152]

And contrary to the opinion of many Englishmen, in the midst of debates over corrupt caucus politics in America, Campbell found American politicians to be practical and fairly virtuous.[153] The Irish Nationalist MP, Justin McCarthy, who had spent a number of years in America in the 1870s,[154] also praised American home rule.

> This plan of Home Rule for Ireland would establish between Ireland and the Imperial Parliament the same relations in principle that

exist between a State of the American Union and the Federal Government, or between any State of the Dominion of Canada and that central Canadian Parliament which meets in Ottawa. I would leave to Ireland the making of her domestic laws, exactly as an American or Canadian local legislature has that power now.[155]

Furthermore, McCarthy called for a chief executive, a bicameral legislature, and a Senate similar to those establishments in the United States.[156] Nor was it only a case of the advocates of Home Rule praising American federal and constitutional examples. Many future Liberal Unionists, especially a body of intellectuals with fervidly held liberal principles, men like A. V. Dicey, Goldwin Smith, E. A. Freeman, and Matthew Arnold, all hailed the conservative virtues of American constitutionalism.[157] All four men had traveled extensively in the United States in the mid-1880s, visiting family, lecturing, or studying certain American developments. They all expressed great respect and enthusiasm for the United States.[158] Although Matthew Arnold, among the four, has a reputation for his critical comments about the depravity and philistinism of American culture, he still could voice praise for federalism.

But here again let us look at what is done by people who in politics think straight and see clear; let us observe what is done in the United States. The Government at Washington reserves matters of imperial concern, matters such as those just enumerated, which cannot be relinquished without relinquishing the unity of the empire. Neither does it allow one great South to be constituted, or one great West, with a Southern Parliament, or a Western. Provinces that are too large are broken up, as Virginia has been broken up. But the several States are nevertheless real and important wholes, each with its own legislature; and to each the control, within its own borders, of all except imperial concerns, is freely committed. The United States Government intervenes only to keep order in the last resort. Let us suppose a similar plan applied in Ireland.[159]

Arnold, like most Liberal students of Irish Home Rule, whether for or against it, made serious studies of 'American Home Rule' (federalism) in the 1880s. For the Gladstonian home ruler, American federalism gave States self-government, while for the Unionist, it bound States to a strong central authority.

Liberal leaders were ever more aided in gaining American opinion on federalism by patriotic Americans. Andrew Carnegie admonished

Englishmen to 'Look at America to-day' in terms of a federal remedy for Ireland in his first article for a British periodical, Morley's *Fortnightly Review.*[160] Carnegie never lost an opportunity to try to persuade his Liberal friends – Gladstone, Morley, and Rosebery – to adopt federalism for Ireland. Edwin L. Godkin also provided an endless and useful flow of information to Liberal leaders on American constitutional practices.[161] He influenced Bryce's views enormously.[162] Gladstone himself sought out North American opinion on Home Rule when, in 1883, he asked the Marquis of Lorne, Governor-General of Canada, for Canadian and American views of federalism, Home Rule, and the Irish question.[163] In the summer, the Prime Minister received his reports: two lengthy surveys by the leading Canadian politicians, Anglin (former Speaker of the Canadian House of Commons) and Costigan (a Cabinet minister).[164] Many more instances could be cited of other Liberal studies of Canadian and American precedents for federal union in the British Isles. At first these references occurred only sporadically in British political debate, but between 1886 and 1893 they became prevalent in Liberal communications and publications. The consolidation of transatlantic liberal friendships in the mid-1880s inspired Liberals to consider seriously some form of American federalism for Ireland.[165]

There were many areas of the American federal or constitutional experience which specifically appealed to Liberals. In the winter of 1880–81, when the Irish turned to obstruction of debate in the House of Commons, the Liberal government examined foreign practices for controlling debate. A Cabinet memorandum circulated in November declared that 'the American Previous Question is a more powerful weapon than the Continental Cloture,'[166] and a year later another 'study praised American clôture.'[167] Bryce was particularly supportive of the American use of the 'previous question' to curtail debate, and Gladstone also considered it in a fairly favorable light.[168] Most Liberals believed that clôture helped the American Senate to preserve its distinguished integrity.

No American institution was more lauded by all British politicians than the Senate. By the mid-1880s, the Senate played a primary role in any positive comment about the American political system. When debate erupted in 1884 over the possible reform of the House of Lords and the passage of the Representation of the People Bill, the Senate was frequently upheld as the ideal higher chamber. Bryce called it 'the sheet anchor of the American system, preventing abuses of power by the Executive,' and restraining the 'impetuosity of the popular

House.'[169] Rosebery boldly introduced a motion for a committee to inspect the efficiency of the Lords.

> Let us compare this Assembly, with these 116 persons, with the most powerful and efficient Second Chamber that exists in the world. I do not suppose anybody conversant with the two Assemblies denies that, in point of weight of power and of authority, the Senate of the United States is the first Second Chamber in the world. Why is it that the Senate should exercise more power than the House of Lords? Why is it that its decisions are decisions from which there is practically no appeal? Why is it that it has greater power entrusted to it?[170]

When Carnegie published his *Triumphant Democracy*, Salisbury's ('The Americans have a Senate – I wish we could institute it here – marvelous in its strength and efficiency') and Gladstone's overflowing commendations of the Senate were displayed on the cover.[171] Throughout the 1880s, the American Senate remained the most brilliant example to British parliamentarians of the efficiency of American institutions.[172] In the final analysis, the debates on the whole Irish Home Rule question, and to a lesser extent on the broader question of growing British democracy, focused Liberal attention on the broad virtues and specific practices of American federalism.[173]

In the winter of 1885, Gladstone retired to Hawarden to consider possible solutions to the Irish question. The country waited anxiously. On 17 December, his son Herbert Gladstone released the dramatic news that his father had opted for Home Rule and self-government for Ireland. The Liberal party was stunned. The eventual proposal as framed in the first bill introduced on 8 April 1886 provided for a separate Irish legislature and executive. They would control all Irish matters, but Her Majesty's government would still retain control over imperial or Crown matters, foreign relations, trade, defense, the post office, and coinage. While there was much that appealed to Irishmen and some Liberals, other Liberals – the Unionists – violently objected to such splitting up of the British empire. The debates on the details of the Home Rule Bill were waged with great intensity. American federalism was also an issue of contention between some Gladstonian and Liberal Unionists, with differing perspectives on the utility of the American experience for British politics.

No leading Liberal was more genuinely ready to support American federalism for the British Isles than Joseph Chamberlain, as has been noted by historian Kendle.[174] Initially, he had adopted the proposal of a form of National Council for Ireland in the winter of 1884–85 as a part of the 'Radical Programme.' This provided for the election of a National Irish Council which would have certain responsibilities for local government which the Imperial Parliament did not have the time to consider. When Chamberlain presented his Irish Central Board scheme to the Cabinet on 9 May 1885, it was rejected by all the peers except Granville though 'supported by Gladstone and all the Commoners.'[175] When he pressed the National Council idea in July, it again gained little following.[176] Then on 17 December came the startling news of Gladstone's conversion to Home Rule.

In the following weeks, Chamberlain turned himself to devise a new and potentially attractive scheme for Ireland. On 26 December, his federal plan based upon the United States was revealed to two of his closest friends: Henry Labouchere and Charles Dilke. 'There is only one way of giving *bona fida* Home Rule, which is the adoption of the American Constitution.'[177] Chamberlain's plan called for a radical reconstruction of the British Constitution. Chamberlain acknowledged as much, and thus saw little chance of its acceptance in Britain. But that did not deter him from formulating a well-designed proposal.

> Is there any other possible arrangement which would secure the real integrity of the Empire for Imperial purposes while allowing Irishmen to play the devil as they liked in Ireland?
>
> Yes, there is; but it involves the entire recasting of the British Constitution, & the full & complete adoption of the American system.
>
> According to this view you might have 5 Parliaments for England, Scotland, Wales, Ulster, & the three other Provinces combined. Each Parliament to have its own Ministry responsible to it & dependent on its vote.
>
> In addition an Imperial Parliament or Reichsrath with another ministry dealing with Foreign & Colonial affairs, Army, Navy, Post Office & Customs.
>
> To carry out this arrangement a Supreme Court or similar tribunal must be established to decide on the … several local legislatures & the limits of their authority.
>
> The House of Lords must go – or you must establish a separate second Chamber for each Legislature.[178]

Chamberlain's plan was truly federal, unlike many of those of the home rulers. It sought to consolidate national unity among a group of separate states, not just Ireland and England. Why Chamberlain did not press forward with this scheme is open to several explanations. In large part, he thought the plan was far too radical, nor was he hopeful that Gladstone would adopt it. To Labouchere, Chamberlain wrote on 27 December 1885:

> I wish someone would start the idea of a Federal Constitution like the United States. I do not believe people are prepared for this solution yet, but it is the only possible form of Home Rule. It is that or nothing. In my opinion Mr. Gladstone cannot carry his or any other scheme just now.[179]

In part, he advocated land reforms as still the fundamental Irish solution. Moreover, he increasingly lost his appetite for politics and his patience with past friends.[180] Between Chamberlain's first and last letters of resignation from Gladstone's Cabinet (15 and 27 March), Harcourt discovered one way that Chamberlain might be induced to remain in the government. The Home Secretary reported to Gladstone that Chamberlain would compromise on the American experience.

> Is it possible [Chamberlain speaking] to discuss the question on the basis of four bodies resembling the State Governments in the US – these bodies to be supreme in all matters referred to them such as all local Govt., Public Works, Education etc. but excluding Imperial Revenue, Taxation, Customs and Excise, Judiciary, Army & Navy, Foreign & Colonial Affairs; Legislation as to Land to be also excluded.[181]

Gladstone rejected such a compromise. Had his own justifications and animosities, like those of Chamberlain, not reached such a severe pitch, he might have more seriously considered aspects of Chamberlain's federal remedy.[182] In fact, in 1893, he himself turned to call for a more blatantly federal solution in the second Home Rule Bill.

Other important Liberals privately admonished Gladstonians to adopt either American or Canadian federalism. Leonard Courtney, the champion of proportional representation, tried to persuade Morley that the Canadian plan was admirably suited to the British experience. Morley assured Gladstone that his 'article is not going to be published.'[183] Carnegie suggested that Gladstone consider that the rights of American States were needed for Ireland. 'Such a measure will strengthen the bonds of union between Ireland and Great Britain; for America has proved through the federal system that the freest self-government of the parts produces the strongest government of the whole.'[184] Finally, William Rathbone, the Liberal MP for Caernarvonshire and a shipowner who had traveled widely in the United States, wrote Gladstone a lengthy memorandum upon the soundness of American practices. He warned that Gladstone's bill needed 'sound precautions against local expenditure and local indebtedness, precautions which at least ten States in the American Union have found it necessary to insert in their constitutions.' Otherwise, 'we shall utterly demoralise the Irish by a lavish system of outdoor relief.'[185] Moreover, an excellent way to place Irish legislation under some control – they certainly would not accept that of the British government – would be to place them 'under restrictions analogous to those enforced by the Supreme Court in America and restrictions as to taxation and debt which the Americans have found it necessary to submit to.'[186] This advice had no evident impact. Gladstone rejected all considerations of American federalism in his Home Rule Bill. In only one instance did Gladstone act upon the advice of American history. The Liberal Prime Minister urged Englishmen to grant Ireland a measure of full autonomy similar to that given to the Southern States during Reconstruction.[187]

Many Liberals had seen the Home Rule crisis in the light of the American experience, and yet British views of American federalism were often confused and inaccurate.[188] However, there could be no hiding the fact that the United States as represented by images, historical analogies, and constitutional precedents had hovered before everyone as a focus of lively debate. However, in June 1886, the Liberals were confused about much more than American federalism. With the defeat of the Home Rule Bill on 8 June, the party was hopelessly divided on many issues and lay in ruins. In its place, an invigorated Conservative party came to power led by the indefatigable Lord Salisbury. The Liberals would return to consider American federalism with more unity of viewpoint, but they would never form another ministry in the nineteenth century solidly based upon Liberal unity.

Conclusion

During Gladstone's second and third ministries from 1880 to 1886, three periods of Anglo-American understanding stood out: the first, in 1881–82 after President Garfield's assassination; the second, in 1884–85 after Grover Cleveland's election; and the third, during the controversy in Great Britain over Gladstone's first Home Rule Bill.

In the winter of 1885–86, Irish-Americans changed their assessments of the Liberal government's Irish policies. The anti-British hostility of the 'dynamiters' and revolutionaries suddenly subsided. Gladstone and Harcourt were no longer universal targets of assassination rhetoric. Instead, Gladstone became as great an idol in the eyes of the Irish in North America as Parnell. 'Generally, despite a few murmurs, the Irish in America supported the bill and praised Gladstone.'[189] In part, this shift in Irish-American views of Gladstone was the product of the Prime Minister's championing of Irish rights. In part, it was also the result of the Irish-American effort itself losing its revolutionary character and adopting constitutional aims. In August 1885, the Irish National League, at a national meeting in Chicago, adopted a Home Rule platform as a solution to the Irish problem. This convention, not surprisingly, was watched closely and its decisions were joyously celebrated by many Liberals.[190] When Gladstone adopted the Home Rule measure in December, it came after a similar conversion by Irish-Americans. Home Rule for Ireland meant not only a settlement for Ireland, but a settlement of the Anglo-American differences over Irish-American issues of the previous six years.

As Gladstone's popularity plummeted in England among Liberals, his reputation soared in the United States among many groups.[191] The waves of Irish-American support for the Irish Home Rule cause were staggering. American financial contributions, which had been substantial during the Land League movement, had dropped drastically from 1882 to 1885. If there was any aid, it was of a clandestine nature and impossible to trace. However, in March 1885, a Parliamentary Fund was established on behalf of Irish Home Rule. Funds poured in. From 1 January 1886 to 26 June 1886, the subscriptions jumped from, £3340 to £66 420 (90 percent came from the United States).[192] But in addition to financial support, flattering petitions rained down upon Gladstone. He received them from such bodies as the Assembly of New York, a mass meeting in Brooklyn, a convention at the University of Michigan, a branch of the Irish National League of America in Jacksonville, Florida, a committee of the Colored Men's Republican Club in Washington, DC, and the Polish National Alliance of the United States.[193] Perhaps the most interesting communication came from a Pennsylvanian Congressman, James Kitson. He had made a study of the popularity of the schemes of Gladstone and Chamberlain with American Senators and Congressmen.[194] The results of his questionnaire were overwhelmingly in favor of Gladstone's course of action. These American views represented an almost complete about-face from the sordid and violent Irish-American messages of the early 1880s. Gladstone was evidently overjoyed. In response to one petition, Gladstone sent a telegram: 'the number & the cordiality of the expressions of approval from America, are most encouraging to H.M. Govt. in their attempt to promote the welfare of the country by their measures in connection with Ireland.' On the draft of the telegram, Gladstone jotted down his feelings, 'Yes, my!'[195]

Throughout the period 1880 to June 1886, the Irish question had stood as a barrier to harmonious relations between Britain and the United States. The Anglophobia of Irish-Americans had peaked in 1884; so too had the obstinacy of the Republican administration of Chester Arthur to help the Liberals stem Irish revolutionary activities. However, by June 1886, neither the Anglophobia of the Irish-Americans nor the Republicans represented barriers to Anglo-American understanding. Both had fallen by the wayside, at least temporarily. Gladstone's Home Rule Bill marked a bold attempt to settle a critical imperial crisis, and in a manner it also happened to represent a bold move to reconcile Anglo-American relations. While Gladstone in 1886 precipitated a period of intense internal struggles in British politics, he had helped create a new era of Anglo-American reconciliation.

Notes

1. A. Ramm (ed.), *The Political Correspondence of Mr. Gladstone and Lord Granville 1876–1886*, 2 vols (Oxford, 1962), i, p. xxx. Other recent studies of this period include Angus Hawkins, 'The Crisis of Liberalism, 1880–6,' *British Party Politics, 1852–1886* (London, 1998), pp. 217–65; T. A. Jenkins, *The Liberal Ascendancy, 1830–1886* (London, 1994), pp. 169–228; and J. P. Parry, *The Rise and Fall of Liberal Government in Victorian Britain* (New Haven, CT, 1993), pp. 274–303.
2. D. Hamer, *Liberal Politics in the Age of Gladstone and Rosebery. A Study in Leadership and Policy* (Oxford, 1972), p. 87.
3. D. M. Pletcher, *The Awkward Years. American Foreign Relations under Garfield and Arthur* (Columbia, 1962); A. Nevins, *Grover Cleveland. A Study in Courage* (New York, 1932); M. Plesur, *America's Outward Thrust: Approaches to Foreign Affairs, 1865–1890* (DeKalb, IL, 1971); and C. Tansill, *The Foreign Policy of Thomas F. Bayard, 1884–1897* (New York, 1940).
4. J. A. Garraty, *The New Commonwealth, 1877–1890* (New York, 1968), p. 279.
5. The six principles were '(1) just legislation and economy at home, (2) to preserve to the nations of the world the blessings of peace, (3) to strive to cultivate and maintain … the Concert of Europe, (4) avoid needless and entangling engagements, (5) acknowledge the equal rights of all nations and (6) the foreign policy of England should always be inspired by the love of freedom.' E. Feuchtwanger, *Gladstone* (London, 1975), p. 191.

6. Hansard, 3rd series, ccliii, 16 June 1880, 106.
7. International bimetallism and international copyright matters prior to 1886 are discussed in Chapter 4, pp. 139–43.
8. The best introductions to Anglo-American politics during the period 1880–86 are C. Campbell, *The Transformation of American Foreign Relations 1865–1900* (New York, 1976), pp. 84–139, and *From Revolution to Rapprochement the United States and Britain, 1783–1900* (New York, 1974), pp. 137–63.
9. Memorandum by North, 10 June 1880, FO 5/1826; cited in Campbell, *From Revolution to Rapprochement*, p. 146.
10. On Lowell at the ministry from 1880–85, see M. Duberman, *James Russell Lowell* (Boston, 1966), pp. 302–38 and C. Norton (ed.), *Letters of James Russell Lowell*, 2 vols (London, 1894), ii, pp. 281–356.
11. The fast friendship of Granville and Lowell is captured in their correspondence with each other, scattered throughout their papers: Lowell Papers and Granville Papers (Public Records Office).
12. Hoppin Diaries, MS Am 986, vol. vii (1881), pp. 15–19.
13. Granville to Lord Thornton, March 1881, cited in P. Knaplund and C. Clewes (eds), 'Private Letters from the British Embassy in Washington to the Foreign Secretary, Lord Granville, 1880-1885,' *Annual Report of the American Historical Association*, vol. i (London, 1941), p. 121.
14. For further references on Lowell's friendly working relations with Liberals, see p. 79.
15. Campbell, *The Transformation of American Foreign Relations*, pp. 91–2.
16. Library of Congress (Blaine Papers): Carnegie to Blaine, 14 Jan. 1883, Reel 10 (340).
17. D. Bahlman (ed.), *The Diary of Sir Edward Hamilton 1880–1885*, 2 vols (Oxford, 1972), i, p. 204.
18. GP, 44173, Granville to Gladstone, 25 Dec. 1881, f. 260. For Gladstone–Granville correspondence over Blaine, see Ramm (ed.), *Correspondence of Gladstone and Granville* , i, pp. 322–4.
19. Granville Papers, Gladstone to Granville, 23 Dec. 1881, 30/29/124.
20. For the history and best recent treatment of the British free trade movement, see Anthony Howe, *Free Trade and Liberal England 1846–1946* (Oxford, 1997), especially, pp. 111–229.
21. Pletcher, 'The Mongrel Tariff,' *The Awkward Years*, pp. 139–57. Henry Hyndman lamented that 'Protection has won all along the line' in the United States in 1881. 'Lights and Shades of American Politics,' *FR*, vol. xxix (Nov. 1881), p. 341.
22. 7 Oct. 1881, in H. Lucy (ed.), *Speeches of Gladstone* (London, 1885), p. 42.
23. Ibid., pp. 42–3.
24. Speech on 'Free Trade and Protection,' at Leeds, 8 Oct. 1881, in Lucy (ed.), *Speeches of Gladstone*, p. 66.
25. Playfair, 'The Industries of the United States in Relation to the Tariff,' *MM*, vol. xlv (Feb. 1882), p. 329.
26. Ibid., p. 336.
27. Ibid.
28. Ibid.
29. J. Welsh, 'English Views of Free Trade,' *NAR*, vol. cxxxv (Nov. 1882), p. 412.

30. Speech on 'Free Trade and Protection' at the Cobden Club dinner, 13 June 1885, in H. Lucy (ed.), *Speeches of the Right Hon. Joseph Chamberlain, M.P. with a sketch of his life* (London, 1885), p. 144. On another occasion, Chamberlain argued that protection would only benefit large landowners, reduce total production, lower wages, and raise prices. Speech on 'Work for the New Parliament' at Birmingham, 5 Jan. 1885, ibid., p. 105.

31. D. A. Farnie, *The English Cotton Industry and the World Market 1815–1896* (Oxford, 1979), pp. 171–205.

32. For other Liberal leaders' views on American protectionism, see: Gladstone, 'Free Trade, Railways, and the Growth of Commerce,' *NC*, vol. vii (Feb. 1880), pp. 367–88; Morley, 'Cobden's First Pamphlets,' *FR*, vol. xxix (May 1881), pp. 641–9; and *PMG*: 4 Nov. 1880 ('Presidential Election and the Tariff'); 16 Dec. 1880 ('American Corn and English Rents'); 4 Feb. 1882 ('Who Benefits by American Protection?'), and 30 Dec. 1882 ('Free Trade in the United States'). American protectionism is treated more fully in Chapter 4, pp. 133–9. For an example of how common it had become to associate British economic depression with American protectionism in 1885, see PP, *Reports, minutes and evidence of the Royal Commission into the Depression of Trade and Industry* (1886), XXI, C. 4621 and C. 4715; (1886), XXII, C. 4715-I; (1886), XXIII, C. 4797 and C. 4893.

33. Martin Crawford argues convincingly upon the fervor of the Anglo-American rapprochement of 1860, interrupted by the outbreak of the Civil War. 'British Travellers and the Anglo-Saxon Relationship in the 1850s,' *JAS*, vol. xii (1978), pp. 203–19.

34. Speech on 'Fair Trade' at Leeds, 7 Oct. 1881, Lucy (ed.), *Speeches of Gladstone*, p. 42.

35. 'President Garfield,' *PMG*, 20 Sept. 1881.

36. 26 Sept. 1881.

37. LP, bMS Am 765, 26 Sept. 1881 (723).

38. R. Horsman, 'Origins of Racial Anglo-Saxonism in Great Britain Before 1850,' *JHI*, vol. xxxvii (July–Sept. 1976), pp. 387–410.

39. BP, MS Bryce 11, Bryce to Gladstone, 31 Oct. 1881, ff. 56–7.

40. BP, MS Bryce 7, E. Freeman to Bryce, 1 Apr. 1882, f. 36.

41. Bahlman (ed.), *Diary of Hamilton*, i, p. 197.

42. Massachusetts Historical Society, Boston (Winthrop Papers): Gladstone to R. C. Winthrop, 9 Dec. 1881 (Reel 33: Jan. 1881–Dec. 1888). Also see Morley's eloquent words on the closeness of Anglo-American relations in 1881: *FR*, vol. xxx (July 1881), p. 136.

43. Bahlman (ed.), *Diary of Hamilton*, i, p. 208.

44. Good introductions to Irish-American, American, and British activities in the 1880s are D. Pletcher, 'The Irish-American Agitators,' *The Awkward Years* (London, 1962), pp. 234–54 and J. L. Hammond, *Gladstone and the Irish Nation* (London, 1964), pp. 163–531.

45. F. Lyons, *Ireland Since the Famine* (London, 1971), p. 168.

46. P. Bagwell and G. Mingay, *Britain and America 1850–1939; A Study of Economic Change* (London, 1970), pp. 114–15. Also see A. Schrier, *Ireland and the American Migration, 1850–1890* (Minneapolis, 1958), *passim*.

47. F. Sheehy-Skeffington, *Michael Davitt. Revolutionary, Agitator and Labour Leader* (London, 1908), p. 78.

48. M. Davitt, *The Fall of Feudalism in Ireland, or the story of the land league revolution* (London, 1904), p. 116.
49. F. S. L. Lyons, *Charles Stewart Parnell* (London, 1977), p. 108.
50. Cited in ibid., p. 111.
51. Davitt, *Fall of Feudalism*, p. 198 and pp. 202–3. Many Irish parliamentary leaders had American families: Parnell, Davitt, and Justin McCarthy were among the most important. Thus, for instance, Parnell had a mother, three sisters, and a brother in America in the 1880s. Lyons quotes a reporter who reported that Parnell referred to his American blood 'with more animation than anything else.' Lyons, *Parnell*, p. 113.
52. Davitt, *Fall of Feudalism*, p. 320.
53. For Ford's part in fomenting Irish-American opposition to British politics, see J. P. Rodechko, *Patrick Ford and his Search for America. A Case Study of Irish-American Journalism 1870–1923* (New York, 1976).
54. C. C. O'Brien, *Parnell & his Party 1880–90*, 2nd edn (Oxford, 1964), pp. 134–5.
55. Davitt, *Fall of Feudalism*, p. 210.
56. Hansard, 3rd series, cclviii, 1 Mar. 1881, 1951. Harcourt also warned the Commons to take the newly formed American Land League seriously. Ibid., 24 Feb. 1881, pp. 1694–7.
57. BP, 11, Bryce to Gladstone, 31 Oct. 1881, ff. 56–7.
58. GP, 44468, Lowell to Gladstone, 24 Jan. 1881, ff. 47–8. Also, see ibid., 44467, 17 Nov. 1880, ff. 3–5.
59. Lyons, *Ireland*, p. 178.
60. Ibid., p. 174.
61. Kenneth Short's *The Dynamite War: Irish-American Bombers in Victorian Britain* (London, 1979) does a very good task of tracing the unfoldings of the revolutionary plots of the Irish-Americans as well as the responses of British officials to those threats to Victorian internal security and peace.
62. Ibid., pp. 259–60.
63. GP, 44196, Harcourt to Gladstone, 13 June 1881, f. 171. See Gardiner, *Life of Harcourt*, i, pp. 428–30.
64. Cabinet Papers, 41/15/24, 13 June 1881.
65. *United Irishman*, 30 Apr. 1881, printed in FO 5/1863 (America 'Fenian Brotherhood. Incitements to Outrages in the Fenian Press in the U.S. 1881–1883').
66. *United Irishmen*, 14 Oct. 1882, printed in ibid.
67. *United Irishmen*, ibid, 5 Jan. 1884, printed in FO 97/475 ('Press Incitements to Outrages. 1885'). Also see Cabinet Papers, 37/10/35, 4 May 1883 ('Extracts from the United Irishman') and *PP, Corrrespondence respecting the Publication in the United States of Incitements to Outrages in England in 1882*, United States, No. 3 (1882), C. 3194.
68. Hansard, 3rd series, cclxvi, 9 Feb. 1882, 290.
69. Harcourt to Vincent, 23 Jan. 1881, cited in S. Jeyes and F. How, *Life of Sir Howard Vincent* (London, 1885), p. 106.
70. HP, Box 8, Gladstone to Harcourt, 21 July 1882, f. 157. *The Molly Maguires* (Philadelphia, 1877) and *The American Irish* (London, 1882).
71. 'The Story of an Irish Secret Society,' 2 Dec. 1882 (supplement).
72. HP, Box 42, Harcourt to Spencer, 31 Mar. 1883, f. 45.

73. GP, 44198, Harcourt to Gladstone, 16 May 1883, f. 71. Also see, Harcourt's letter to Gladstone, 27 Nov. 1882: 'The only practical suggestion I can make is an immense increase of the detective Police force of Dublin so that every-one of the suspected persons should be followed every where & their occu-pations and houses searched day & night & that they should never be allowed to be out of sight & guard for a moment ... No man could be able to long stand this perpetual supervision. His nerves would break down under it ... In America as I think in England in such a state of things the whole town would constitute itself a *Vigilance Society* to watch & if necessary lynch these villains.' Ibid., 44197, ff. 149–50.

74. Ibid., 44198, Gladstone to Harcourt, 18 May 1883, f. 76.

75. Short, *The Dynamite War*, pp. 71–101.

76. HP, Box 103 ('Home Office. Irish Secret Service-Correspondence with E. G. Jenkinson, 1882–3'); Box 104 ('Home Office. Irish Secret Service-Correspondence with E. G. Jenkinson, 1884–5'); and Box 105 ('Home Office. Irish Secret Service-Correspondence with Sir R. Anderson (1882–4) and N. Gosselin (1883–4)').

77. FO 5/1820 ('America. Fenian Brotherhood. 24 Aug. to 31 Dec. 1882'); FO 5/1848 ('America. Consuls General at New York. Archibald, Booker, Edwards (Political Consular) Jan. to Dec. 1883'); and many other such FO 5 reports. HP, Box 96, 'John Rose's reports on Secret Consular Agencies in the United States', 13 Sept. 1882, ff. 131–41.

78. Hamer, *Liberal Politics in the Age of Gladstone*, pp. 79–98.

79. HP, Box 97, Harcourt memorandum, 3 Mar. 1883, f. 23. Also see, Cabinet Papers: 37/10/25, 1 Mar. 1883 ('Memorandum on the Police Authority in the new Municipality of London') and 41/17/2, 17 Mar. 1883.

80. HP, Box 42, Harcourt to Spencer, 14 June 1883, f. 109.

81. Morley, 'England and Ireland,' *FR*, vol. xxix (Apr. 1881), pp. 407–25; 'Some Irish Realities: An Historical Chapter,' *FR*, vol. xxxi (Mar. 1882), pp. 380–99; and 'Irish Revolution and English Liberalism,' *NC*, vol. xii (Nov. 1882), pp. 647–9.

82. PP, *Correspondence respecting the imprisonment in Ireland under the Protection of Person and Property (Ireland) Act 1881 of Naturalized Citizens of the United States*, United States, No. 2 (1882), C. 3193.

83. Hoppin's Diaries, MS Am 986, vol. ix (1882), Lowell to Hoppin, 29 and 30 Aug. 1882, pp. 53–5 and FO 5/1820 (1882), pp. 42–3 and 150–1.

84. PP, *Correspondence with the United States respecting the sentence passed upon the Convict O'Donnell*, United States, No. 2, (1884), LXXXVII, C. 3835; HP, Box 97, Lowell to Granville, 12 Dec. 1883, ff. 192–3; and Pletcher, *The Awkward Years*, pp. 244–6.

85. HP, Box 97, Selborne to Harcourt, 13 Dec. 1883, f. 194.

86. Ibid., Box 42, Harcourt to Selborne, 23 Dec. 1883, f. 145.

87. Short, *The Dynamite War*, p. 168.

88. Also see, *PP, Report of the Royal Commission on Extradition*, (1878), XXIV, C. 2039.

89. FO 5/1864 ('America, Extradition of Criminals, Jan. to Dec. 1882') and FO 5/1896 ('America, Extradition of Criminals, 1884').

90. Pletcher, *The Awkward Years*, p. 252.

91. The tenth article of the Webster-Ashburton Treaty was altered to incorporate a large list of extraditable crimes. See 'Extradition Convention between the United States of America and her Britannic Majesty,' concluded at Washington, 12 July 1890 (subsequently ratified) in the Library of Congress, Washington (Henry White Papers): Box 13 (1889).

92. HP, Box 97, Lowell to Harcourt, 7 Aug. 1883, ff. 139–9. Also, see ibid., Coleridge, Selborne, Lowell, and Harcourt letters, July–Aug. 1883, ff. 123–45; Cabinet Papers, 41/17/18, 9 Aug. 1883; and C. Russell, *Diary of a Visit to the United States of America in the Year 1883* (London, 1910).

93. M. Willoughby, *With Mr. Chamberlain in the United States and Canada, 1887–88* (London, 1914), pp. 29–31. Threats of assassination of British politicians by the American-Irish did not entirely end in the 1880s. Thus, for instance, there was a major plot to assassinate Chamberlain in 1897 (Ch.P, JC 3/12/1–20).

94. Cabinet Papers, 37/10/34, 5 May 1883; 37/10/36, 7 May 1883; 41/17/8, 7 May 1883; 41/17/2, 17 Mar. 1883; and 41/17/6, 23 Apr. 1883.

95. HP, Box 98, Harcourt to Cabinet, Feb. 1884, f. 47. Interestingly, this memorandum was thought to be highly sensitive by Loulou Harcourt, who instructed Gardiner, Harcourt's biographer, to read but not to publish it.

96. Ibid., Box 43, Spencer to Harcourt, 29 Feb. 1884, f. 51.

97. Ibid., Box 98, 'Confidential draft of despatch from Granville to Sackville-West,' 13 March 1884, ff. 114–18.

98. Ibid., Box 99, Frelinghuysen to Lowell, 24 Nov. 1884, f. 28.

99. Short, *The Dynamite War*, p. 216.

100. Blaine Papers, Gladstone to Blaine, 6 Oct. 1884 (Container 34), Reel 17/21.

101. MM, vol. 1 (Aug. 1884), p. 320. Morley was the author of the regular 'Review of the Month' at this time.

102. God.P, Bryce to Godkin, 12 Nov. 1884 (85).

103. HP, Box 104, E. Watkin to Harcourt (enclosure: J. Moore to Watkin), 3 Jan. 1885, f. 104.

104. Kelley notes that 'In the decade when Gladstone was fighting for the Irish in the British Parliament, therefore, Cleveland and the Democrats played the same role in the United States.' R. Kelley, *The Transatlantic Persuasion: the Liberal-Democratic Mind in the Age of Gladstone* (New York, 1969), p. 305.

105. HP, Box 104, 3 Jan. 1885, f. 110.

106. Ibid., ff. 108 and 110–11.

107. RP, 10081, T. Bayard to Rosebery, 7 Mar. 1884, ff. 7–8. Bayard actually used private channels to convey his pro-British and pro-Rosebery sympathies from time to time. J. Moore wrote Rosebery on 13 Feb. 1886: 'I have come to the conclusion that Mr. Bayard wished you to know some "snatches" & "patches" of his sentiment but perhaps owing to his position he would not like to communicate personally. Well then. Mr. Bayard began a sort of oration by showing how happy it must be for two such great countries to have men preside over the destinies of foreign affairs who know each other personally. And, as he said on his part, has, as the Scotch would say "a warm corner" for you.' Ibid., 10085, f. 65.

108. FO 97/475, Harcourt to J. Pauncefote, 9 Mar. 1885.

109. Ibid., Gladstone to Granville, 20 Feb. 1885.

110. The major bill, introduced by Senator Edmunds, finally perished in Committee.
111. Cited in Campbell, *The Transformation of American Foreign Relations*, p. 66.
112. HP, Box 99, 'Draft of proposed answer to Mr. Frelinghuysen's despatch,' 12 Feb. 1885, ff. 7–10.
113. Some of George's most important articles included: 'England and Ireland: An American View,' *FR*, vol. xxxi (June 1882), pp. 780–94; 'The Common Sense of Taxation,' *NAR*, vol. cxxxiii (July 1881), pp. 65–74; 'Money in Elections,' *NAR*, vol. cxxxvi (Mar. 1883), pp. 201–11; 'Overproduction', *NAR*, vol. cxxxvii (Dec. 1883), pp. 584–93; 'England and Ireland,' *NAR*, vol. cxlii (Feb. 1886), pp. 185–93; and 'More About American Landlordism', *NAR*, vol. cxlii (Apr. 1886), pp. 387–401.
114. E. P. Lawrence, *Henry George in the British Isles* (East Lansing, MI, 1957), p. 3. I am indebted to Mr Lawrence's discussion of George's British activities.
115. During his trips to the British Isles – 1881–82, 1883–84, 1884–85, 1888, 1889, and 1891 – George associated almost predominantly with Irish and Scottish nationalists, such as Parnell and Davitt, or radicals, such as Hyndman and Alfred Wallace. See E. P. Lawrence's, 'Henry George's British Mission,' *American Quarterly*, vol. iii (1951), pp. 232–43.
116. George, *Progress and Poverty*, 5th edn (New York, 1883), p. 295.
117. George, *The Irish Land Question* (New York, 1881), p. 30.
118. An interesting analysis of the content of George's ideas is to be found in J. B. Ward's 'Land Reform in England, 1880–1914' (Reading University PhD thesis, 1976).
119. Lawrence, *George in the British Isles*, p. 7.
120. Gladstone to H. George, 11 Nov. 1879, cited in H. George Jr, *The Life of Henry George* (New York, 1900), p. 323.
121. *The Times*, 28 Feb. 1891.
122. Duke of Argyll, 'The Prophet of San Francisco,' *NC*, vol. xv (Apr. 1884), pp. 557–8.
123. *Industrial Remuneration Conference. The Report of the Proceedings and Papers ...* (London, 1885), p. 358.
124. New York Public Library, New York (George Papers): H. George Jr to H. George, 25 July 1891 (1891 folder) and George to P. Ford, 22 Apr. 1882, cited in George Jr, *Henry George* , p. 371.
125. George Papers, George to T. F. Walker, 27 Mar. 1883 (1883 folder).
126. Ibid.
127. Ch.P, Morley to Chamberlain, 24 Dec. 1882, JC 5/54/466. Hamer, *Morley*, p. 139.
128. Morley, 'England and Ireland,' p. 422.
129. *PMG*, 10 Nov. and 2 Dec. 1882 ('The New Gospel of American Socialism').
130. Ch.P, Morley to Chamberlain, 24 Dec. 1882, JC 5/54/466.
131. Ibid., Chamberlain to Morley, 26 Dec. 1882, JC 5/54/568.
132. *PMG*, 24 Jan. 1883.
133. Ibid., 29 Jan. 1883.
134. 'Labourers' and Artisans' Dwellings,' vol. xxxiv (Dec. 1883), p. 762.
135. *PMG*, 24 Jan. 1883.

136. See in particular Lawrence, 'His Influence on Chamberlain,' *George in the British Isles*, pp. 89–108.
137. Chamberlain, 'A Radical View of the Irish Crisis,' *FR*, vol. xxxix (Feb. 1886), p. 284.
138. Lawrence, *George in the British Isles*, p. 93.
139. *The Radical Programme by Chamberlain, Morley and Others* (London, 1885), ed. D. A. Hamer (London, 1971), p. xx.
140. Ibid., p. 55.
141. *PMG.*, 13 Apr. 1885; cited in Lawrence, *George in the British Isles*, p. 100.
142. For instance, see Samuel Smith, *My Life-Work* (London, 1902), pp. 148–51 and 501–22.
143. Lawrence, *George in the British Isles*, pp. 111–28. There is evidence that some of George's ideas and schemes were considered during the debate over the Newcastle Programme in 1891.
144. Morley to Chamberlain, 10 Oct. 1877, cited in Hamer, *Morley*, p. 162.
145. Bryce (ed.), *Handbook of Home Rule* (London, 1887), p. 39.
146. H. Tulloch, 'The Anglo-American Background to James Bryce's *American Commonwealth*,' (Cambridge University PhD thesis, 1974), p. 221.
147. Ibid., p. 175.
148. The best treatment of the impact of federalism upon British politics, its various precedents and foreign analogies, is John Kendle's *Ireland the the Federal Solution. The Debate over the United Kingdom Constitution, 1870–1921* (Kingston and Montreal, 1989). Liberals studied constitutional precedents of other countries in addition to the United States thus, Canada, Sweden, Denmark, Switzerland, Norway, and Austria-Hungary to name several.
149. Lord Blandford, 'Home Rule,' *NC*, vol. xi (June 1882), pp. 39–40.
150. R. J. Hind, *Henry Labouchere and the Empire 1880–1905* (London, 1972), p. 98.
151. *Truth*, 27 Oct. 1881, p. 540, cited in Hind, *Labouchere*, p. 60. Also see *Truth*, 6 Nov. 1884, p. 711, in ibid., p. 64.
152. G. Campbell, *White and Black, the Outcome of a Visit to the United States* (London, 1879), pp. 71–2. Parts of this book were first published in *FR*, vol. xxv (Mar.–Apr. 1879), pp. 449–68 and 588–607.
153. Ibid., pp. 73–7.
154. McCarthy devotes an exceptionally large amount of his autobiography to American references. *Reminiscences*, 2 vols (London, 1899), i, pp. 190–308, and ii, pp. 1–23 and 61–88.
155. McCarthy, 'Home Rule,' *NC*, vol. xi (June 1882), p. 863.
156. Ibid., pp. 866–8.
157. H. Tulloch, 'Changing British Attitudes towards the United States in the 1880's,' *Historical Journal*, vol. xx (1977) pp. 825–40 and C. Harvie, 'Ideology and home rule: James Bryce, A. V. Dicey and Ireland, 1880–1887,' *EHR*, vol. xcii (Apr. 1976), pp. 298–314.
158. There are innumerable examples of the four intellectuals' serious interests in the United States. See A. Haultain (ed.), *A Selection from Goldwin Smith's Correspondence. Comprising letters chiefly to and from his English friends written between the years 1846 and 1910* (New York, 1913); E. A. Freeman, *Some Impressions of the United States* (London, 1883), pp. 110–14 and 268–85; A. V. Dicey, *Introduction to the Study of the Law of the Constitution*, 9th edn

(London, 1914), pp. 175–80; and M. Arnold, *Civilization in the United States* (London, 1888).

159. Arnold, 'A Word More About America,' *NC*, vol. xvii (Feb. 1885), p. 231. Also see, Arnold, 'A Word About America,' *NC*, vol. xi (May 1882), pp. 680–96. B. E. Lippincott put Arnold's admiration for American democracy this way: 'He found American democracy to work naturally, in contrast to the the English, which worked under tension and strain; American democracy, unlike the English, enjoyed social equality.' *Victorian Critics of Democracy* (New York, 1964), p. 108.

160. 'As Others See Us,' vol. xxxi (Feb. 1882), p. 161.

161. E. L. Godkin, 'An American View of Ireland,' vol. xii (Aug. 1882), pp. 175–92.

162. See Chapter 4, pp. 124–33.

163. GP, 44480, Lorne to Gladstone, 1 May 1883, ff. 274–5.

164. Ibid., 44482, Lorne to Gladstone, 20 July 1883, ff. 139–51 (enclosures).

165. See Chapter 4.

166. HP, Box 313, 'Cabinet memorandum,' 24 Nov. 1880, f. 22.

167. Ibid., 'Confidential: Memorandum on the various proposals of Sir Erskine May,' 21 Dec. 1881, f. 142.

168. *Hansard*, 3rd series, cclxvii, 20 Mar. 1882, 1379–80 and GP, 44625, 'Notes on cloture,' ff. 106–19. By 1890, obstructionism had become so common in both the House of Representatives and Commons, that there were unanimous Anglo–American calls to curtail 'filibustering' tactics. See J. Bryce, 'A Word as to the Speakership,' *NAR*, vol. cli (Oct. 1890), pp. 385–98; J. Chamberlain, 'Shall We Americanise Our Institutions?' *NC*, vol. xxviii (Dec. 1890), pp. 861–75; and H. C. Lodge, 'Parliamentary Obstruction in the United States,' *NC*, vol. xxix (Mar. 1891), pp. 423–8.

169. 'Do We Need a Second Chamber?' *CR*, vol. xlvi (Nov. 1884), p. 730.

170. Hansard, 3rd series, cclxxxix, 20 June 1884, 941.

171. Salisbury's speech at Glasgow, cited in *The Times*, 2 Oct. 1884. See Chamberlain's startled reaction to Salisbury's remarks (DP, 43886, Chamberlain to Dilke, 3 Oct. 1884, f. 218). Salisbury was certainly no friend in general to the United States. At Edinburgh, on 23 Nov. 1882, he declared: 'I confess I do not often envy the United States, but there is one feature in their institutions which appears to me the subject of the greatest envy – their magnificent institution of a Supreme Court.' A Carnegie, *Triumphant Democracy or Fifty Years March of the Republic* (London, 1886), p. 369.

172. The American institution second only to the Senate in British parliamentary opinion was the Supreme Court. See note 171 and GP, 44255, Morley to Gladstone, 5 Oct. 1887, f. 222.

173. A leading work upon the American federal aspects of Irish Home Rule was by H. Maine, *Popular Government* (London, 1885). There were many articles by such men as Freeman, Maine, E. L. Godkin, Morley, Goldwin Smith, Justin McCarthy, Matthew Arnold, Henry George and many others, upon federalism in the Liberal periodicals in 1885–86. Also see, Alan Diamond (ed.), *The Victorian Achievement of Sir Henry Maine: A Centennial Reappraisal* (Cambridge, 1991) and John Burrow, 'Some British Views of the United States Constitution' in R. C. Simmons (ed.) *The United States Constitution: The First 200 Years* (Manchester, 1989).

174. Kendle noted in *Ireland and the Federal Solution*, 'by the end of 1885 he [Chamberlain] was increasingly attracted by a federal solution modelled on the constitution of the United States,' p. 24.
175. Ibid., p. 28.
176. For Chamberlain and the National Council Plan, see T. W. Heyck, *The Dimensions of British Radicalism. The Case of Ireland 1874–95* (Urbana, IL, 1974), pp. 97–105.
177. Chamberlain to Labouchere, 26 Dec. 1885, cited in A. Thorold, *The Life of Labouchere* (London, 1913), p. 272.
178. DP, 43887, Chamberlain to Dilke, 26 Dec. 1886, ff. 224–5, cited in D. Judd, *Radical Joe: A Life of Joseph Chamberlain* (London, 1977), p. 134.
179. Chamberlain to Labouchere, cited in Thorold, *Labouchere*, pp. 272–3.
180. Garvin, *Life of Chamberlain*, ii, p. 306. Another explanation is put forward by T. J. Dunne. He argues that Chamberlain never seriously considered a plan based on American federalism because he did not want to give American-type states rights to Ireland and because he wished to consider the desires of the Irish Majority. 'Ireland, England & Empire 1868–86; the ideologies of British political leadership' (Cambridge Univ. PhD thesis, 1975), pp. 230–2.
181. HP, Box 59, 'Memorandum of conversation with Mr. Chamberlain at Mr. Gladstone's request,' 20 Mar. 1886, ff. 124–5.
182. See Chamberlain's reminiscences in 1888 upon the failure of the federal scheme for Ireland, Chapter 4, p. 127.
183. GP, 44255, Morley to Gladstone, 28 Feb. 1886, f. 59.
184. Ibid., 44492, Carnegie to Gladstone, 25 Jan. 1886, f. 71. Also see, Carnegie, 'Democracy in England,' *NAR*, vol. cxlii (Jan. 1886), pp. 74–80 and GP, 44492, Lorne to Gladstone, 20 Sept. 1885, ff. 102–8 ('Irish Notes (from an American point of view)').
185. GP, 44497, 'Memorandum on some Points with Reference to the Government of Ireland Bill,' Apr. ?, 1886, ff. 327–8.
186. Ibid., ff. 331–2.
187. Speech in the House of Commons, 13 Apr. 1886, in A. Hutton and H. Cohen (eds), *Speeches and Public Addresses of the Right Hon. W.E. Gladstone, M.P. (1886–88)*, vols ix–x (London, 1892–94), ix, p. 63. Also see Chamberlain's references to American history, which urged Britons to preserve the Union. Chamberlain's speech at Birmingham, 17 Dec. 1885, cited in Garvin, *Life of Chamberlain*, ii, p. 140.
188. Kendle, *Ireland and the Federal Solution*, pp. 36–56, for British consideration of American and foreign precedents in 1885–86, and for Gladstone's examination of constitutional precedents and history. During the debate in the House of Commons, only Chamberlain really spoke clearly on a measure of federalism to be adopted in a final bill.
189. O'Brien, *Parnell, 1880–1890*, p. 187.
190. Ibid., p. 195.
191. For American views on Gladstone, see Moncure Conway, 'Gladstone,' *NAR*, vol. cxxxvi (Mar. 1883), pp. 223–36. He indicates that Americans had a tendency for 'Gladstone-worship' (p. 228). It was the common assumption in political circles in London that all Americans were friendly to Gladstone and Home Rule. Thus believed Chauncey Depew, *My Memories of Eighty Years* (New York, 1922), p. 263.

192. O'Brien, *Parnell, 1880–1890*, p. 266. 'Subscriptions to the Parliamentary Funds, 1885–1889':

1 January	1886	£3 340	19 November	1886	£97 967
17 March	1886	£10 175	31 December	1886	£99 302
12 May	1886	£17 757	1887		£1 10 064
23 June	1886	£52 930	1888		£1 19 441
26 July	1886	£66 420	1889		£1 25 654*
4 August	1886	£73 826			
31 August	1886	£90 581			

*£102 000 of this amount came from the United States; £11 500 from Australasia; and £2 000 from Canada.)

193. GP, 44496, New York Assembly to Gladstone, 12 Apr. 1886, ff. 239–40; Brooklyn meeting to Gladstone, 30 Apr. 1886, ff. 70–4; University of Michigan to Gladstone, 5 June 1886, ff. 353–6; and Irish National League of Jacksonville to Gladstone, 6 May 1886, ff. 366–7; and 44498, Colored Men's Republican Club to Gladstone, 25 June 1886, ff. 58–9; and Polish National Alliance to Gladstone, 7 July 1886, ff. 152–8.

194. The three questions were: '1. Do you approve of Mr. Gladstone's Home Rule Bill? 2. Do you approve of Mr. Chamberlain's course? 3. Is the opinion of the majority of the voters you represent in Congress for or against the Bill?' Ibid., 44498, Kitson to Gladstone, 28 June 1886, ff. 70–1. One hundred and twenty-three Congressmen responded. Only 'one or two' did not support Gladstone.

195. Ibid., 44497, 30 Apr. 1886, f. 74.

4
Gladstonian Liberalism, Home Rule, and American Politics and Society, 1886–1892

A memorable period in our history now followed, extending over seven years. The theater was small in its proportions, but keen audiences watched it all over the English-speaking world. Scenes were constantly shifted; the main course of action was diversified by exciting underplots. The sanctity of law was violently strained, so was the fundamental machinery of government.[1]

Introduction

Thus wrote John Morley about the turbulent period in British politics from June 1886 to April 1892. The Liberal party lay split asunder; its members earnestly searched for Irish solutions, new programs, or any plan that would draw back the Liberal Unionists into the party fold. The answers were neither easy nor apparent. Meanwhile, the Conservative government under Salisbury clearly directed the country's progress. It tackled a whole range of domestic, foreign, and imperial problems with considerable success. The Chief Secretary of Ireland, A. J. Balfour, held the Irish in check with a dual policy of strong coercion and remedial land purchase legislation. Conservatives also were responsible for a stream of domestic measures: the Local Government Act, the Technical Instruction Act, the Housing of the Working Classes Act, and a Factory Act, among others. Moreover, Salisbury demonstrated an expertise in foreign affairs. Britain consolidated a number of alliances with European nations and established closer imperial connections in Africa, the Far East, and elsewhere. The period of Salisbury's second ministry was particularly active in the area of foreign affairs. Relations with the United States were no exception.[2] American–Canadian–British fishery disputes, the Sackville incident, the Bering Sea seal controversy, and questions of Canadian autonomy all exasperated Anglo-American relations. For the most part, Salisbury handled these all with consummate skill. When, following the election of 1892, the Liberals turned to form the last Gladstonian ministry, there were no outstanding Anglo-American difficulties of any magnitude.

Liberal leaders pursued a wide variety of intellectual interests in the United States from 1886 to 1892. They seldom concerned themselves with opposition to Salisbury's American policies; instead they studied a variety of American themes and developments. In contradistinction to their last period of opposition, the Liberals' American analyses were detailed, superior, and often historic events in themselves. James Bryce's *American Commonwealth* and Gladstone's periodical articles captured the audiences on both sides of the Atlantic and symbolized Liberal attention directed 'across the sea.' These were also the years when a transatlantic liberal community was formed, when Rosebery, Morley, Gladstone, and Bryce, in particular, had extensive contacts and associations with Americans and American issues within the context of associations in both the British Isles and the United States. Andrew Carnegie too emerged as a central Anglo-American personality and force.

The range of American themes that captivated the Liberals' attention had broadened significantly since the 1870s. This trend is most clearly evident in the pages of British periodicals. Table 4.1 indicates that there were two-and-a-half times more American related articles printed in the *Nineteenth Century* between 1888 and 1898 than between 1877 and 1887. From about 1885, articles covered such various issues as American labor, women, history, blacks, and copyright.

The temper and forms of attention constituted a distinct break with the past. Previously, American articles had usually consisted of traveler's impressions or casual discussions of politics, with periodic articles on literature and history. Moreover, the authors of these articles in the 1880s and 1890s were now the leading political figures. American articles were no longer the domain of Englishmen, but also of American authorities. Gladstone, Chamberlain, Morley, Goldwin Smith, Bryce, Henry Cabot Lodge, George Smalley, Matthew Arnold, Edwin Godkin, E. J. Phelps, Playfair, and Chauncey Depew all wrote for the review. The events which drew the most attention in Britain were the presidential elections, especially those of 1888, 1892 and 1896. While the figures in Table 4.1 are not conclusive regarding the number of American articles published by the *Nineteenth Century* because many articles lacking

Table 4.1   American articles in the Nineteenth Century

Theme	1877	78	79	80	81	82	83	84	85	86	87	88	89	90	91	92	93	94	95	96	97	98	Totals
Politics	1	1				2			2	3		1	1	2	2	2	2	3		4	2	3	31
Travel views		5	1			2	1		1	1		2			1	3	2		1				20
Irish-American				1	1		1	1			1				1	1		1	1				9
Agriculture			1		1		1		1			1	1			1						1	8
Finance – Currency									1							1	1	2		1	1		7
Trade protection											1				2		1	1	1				6
Others					1	1		1	2	1	10		3	3	3	3	4	3	3	7	2	4	51
	1	6	2	1	3	5	3	2	7	5	12	4	5	5	9	11	10	10	6	12	5	8	132

'America' or 'The United States' in their title could qualify as American articles, they clearly represent a pattern evident in other major Liberal periodicals during this same period.[3]

It is the purpose of this chapter to look at Liberal treatment of the most important American topics between 1886 and 1892. These included federalism and the Constitution, commercial trade policies such as protectionism, and financial and economic matters such as bimetallism. At the same time, Liberal support for the Anglo-American copyright movement is symbolic of their active concern for improved Anglo-American understanding. Finally, while the decade cannot be understood without reference to the publication in 1888 of James Bryce's seminal work *The American Commonwealth*, so too Gladstone's American articles stamped him as an equally important spokesperson and English commentator upon the United States and American affairs. The *North American Review* became a notable voice for the espousal of opinion on a wide variety of transatlantic liberal issues and activities, articles frequently authored by a core group of British and American liberals.

American federalism reconsidered

The increased Liberal interest in American federalism and the Constitution was easily predictable. It had been keen during the debate on Gladstone's first Home Rule Bill from December 1885 through April 1886, and since the Irish Home Rule issue continued to dominate the years between Gladstone's third and fourth ministries, histories and institutions remained central Liberal interests. Their studies were not then, nor are they now, entirely evident. Most of the major Gladstonian Liberals wished to keep points of argument hidden from the public eye,[4] which meant that their observations dealing with American aspects of Irish Home Rule often were either buried in private communications or merely alluded to in public addresses. Nonetheless, the American union emerged for them as a realistic possible 'practical point of departure.'[5] Secondly, a spate of lengthy disputations by Home Rule opponents against the inexpediency of adopting American federal practices regarding Ireland spurred a strong Gladstonian Liberal rebuttal. Sir Henry Maine's *Popular Government* and A. V. Dicey's *The Law and Working of the Constitution*, both published in 1885, stirred strong Liberal retorts. Gladstone, Morley, and Bryce led the counterattacks. Finally, rising debates over Scottish and Welsh nationality, the British empire, imperial unity, the Imperial Federation, and the Empire Trade

Leagues, all dwelt at times upon the American federal model. In short, between 1886 and 1892, there was a host of British movements which saw the American federal plan as the possible best means for strengthening British central control over her empire while devolving limited self-government to the various parts.[6]

Throughout 1886 and 1887, Gladstonian Home Rulers vigorously debated their opponent's declarations that American federalism was inappropriate for Ireland. In the process of such disputations, it seems that Liberals, at first themselves not strict advocates of the model of American federalism, increasingly moved to consider the real possibilities raised by the case of the United States. Maine's and Dicey's books 'stimulated a major reappraisal of the American Constitution which in turn transformed and coloured the Englishman's conception of America.'[7] Morley, Goldwin Smith, and Godkin all took Maine to task in articles.[8] One historian has called Maine 'probably the most searching critic of democratic optimism in the Victorian era.'[9] There can be no question as to why he drew the striking criticisms of many democratic Liberals. Maine had described how democracy had failed everywhere and would continue to be 'fragile.' It had worked alone in the United States because of 'the great portion of the British institutions which were preserved in' the American Constitution and because of 'the sagacity' of American statesmen.[10] Godkin argued that since the United States was the 'one country in the world in which Popular Government' existed successfully, other countries should take heart in the ultimate prospects for democracy and federalism.[11] Morley underlined Maine's negative, critical, and blind views towards the American experience.

But on the one great question on which the Constitution of the United States might have been expected to shed light – the modification of the House of Lords – Sir Henry Maine explicitly admits (p. 186) that it is very difficult to obtain from the younger institution, the Senate, any lessons which can be of use in the reconstruction of the older.[12]

While Maine discussed federalism in a generally critical fashion, Dicey directly attacked federalism. 'A Federal Government is, of all constitutions, the most artificial.'[13] In the United States, Dicey argued, federalism had slowed legislation, produced a lack of Congressional vigor, hindered reform, weakened central authority, and precipitated the Civil War.[14] 'This is no future or imaginary peril; the mere proposal of Home Rule, under something like a Federal form, has already made it an immediate and pressing danger.'[15] Even more than Maine's work, Dicey's triggered vigorous Liberal responses. Gladstone urgently believed that Liberals for Home Rule should pursue 'a literary campaign to convince the people through books or newspapers.'[16] When they had collected their views together, in the *Handbook of Home Rule*, the case of the United States again figured. In fact, the American aspect of Dicey's original attack on home rule immensely disturbed Bryce (the editor of the essays). As a result, he went out of his way to ensure that the Liberal position on American home rule became one of the strongest arguments in his book. Thus, he turned to his friend Godkin. The latter had already published an excellent article on 'American Home Rule' in the *Nineteenth Century* in June 1886,[17] which had drawn wide praise from Liberals, including such aristocrats as Lord Spencer and Matthew Arnold.[18] This Bryce republished. At the same time, he spurred Godkin to write a second article in which he specifically attacked Dicey's American points in more detail. Godkin quoted at length from *The Federalist Papers* and the Constitutional Convention to show that Dicey's attacks on American federalism were similar to those of the founding fathers themselves. Yet, American history had demonstrated these fears to be groundless.[19] A unique feature of American federalism was that it protected minority rights, these being guaranteed by the contract between the people and the central government.[20] In the end, Godkin argued that though no federal or Home Rule scheme for Ireland would be faultless or American, the American experience was pertinent to any new practical constitution for contemporary Ireland and Great Britain.[21] British Liberals accepted Godkin's position that the mechanism of American federalism was applicable to Ireland.

One major reason why Gladstonian Liberals examined American federalism was that they realized it might produce a reconciliation with Chamberlain and the Liberal Unionists. As early as August 1886, Gladstone admitted to Harcourt that 'it might be possible for the new people to frame some initial plan of federation, and begin by dealing with the Irish part of it. This mode, if possible, would correspond with one at least of Chamberlain's many declarations.'[22] Finally, in January 1887, a group of leading Gladstonian Liberals and Liberal Unionists came together at Harcourt's Grafton Street house. Gladstone and Morley were conspicuously absent. Were there any grounds for a compromise between Liberal camps? Ireland was the central issue. Federal solutions, while not the only ones, did emerge as a possible point of common ground.[23] Harcourt reported respectively to Gladstone and Morley that

Chamberlain accepted an Irish legislature with the Canadian 'provincial power specifically defined' and American safeguards for education.[24] Chamberlain himself acknowledged that federalism for Ireland seemed indeed practical. In the midst of his official duties during the Washington Fishery Conference in January 1888, he remarked to Morley: 'The Canadian Federal Scheme which at one time I hoped would emerge from the Round Table Conference, but which disappeared in that unfortunate negotiation, would satisfy every American I have met, even the most advanced.'[25] Gladstone and Chamberlain both in their own ways favored federalism for Ireland, either on the American or Canadian plan. But regardless of intellectual agreement, personal differences and ambitions clashed. By the middle of 1887 compromise was impossible.

However, Gladstone moved increasingly towards federalism along American lines from 1887 to 1890. Such a plan became practical as Gladstone moved to accept Irish representation in Westminister. Many constitutional experts tried to persuade Gladstone of the beneficence of American expedients. The Welsh MP William Rathbone thought that a Supreme Court similar to that of the United States would be particularly desirable in Ireland, especially since it could protect the protectionist and Northern minority.[26] In October 1887, Gladstone asked Morley for information regarding the American states, and especially the 'working of the clauses as to contracts.' In response, Morley praised the Supreme Court highly and added: 'I shall probably be able to send you in advance a small book which is an excellent account of the American system for Irish application.'[27] In the same month, the former American Minister, Edwards Pierrepont, forwarded copies of the New York and United States Constitution for Gladstone's study.[28] That all these influences had in fact worked upon Gladstone became evident in March 1888. On 10 March, Gladstone met Parnell privately to discuss a practical scheme. Two days before the meeting Gladstone had made a series of notes. One point ran: 'Does the idea of the American Union afford a practical point of departure?'[29] This was not merely the subject of a possible casual question. In fact, it was likely the major reason for the meeting. Again, Gladstone had it in his mind that the opponents of Home Rule might accept federalism.

> My chief point with him [with Parnell] was that impressed in No. 5, on this ground, that the opponents never so far as I know have condemned the American system as a possible basis of a plan of Home Rule; and I have always held the hopes that it might in case of need supply at least a [start] in point of consistency. I said I was

aware of no difficulty unless it should be found to lie in the inca-
pacity to touch contracts. On the practical working of which I had
not been able to obtain sufficient information.[30]

Gladstone recorded that Parnell 'thought this idea might be made
a groundwork.'[31] Finally, one further event occurred which marked
Gladstonian sympathy for American federalism.

In the fall of 1888, Bryce published his three-volume work, *The
American Commonwealth*, and his name became strongly linked to
American history through an increasing plethora of American associations (see Table 4.2). In Gladstone's view, the book was 'an event in the
history of the United States, and perhaps in the relations of the two
countries.'[32] It stimulated immense interest in both countries with
respect to the politics and society of the United States. It also was obvious that a central concern of the author was the benefits of federalism.
His first volume dealt almost solely with the topic. 'Nevertheless the
rigid Constitution of the United States has rendered, and renders now,
inestimable services.'[33] To those critics who argued that federalism had
produced a major civil war, Bryce defiantly wrote:

> It may be answered not merely that the National government has
> survived this struggle and emerged from it stronger than before, but
> also that Federalism did not produce the struggle, but only gave to it
> the particular form of a series of legal controversies over the Federal
> pact followed by a war of States against the Union.[34]

Moreover, the victory of the North and Reconstruction had been a victory for federalism. Many prominent Englishmen, such as Frederic
Harrison and Goldwin Smith, turned to take note of Bryce's masterful
discussions of 'American Home Rule.'[35] In effect, Bryce's work linked
Gladstonians with American self-government.

It is apparent that Liberals lauded American federalism for a variety
of reasons. It was a compromise solution as well as a centralizing
scheme. It provided for limited devolution. Yet in retrospect their adulation was based primarily upon a historical comparison. Liberals saw
themselves as similar to the American founding fathers. They were to
model their positions in keeping with the style though not necessarily
the content of Washington, Jefferson, and Hamilton. In 1889,
Gladstone extolled the 'extraordinary history' of the American

Table 4.2 Bryce's American associations, 1870–98

Major friendships		Years of association
*Eliot, Charles W.	President of Harvard	1871–97
Garrison, William	Journalist with *The Nation*	1881–98
*Godkin, Edwin L.	Editor of *The Nation* and Mugwump	1882–98
Higginson, Thomas	Author and reform-Republican	1878–98
*Holmes, Oliver W. Jr.	Lawyer and judge	1871–98
Johnson, Robert U.	Secretary of the Amer. Copy. League	1884–98
Low, Seth	New York municipal reformer	1887–97
Lowell, James R.	Author, diplomat, and Mugwump	1880–91
*Norton, Charles	Author, Harvard Prof., and Republican	1884–98
*Roosevelt, Theodore	New York politician and Republican	1886–98
Villard, Henry	Railway owner and businessman	1884–98
Whitman, Sarah	Member of Brahmin group	1882–98

Minor friendships	Years of association	Minor friendships	Years of association
Abbot, Edwin Hale	1886–93	*Holmes, Oliver W.	1871–86
Abbott, Lyman	1895–96	*James, Henry	1880–98
Adams, Herbert	1882–96	James, William	1882–98
*Atkinson, Edward	1885	Kearney, Dennis	1889–90
Bacon, Theodore	1887–97	Lea, Henry C.	1870–98
Baldwin, Simeon	1886 and 1893	*Longfellow, Henry	1871
*Bancroft, George	1881	MacDermott, Edward	1890–98
*Bayard, Thomas	1883	MacVeagh, Wayne	1897
Bishop, J. B.	1888–94	Macy, Jesse	1887–97
Brace, Charles L.	1884–90	Moses, Bernard	1885–87
Bradford, Gamaliel	1884–96	Putnam, George	1891–98
Brown, Frederick	1884–97	Reed, Thomas	1891
Butler, N. M.	1891–98	Rosengarten, J. G.	1887–93
*Carnegie, Andrew	1891–98	Schurz, Carl	1884–98
Collyer, Robert	1871–89	*Shaw, Albert	1885–98
Edmunds, George F.	1885	Stanton, Theodore	1887
Eggleston, Edward	1889–96	Stillman, W. J.	1887–98
*Emerson, Ralph W.	1870	Thayer, James B.	1882–98
*George, Henry	1884	Washburn, George	1887–98
Gilder, Richard W.	1880–98	White, Andrew	1883–98
Gilman, Mrs E. D. W.	1883–89	*White, Henry	1890–98
Goodnow, Frank	1888–96	Wilson, William L.	1892–96
Hay, John	1887–98	Wilson, Woodrow	1888–98

An astrisk (*) indicates that I have consulted the private papers of these individuals for Bryce references. A major friendship is defined as one with whom Bryce had personal associations, private correspondence, and a certain level of intimacy. The years relate to the approximate time of Bryce's friendship with each American. They are based primarily upon his letters to and from the individual. If the conclusive year is 1898, this indicates that usually the relationship continued past that date. Some minor nineteenth century friendships became major after 1900.

Revolution.[36] In George Washington, he found a model for his own actions and a statesman second to none.

> When I first read in detail the life of Washington, I was profoundly impressed with the moral elevation and greatness of his character: and I found myself at a loss to name among the statesmen of any age or country many, or possibly any, who could be his rival...I will then say that if, among all the pedestals supplied by history, I saw one higher than all the rest, and if I were required at a moment's notice to name the fittest occupant for it, I think my choice, at any time during the last 45 years, would have lighted, and it would now light, upon Washington.[37]

Morley also praised the founding fathers. When asked by James Knowles, the editor of the *Nineteenth Century*, to review any important book, he significantly chose one on the American Revolution: James Fiske's *The Critical Period of American History*. Morley saw Fiske's work as a necessary companion to Bryce's work, the latter of which he thought weak on the origins of the United States. While Morley conceded that Liberals might not find the exact solutions to Ireland in American expedients, they would find in the American Revolutionary experience 'everything to learn from the temper in which a serious piece of political business was done; practical and politic, yet firm to principles; deliberate, yet energetic; supple, though tenacious; elastic, versatile, and abounding in ingenious resource.'[38] Other Liberals praised the first Americans. The historian E. A. Freeman called Washington 'the Expander of England' and Playfair extolled the great triumphs of the signing of the Constitution at the Centennial Celebration in Philadelphia in 1887.[39] Between 1887 and 1890, the Irish Home Rule question clearly motivated Liberal leaders to consider the precedent of American constitutional history much more seriously than in 1885–86.

Other British movements also focused Liberal attention on American federalism. This was especially the case with the Imperial Federation League. Rosebery, Bryce, Dilke, and the academics J. A. Froude and J. R. Seeley all were thoroughly dedicated advocates of unification of the British empire. From 1886 to 1892, Rosebery was President of the League and a leading campaigner 'to secure by Federation the permanent unity of the Empire.'[40] Yet neither Rosebery nor most of his cohorts were sure as to how imperial federation could be achieved.[41] It seemed that the best way must lie with some federal precedent already tested like that of the United States. Rosebery spoke:

> Take the two great Federal States that have been last founded in the world – take the United States – I venture to say that the federation of the British Empire can be carried out with infinitely more ease, given goodwill on all sides, than, the United States encountered in their formation.[42]

Seeley and Froude, who both had given federalism more penetrating considerations than Rosebery, also were lavish in their praise for American federalism.

> But the greatness of the United States is the best proof that a state may become immensely large and yet prosper. The Union is a great example of a system under which an indefinite number of provinces is firmly held together without any of the inconveniences which have been felt in our Empire. It is therefore the visible proof that those inconveniences are not inseparable from a large Empire, but only from the old colonial system.[43]

> The problem of how to combine a number of self-governed communities into a single commonwealth, which now lies before Englishmen who desire to see a federation of the empire, has been solved, and solved completely, in the American Union.[44]

Yet many imperial federationists stumbled in trying to devise an exact plan for their union. A fundamental problem was whether or not their union could, would, or should be a racial organization. As federation debates continued, it became increasingly more practical to consider an Anglo-Saxon alliance than a specifically British imperial alliance. Anglo-Saxonism was an expanding force in the 1880s, demonstrated by British dominance of the world, rising American power, and even bolstered by English reactions to Irish nationalism.[45] In any Anglo-Saxon alliance, it was blatantly clear that the United States could not be omitted. When Rosebery proposed major reasons for an imperial federation, themes of Anglo-Saxonism and Anglo-American understanding stood out. First, it would moderate difficult American–Canadian relations. Second, it would 'secure an enormous area throughout the world for peace and commerce.' Third, 'we should be a beneficial friend to the United States and not a mere collection of scattered relations.' Finally, federation would consolidate the Anglo-Saxon race.[46] The whole imperial federation movement leaned towards Anglo-Saxonism. A federation based on race appealed to the broadest group of Anglo-Americans: Chamberlain, Dilke, W. Stead, Carnegie, Albert Shaw, and even Gladstone.[47]

Gladstone expressed his views on racial federation and Anglo-Saxonism most definitively in 1889, drawn towards more extensive studies of the United States and influenced by his friendship with Andrew Carnegie. Throughout the 1880s, he had become increasingly intrigued by statistical studies of Anglo-Saxon population growth. The facts led to one logical conclusion: that Britain and the United States would dominate the next century. An early version of these views was sketched out in a letter to Smalley in 1884,[48] and in 1889 they formed a topic for an article. Gladstone's studies of the population estimates of Barnham Zincke, Thomas Jefferson, and a Captain Imlay led him to estimate that the United States could have between 600 and 700 million people in 1980![49] No country, neither Britain, France, Russia, Germany, nor even China would be so numerically strong. He believed that it would be foolish to construct any artificial alliances within the British Empire that did not have at its core the grand, natural, and moral union of England and America.

> They are being drawn nearer and nearer to one another, not by any artificial contrivances, but with 'the cords of a man'... All my life long, I have, in a wide and varied circle, seen and shared the intercourse between the two countries. It is not the same as it was. It has been visibly softened, mellowed, ripened. An American stranger is to us more and more like a British stranger, and I hope that a British stranger is to them more and more like an American stranger. If there is a space between, it is a narrowing space. The great idea of common inheritance, and to a larger extent of common prospects, more and more regulates our relations, and makes easy and familiar the conditions of mutual approach.[50]

In the case of an English-speaking union, Gladstone did seem to 'put much more store on order and stability than on national liberty.'[51]

Between 1886 and 1892, the Liberal leaders' preoccupation with federal prospects for Irish Home Rule, imperial federation, and Anglo-Saxonism led them constantly to study American federalism and the Constitution. One political scientist has claimed that 'the Constitution of the United States of America was unsuitable for his [Gladstone's] purposes because it did not secure sufficient power to the federal government.'[52] That federal plans for Britain did not materialize, even though the Gladstonians' move towards limited Irish representation at Westminister was implicitly federalist in nature, should not obscure the Liberals' serious study of American federalism. In 1890–91, Liberal attention to American precedents diminished. The Parnell divorce crisis dealt Home Rule 'a severe blow'[53] and the Newcastle Programme focused on a broad spectrum of Liberal party issues. In 1892, however, American federalism would have one final nineteenth-century discussion in the Home Rule Bill debate.

American protectionism and tariffs reconsidered

American protectionism became a central issue in British political life between 1886 and 1892. During these years in 1890, the United States passed the controversial McKinley Tariff, waged two presidential elections on the tariff (1888 and 1892), and moved consistently towards higher tariffs. American trade policies profoundly affected British trade, agriculture, and business and these impacted considerably upon British political and economic reality as the Great Depression continued in the late Victorian age. Within Britain, many called for retaliatory measures: preferential treaties, imperial commercial reciprocity, or even imperial commercial confederation. These aims were taken up by such bodies as the Fair Trade League, the Imperial Federation League, the Conservative Protectionist Association, and the Bimetallist League. Most of these movements were led by businessmen, and Conservatives such as Howard Vincent, Louis Jennings, and Earl Dunraven were some of the most active leaders.[54] There were many instances of meetings or commissions focusing on the protectionist stances of the United States: the Royal Commission on Trade and Depression, the Royal Commission on Gold and Silver, the Colonial Conference in 1887, the National Union of Conservative Constitutional Associations in 1887, and a Sugar Convention in 1888. Thus, for instance, the Liberal MP A. O'Connor described the impact of American duties on Sheffield to the Commission on Trade and Depression in 1886:

> Then there are the American duties. I had a fine trade with America about 25 years ago – a magnificent trade. I had an agent there who was paid 400 l. a year to keep stock there, and who did a big business. It is all gone, and I do not send six-pennyworth to the United States today. That is one cause for the depression of the trade of Sheffield; and other firms are similarly situated with myself.[55]

In their arguments against protectionism, Liberal leaders had somehow to explain that the tremendous American commercial progress had been the result of other factors such as her huge internal markets rather than her high tariff policies. Many Liberals only turned with great difficulty to the issue of protectionism. In 1886, Gladstone, Shaw-Lefevre, William Fowler, and Thomas Farrer all refused to serve on the Royal Commission on Trade and Industry.[56] Bryce hardly mentioned protectionism at all in *The American Commonwealth*, although he acknowledged 'Free Trade v. Protection' as 'another burning question, and has been so since the early days of the Union.'[57] Two formerly active important Liberals, Chamberlain and Dilke, increasingly toyed with protectionism for Great Britain in the form of preferential treaties.[58] Harcourt said little in depth about protection. In the end, Gladstone, Playfair, and the non-parliamentarian T. H. Farrer argued most vigorously about the encroaching threat of American trade policies.

Lyon Playfair and the permanent secretary of the Board of Trade from 1865 to 1886, T. H. Farrer, formulated the most complete positions against American protectionism before the McKinley Act burst upon the British scene in 1890. Both Playfair and Farrer had extensive personal knowledge of the United States and associations with American free-traders.[59] Thus Farrer urged Edwin Godkin: 'If you adopt Free Trade – or approach it – it will do much to solve all these [Anglo-American] questions in the best manner.'[60] Playfair was disturbed that Liberal leaders were apt to ignore the issue of protectionism or 'fair trade,' and he tried to rejuvenate Liberal commitment to free trade.[61] In November 1887, Playfair warned Gladstone of protection's great new popularity:

> Three years ago Free Trade was advancing in the U.S. Now there is a strong reaction and Protection is rampant. There is now no party and very few individuals dare announce Free Trade doctrines. The reason for this is that the South which was formerly wholly agricultural & Free Trade in opinions has now become largely manufacturing & has veered round to protection.[62]

Farrer argued many times against American protectionism.[63] The gist of his arguments was that protection had hindered trade and manufactures in all countries; certainly in France, Germany, and the United States. Moreover, protectionism was dangerous because it threatened to stimulate a trade war between Great Britain and the United States that would inevitably cloud over Anglo-American relations. He emphasized that 'the United States ... in spite of their monstrous Protective system, are still our best customers as well as our nearest of kin.'[64] Playfair agreed completely with Farrer. In his statements on American protectionism, he often focused upon British and American wages. To those critics who argued that protection led to high wages, Playfair countered that American unprotected industries had higher wages than protected ones.[65] Moreover, protection was both dangerous and immoral. 'Protection leads to Socialism and tends even to Communism... Protectionists live on the product of the labour of others. In the United States one protected labourer is supported by a tax on seventeen unprotected.'[66] Finally, British wages had increased by 39 percent between 1850 and 1883, American by only 30 percent.

Test the whole question, in any way you choose, by real wages, by savings, by commercial prosperity, by population, by reduction in pauperism and crime, and you will not find the slightest support from American experience that Free Trade is a delusion, that Protection adds to the remuneration of labour, or that it acts in any other way than as a drag upon the development of nations.[67]

When, in the presidential election of 1888, the American people rejected the free trader President Cleveland, Gladstone tackled the perplexing question of American protectionism. Perhaps in a moment of sarcasm directed towards Chamberlain, he called his unpublished paper on American protection 'For Fair Play All Round.' Chamberlain had called his 1885 Irish central board scheme 'Home Rule All Round.' In fact Gladstone saw protection strictly as a policy for the privileged. He called it 'a Pandora's box, of which the principal contents are waste for the nation, forced upon its victims, and something dangerously near, demoralization for its favourites, whom it endows with the fruits of industry and enterprise of other people.'[68] The great fault was that the majority paid for the profits of a small manufacturing minority. While the United States gave attention to capitalists in regard to 'labour saving machines,' they abandoned the interests of the workmen. Moreover, foreign labour was used to keep the condition of American labour depressed. In the end protection produced great wealth for industry and capitalists, but destroyed basic class relationships and enslaved workers. In Gladstone's view, the United States could not live up to its majestic future so long as she followed trade policies that weakened the very social and moral fibers of the country.[69]

In 1890, American protectionism aroused British political opinion as never before, when after vigorous debate the Congress passed the

protectionist McKinley Tariff. 'In 1890 McKinley precipitated something of an imperial crisis by the announcement of a new and more
protective United States tariff.'[70] While some of the duties were low-
ered (in the case of sugar repealed), most were raised; this included for
the first time rates on agricultural products. The immediate result of
the tariff insofar as the United States was concerned was to raise customs rates to over 49 percent for the fiscal period 1892 to 1894.[71] In
Britain, industry and agriculture reacted with horror, shutting down
enterprises and calling for retaliatory measures. The North of England,
Bradford, Sheffield, Leeds, and other cities, were hit particularly hard.
Calls for retaliation filled every paper and received some solid support
in Parliament, for the first time from some Liberals as well as
Conservatives.[72] While the monthly publication of the *Journal of the
Board of Trade* had essentially passed over the agitation in America on
the McKinley Act, it turned after the act took effect in October to
expose the harm wrought upon Great Britain.[73] Gladstone, Playfair,
and Farrer once more came to the defense of free trade and, at the
same time, came to calm those who wished to retaliate against the
United States.

Even before the passage of the McKinley Act, Gladstone had jumped
into the Anglo-American debate about the proposed measure. In fact,
he contributed an article on the defense of free trade to the *North
American Review* in January 1890 which created a tremendous sensa-
tion, especially in America. Part of the reason why the article had such
an impact was attributable to the publicity efforts of the editor, Lloyd
Bryce. With Gladstone's consent, he had obtained a stirring article for
protection by the Anglophobic Secretary of State James Blaine and
printed the two articles alongside each other. The headlines ran
'A Duel.'[74] As Lloyd Bryce reported to Gladstone: 'I am satisfied that
this controversy will be one of the most important discussions in the
history of periodical literature.'[75] He was not mistaken.

Gladstone approached his defense of free trade in the United States
with great caution. Obviously conscious of his ill-timed remarks of
1862, he wrote that 'To interfere from across the water in such a controversy is an act which may wear the appearance of impertinence.'[76]
Nonetheless, he tackled the hard issues. The reason the United States
prospered, he held, was not because of her protectionist policies but
because of a host of other unique advantages. These included her
immense capital, vast territory, great industry, superior natural wealth,
and an isolated international position. Thus the United States was able
to surpass Great Britain in almost every aspect of 'cheapness.' Finally,

two additional developments greatly aided the United States. First, British free trade had given American growth a gigantic boost. Second, the American inventive faculty was second to none. However, Gladstone saved the greatest danger to last, namely that protectionism would lead to moral as well as economic decay. 'I urge, then, that all protection is morally as well as economically bad.'[77] Protection was destructive of the 'liberal spirit.' Since the United States had been founded on political, religious, and economic freedom, Gladstone thought it was hypocritical for her to claim to be the protector of such liberties while she curtailed the industries of her people. If the United States wanted to maintain her rising international status, she would have to protect economic and moral freedom equally.

> The American love of freedom will, beyond all doubt, be to some extent qualified, perhaps in some cases impaired, by the subtle influence of gold, aggregated by many hands in vaster masses than have yet been known.
> But, to rise higher still, how will the majestic figure, about to become the largest and most powerful on the stage of the world's history, make use of his power? Will it be instinct with moral life in proportion to its material strength![78]

The American response to Gladstone's article was extensive, and Gladstone himself feared that Americans had resented his views. Lloyd Bryce assured him he was mistaken. He wrote '... in the thousands of newspaper articles which I have read on the Duel, I have not yet seen a single criticism hostile or discourteous to you.'[79] The *North American Review* became an instrument for reply to Gladstone from many Americans: McKinley himself; Justin Morrill, author of a tariff; Congressman Roger Mills; and Carnegie. They all, including Blaine, were very courteous towards Gladstone and indeed pleased that the most prominent living British Liberal had voiced his views and engaged in 'a duel.' Most authors debated various matters of detail with Gladstone. Blaine was able to mount a sharp opposing view, and had had a singular polemical advantage in having a proof of Gladstone's article when he wrote his.[80] Mills upbraided Blaine on many of the same points which Blaine had marshaled against Gladstone.[81] Morrill, who found nothing striking in Gladstone's arguments, asserted that they had 'been heard by me so often from our Democratic revenue-reform friends that the refrain, if not a bore, excites neither delight nor alarm.'[82] Even Carnegie, while he had some sympathy for free trade in Britain, claimed that Gladstone's call for American free trade was based upon a misreading of American facts. Carnegie also thought that Gladstone's article would have little effect on 'the question of protection as it interests the United States.'[83] Carnegie may have been right that Gladstone was unable to stem the inevitable move towards protectionism, but he was mistaken about Gladstone's influence. He himself, like many prominent Americans, had been stirred to address protectionism as an Anglo-American issue. In acting as a catalyst for Anglo-American understanding, Gladstone forced many Americans to reconsider the consequences of their unilateral actions.

As previously mentioned, Playfair joined Gladstone in conciliating an outraged British industrial and agricultural population. Immediately after the McKinley Tariff began taking its toll upon British commerce in October 1890, Gladstone and Playfair made important speeches on the McKinley Tariff in the disturbed Northern Midlands. Playfair's comments were particularly knowledgeable. He had been in the United States during the passage of the McKinley Act and had given it 'close study.'[84] He urged that American commercial policy was fundamental for Englishmen to understand. 'If they be right in principle and successful in practice, the whole commercial policy of the United Kingdom is founded on a gigantic error, and must lead to our ruin as an industrial nation.'[85]

Both Gladstone and Playfair argued that throughout American history, protectionism had consistently hurt the United States more than it had Great Britain. Gladstone declared: 'Substantial injury cannot be done to us, though occasional injury may here and there result.'[86] While it seemed logical that the two Liberal leaders might well have been pessimistic about the course of American events, they were, on the contrary, calmly optimistic. The protectionist Republicans had suffered heavy defeats in the 1890 fall elections and to Playfair this seemed to inaugurate a move towards free trade. 'The Republicans, who were in a small majority in the House of Representatives, and carried the McKinley Act by high-handed means, have been hopelessly defeated at the polls, and the Democrats have now an overwhelming majority.'[87]

In their respective conclusions, Gladstone and Playfair made grand perorations about the need for unity between Britain and America. No temporary difficulty, including protectionism, should ever stand in the way of the natural intercourse between the two countries. Gladstone put it this way:

Let us rely upon it that the light will come in upon the dark places – that a people so acute, a people with so remarkable a history, and a people of destinies yet more wonderful and grand than the history which it has already recorded – they will find their way to the results that are best for themselves, and they will find it more easily, more readily, and more effectually in proportion as they are left more respectfully to themselves, in proportion as we show, that much as we value their commerce, we value their friendship and regard still more; ... [88]

From the fall of 1890 to the end of 1892, Liberal leaders continued to look optimistically upon the course of American politics, especially with regard to protectionism. The McKinley Act came under increasing criticism in the United States, for the country was suffering a trade depression. In November 1892, only a few months after the Liberal victory in England, the free trade party of the Democratic Cleveland scored a resounding victory at the polls. Liberal leaders were gleeful. Playfair, who was again in the United States, reported eagerly to Gladstone. 'I have thoroughly studied the operation of the McKinley Act during my stay. It is breaking its own back very rapidly.'[89] Bryce also congratulated his free trade friend, Godkin, on the Democratic victory.[90] The period from 1886 to 1892 clearly reinforced the ideological position of transatlantic liberals over free trade. One historian has declared that 'Grover Cleveland had become a Gladstonian Liberal, American-style.'[91] It is equally true that some prominent Liberal leaders became Cleveland Democrats, British-style.

American currency and bimetallism

A major corollary to the Liberal interest in American protectionism was their attention to American financial and monetary policy. Bimetallism – the use of both silver and gold with parity between the two metals – and international bimetallism – international agreement on the value of silver and gold used in international transactions – like protectionism burst upon the British political scene between 1886 and 1892, as a result of falling prices, the low value of silver, and depressed conditions of agriculture.

Any consideration of either bimetallism or international bimetallism involved the United States. Not only were they the major power committed to a gold and silver system, but they had been the main movers, along with the French, for International Monetary Conferences throughout the 1870s and 1880s. Two such conferences were held in Paris in 1878 and in 1881, followed by two more in 1888 and 1892.

As historian E. H. H. Green notes, representatives at the conferences included individuals from the United States, Britain, France, Belgium, Italy, Denmark, Germany, and other nations – and British representatives Balfour, Goschen, H. H. Gibbs, and Alfred Rothschild.[92] The conferences made little progress because of the lack of cooperation by the hardened monometallic British.[93] In 1885, a secret mission by the former New York journalist, Manton Marble, on behalf of President Cleveland, found hardly any bimetallic sympathies among British leaders.[94] But whereas the monometallic Liberal leaders had largely ignored the views of the silver advocates before 1886, they were forced by worsening economic conditions and foreign pressure to examine the issue seriously from 1886 to 1892. In this the silver-based economy of India also played a major role. The free trade propagandists Gladstone, Playfair, and Farrer were now also the main Liberal exponents for gold monometallism.

While to a great extent bimetallism 'was never more than an academic proposition,'[95] it gained increasing credibility and attention in the late 1880s. Even though the Royal Commission on Trade Depression had considered many currency issues, in 1886 another commission was appointed specifically to inquire into the relative value of silver and gold and to find the reason for falling prices. The Royal Commission on Gold and Silver included such prominent Liberals as Joseph Chamberlain, Sir John Lubbock, and Leonard Courtney as well as some sympathizers with bimetallism, Henry Chaplin, Arthur Balfour, and William Houldsworth. Throughout the proceedings, American facts and experience played a large part.[96] As historian Anthony Howe has noted 'More widely, as an international cause, bimetallism seems on the whole to have won the support of liberal political economists, for example, in America, Japan, and Australia.'[97] Thus, for instance, the Commission sought the advice of the American economic authorities David A. Wells and S. Dana Horton.[98] The conclusions of the Commission were inconclusive. Surprisingly, the members were not very critical about silver schemes. The cause of bimetallism in Britain continued to advance. In 1881, the International Monetary Standard Association was formed, which evolved in 1886 into the Bimetallic League under the leadership of the banker Henry H. Gibbs and the Conservative MP Henry Chaplin.[99] It was very active well into the mid-1890s, and was so successful in five months in 1894 that it was able to raise a guarantee fund of £100 000.[100]

While there was some real dispute among many observers as to the true strength of bimetallism in Britain, Gladstone and Playfair had notably taken up the attack by 1890. When Marble revisited Great

Britain in 1886 on private business, silver agitation was much greater than in the year previous. He found 'It is extraordinary the change which has come and which is avowed.'[101] On the other hand, Edward Atkinson made another secret mission on behalf of President Cleveland to test the strength of bimetallism – this in 1887. As he saw it, there was 'no indication that the subject of bimetallism has received any intelligent or serious consideration outside of a small circle in each country.'[102] T. H. Farrer also reported: 'There is not – as far as I can see – the least hope of bimetallism making its way here.'[103] Yet when Playfair made an address to the Political Economy Club in January 1889, it was on 'Bimetallism.' While he could not contemplate any desire upon the part of Great Britain to tamper with the gold standard, he expressed real concern over the silver agitation. Much of his talk was addressed to the advanced state of silver in the United States.[104] Free silver and soft money had become central issues supported by such important bodies as the Knights of Labour and the Farmer's Alliances.

Elsewhere, Playfair declared 'The political education of the masses must be at a low ebb when such wild-cat projects are even conceivable, and it is a serious duty of intelligent Americans to undertake an educational campaign upon currency questions.'[105] Despite such discouraging conditions in America, he praised the majority of its citizenry for being level-headed. Further, he thought it was erroneous to believe that by increasing the currency in circulation (a silver argument), prosperity would increase. Britain's prosperity had grown from 1879 to 1889 despite falling currency circulation.[106] Gladstone also, in a series of notes on bimetallism written in April 1889, argued that gold had 'stood the trial.' It had '*maximum of stability.*'

> There is such a commodity: and it is gold: the most ductile, indivisible, incorruptible, and perhaps the least easily imitable of substances: but above all, and this is the essential point, the most constant in its value: which has undergone no serious change say within the last hundred years[107]

Moreover, Gladstone like Playfair argued against adoption of silver merely because other countries, the United States for one, had tried such a system.

> I object to making the standard of value to be maintained in this country dependent on the consent of other nations. The political economy of England is the standard bearer of the world. She is at issue with most other nations as to the laws of trade: and I am not

much disposed to be their pupil as to the laws of currency. They do not inspire me with the requisite confidence to induce me to subject our ideas to compulsory modification by theirs.[108]

When bimetallism became the end of vigorous debate in the Commons on 4 June 1889 and on 18 April 1890, Lyon Playfair, Harcourt, and other Liberals denounced any consideration of adopting American 'silver currency fanaticism' in Great Britain.[109] The currency systems of Britain and America continued to diverge. In 1890, the Congress passed the Sherman Silver Purchase Act, while in 1890, on the other hand, the bimetallists were defeated overwhelmingly in a motion in the House of Commons.

The gloomy situation in the United States slowly changed. Early in 1891, the former President Cleveland came out for gold despite the warnings of Western Democrats.[110] With his great triumph at the polls in 1892, gold and free trade both gained similar victories. Playfair, his view sustained, recalled that 'Last spring the English Bimetallic League trumpeted loudly their joy when they saw the price of silver rising under the new demand of the United States for 'a silver currency.'[111] Nonetheless, the good sense of the American people had prevailed. Certainly now, there were important lessons to be learned from across the sea. 'Bagehot was right when he said that the astounding experiments of American legislation were important in their failures because they established the stable truths of political economy.'[112] Gold like free trade easily identified British Liberals with the Cleveland Democrats in 1892. As noted by historian Anthony Howe, 'The gold standard, like free trade, seemed part of the social contract upon which the Victorian state was based.'[113]

Anglo-American copyright

During the period between 1886 and 1892, many other American issues appeared to engage the serious attention of Liberal leaders for the first time – arbitration, women's rights, labor, urban development, and temperance. These continued to evolve in the 1890s. Thus they are treated in subsequent chapters. However, one issue emerged and was settled in these years, and it symbolized the Liberal involvement in tying the two Anglo-Saxon countries into one harmonious and friendly entity. That issue was copyright, and characteristically, both Bryce and Gladstone played central roles in its settlement.

Anglo-American copyright had been a major problem throughout the nineteenth century. American publishers persisted in publishing cheap editions of European authors, or pirated works as they were known.[114] In the 1870s and 1880s, British authors and publishers began to gain some support from Americans for reform of the existing arrangements.[115] In 1876, a Royal Commission was appointed on copyright and its report underlay the enormity of the pending difficulties; 'that the United States is of all nations the one in which British authors are most concerned, – the nation in regard to which the absence of a copyright convention gives rise to the greatest hardships.'[116] Both Liberals and Americans gave important testimony before the Commission. Matthew Arnold, Edward Dicey, Charles Trevelyan, Thomas Huxley, Herbert Spencer, Thomas Farrer, the American publisher George Putnam, and George Smalley were star witnesses.[117] British opinion was largely unanimous for a change, but it was necessary for a simultaneous movement in the United States for the Anglo-American copyright agreement to make headway.[118] That point was reached in the mid-1880s.

The moving force behind the copyright reform in the United States was the American Copyright League, and in particular the New England journalist with the *Century Magazine*, Robert Underwood Johnson. In 1888, he became the secretary of the League. He had close associations with the Washington political world. On 12 January 1884, the American Copyright League passed a resolution which pressed the Department of State 'to complete an International Treaty with Great Britain, securing to the authors of each country the full recognition of property rights in both countries.'[119] Thereafter, Johnson lobbied throughout the East Coast. Moreover, he began reporting the American progress to his friend James Bryce. British Liberals came to have a special impact on the American movement after 1887.

In 1887, British Liberals both aided and confused the Anglo-American copyright issue. James Knowles, editor of the *Nineteenth Century*, triggered a host of prominent British reactions to American actions when he published a letter on the copyright plan of the American Pearsall Smith. Johnson described the plan as one which would permit 'anyone to publish an author's book by merely purchasing royalty stamps from him.'[120] Gladstone, the Duke of Argyll, Archdeacon Farrar, Justin McCarthy, Thomas Farrer, Matthew Arnold, and Thomas Huxley all responded to Smith's scheme in Knowles journal under a joint article, 'An Olive Branch from America.'[121]

Most Englishmen supported the aim of the copyright movement but were divided on their support for specific details. Gladstone's position emerged as critical, and he called Anglo-American copyright a vital concern. 'The literary question between England and the United States enters into the general relations of the two countries; and tends, within a limited but important sphere, to a disagreeable friction.'[122] While Gladstone's broad support for copyright seemed plain enough, it was construed in the United States as specific endorsement of Smith's royalty plan, which was opposed by the American Copyright League. Johnson was most disturbed. He wanted a fairer and more general agreement. Therefore, he put pressure on Bryce to have Gladstone clarify his position. Bryce wrote to Gladstone: 'A telegram just received from America begs me to convey their view of theirs to you, as they seem to fear that you may be inclined to lend the weight of your countenance to the Pearsall Smith plan.'[123] While Gladstone and Bryce discussed various alternative actions, Gladstone curiously withheld endorsement from Johnson. His ambiguous stance continued to create problems for the American Copyright League until 1890.

In 1890–91, an Anglo-American copyright agreement was finally achieved. It owed most to Johnson, who gained the support of such prominent Senators as Platt, Lodge, and Sherman. He continued to work closely with Bryce, requesting information and hoping that the British position would fall into line. As success seemed imminent in February 1890, he strove to get a letter from Gladstone. Opponents of copyright had continued to cite Gladstone's views as reasons to defeat a larger measure.[124] In April, Gladstone finally replied. Any minor disagreements on proposed legislation were insignificant compared to the goodwill that would arise.

On 8 April 1890, Gladstone's views were printed in the *New York Tribune:*

> I set so high a value upon the recognition by the United States of the principle of international copyright, a principle which has been now almost universally adopted in Europe, that although I regret some of the provisions of the Bill now before Congress which you have sent to me, I cannot refuse to express my sympathy with the efforts which American authors have so perseveringly made to procure legal protection for the rights of foreign authors, ...
>
> It is quite erroneous to suppose that I have formed any opinion in favour of the Royalty scheme as against the bill.[125]

Gladstone's letter evidently greatly encouraged the American copyrightists. Johnson reported to Bryce that 'it adds great strength to our prospect of success.'[126] Success finally was achieved. On 4 March 1891,

President Harrison signed a Copyright Bill thus ending years of literary disunity between Britain and America. In the aftermath of the American success, American copyright leaders turned to insure that there were no other difficulties across the Atlantic. George Putnam, Senator Eggleston, and the publisher M. Appleton all journeyed to England to meet with groups and put pressure upon the government. Johnson worked through his ever faithful correspondent, Bryce.

> Much was made here of English opposition – both in Committee and on the floor of Congress, and if they should get a catchword it might make it necessary for us to fight hard to retain what we have won ... The difficulty is to get wind of official action before it is taken. Can you do this on your side?[127]

In the end, while the Conservative government was slow to react to American overtures, they acceded to the efforts of the Anglo-American movement. Throughout, Liberal politicians, academics, and authors had kept up a steady stream of contributions in the form of letters and articles on behalf of agreement.[128] These certainly had a strongly favourable impact. Yet, it is to Bryce that the last accolade due an Englishman must be given. Johnson praised him. 'What has been done on your side has been largely due to your effort and politic action, and I am sure I speak for the whole of our Executive Council in thanking you very heartily for what you have done.'[129] On 1 July 1891, the Anglo-American agreement took effect.

Gladstone: American activities and political issues

Between 1886 and 1892, Gladstone played a unique and important role in Anglo-American history. He turned to address a series of American social and moral problems which attracted enormous attention on both sides of the Atlantic. His contributions on free trade, the English-speaking union, and copyright have already been noted. Yet he made many more. During his six-year absence from office, Gladstone contributed no less than a dozen articles to the *North American Review*, the *Youth's Companion*, and the *Nineteenth Century*[130] that dealt with Anglo-American topics. Fundamentally, Gladstone was disturbed by moral and social decay in the United States, and in his essays he sought to draw attention to specific problems and to inspire efforts for reform. Thus, in a sense, Gladstone played the role of an American patrician muckraker; and among his many close American friendships and associations none was more important than that with the American industrialist Andrew Carnegie (see Table 4.3).

Gladstone had extolled Bryce's *American Commonwealth*, but he also regretted its limitations. To Bryce, he wrote that it was 'a great book' and 'an event in the history of the United States, and perhaps in the relations of the two countries.'[131] But to Mary Sands, the wife of the American free trader Mahlon Sands, he said that Bryce's book had ignored important social developments. Mrs Sands, after an intimate discussion with Gladstone, reported to her brother-in-law, Godkin: that the GOM 'regretted to find it chiefly a political study, & much wished to see a picture of the social development of America.'[132]

No issues concerned Gladstone more deeply throughout his life than those revolving around religion, and as the century progressed, the decline of religious values in the world distressed him. The conflict between Christianity and Darwinism brought his anxieties to a head. In the United States, the battle had been particularly intense: Spencerians and Darwinists like Josiah Strong, William Fiske, and William G. Sumner had made resolute progress with their atheistic ideas.[133] Evolution had been used by many Americans as proof of their march towards unlimited future greatness. No figure was more prominent in devastating attacks on Christianity than the freethinker and agnostic Colonel Robert Ingersoll. The controversy surrounding him reached something of a peak in 1887 in the pages of the *North American Review*, where he engaged in a fierce debate with the Rev. Henry Field, brother of Gladstone's good acquaintance Cyrus Field.[134] Ingersoll defiantly attacked Christianity and the past. 'The most religious nations had been the most immoral, the cruelest and the most unjust. Italy was far worse under the Popes than under the Caesars.'[135] Religion was a harmful force. 'Religion has been the enemy of social order, because it directs the attention of man to another world. Religion teaches its votaries to sacrifice this world for the sake of that other. The effect is to weaken the ties that hold families and States together.'[136] Against such contentions, Field argued for the stability and morality that Christianity brought the Western world.

In December 1887, the editor Thorndike Rice asked Gladstone for an article on his 'belief in Christian Revelation, and using Mr Ingersoll and Dr Field as the John Doe and the Praetorial Doe of the case.'[137] Rice emphasized the enormous American interest in the Ingersoll–Field debate and Ingersoll's prominence. 'Mr. Ingersoll is without question the infidel who commands the largest following of any single individual of

Table 4.3 Gladstone's American Associations, 1860–98

Friendships		Years of association
*Carnegie, Andrew	Industrialist and Republican	1882–98
*Lowell, James R.	Diplomat, author, and Mugwump	1880–85
*Motley, John L.	Diplomat and historian	1870–73
Nevin, Robert	Clergyman and friend of Dollinger	1875–86
Rice, Allen Thorndike	Journalist: editor of *NAR*	1877–89
Rideing, William	Editor of *YC* and *NAR*	1887–97
Sands, Mrs Mary	English woman married to American reformer, Mahlon Sands	1884–95

Acquaintances	Years of association	Acquaintances	Years of association
Adams, Charles F.	1867–74	*Hoppin, William	1877–87
*Bancroft, George	1882	Hurlbert, William	1887
*Bayard, Thomas F.	1893–97	Johnson, Reverdy	1868–74
Beecher, Henry Ward	1886	Kelley, Eugene	1886
*Blaine, James G.	1881–87	Lee, Margaret	1888–89
Bryce, Lloyd	1889–97	*Marble, Manton	1886
Burritt, Elihu	1876	Metcalf, Loretus	1887
Coxe, Arthur Cleveland	1861–96	Phelps, Edward J.	1885–89
Crawford, Theron C.	1887	Pierrepont, Edward	1881–87
*Dana, Richard H. Jr	1860–76	Pomeroy, Henry S.	1888–91
Depew, Chauncey	1895–97	Pulitzer, Joseph	1895
Doane, George W.	1841–56	Schenck, Robert	1872–76
Donnelly, Ignatius	1887–88	Schuyler, Eugene	1876
*Eliot, Charles W.	1878	Sherman, William T.	1872
Ewarts, William M.	1877–87	*Smalley, George W.	1872–90
Field, Cyrus	1862–86	Smedes, Susan	1889–91
Field, Eugene	1890	Stillman, William J.	1882
*Fish, Hamilton	1868–90	Story, William W.	1888
Girard, Pierre	1872–76	*Sumner, Charles	1857–71
*Godkin, Edwin L.	1889–95	*Ward, Samuel	1879–83
Greeley, Adolphus	1888	*Wells, David A.	1867
Hale, Horatio	1886–88	*White, Henry	1883–98
*Hay, John	1887–97	*Winthrop, Robert	1870–82
Hearst, William R.	1897	Yarnell, Elis	1864–74
*Holmes, Oliver W.	1891		

An asterisk (*) indicates that I have consulted the private papers of these individuals for Gladstone references, and in particular with reference to friendships. The approximate years of associations are based primarily on the correspondence of the Gladstone Papers in the British Museum, and in some cases may have been more extensive than the years listed here; references have also been checked in *The Gladstone Diaries*.

his school in this country, and from likely in the world. He is a lawyer of great celebrity, and without a peer among our orators.'[138] Gladstone accepted the offer.

As with the free trade–protection debate, Gladstone's presence in the Ingersoll–Field controversy sparked a wider interest than the original debate. In a sense, the Gladstone–Ingersoll controversy paralleled the debate between the Darwinian Thomas Huxley and Gladstone in the late 1880s and early 1890s.[139] The news of Gladstone's impending article triggered various reactions. A Congregationalist minister from Iowa thanked Gladstone for his attention to Ingersoll's 'irreligious views.'[140] On the other hand, the prominent Bishop of Western New York, Cleveland Coxe, warned Gladstone not to participate. The former Prime Minister's words would give Ingersoll a recognition that he in no way deserved.

> Over & over again have those whom he has indirectly challenged declined to have any thing to do with him. Something besides this – he had continued 'to get you to meet him' – because it recognizes him as a foreman not unworthy of the steel of the foremost man in European public life – & a Christian. We should never hear the last of it & your recognition will gain him admission to scenes & circles, where his power to ruin our youth will be immense. Never was there so plausible a scoffer; never one so unprincipled & audacious. He has peddled his blasphemies over all our cities, great towns, & has sown the seeds of another 'French Revolution.'[141]

American subscription agencies were delighted with the prospects of a great debate which would produce commercial benefits.[142] Finally, British audiences also took a keen interest in the gladitorial contest.[143]

Gladstone's article on Ingersoll appeared as the feature in the May 1888 edition of the *North American Review*.[144] In it, Gladstone sought to avoid direct comments on the Field–Ingersoll debate or the state of American religion; rather, he defended the spirit and value of Christianity. Nonetheless, he made sharp references to religious and moral decay in both England and America when he wrote that 'the human constitution [lay] in its warped, impaired, and dislocated condition.'[145] Nor did Gladstone altogether restrain from upbraiding Ingersoll:

> Colonel Ingersoll writes with a rare and enviable brilliancy, but also with an impetus which he seems unable to control. Denunciation, sarcasm, and invective, may in consequence be said to constitute the staple of his work; and, if argument or some favorable admission here and there peeps out for a moment, the writer soon leaves the

dry and barren heights for his favorite and more luxurious galloping grounds beneath.[146]

Most of Gladstone's article was a closely argued fundamentalist interpretation of Genesis and Revelation. Ingersoll did not wait long to respond.[147] In June, his rebuttal appeared, and it was better mannered than that to Field; Gladstone was a man he deeply respected.[148] Yet Ingersoll wasted no efforts in clinically dissecting Gladstone's arguments. He disagreed with Gladstone's derogation of the contemporary human condition.[149] As with Gladstone, the bulk of his article was devoted to specific Biblical analysis. He attacked the 'falsity,' 'wickedness,' and 'foolishness' of the 'sacred volume.'[150]

The Gladstone–Ingersoll debate spurred a quick and heated response on both sides of the Atlantic. In July 1888, a group of distinguished American clergymen contributed their views.[151] In September, the Archbishop of Westminster, Henry Manning, defended Gladstone.[152] In Britain, the debate was followed attentively. Various religious leaders thanked Gladstone for his efforts, and the *Congregationalist Review* published a reprint of Gladstone's article.[153] The content of the various defenses or attacks on Gladstone's position, while interesting, were not usually original; for our purpose they are not vital issues.[154] The point to underline was that Gladstone had publicly confronted the foremost American anti-religious leader, known as 'The Great Agnostic.' He had defended moral and religious standards; his purpose was to redefine the faith and, hopefully, to modify the socio-religious climate of the United States.

Gladstone had a second major interest in American society in the late 1880s – divorce. The rising incidence of divorce in America threatened to destroy the family structure and ultimately society itself, so believed Gladstone. In September 1888, he received a copy of *The Ethics of Marriage* by an American clergyman Henry Sterling Pomeroy. The work tracing the dramatic rise of divorce filled Gladstone with horror.[155] Pomeroy also described the increase in Malthusianism in America, or the practice of sexual restraint to prevent population increases. British secularists Annie Besant, Charles Bradlaugh, and George Holyoake, according to Pomeroy, had 'wrought untold evil in America' because of their flirtation with Malthusianism.[156] While Gladstone did not respond favorably to Pomeroy's request to write an introduction for a future work (*The Malthusian Idea*), he reacted with alarm to the problem. 'I am appalled by the scene which you open. I had heard of the mischief but not of its extent. Although I admit that what I have recently learned about Divorce in America had filled me with alarm.'[157] By November, Gladstone's interest in divorce had expanded significantly. To Sir Walter Phillmore, ecclesiastical lawyer and of the Admiralty Court, he wrote: 'This question of marriage is looming more and more gigantic. I almost believe it is the one cardinal test of the Christian civilization.'[158]

In 1889–90, Gladstone made several strong public pronouncements against divorce and for family unity. First, he reviewed a work, *Faithful and Unfaithful*, by the American novelist Margaret Lee. Here he emphasized that 'the present social life of America offers at all points a profoundly important field of observation.' He singled out for attention the alarming facts that one marriage in every ten was dissolved in Connecticut, and one in every seven in California.[159] Gladstone thought the book so important that he persuaded Alexander Macmillan to publish it in Great Britain.[160] Second, Gladstone wrote an introduction for a pamphlet by Henry Pomeroy, 'Is Man too Prolific?' He had also proved of immense service to Pomeroy by introducing him to British leaders on the latter's British visit in the fall of 1890.[161] Third, Gladstone responded to a questionnaire-letter drawn up by the Secretary of the American Divorce Reform League, Samuel Dike, which had been published in the *North American Review*. The Secretary decried the rise in American divorce from 9937 in 1867 to 25 535 in 1886.[162] Gladstone was only one of the prominent leaders who responded to Dike's letter.[163] He turned yet again to the important lessons of the United States.

> For I incline to think that the future of America is of greater importance to Christendom at large than that of any other country; that that future, in its highest features, vitally depends upon the incidents of marriage; and that no country has ever been so directly challenged as America now is to choose its course definitively with reference to one, if not more than one, of the very greatest of these incidents.[164]

Many other respondents to Dike's letter agreed with Gladstone: that the rise of divorce would lead to the alarming collapse of the family structure. However, Ingersoll typically argued against the grain. He claimed that divorce was a justifiable way for women to preserve their individuality and hence maintain family unity.[165] Margaret Lee disagreed with Ingersoll. Both woman and man should honor the initial marriage contract. 'A republic owes its existence and its continuance to the personal purity of its people. Divorce is the disintegrating wedge, and no time should be lost in forcing it out.'[166] Gladstone's part in the American divorce reform movement cannot be measured in the outcome of legislation. That was not substantially forthcoming until the twentieth century. Yet Gladstone's advocacy gave the movement some publicity and indirectly spurred it much further forward than would have been the case had he not participated. Samuel Dike, the Secretary of the Divorce Reform Movement, was the first to acknowledge Gladstone's impact. Pomeroy reported back to Gladstone: 'Dr. Dike referred to the great service rendered to the Divorce Reform Movement by your written words.'[167]

Gladstone played an important role in one more Anglo-American controversy in the years 1889–90, and again the pages of the *North American Review* presented the issue. The rapid industrial progress of the United States and the accumulation of capital that symbolized the Gilded Age had produced immensely wealthy individuals. It was not clear what they might do or ought to do with their fortunes. The problem emerged conspicuously when Andrew Carnegie presented a new theory: that wealthy individuals will administer their fortunes so as to promote the welfare of the community at large.[168] He outlined the seven best ways to dispose of this wealth.[169] Carnegie's views enjoyed an enormous attention in Great Britain, especially after they were reprinted in the *Pall Mall Gazette*. The editor Stead entitled them 'The Gospel of Wealth.'[170] Gladstone was extremely impressed by Carnegie's plans, which managed to bypass the problems inherent in many charity programs. Gladstone was moved to superlatives:

> This self-made *millionaire* has confronted the moral and social problem of wealth more boldly, so far as I know, than any previous writer. He may, like the rest of us, have his infirmities; but his courage and frankness, both of them superlative, are among the attendant virtues, which walk in the train of a munificence not less modest and simple than it is habitual and splendid.[171]

Gladstone called for an association to carry Carnegie's views into practice, one that would regulate the dispensation of fortunes.[172] The Liberal leader's endorsement of Carnegie's idea appears to have been genuine and not merely the result of Carnegie's philanthropic relations with Gladstone. In June 1890, Carnegie had secretly helped Gladstone to save Lord Acton's library from being auctioned to pay debts.[173] Proof of Gladstone's genuine estimation for Carnegie was perhaps best indicated when Gladstone selected the life of the millionaire, steel owner, and scientist Sydney Thomas to extol in the pages of the *Youth's Companion*.[174] The lives of Thomas and Carnegie were very similar, though the former died tragically a young man while the latter lived to an old age. Gladstone thought that Thomas was a man 'to whom I really look up with romance.'[175] The same could be said of his estimation for Carnegie.

Between 1890 and 1892, Gladstone took pride in the fact that Carnegie's 'Gospel of Wealth' found favor with various British leaders. The whole idea was very controversial and it was debated in great detail on both sides of the Atlantic. Thus for instance, Edward Phelps (former American Minister in Britain), Godkin, Ingersoll, Cardinal Gibbons, and Carnegie himself debated the concept of 'wealth' in Liberal periodicals.[176] But it was Gladstone who was the main proponent in England. In private he worked for the formation of an association inspired by Carnegie's views. In March 1892, he reported on his progress to Carnegie. 'I am disappointed in the non-effect of my appeal for *names* of adherents to the principle, made through the *Nineteenth Century*.'[177] On the other hand, Gladstone had found warm support from such leaders as Lord Meath, the Rothschild family, the Archbishop of Canterbury, and Cardinal Manning. Manning's sudden death in 1892 significantly depleted the ranks of Gladstone's supporters; so much so, that Gladstone acknowledged that the time was not right for further organization. 'Only at some day of leisure, if it ever comes, can I venture even to meditate upon the possibility of an organization; but I continue ever more conscious than ever.'[178] It was an underlying element of Gladstone's admiration for Carnegie that the American not only spoke of the need for moral, religious, and philanthropic leadership but actually produced the specific schemes that elevated the condition of the people. Only with such leaders, believed Gladstone, could the United States and Great Britain save themselves from the threatening forces of those with 'wealth.' To Carnegie, he wrote, 'Wealth is at present like a monster threatening to swallow up the moral life of man. You by precept and by example have been teaching him to disgorge. I for one thank you.'[179]

Conclusion

The period between 1886 and 1892 was therefore marked by a series of significant studies of the United States by leading Liberals. Most of the instigating American issues, like protectionism, federalism, bimetallism, divorce, wealth, or copyright, were analogous to problems that faced Liberals in Great Britain. Partly because the Liberals were out of office, they were able to devote considerable time to these American preoccupations. Liberal faith in the great future of the United States developed despite their disappointment in certain practices common there. Belief in Anglo-Saxon racial supremacy carried more weight than isolated though important pressures generating hostile trade and financial policies. Gratefully, in the fall of 1892, the election of Cleveland, a free trader and monometallist, to a second term reaffirmed to Liberals that common sense still reigned supreme in America. Finally, these were the years when both Bryce and Gladstone made great contributions to Anglo-American history. While Bryce's *The American Commonwealth* far surpassed any British study of the United States, Gladstone through his articles challenged popular thinking in a way that the still young Bryce could not have. Gladstone's impact on history was immediate, Bryce's would grow as the brilliance and appreciation of his work became established. The importance of the United States to Liberal leaders was nowhere more aptly stated than by Gladstone. In the early 1890s, he instructed Morley in what he considered the first object of study for every young man: 'the history and working of freedom in America.'[180]

Notes

1. Morley, *Recollections*, 2 vols (London, 1917), i, p. 217.
2. J. A. S. Grenville, *Lord Salisbury and Foreign Policy, the Close of the Nineteenth Century* (London, 1964) and N. E. Johnson, 'The Role of the Cabinet in the Making of Foreign Policy 1885–95, with special reference to Lord Salisbury's second administration' (Oxford Univ. DPhil thesis, 1971).
3. Further evidence that the United States figured prominently in British discussions of their own problems can be seen in the large space devoted to American references in collections of essays published during this period: E. Carpenter, *Civilization: Its Cause and Cure, and Other Essays* (London, 1889); Playfair, *Subjects of Social Welfare* (London, 1889); G. Smith, *Essays on Questions of the Day. Political and Social*, 2nd edn (New York, 1894); and Thomas Farrer's articles (see notes 59 and 63).
4. D. Hamer, *Liberal Politics in the Age of Gladstone and Rosebery. A Study in Leadership and Policy* (Oxford, 1972), p. 161.
5. GP, 44773, 'Gladstone Memorandum,' 8 Mar. 1888, f. 50. James Bryce and Edwin Godkin had a fascinating and close friendship, with much correspondence in the 1880s about American matters. Thus, Bryce admitted to Godkin as early as August 1882, 'Personally, I feel drifting towards some sort of Home Rule but don't like to admit it' (God.P, Bryce to Godkin, 18 Aug. 1882 (78)). For the Bryce–Godkin friendship, see H. Tulloch, *James Bryce's American Commonwealth: The Anglo-American Background* (Woodbridge, 1988), pp. 94–9.

J. Bryce's *The American Commonwealth*, 3 vols (New York, 1888) owed a great deal to the American Mugwump tradition (Seth Low, Dennis Kearney, Richard Gilder, and Frank Goodnow) and especially Edwin Godkin; to whom he wrote 'how much more I am indebted to you than to any other source for the views I have formed, both to your letters and talk and to the Nation articles' (God.P, Bryce to Godkin, 22 Oct. 1888 (105)).

6. J. Kendle, *Ireland and the Federal Solution: The Debate over the United Kingdom Constitution, 1870–1921* (Kingdom and Montreal, 1989), pp. 57–74.

7. H. Tulloch, 'The Anglo-American Background of James Bryce's *American Commonwealth*' (Cambridge University PhD thesis, 1974), p. 176.

8. Essay IV, 'The Constitution of the United States' in H. Maine's *Popular Government* (London, 1885), (pp. 196–254) roused particularly strong responses from Godkin and Morley. Godkin, 'An American View of Popular Government,' *NC*, vol. xix (Feb. 1886), pp. 177–90 and Morley, 'Sir H. Maine on Popular Government.' *FR*, vol. xxxix (Feb. 1886), pp. 153–73.

9. B. Lippincott, *Victorian Critics of Democracy* (Minnesota, 1938), p. 167. Lippincott also found many weaknesses in Maine's attacks on democracy (pp. 189–206).

10. Maine, *Popular Government*, p. 253.

11. Godkin, 'An American View of Popular Government,' p. 182. Maine responded to this article with one of his own. In it, he claimed that all along he had sought to claim how admirably American democracy/federalism had coped with government. However, he also pointed out that violent riots in California against Chinese immigration were representative of the evil characteristic of democracy. 'Mr. Godkin on Popular Government,' *NC*, vol. xx (Nov. 1886), pp. 375–6.

12. Morley, 'Sir H. Maine on Popular Government,' pp. 155–6. Goldwin Smith came to the support of Godkin and Morley in his denunciations of Maine's thesis. 'The Moral of the Late Crisis,' *NC*, vol. xx (Sept. 1886), pp. 313–21.

13. A. V. Dicey, *England's Case against Home Rule* (London 1886), p. 178.

14. Ibid., pp. 169–74.

15. Ibid., p. 189. Also see, A. V. Dicey, 'Can the English Constitution be Americanized?' *The Nation*, vol. xlii (Jan. 1886), p. 73. Dicey also wrote in *The Nation*: 'The plain truth is that educated Englishmen are slowly learning that the American republic affords the best example of a conservative democracy; and now that England is becoming democratic, respectable Englishmen are beginning to consider whether the Constitution of the United States may not afford means by which, under new democratic forms, may be preserved the political conservatism dear and habitual to the governing classes of England.' 21 Jan. 1886; cited in Tulloch, *James Bryce's American Commonwealth*, p. 114.

16. God.P, Bryce to Godkin, 1 Aug. 1886 (93).

17. Godkin, vol. xix, pp. 793–806.

18. God.P, Spencer to Godkin, 9 Aug. 1886 (979) and M. Arnold to Godkin, 3 Oct. 1887 (29).

19. Godkin, 'A Lawyer's Objections to Home Rule,' in J. Bryce, *Handbook of Home Rule* (London, 1887), pp. 136–9. Also see, Bryce to Godkin, 29 May 1887 (97).

20. Godkin, 'A Lawyer's Objections to Home Rule,' p. 142.

21. Ibid., pp. 143–4.
22. 2 August 1886, cited in Gardiner, *The Life of Sir William Harcourt*, 2 vols (London, 1923), ii, pp. 4–5.
23. Surprisingly, Michael Hurst has little to say about the role of federalism at the Round Table Conference in his *Joseph Chamberlain and Liberal Reunion, the Round Table Conference of 1887* (London, 1967).
24. HP, Box 11, Harcourt to Gladstone, 14 Jan. 1887, f. 36 and Box 16, Harcourt to Morley, 17 Jan. 1887, f. 83.
25. Ch.P, Chamberlain to Morley, 3 Jan. 1888, JC 5/54/716.
26. GP, 44500, Rathbone to Gladstone, 18 Mar. 1887, ff. 164–5. Also see, Hansard, 3rd series, cccxxvi, 11 June 1888, 1726–7.
27. GP, 44255, Morley to Gladstone, 5 Oct. 1887, f. 222.
28. Ibid., 44502, E. Pierrepont to Gladstone, 25 Oct. 1887, ff. 59–60. Pierrepont also reported to Gladstone on a meeting Disraeli had had with the Queen in 1877. The Conservative Prime Minister had advocated a federal solution to Ireland, similar to the relationship between New York and the United States Government. Ibid., 44501, 30 Sept. 1877, ff. 321–5. Further articles that Gladstonian Liberals examined were: Marquis Lorne, 'Transatlantic Lessons on Home Rule,' *CR*, vol. 1 (July 1886), pp. 128–36; Albert Shaw, 'The American State and the American Man,' *CR*, vol. li (May 1887), pp. 694–711; G. Smith, 'The Canadian Constitution,' *CR*, vol. lii (July 1887), pp. 1–20; E. L. Godkin, 'American Opinion on the Irish Question,' *NC*, vol. xxii (Oct. 1887), pp. 285–92; C. R. Lowell, 'English and American Federalism,' *FR*, vol. xliii (Feb. 1888), pp. 189–95; E. J. Phelps, 'The Constitution of the United States,' *NC*, vol. xxiii (Feb. and Mar. 1888), pp. 297–316 and 441–57; and Albert Shaw, 'The American State Legislatures,' *CR*, vol. lvi (Oct. 1889), pp. 555–73.
29. GP, 44773, 'Gladstone Memo,' 8 Mar. 1888, f. 46. See H. C. G. Matthew, *The Gladstone Diaries, Vol. XII. 1887–1891* (Oxford, 1994), pp. 104–5 for the complete letter. Also see, ibid., 'Irish Government. Points prepared for Conversation. Dec. 18, 89,' pp. 252–4.
30. GP, 'Gladstone Memo,' 10 Mar. 1888, f. 50.
31. Ibid. In the same year, Gladstone argued: 'But what America supplies is an example, on the largest scale, of a successful division between Imperial and local functions, even in a case where the central power is secondary, and is limited to certain stipulated offices.' 'Further Notes and Queries on the Irish Demand,' *CR*, vol. liii (Nov. 1888), p. 332.
32. BP, 10, Gladstone to Bryce, 3 Oct. 1889, ff. 93–4. Bryce acknowledged that it was Gladstone who 'at Hawarden in January 1884' urged him to write 'a survey of American political and social life.' BP, 12, Bryce to Gladstone, 15 Oct. 1889, f. 16.
33. *The American Commonwealth*, i, pp. 536–7.
34. Ibid., i, p. 462.
35. Harrison, 'Mr. Bryce's American Commonwealth,' *NC*, vol. xxv (Jan. 1889), pp. 140–8 and Smith, 'The American Commonwealth,' *MM*, vol. lix (Feb. 1889), pp. 241–53.
36. Speech at Saltney, 26 Oct. 1889, cited in A. Hutton and H. Cohen (eds), *The Speeches and Public Addresses of the Right Hon. W.E. Gladstone M.P.* vols ix–x (London, 1892–94), p. 138.

37. GP, 44487, Gladstone to Smalley, 4 Oct. 1884, f. 258.
38. Morley, *NC*, vol. xxv (Aug. 1889), p. 327. The American publishers Dodd, Mead & Co. asked Morley to write a life of Washington. Though tempted, he declined. Ironically, when he received the request, he was in the middle of reading a life of Washington. RP, 10045, Morley to Rosebery, 25 Jan. 1890, ff. 166–8.
39. E. A. Freeman, *Greater Greece and Greater Britain, and George Washington the Expander of England* (London, 1886), especially pp. 100–3, and W. Reid, *Memoirs and Correspondence of Lyon Playfair* (London, 1899), i, pp. 361–4. Also see, G. Smith, 'American Statesman,' *NC*, vol. xxiii (Jan. 1888), pp. 93–114 and (June 1888), pp. 881–92 and vol. xxiv (Aug. 1888), pp. 262–75.
40. *Report of the Westminster Palace Hotel Conference, 29 July 1884, London* (London, 1884) (Rhodes House Library, Oxford).
41. M. D. Burgess, 'Lord Rosebery and the Imperial Federation League, 1884–1893,' *The New Zealand Journal of History*, vol. xiii, no. ii (Oct. 1979), p. 170.
42. Speech at Edinburgh and East of Scotland Branch of the Imperial Federation League, 31 Oct. 1888, RP, 10176, ff. 6–7.
43. Seeley, *The Expansion of England. Two Courses of Lectures* (London, 1883), p. 160. Deborah Wormell discusses Seeley's almost blind adulation of many American institutions: *Sir John Seeley and the Uses of History* (Cambridge, 1980), p. 162.
44. J. Froude, *Oceana, or, England and Her Colonies* (London, 1886), p. 304. For Froude's American relationships, including close friendships and lecture tours, see W. Dunn, *James Anthony Froude. A Biography*, 2 vols (Oxford, 1961–63).
45. For the origins and development of Anglo-Saxonism in Britain in the nineteenth century, see: R. Horsman, 'Origins of Racial Anglo-Saxonism in Great Britain Before 1850,' *Journal of the History of Ideas*, vol. xxxvii (July–Sept. 1976), pp. 387–410; and L. P. Curtis, *Anglo-Saxons and Celts: A Study of Anti-Irish Prejudice in Victorian England* (London, 1968), especially pp. 98–107.
46. Speech at Edinburgh, 31 Oct. 1888, cited in RP, 10176, f. 9. Also see speech to Leeds Chamber of Commerce, 11 Oct. 1888, cited in ibid., ff. 1–4.
47. Chamberlain: *New York Herald*, 3 Mar. 1888; *The Times*, 18 Feb. 1888; *Birmingham Daily Gazette*, 29 Mar. 1888; and *Birmingham Daily Post*, 9 Jan. 1889; Dilke, *Problems of Greater Britain*, 2 vols (London, 1890); Stead, *RR*, vol. i, no i (Jan. 1890), pp. 15–20; Carnegie: 'Imperial Federation: An American View,' *NC* , vol. xxx (Sept. 1891), pp. 490–508; and Shaw, 'An American View of Home Rule and Federation,' *CR*, vol. lxii (Sept. 1892), pp. 305–18.
48. GP, 44547, Gladstone to Smalley, 4 Oct. 1884, ff. 120–1. This letter is the subject of an article by F. Herrick, 'Gladstone and the Concept of the "English-speaking Peoples,"' *JBS*, vol. xii (1972), pp. 150–6.
49. 'The Future of the English-Speaking Races,' *YC*, vol. lx (1 Nov. 1888), p. 558.
50. Ibid.
51. K. Sandiford, 'Gladstone and Liberal-Nationalist Movement,' *Albion*, vol. xiii, no. i (Spring 1981), p. 28. W. T. Stead also argued frequently on behalf of 'English-speaking unions' in his *Review of Reviews* and *James Russell Lowell. His Message, and How it Helped Me* (London, 1892).

52. V. Bogdanor, *Devolution* (Oxford, 1979), p. 16.
53. Hamer, *Liberal Politics in the Age of Gladstone*, p. 169.
54. B. Brown, *The Tariff Reform Movement in Great Britain, 1880–1895* (New York, 1943), pp. 58–84. Also see, Anthony Howe, *Free Trade and Liberal England 1846–1946* (Oxford, 1997).
55. PP, *Depression of Trade and Industry. Second Report: Minutes of Evidence and Appendix, Part I* (1886) XXI, C. 4715, p. 251.
56. Brown, *The Tariff Reform Movement*, pp. 63–4.
57. ii, p. 350.
58. See Chamberlain's speeches during his 1888–89 American trip in Maycock, *Mr. Chamberlain in the United States* and Dilke's *Problems of Greater Britain*, 2 vols (London, 1890), especially ii, pp. 332–57.
59. Farrer was a keen student of the United States with many close American friends. In 1886, he had made a fact-finding American visit and he was particularly intimate with E. Godkin, E. Atkinson, D. A. Wells, and the expatriated G. Smith. Godkin greatly enjoyed his stays with Farrer at Abinger Hall from 1889 onwards. D. A. Wells, in particular, encouraged Farrer and other Britons to look at the American impact upon the British trade depression. 'The Great Depression of Trade,' *CR*, vol. lii (Aug. and Sept. 1887), pp. 275–93 and 381–401, and 'The Fall of Prices,' vol. lii (Oct. and Nov. 1887), pp. 523–48 and 628–43.
60. God.P, Farrer to Godkin, 12 Oct. 1887 (275).
61. W. Reid, *Memoirs of Playfair*, p. 367.
62. GP, 44280, Playfair to Gladstone, 30 Nov. 1887, f. 221.
63. Farrer, *Free Trade versus Fair Trade* (edns 1882, 1885, and 1886); *The State and its Relation to Trade* (1883); *Shall We Retaliate on Sugar Bounties?* (1888); *The Sugar Convention* (1889); *The Sugar Convention and Bill. Letters to The Daily News* (1889); and *Retaliation and Commercial Federation* (1891) (pamphlets: Bodleian Library, Oxford).
64. Farrer, *The Sugar Convention*, p. 68.
65. Speech on 'The Effect of Production on Wages' at Leeds, 1 Dec. 1888, cited in Playfair, *Subjects of Social Welfare* (London, 1889), pp. 166–9.
66. Ibid., p. 181.
67. Ibid., pp. 181–2. For other comments by Playfair about American protectionism see 'Depression of Agriculture and Trade,' *Subjects of Social Welfare*, pp. 107–25 and 'The Presidential Election in the United States,' *NC*, vol. xxiv (Dec. 1888), pp. 785–98.
68. GP, 44773, 'Paper on Protection in America: For Fair Play All Round,' Apr. 1889, f. 96. See H. C. G. Matthew, *The Gladstone Diaries. Vol. XII. 1887–1891*, pp. 169–70. Gladstone delayed his article, eventually published in 1890, because 'it would have been impertinent of me … to accept the invitation of Mr. McKay whilst the Presidential contest was yet pending' (*NAR*, cl. 2).
69. GP, 44773, 'Paper on Protection in America,' ff. 96–100, *passim*.
70. L. Trainor, 'The British Government and Imperial Economic Unity, 1890–1895,' *HJ*, vol. xiii, no. i (1970), p. 69.
71. H. Faulkner, *Politics, Reform and Expansion, 1890–1900* (New York, 1963), pp. 105–8.
72. Brown, *The Tariff Reform Movement*, pp. 74–80.

73. vol. ix (July–Dec. 1890), pp. 399–401 and 715–30.
74. Gladstone and Blaine, 'A DUEL. Free Trade – The Right Hon. W. E. Gladstone and Protection – The Hon. James G. Blaine,' *NAR*, vol. cl (Jan. 1890), pp. 1–50.
75. GP, 44508, L. Bryce to Gladstone, 12 Nov. 1889, f. 136.
76. Gladstone, 'Free Trade,' p. 1.
77. Ibid., p. 25.
78. Ibid., p. 26.
79. GP, 44510, L. Bryce to Gladstone, 6 May 1890, f. 10.
80. Blaine, 'Protection,' pp. 27–54.
81. R. Mills, 'The Gladstone–Blaine Controversy,' *NAR*, vol. cl (Feb. 1890), pp. 163–5.
82. J. S. Morrill, 'Free Trade or Protection. A Continuation of the Gladstone–Blaine Controversy,' *NAR*, vol. cl (Mar. 1890), p. 281.
83. Carnegie, 'Summing Up the Tariff Discussion,' *NAR*, vol. cli (July 1890), p. 53. William McKinley defended protection in 'The Value of Protection,' *NAR*, vol. cli (June 1890), pp. 740–8.
84. Speech on 'The Tariffs of the United States in Relation to Free Trade,' at Leeds, 13 Nov. 1890, cited in *23 Pamphlets on Free Trade (1889–96)* (Bodleian Library, Oxford), p. 3.
85. Ibid.
86. Speech on 'Free Trade and the McKinley Tariff,' at Dundee, 29 Oct. 1890, cited in Hutton and Cohen (eds), *Speeches of Gladstone*, p. 299.
87. Playfair, 'The Tariffs of the United States,' p. 26.
88. 'Free Trade and the McKinley Tariff,' p. 300.
89. GP, 44280, Playfair to Gladstone, 1 Nov. 1892, f. 233.
90. God.P, Bryce to Godkin, 8 Nov. 1892 (131). For further British and American liberal views, increasingly optimistic over the defeat of protectionism in the United States, see A. Shaw, 'The American Tariff,' *CR*, vol. liv (Nov. 1888), pp. 683–94; G. Smith, 'The American Tariff,' *MM*, vol. lxii (Sept. 1890), pp. 350–6 and 'Exit McKinley,' *MM*, vol. lxiii (Jan. 1891), pp. 161–9; and R. Donald, 'McKinleyism and the Presidential Election,' *CR*, vol. lxii (Oct. 1892), pp. 489–504.
91. R. Kelley, *The Transatlantic Persuasion: The Liberal-Democratic Mind in the Age of Gladstone* (New York, 1969), p. 302. Also see, J. Sproat, *'The Best Men'. Liberal Reformers in the Gilded Age* (New York, 1968), pp. 170–203.
92. For a discussion of these conferences, see H. B. Russell, *International Monetary Conferences* (New York, 1898), *passim*. See also, J. P. Nichols, 'Silver Diplomacy,' *Political Science Quarterly*, xlviii (1933). See note 100 for more on the study of bimetallism.
93. PP, *Report of Committee at the International Monetary Conference (Paris)*, (1879–9) XXI, C. 2196 and *Report of Committee at the International Monetary Conference, Paris* (1881), LXXV (409).
94. Marble's detailed report of his interview with Gladstone is particularly fascinating. Bayard Papers, Box 213, Marble to T. Bayard, 29 July 1885.
95. P. Ghosh, 'Fair Trade Revisited, 1874–1895,' seminar paper delivered at British Modern History Seminar, Oxford, in winter of 1977.
96. PP, *First Report of the Royal Commission appointed to inquire into the recent changes on the relative value of the precious metals* (1888) XLV, C. 5248; *Second*

Report (1888) XLV, C. 5248; and *Final Report* (1888) XLV, C. 5512. Also see, R. Lethridge, 'Bimetallism,' *National Review*, vol. xliii (Sept. 1886), pp. 164–80.
97. *Free Trade and Liberal England, 1846–1946*, p. 200.
98. PP, *Final Report* (1888) XLV, C. 5512, pp. 280–1, 539–46, and 553–4. Also see D.A. Wells, 'Bimetallism,' *CR*, vol. lii (Dec. 1887), pp. 795–814.
99. *The Proceedings of the Bimetallic Conference held at the Westminster Palace Hotel, December 13th, 1888* (Manchester, 1889).
100. E. H. H. Green, 'Rentiers versus Producers? The Political Economy of the Bimetallic Controversy c. 1880–1898,' *EHR*, vol. ciii (July 1988), p. 589. This article is the main comprehensive treatment of the bimetallic controversy and confirms that the interest was great in the subject and generated a vast body of literature during these years. There has been a subsequent debate: see A. C. Howe, 'Bimetallism, c. 1880–1898: a controversy re-opened?' *EHR*, vol. cv (April 1990), pp. 377–91 and E. H. H. Green, 'The Bimetallic Controversy; empiricism believed or the case for the issues,' *EHR*, vol. cv (July 1990), pp. 673–83.
101. Marble Papers, 64, Marble to Rosebery, 9 Oct. 1886, f. 13778. Also see GP, 44498, Marble to Gladstone, 9 Oct. 1886, ff. 84–7.
102. E. Atkinson, *Report Made by Edward Atkinson of Boston, Mass., to the President of the United States, upon the present state of Bimetallism in Europe* (Washington, DC, 1887), p. 6.
103. God.P, Farrer to Godkin, 4 May 1887 (273). Farrer was very concerned about the increasing strength of silver in the American West and South. He asked Godkin to keep him posted on American events. See God.P., Farrer to Godkin, 8 Apr. and 12 Oct. 1888 (274–5).
104. Cited in Playfair, *Subjects of Social Welfare*, p. 195.
105. Playfair, 'The Demas Invitation to Abandon Gold for Silver in the United States,' *Ne.R*, vol. iv (May 1891), p. 121.
106. Ibid., pp. 121–2.
107. GP, 44773, 'Notes on Bimetallism,' April 1889, f. 106.
108. Ibid., f. 107. Mr. Gladstone may have met and talked inevitably with Mr. Atkinson, 15 November 1889. See H. C. G. Matthew, *The Gladstone Diaries. Vol. XII. 1887–1891*, p. 244.
109. Hansard, 3rd series, cccxxxvi, 4 June 1889, 1869–1923 and cccxliii, 18 Apr. 1890, 815–912.
110. Faulkner, *Politics, Reform and Expansion*, pp. 120–1.
111. Playfair, 'The Demas Invitation,' p. 127.
112. Ibid. For other British views of American currency and tariff issues in 1892, see Farrer, 'English Views of the McKinley Tariff,' *The Forum*, vol. xiv (1892), pp. 310–23.
113. *Free Trade and Liberal England, 1846–1946*, p. 203.
114. For general background on transatlantic literary relations, see A. J. Clark, *Movement for International Copyright in Nineteenth Century America* (New York, 1960).
115. An interesting work discussing Anglo-American publishing problems between 1870 and 1900 is D. Welland, *Mark Twain in England* (London, 1978).
116. PP, *Reports, minutes, and evidence of the Royal Commission on laws regulating home, colonial and international copyrights* (1878) XXIV, C. 2036, p. xxvi.

117. Ibid., especially pp. 64–95 and 202–10.
118. British Liberals frequently pressed for Anglo-American copyright agreement. See, for instance, E. Dicey, 'The Copyright Question,' *FR*, vol xix (Jan. 1876), pp. 126–40; T. H. Farrer, 'The Principle of Copyright,' *FR*, vol. xxxviii (Dec. 1878), pp. 836–51; Leonard Courtney, 'International Copyright,' *MM*, vol. xl (June 1879), pp. 61–6; and M. Arnold, 'Copyright,' *FR*, vol. xxvii (Mar. 1880), pp. 319–34.
119. BP, USA 7, American Copyright League to the Department of State, 12 Jan. 1884, f. 4.
120. Ibid., R. U. Johnson to Bryce, 8 Feb. 1887, f. 14.
121. *NC*, vol. xxii (Nov. 1887), pp. 610–24. Pearsall's letter precedes the British responses (pp. 602–10).
122. Ibid., p. 611.
123. BP, 11, 11 Dec. 1887, ff. 188–9.
124. Ibid., USA 7, R. U. Johnson to Bryce, 21 Feb. 1890, ff. 17–18 and 12, Bryce to Gladstone, 2 Mar. 1890, ff. 30–1.
125. *New York Tribune*, 8 Apr. 1890.
126. BP, USA 7, R.U. Johnson to Bryce, 15 Apr. 1890, f. 19.
127. Ibid., 30 Apr. 1891, ff. 33–4.
128. E. A. Freeman, 'International Copyright,' *The Nation*, vol. lii (1890), pp. 259–61; Edmund Gosse, 'The Protection of American Literature,' *FR*, vol. xlviii (July 1890), pp. 56–65; and Frederick Pollock, 'Anglo-American Copyright,' *CR*, vol. lix (Apr. 1891), pp. 602–8.
129. BP, USA 7, R. U. Johnson to Bryce, 7 July 1890, f. 54. Also see, PP, *Correspondence relating to copyright correspondence between the United States and Great Britain* (1890–1), LXXXIII (671).
130. See P. Metcalf, *James Knowles. Victorian Editor and Architect* (Oxford, 1980) for detailed studies of Gladstone's relationship with the *Nineteenth Century*, especially pp. 274–351.
131. BP, 10, 3 Oct. 1889, ff. 93–4.
132. God.P, M. Sands to E. Godkin, 20 Nov. 1888 (925).
133. British and American reactions to Darwinism were well intertwined. See R. Hofstadter, *Social Darwinism in American Thought*, 2nd edn (New York, 1969); C. E. Russett, *Darwin in America: The Intellectual Response 1865–1912* (San Francisco, 1976); and J. R. Moore, *The Post-Darwinian Controversies: A Study of the Protestant Struggle to Come to Terms with Darwin in Great Britain and America 1870–1900* (Cambridge, 1979).
134. The Field and Ingersoll articles first appeared in the *NAR* from August 1887 through January 1888 (vol. cxlv–vi). The articles by Field, Ingersoll, Gladstone, and others which constituted the debate are in *The Works of Robert G. Ingersoll*, 12 vols (New York, 1902), vi, pp. 121–396.
135. Ingersoll, 'A Reply to the Rev. Henry M. Field, D.D.', vol. cxlv (Nov. 1887), p. 481.
136. Ibid.
137. GP, 44502, Rice to Gladstone, 2 Dec. 1888, f. 165.
138. Ibid., f. 166.
139. Metcalf, *James Knowles*, pp, 308–36 and Moore, *Post-Darwinian Controversies*, pp. 65–8.
140. GP, 44503, C. O. Brown to Gladstone, 21 Mar. 1888, f. 105.

141. Ibid., C. Coxe to Gladstone, 19 Apr. 1888, ff. 178–9.
142. Ibid., H. L. Viller to C. Coxe, 17 Apr. 1888, sent to Gladstone by Coxe, 18 Apr. 1888, f. 187.
143. Ibid., H. Smith to Gladstone, 30 May 1888, ff. 278–80.
144. The Gladstone–Ingersoll debate is covered briefly in O. Larson, *American Infidel: Robert C. Ingersoll. A Biography* (New York, 1962), pp. 222–5 and C. H. Cramer, *Royal Bob: The Life of Robert G. Ingersoll* (New York, 1952), pp. 161–5.
145. 'Colonel Ingersoll on Christianity,' vol. cxlvi (May 1888), p. 482.
146. Ibid., p. 483.
147. In private, Ingersoll denounced Gladstone as a 'sentimentalist.' Ingersoll to G. S. Pike, 23 May 1888, cited in *Works of Ingersoll*, viii, p. 297.
148. See Ingersoll's unpublished and undated interview with Gladstone, cited in ibid., ix, pp. 400–2.
149. 'Col. Ingersoll to Mr. Gladstone,' *NAR*, vol. cxlvi (June 1888), p. 615.
150. Ibid., p. 618.
151. Phelps, Collyer, Mendes, and Courdet, 'The Combat for the Faith: The Field–Ingersoll–Gladstone Controversy,' *NAR*, vol. cxlvii (July 1888), pp. 1–36.
152. 'The Gladstone–Ingersoll Controversy,' *NAR*, vol. cxlvii (Sept. 1888), pp. 241–69. Also see Ingersoll, 'Rome or Reason? A Reply to Cardinal Manning,' *NAR*, vol. cxlvii (Oct. and Nov. 1888), pp. 394–414 and 503–24.
153. GP, 44504, J. Guiness Rogers to Gladstone, 11 June and 6 July 1886, ff. 14 and 87.
154. See the Huxley–Ingersoll correspondence over their separate conflicts with Gladstone over Christianity, *Works of Ingersoll*, viii, pp. 309–11.
155. Gladstone wrote to Bryce that divorce was the one great question which needed more treatment than it had received in *The American Commonwealth*. BP, 10, 3 Oct. 1889, f. 94.
156. GP, 44504, Pomeroy to Gladstone, 22 Sept. 1888, f. 275.
157. Ibid., 44505, Gladstone to Pomeroy, 23 Oct. 1888, f. 40. Gladstone did not write the introduction for fear of alienating American opinion.
158. Ibid., 27 Nov. 1888, f. 168.
159. 'Divorce – A Novel,' *NC*, vol. xxv (Feb. 1889), p. 214.
160. Macmillan Co. Papers, 55243, Gladstone to Macmillan, 20 Dec. 1888, f. 39. See Lee's overwhelming appreciation of Gladstone's efforts, which she thought would add tremendous support for their movement. GP, 44506, Lee to Gladstone, 16 Feb. 1889, ff. 55–7.
161. GP, 44510, Pomeroy to Gladstone, 29 Aug. and 5 Sept. 1890, ff. 240–1 and 249.
162. Dike, 'Is Divorce Wrong?' *NAR*, vol. cxlix (Nov. 1889), p. 614 and Gladstone, 'The Question of Divorce,' *NAR*, vol. cxlix (Dec. 1889), pp. 641–4.
163. Others included Ingersoll, Margaret Lee, Supreme Court Justice Joseph Bradley, and Senator Joseph Dolph. Ibid., vols. cxlix–cxlx (Nov. 1889–Feb. 1890).
164. Gladstone, 'The Question of Divorce,' p. 641.
165. Ingersoll, 'Is Divorce Wrong?' *NAR*, vol. cxlix (Nov. 1889), p. 6.
166. M. Lee, 'Final Words on Divorce,' *NAR*, vol. cl (Feb. 1890), p. 264.

167. GP, 44510, H. Pomeroy to Gladstone, 29 Aug. 1890, f. 240. See S. W. Dike, 'The Problem of the Family in the United States,' *CR*, vol. lxiv (Nov. 1893), pp. 724–36.
168. Carnegie, 'Wealth,' *NAR*, vol. cxlviii (June 1889), pp. 653–64.
169. Ibid., 'The Best Fields for Philanthropy,' *NAR*, vol. cxlix (Dec. 1889), p. 692.
170. Gladstone received advance copies of Carnegie's articles. In fact, he was asked to help edit them as well as to write a review upon them by E. T. Cook of the *Gazette*.
171. Gladstone, 'Mr. Carnegie's "Gospel of Wealth": A review and a recommendation,' *NC* , vol. xxviii (Nov. 1890), p. 681.
172. Ibid., p. 692. Gladstone wrote in depth to E. T. Cook on Carnegie's 'Gospel of Wealth': 'I follow Mr. Carnegie in nearly everything he affirms and recommends. My main reservation is prompted by his language respecting the endowment of twenty millions (of dollars) granted with a splendid munificence to Stanford University. My mind is possessed with much misgivings…about the wholesale endowment of offices and places…I have doubts whether it does not raise the market price of the higher education, which it aims at lowering…' Letter in the New York Public Library, and *PMG*, 1 Jan. 1890, cited in H. C. G. Matthew, *The Gladstone Diaries, XII. 1887–91*, p. 257.
173. See GP, 44510 for letters between Gladstone, Carnegie, and lawyer W. D. Freshfield, June and July 1890. See also Owen Chadwick, 'The Acton Library,' in Peter Fox (ed.), *Cambridge University Library: The Great Collections* (Cambridge, 1998), pp, 136–52 and Owen Chadwick, 'With Gladstone,' in *Acton and History* (Cambridge, 1998), pp. 139–85.
174. Gladstone, 'A Rare Young Man' [Sydney Gilchrest Thomas], vol. lxv (Aug. 1892), pp. 402–3.
175. GP, 44513, Gladstone to Carnegie, 3 July 1891, f. 1.
176. A. Carnegie, 'The Advantages of Poverty,' *NC*, vol. xxix (Nov. 1891), pp. 367–85; Gibbons, 'Wealth and Its Obligations,' *NAR*, vol. clii (Apr. 1891), pp. 385–94; Henry Potter, 'The Gospel of Wealth,' *NAR*, vol. clii (May 1891), pp. 513–22; Edward Phelps, 'Irresponsible Wealth,' *NAR*, vol. clii (May 1891), pp. 523–34; R. Ingersoll, 'Is Avarice Triumphant,' *NAR*, vol. clii (June 1891), pp. 671–81; A. Carnegie, 'The A B C of Money,' *NAR*, vol. clii (June 1891), pp. 723–50; and E. L. Godkin, 'The Economic Man,' *NAR*, vol. cliii (Oct. 1891), pp. 491–503.
177. New York Public Library, New York (Gladstone Collection): Gladstone to Carnegie, 8 Mar. 1892.
178. Ibid.
179. Ibid., 19 Aug. 1892.
180. J. Morley, The *Life of William Ewart Gladstone*, 3 vols (London, 1903) iii, p. 491.

5
Liberal Ministries, Ideas, and Andrew Carnegie, 1892–1895

Introduction

In the summer of 1892, following the general election, the Liberals returned to office under their venerable veteran leader Gladstone. Their majority was based tenuously upon the Irish Nationalists as there had been no reconciliation with the Liberal Unionists and Chamberlain. Despite their party's eagerness to produce legislative reforms, the Liberal leaders found the trial of governing more difficult than in 1886. While the Newcastle Programme of 1891 had emphasized a broad progressive platform, Gladstone and his Chief Secretary for Ireland, John Morley, both advocated the single overriding issue of Irish Home Rule. The Chancellor of the Exchequer, Harcourt, eventually advocated local option for the drink trade and reform of the death duties. The Foreign Secretary, later Prime Minister, Rosebery, supported reform of the House of Lords, but his primary enthusiasm was directed towards a more active imperial and foreign policy. However, it was Gladstone who inevitably dominated the content and tone of Liberal affairs, and it was Home Rule that consumed him.

In February 1893, Gladstone introduced his second Home Rule Bill to a packed House of Commons; it was a bill which now provided for the inclusion of 80 Irish MPs at Westminster. After a rancorous and lengthy period of debate, the bill was passed by the House. On 8 September, it was promptly vetoed by the Lords. Thereafter it was only a matter of time before Gladstone retired, for with the defeat of Home Rule he had lost much of his incentive for leadership. Moreover his health was delicate, and in March 1894, Rosebery became Prime Minister. Despite some optimism in the Liberal party, the animosities between the leaders, especially between Rosebery and Harcourt, only grew fiercer and more bitter. The discord thoroughly obstructed the course of government and it was only a matter of time before the Conservatives were returned to power. In June 1895, the Liberals were defeated overwhelmingly at the polls; even Morley lost his seat at Newcastle and Harcourt his at Derby. The party left office disenchanted and dispirited, with a lengthy period of opposition stretching ahead.[1]

Since the 1880s, the Liberal leadership had changed substantially. By 1892, the party had been deprived of the hard-working services of Granville, while Chamberlain, Hartington, Forster, and Argyll had seceded. Dilke had rejoined the Liberal party in 1892, or its radical fringe, but his presence had little political impact. Parnell's death, too, in 1891 had produced a weakened association between the Liberals and the Irish Nationalists. There was no doubt as to the four leading Liberals: Gladstone, Rosebery, Harcourt, and Morley. They were supported by a body of older and experienced past and present Gladstonian Cabinet members, such as Lord Spencer, Lord Kimberley, G. A. Shaw-Lefevre, A. J. Mundella, James Bryce, and Henry Fowler. In addition, they could count upon a group of younger Liberal imperialists, often of radical inclinations, Henry Asquith, Richard Haldane, A. H. D. Acland, Edward Grey, Ronald Munro-Ferguson and Tom Ellis, the new junior whip. Each had his own remedy for the ills of the party, but Gladstone, Rosebery, and Morley stood quite firmly opposed to larger commitments to social reform. Much of the energy and reform impulses – historically associated with the Liberal party – came from a mixture of radicals, Liberal journalists and London leaders sympathetic to the strains of liberalism. Thus Henry Labouchere, T. H. Farrer, Bertram Currie, Liberal Unionist Sir John Lubbock, Sir Lyon Playfair, William T. Stead, James Knowles, and Henry Massingham had strong reservations about the direction of the Liberal party. Nonetheless, they maintained friendly associations with its leaders and influenced the composition and temper of the party.

During the Gladstone and Rosebery ministries of 1892–95, concern with the United States took a modest place compared with the momentous party and national issues at hand. Anglo-American diplomatic incidents of some importance had transpired during Salisbury's government, but these had been solved amicably, though not without some degree of friction. The Washington Fishery Treaty Conference of 1887–88 produced a *modus vivendi* over fishery relations between Canada, Britain, and the United States; the dismissal of the British Minister Lionel Sackville-West had been endured; British and American expansionist drives had been balanced in South America, the Caribbean, and the Far East; and the Bering Sea seal controversy had been settled just prior to the Liberals coming to office.[2] There were no comparable incidents during the Liberal ministry from 1892 to 1895, and on the face of it, there would seem to have been very few American problems. However, closer examination of a wide variety of sources does indicate that the United States occupied the minds of Liberal leaders, in some cases to a greater extent than ever before. In the first place there were American aspects to British foreign policy, most notably over American territorial expansion, international bimetallism, and arbitration treaty negotiations. Second, a host of American features surfaced in the Home Rule debate of 1893. Third, the simultaneous outpouring of Anglo-American calls for currency reform – usually international bimetallism – as a remedy for financial crisis and depression gave an American cast to serious financial issues. Fourth, the Liberal leaders paid increasing attention to American labor and municipal affairs, and took some notice of civil service reform, the condition of the blacks, temperance reform, and women's suffrage. While many of these latter issues had interested Liberals during the 1880s, it was not until the 1890s that evidence existed to suggest that they were more than transient concerns. And lastly, by 1892, Andrew Carnegie's important relationship and involvement with William Gladstone and John Morley underlined a close affinity between American and British liberalism, and warm significant transatlantic friendships.

American foreign policies

While no major Anglo-American diplomatic incidents took place during the Gladstone–Rosebery ministry, the leaders still were responsible for framing positions with regard to changing American foreign policy aims. In the 1890s, the United States had become inspired with a new and larger sense of its destiny and place in the world. Territorial, commercial, and imperial expansion comprised a new value for American businessmen, diplomats, and governments. In 1894, for the first time in the nineteenth century, exports of manufactured goods surpassed imports. Spencerian ideas and Social Darwinism precipitated Americans into a new surge of competition with other nations and peoples. Anglo-Saxon racism was popularized significantly by gifted authors like Captain A. T. Mahan and Josiah Strong.[3] 'In the 1890s Anglo-Saxonism was pervasive and deep rooted in American thinking; its consequences for foreign policy were enormous.'[4] The United States had declined countless opportunities to expand her empire in the earlier part of the century in Hawaii, Samoa, and the Far East. In the 1890s, this all changed. A Republican Congress and an excited American public pressured the reluctant President Cleveland to alter long-held isolationist stances. The Liberal government of 1892–95 was the first British administration to have to construct towards the United States a foreign policy affected by these changing American attitudes regarding the world. The issues which faced the Liberal leaders came to a focus at the Bering Fishery Tribunal in Paris, the International Monetary Conference in Brussels, in a few minor Irish-American incidents, in the proposed United States' annexation of Hawaii, and in its activities in South America.

The American foreign policy of the Liberal government from 1892 to 1895 was almost wholly constructed by the two foreign ministers, first Rosebery and then during Rosebery's premiership, Kimberley.[5] Under these two imperialistic peers, British foreign policy moved increasingly away from Cobdenite–Gladstonian principles of non-intervention, national self-determination, and free trade. Gladstone seemed not to mind this relinquishment of policy control. Henry White, amazed to discover in 1893 that Gladstone knew nothing about the past negotiations regarding an Anglo-American extradition treaty during his 1886 ministry, reported 'I know he [Gladstone] leaves everything concerning foreign affairs to Rosebery.'[6]

On the other hand, both Harcourt, the Chancellor of the Exchequer, and Asquith, the Home Secretary, took some part in formulating official policies towards the United States. Harcourt was responsible for the British position during the Brussels Monetary Conference and Asquith for negotiations over Irish-American imprisonments in British jails. Rosebery and Kimberley worked through official diplomatic channels, while Harcourt and Asquith often resorted to informal influence through American friendships. White played a large role, along with Harcourt and Asquith, in solving Anglo-American differences over Brussels and the Irish-Americans. In fact, a solution to the imprisonment of Irish-Americans in 1892–93 – the sort of problem which had raised immense difficulties for the Liberal government in the 1880s – was settled almost entirely through Asquith's and White's friendship. The issue did not come up either in Cabinet meetings or in important Foreign Office memoranda.[7]

While various Gladstonians did not object in principle to freeing some of the dynamiters, they perceived 'that a general release of the dynamiters would be sufficient to turn the Government out of office.'[8] In the end, the American and British governments appear to have abided largely by White's and Asquith's advice; there was little public or official notice of the various solutions to the Irish-American dynamiters' problem in 1893.[9] Throughout the two Liberal ministries, Asquith and particularly Harcourt, maintained close personal American friendships which underlined desires for larger Anglo-American accords.

Liberal leaders more or less ignored the new American aggressive spirit demonstrated in their activities in Hawaii and South America. This lack of Liberal interest in American foreign policy is also noticeable in the absence of concern over the Bering Sea negotiations in 1893. The Paris tribunal met from March until August – it awarded Britain the sum of $473 151 in August – but the issue, as one historian has noted, surprisingly received hardly any attention at all in Liberal cabinets between 1892 and 1894.[10] In 1893, a revolution in the Hawaiian Islands led to a combination of Hawaiian revolutionaries and American expansionists trying to push through the Senate legislation aimed at annexing the islands. A few Anglo-American liberals, E. L. Godkin and William P. Garrison, and James Bryce, watched the issue closely. They praised President Cleveland when he successfully defeated the effort. Thus in Garrison's view, he became as great a President as Abraham Lincoln.[11] Other Liberals maintained an aloof silence, typical of almost all leading parliamentarians. 'Rosebery has been judicious in observing such complete silence; and on the whole our press has taken the matter quite quietly, partly not thinking the thing could go on, partly not caring.'[12] Dr J. Smith, who has made an extensive study of Anglo-American rivalries in Latin America in the later nineteenth century, underlines Liberal disinterest in American moves in Brazil, Nicaragua and other similar places.

> In spite of occasional alarmist dispatches from Washington, the British government tended to discount these American threats and suspicions... Though they were no doubt aware of American commercial designs on Brazil, British officials were not particularly concerned and certainly never sought to exploit the situation in order to gain anything at all.[13]

Similarly, historian Paul Kennedy found no trace of British concern over American and German designs upon the Samoan Islands in the early 1890s.[14] In general, whether in Central or South America, the Hawaiian or the Samoan Islands, Liberals as with other groups in England ignored American expansionist objectives. If there was any method in such a stance it was that the best thing for Anglo-American relations was to do and say nothing. Perhaps Kimberley best summed up the British attitude: 'We have no real interest in the Mosquito [Nicaragua] except to avoid the annoyance such insects inflict on us in consequence of our old engagements – and, what is more important, to avoid ruffling the U.S. susceptibilities.'[15]

In the winter of 1894–95, some Liberal leaders awoke to the importance of framing a more precise foreign policy with regard to American aims in South America. Nicaragua unilaterally took over the Mosquito Coast, which Britain had for years protected, ostensibly in the interest of the native Indians. She expelled the British consul at Bluefields as well as other British and American citizens, actions which deeply perturbed the British government. From August 1894 to February 1895, she considered various options for action and collected information. Carnegie warned Morley: 'You are playing with fire in Nicaragua. There is no question short of rebellion, upon which the American people can be so influenced, as that of a European power touching one of our Sister Republics.'[16]

Despite the warning, Britain moved ahead with an aggressive policy towards the Nicaraguans. On 26 February, she demanded an apology and reparations, and on 27 April, British marines seized the town of Corinto. Although the American press and public raged against the British affrontery, Secretary of State Walter Gresham prevailed. The United States did not intervene.[17] Nonetheless, the Corinto affair produced a significant division in the American foreign policy of the Liberal government.

A major clash between Harcourt and Rosebery over British policy regarding Nicaragua occurred in April 1895. It paralleled the vicious battles between the two Liberal leaders at the same time over other issues. According to Peter Stansky, 'Disagreement over Egypt and the Nile was the major contention between Harcourt and Morley – but practically any issue, foreign or domestic, could serve them as a battlefield.'[18] At a Cabinet meeting on 21 November 1894, it had been agreed 'to send instructions to seize the port of Corinto on the Pacific coast, until reparation is given by Nicaragua for its ill-treatment of British subjects.'[19] On the other hand, there evidently had been some tacit understanding between Harcourt and Rosebery not to act more aggressively in the future without calling a Cabinet meeting. By April 1895, Rosebery and Harcourt were on such poor terms that Rosebery did not want to jeopardize governmental policy by divisive formal meetings. The Prime Minister was adamant that Britain should not let insignificant Latin American republics get away with aggression against Great Britain. No concessions were to be made,[20] Kimberley supported his chief:

> The question is not easy to dispose of. If whenever one of these petty S. Americans ill treats British subjects we submit the question of redress to arbitration, we shall have no end of trouble. The insolence of these wretched little States is beyond bearing, and Nicaragua is perhaps the worse of them. Nothing but a sharp lesson from time to time will keep them in order, or secure decent treatment for foreigners.[21]

Harcourt meanwhile stood unequivocally for arbitration between Nicaragua and Great Britain. 'We are always making loud professions of our readiness to adopt arbitration in place of force and if we refuse it in a case of this kind, which is trumpery enough, the hypocrisy of such pretences will become apparent.'[22] When Rosebery refused to convene a Cabinet meeting and instead went forward with the order that led to the seizure of Corinto by British marines on 27 April, Harcourt's wrath against Rosebery reached new heights.[23] He appealed to Kimberley:

> After the assurance you had given me that the Cabinet should be consulted before forcible measures were resorted to in Nicaragua I can only regard your letter of the 17th [April] received to-day (to employ your favourite phrase) as a highly 'unfriendly' proceeding.
>
> The refusal of Lord Rosebery to reserve a question of this importance for the Cabinet on the request of the Foreign Secretary and the remonstrance of the Leader of the House of Commons is according to my experience without precedent.[24]

Harcourt was not aware that Kimberley supported Rosebery.

The Harcourt–Rosebery discord was significant. The whole question of Anglo-American arbitration had become caught up in a personal battle between the two Liberal leaders over Nicaragua. Only with this in mind is it possible to understand why Harcourt became so active on behalf of Anglo-American arbitration over Venezuela in 1895–96, and why Rosebery was so relatively silent. Arbitration had become very much Harcourt's policy early in 1895. The sad irony of the whole Nicaraguan business was that, had there not been a Rosebery–Harcourt imbroglio, an important Anglo-American settlement might well have come to pass. In April 1895, the American Secretary of State Gresham

sent a private and highly confidential letter to Rosebery in which he outlined the American government's desire for a full understanding with
Britain. It urged Anglo-American cooperation over the two countries'
activities in the South American area. It was a remarkably direct and
unusual move, one apparently which until now has been buried in the
private correspondence of Sir Cecil Spring-Rice.[25] Evidently, Rosebery
did not make known the offer to Harcourt or other leading Liberals.
Thus the Liberal party in their closing months of office ignored an
opportunity to repair personal as well as Anglo-American animosities,
and to stamp their name on a diplomatic arbitration with the United
States which was to become a Unionist achievement in 1896.

Irish Home Rule: American federal and constitutional experiences

During most of the fourth Gladstone ministry the main issue was Irish
Home Rule. It stood firmly centered in the minds of Gladstone and
Morley and 'obstructed' social reforms, temperance, Welsh disestablishment and other measures.[26] As the previous chapter traced, Liberal
leaders carefully weighed the American federal and constitutional
experience in their search for remedies for the constitutional reconstruction of Ireland. At one point in 1888, even Parnell and Gladstone
had considered the American system as 'a practical point of departure'
for Irish Home Rule.[27] In February 1893, Gladstone presented the
Second Bill to the House in a magisterial and moving speech. Both
prior to its introduction and in its aftermath, American parallels, precedents, and analogies again assumed specific importance in debates in
the House, newspapers and periodicals. While it would be inappropriate to attach great significance to these, they were nonetheless
contributing currents in the mainstream of the debates.[28]

The Gladstonian Liberal and Liberal Unionist debate on the American
background to and presence in the Home Rule question was portrayed
strongly by a confrontation between Gladstone and the Duke of Argyll.
In the fall of 1892, they clashed angrily in the pages of the *North
American Review* in a conspicuous and well publicized confrontation.
The editor, Lloyd Bryce, precipitated the incident when he asked Argyll
for an article which placed the Home Rule question fairly before
Americans. Argyll responded enthusiastically, glad to address friends
whom he believed misconstrued the whole matter of Irish Home
Rule.[29] The aristocratic Scottish landowner stressed the conception that
the British were fighting to save the union just as the North had done

in the 1860s. 'Americans, therefore, may depend upon it that we feel that we are fighting the same battle they fought against "Secession," and against the breaking up of our national unity.'[30] Argyll further implied that Gladstone, hostile to the objectives of the North in 1862 and now opposed to union in Britain in 1892, was a traitor in both instances. Finally, Argyll warned Americans that Gladstone wanted to give Ireland far more autonomy than that given to American states. The Liberal chief had made no provision for protecting minorities and his references to Irish history were inaccurate.[31]

It is doubtful whether anybody could have written an article more galling to Gladstone's sensitivities. Argyll, who had been an old friend of Gladstone's until 1886, had spitefully resurrected his 'misdeed' of 1862. Gladstone minced no words in his reply. First and foremost, he contended that in his aims he had the unanimous support of the American people, despite what Argyll claimed. He cited the report of a prominent American Republican (probably Carnegie) who had told him that twelve and a half out of thirteen million American voters 'would be favorable to the cause of Ireland.'[32] Gladstone attacked Argyll for ignorance of American constitutional history.

> The writer thinks that the rights of the American States are those which the Federal constitution 'gives' to them, and seems unaware that the powers of the Federal constitution are exclusively powers given, or in the language of the constitution itself, 'delegated' to it by the States, who acquired their respective sovereignties by the Declaration of Independence and the treaty that put an end to the war … If the Duke has read those amendments, which may be doubted, he must be aware that among the fifteen articles of which they consist, there is not one which could gall the withers of the Irish Nationalism [sic], least of all those which relate to slavery. Article XIII prohibits slavery and involuntary servitude except for crime; and Article XV provides that personal rights are not to be denied or abridged on account of race, color, or previous condition of servitude.[33]

Whereas Argyll had underlined the parallels between America in 1862 and Britain in 1892, Gladstone drew the analogy between the States in the 1780s and Britain in 1892. It was, as he saw it, a matter of two peoples equally searching for self-government in the face of repressive governmental attitudes. In conclusion, Gladstone praised the whole American experience as a model for the Liberals' own plan. Support for his argument came from Argyll's own words, taken from a letter to *The Times* in 1885. 'The United States alone, of all the nations of the earth, must in this matter be our great exemplar.'[34]

In the months between the Gladstone–Argyll altercation and Gladstone's Home Rule Bill introduced on 13 February 1893, Americans and Englishmen argued repeatedly over the American references. Nobody was more bitter than the expatriated Liberal Unionist Goldwin Smith. In a series of letters in *The Times*, he thoroughly denounced Gladstone for confusing and alienating Americans with appeals to their pro-Irish sympathies.[35]

Albert Shaw, a regular writer on American affairs for Percy Bunting's *Contemporary Review* during this period, argued strongly on behalf of Gladstone. Americans, he wrote, 'agree with an absolute unanimity' about Home Rule. They did so because of their unwavering belief in the 'federative balance.' 'It is the sense of reasonableness and fair play, guided by the practical knowledge of federal government in the United States, that has always made Americans so perfectly sure that they favoured Home Rule for Ireland.'[36] Shaw went even further than Gladstone when he called for the development of federation among members of the British Empire, perhaps of the English-speaking races.[37] An unidentified author, T. Raleigh, responded to Shaw's article with a lengthy and trenchant rebuttal. Even the inveterate supporter of a federal Home Rule plan, W. T. Stead, found Raleigh's arguments substantial particularly in the second half of his essay.[38] Did Great Britain want a system where there would be forty legislative bodies, marriage laws, and so forth, creating, unavoidably, a most cumbersome administration? Raleigh blamed federalism in the United States for many of the country's social and political evils: complex laws, a 'spoils system,' high homicide rates, poor prison conditions, and defective state ballot laws. 'These examples (it would be easy to add to their number) may serve to illustrate some of the weaknesses of American Home Rule.'[39] Yet, Stead was in the end unconvinced by such observations and confident in federal solutions. He suggested that federalism might serve to bring about a reconciliation both of Chamberlain and the Gladstonians, as well as between the United States and Great Britain.

> Mr. Chamberlain, it may be replied, sees that the American State system supplies us with invaluable hints as to the necessary decentralisation of our Constitution. The promotion of the *rapprochement* between the American Republic and the British Empire cannot

better be pursued than by the attempt to graft the federal principle upon the English chaotic and paralytic centralisation system. There can be no doubt about the fact, that if we are not to break up the Empire, we must Americanise our Constitution. Mr. Gladstone dimly sees this. Mr. Morley is groping towards it. Why should not Mr. Chamberlain boldly face the situation, and abandoning his perilous sojournings among the tents of Kedar, return to the Liberal party in order to enable them to carry out this great ideal?[40]

In the period preceding the introduction of the Second Home Rule Bill, Gladstone and his opponents continued to focus on the federal and American aspects of possible legislation. Gladstonians in general admired the American experience, while Liberal Unionists and Conservatives usually remained critical, favorable to the United States in only one instance. 'The cause of the Unionist Party is Lincoln's cause – the supremacy of the National Government is a matter of national concern; and when we have won our battle Mr. Shaw and his countrymen will see that we were right.'[41]

On 13 February 1893, Gladstone presented his Second Home Rule Bill. It was very much like his first measure except that 80 Irish MP's were to be included in the Westminster Parliament. They would be free to vote on Irish as well as imperial matters, but not on issues specifically related to Scotland, England and Wales. This proposal constituted a distinct move towards federalism. Control was to be maintained by a central government, with Ireland and England maintaining separate authority to legislate over their own local affairs. It was a limited call for federalism, in that Scotland, Wales, Canada, Australia, and other parts of the Empire would not enjoy similar relationships to the central government. The *Spectator* reported Gladstone's measure as 'The Creeping-On of Federalism,'[42] and *The Times* deplored his use of 'well-worn examples of federal and autonomous Governments.'[43]

In the immediate aftermath, Conservatives and Liberal Unionists reacted with alarm at the inaccurate use of the American federal comparison. Salisbury declared that he was 'absolutely ignorant' of federal parallels and that it was foolish to contend such issues. 'But is it the American Constitution which is to appear in this measure "to amend the provision for the government of Ireland?" '[44] Balfour spoke much more derisively in the Commons.

A Federal Government may be good. Colonial Government may be good. The British Constitution as it stands may be good; but this bastard combination of the three is ludicrous and impossible, and the very attempt to force it down our throats appears to me to argue an ignorance of the past patent lessons of history which I am surprised at in the gentlemen of the learning of those whom I see opposite me.[45]

On the other hand, Liberals defended the use of historical, federal, and American analogies. Bryce, the unquestioned authority on American matters, objected vehemently to Balfour's constant negative references to foreign federal precedents, such as those of Germany, Austria-Hungary, and the United States. He asked Balfour: '... – did he not know that the United States hold together their vast territories, from the Atlantic to the Pacific, because they have embodied in their Constitution a far more complicated system of local autonomy than that to which the right hon. Gentleman objects in this Bill.'[46]

In subsequent Commons debate on the bill, other Liberals, such as Labouchere, Rathbone, and Courtney, as well as Bryce, continued to refer to various positive qualities of the American federal experience.[47] The Conservatives did not relent in their attack. Balfour declared: 'I do not believe that this childish imitation of the American Constitution is either fitted to the needs of our people or commends itself to the judgement of our people.'[48]

The specific reasons why American federalism differed from Gladstone's bill and why federalism was not applicable in Great Britain were put best by Gladstone's fierce antagonist Goldwin Smith. In one of a remarkable series of attacks upon Home Rule in the *Pall Mall Gazette* (no longer Liberal since Henry Cust assumed the editorship),[49] Smith argued that 'no example can be less pertinent than that so persistently urged of American or Canadian federation.'[50] In the New World, states and provinces were taxed locally and federally and while running their own affairs had equal shares in the central government. 'What Mr. Gladstone proposes is to place Ireland on the footing of a vassal kingdom without any share in the central government or the highest functions of the nation, and paying a tribute in the expenditure of which it is not to have a voice.'[51] Smith deplored the fact that the Irish MP's were not free to vote on army, navy, customs, trade, or foreign relations, while Ireland herself was taxed for the maintenance of the central government. He concluded his article with vicious personal attacks on Gladstone, whose popularity in America was due not to the merits of his proposal but to traditional hatred of Britain.[52] On the whole, Smith, Balfour, and Salisbury steadily opposed the Gladstonians' federal and American references. They also made the mistake of the Gladstonians themselves. They did not always bother to distinguish whether they were referring to specific American experiments or federalism generally. Their opposition thus often tended to take on the character of opposition to the United States and federalism, as well as to Gladstone's bill.

Chamberlain's position cannot be ignored. In 1886, he flirted with federalism and Home Rule all round, but in 1893, he chose to ignore references to federalism and the possible constitutional qualities of the United States. Privately, he had checked on certain facts about the Constitution at least once with Henry White,[53] but he did not mention federalism as such or the United States in two lengthy articles which he published upon Home Rule.[54] On one occasion Chamberlain criticized Bryce for a reference to the American Constitution which only demonstrated his own ignorance; and on another he referred Parliament to the authority of Bryce.[55] Chamberlain's earlier sympathy with federalism had been usurped by the Gladstonians. Certainly, he preferred not to raise the issue or openly attack a position which he had earlier supported. His opposition thus centered on specific weakness of financial clauses and the lack of provisions for Ulster.

Between 1892 and 1894, there was a shift of Conservative and Liberal Unionist opinion towards the American Constitution and the use of the American analogy for the British experience in one particular case. While the Home Rule Bill passed the second reading in the Commons by 347 to 304 and the third by 301 to 267, it was defiantly defeated in the Lords on 8 September 1893 by 419 to 41. Liberals turned increasingly to focus all their frustrations and energies on the Upper House. Even for leaders like the aristocratic Rosebery, the reform of the Lords became a central issue. The Conservatives and Liberal Unionists discovered the merits of the protection against hasty constitutional amendments in the American Constitution. Before the high-water mark of the debate in the autumn of 1893, Salisbury had underlined the conservative virtues of the United States. In an important article in November 1892, he pointed out: 'I wish to invite more attention than I think has hitherto been given to the legislation of other democratic countries on the question of Constitutional Revision.'[56] He also defended the 'inconsistencies' of the British Constitution against the 'more exact methods of Belgium or the United States' because the former '*as a whole* ... succeeded.'[57] The American Constitution and Home Rule became a topic of debate in the Lords in July 1893, when the Duke of Argyll introduced a motion specifically on that topic. Argyll argued that 'If we had to break up our old Constitution and frame a new one, as the Government were now doing, and if, above all, we were to frame that Constitution upon a Federal basis, then America must be our great example.'[58] The Duke of Devonshire joined in the chorus of praise. The Thirteenth, Fourteenth and Fifteenth Amendments protected minorities in a fashion which Gladstone's Home Rule measure did not.[59] Conservatives and Liberal Unionists used the American paradigm when they saw its benefit to their own legislative and constitutional designs.

Yet for all the Liberal Unionist and Conservative praise of particular features of the American Constitution which made changes slow and careful, they dreaded fundamental changes in their own British constitutional practices. It would never have been possible for them to entertain the kind of praise of the American Constitution to which the Liberals had resorted, for such would have been tantamount to supporting the position of Irish Home Rule. The Home Rule Bills had helped significantly to bond Gladstonian Liberals still further with the American experience. With the defeat of the Home Rule question, and the demise of the House of Lords reform debate in 1894, the interest in American federalism and the Constitution quickly died out. It did not flare up to a comparable level until the twentieth century, when the issue of Irish nationalism was again revived.[60]

Silver, bimetallism, and currency issues

During the period from 1892 to 1895, the depression of industry and agriculture worsened simultaneously in both Great Britain and the United States. More and more, economic experts turned away from a belief that the cause of the depression was due to import and export imbalances between protectionist countries like America and free trade England, and towards the belief that the distresses centered on the currency or monetary question. The 'silver problem' was almost in some ways as great in the United States. In Britain, silver prices continued to fall in the early 1890s; by 1893 they stood at 'the outrageously low figure of $36\frac{5}{16}$ d. per ounce (it had been $50\frac{1}{2}$ d. in 1884 and $60\frac{5}{16}$ d. in 1872).'[61] With India based on a silver currency and Northern England (Lancashire and Manchester) dependent on Indian trade, there were groups in Great Britain who strongly supported silver as a solution to an imperial crisis of serious magnitude.

The United States suffered the collapse of the railway-building industry, numerous banking failures, extensive labor unrest, and, in 1893, a Wall

Street panic. All this was due, many thought, to falling silver prices and the high price of gold. The Western and Southern States protested the loudest, while the Populist Party and Farmer's Alliance organizations enjoyed peaks of popularity. In the 1892 election the Populist Party had won 22 electoral and one million popular votes.[62] In the face of these events, Anglo-American attention cast about to explore immediate remedies. Increasingly, the solution was seen in terms of currency rather than tariff reform. 'Sufferers from the crisis were crying for a single solution, and their confusion over its causes only heightened their dogmatism about its cure.'[63] Liberal leaders were pestered by a problem of a strange and almost mysterious nature, and it was fraught with aspects that reflected the American situation.

Leading commercial groups and economic authorities leaned toward the persuasion that the solution to the depression lay in joint Anglo-American action rather than in unilateral currency management. This meant growing sympathy for international bimetallism: the use of a gold and silver system where the values of both metals were fixed by governmental statute. In Britain, the activities of the Bimetallic League expanded conspicuously. As early as 1888, it numbered approximately sixty parliamentarians in its organization.[64] Resolutions in favor of international bimetallism were passed in 1892 by the Manchester Chamber of Commerce, the Chamber of Edinburgh and Leith, the East India and China Section of the London Chamber and a Parliamentary Committee of the Trades Union Congress in London.[65] In the United States, the Pan-American Conference in Washington in 1890 recommended the convening of a commission of North and South American representatives. In 1891, it urged an international conference to be held in Paris or London 'to consider bimetallism and the equalization of gold and silver, to be fixed by international agreement, and the universal assimilation of monetary types both of gold and silver and their legal international circulation for all purposes.'[66]

President Cleveland was a hard money man, but he realized that international bimetallism, if and only if other countries cooperated, was better than any unilateral bimetallic proposals. In the spring of 1892, Salisbury, Balfour, and especially Henry Chaplin were all fairly favorable to international bimetallism.[67] There were thus no difficulties in accepting the American proposals for an international conference. On the other hand, Chancellor of the Exchequer Goschen adhered to monometallic principles. He prevented the conference from meeting in London and forced the United States to alter the wording of the proposed meeting. The conference would meet not to discuss 'bimetallism' as the Americans wished, but to inquire into 'what measures, if any, could be taken with reference to a larger use of silver in the systems of currency of leading nations.'[68] Each country appointed three commissioners and the meeting place was set for Brussels. It was to be the fourth such conference at which British and American representatives had confronted each other's different monetary systems since 1878.[69]

In the winter of 1892, the new Liberal government had to finalize plans for the international conference. While he carefully consulted Gladstone at times, Harcourt managed the details of the preparations with painstaking care. He neither wanted to alienate the increasing number of bimetallists within his own party and the American hosts, nor move away from rigid Liberal gold orthodoxy. Goschen had appointed a monometallist (Bertram Currie),[70] a bimetallist (the Indian Civil Servant, William Houldsworth) and a middle-of-the-roader and businessman (Charles Freemantle). The Liberal government reconstituted the British delegation which was originally essentially balanced, and hence dangerously near the bimetallist position. Gladstone warned that 'we cannot put ourselves in the position of receiving a report more or less Bimetallistic signed by a majority of British Commissioners. We must carefully avoid stopping the Commission. I incline to appointing new men rather than restricting the voting subjects.'[71] After unsuccessful attempts to get the Liberal monometallic expert, T. H. Farrer, to join the delegation, Harcourt finally proposed two monometallists, the Comptroller of the National Debt, Sir Charles Rivers Wilson, and the London banker, Alfred de Rothschild. The Americans did not object; they simply added more 'silver men' to their bimetallic delegation. Harcourt gave all the delegates explicit instructions and kept in close touch with London financial authorities, especially Farrer and various Rothschilds.[72] To Freemantle, Harcourt wrote:

> We ought carefully to avoid any appearance of a desire prematurely to break up the Conference by an *alienation* of any kind – a proceeding which would give great offence both to the United States & the Government of India which we are specially bound to regard.[73]

When the American delegation passed through London on their way to Brussels, Harcourt enlisted the services of his friend Henry White to give dinners on behalf of the Americans. 'I must not be outdone by the U.S. in courtesy & hospitality to the Monetary Delegates.'[74] On

18 November, a dinner was held at the Savoy Club for the British and American delegates.[75] It is hard to imagine anybody outdoing Harcourt in the great care he took both to bring about the failure of the Conference and at the same time to ensure that it produced a high degree of good feeling between the United States and Great Britain.

Liberal bimetallists were deeply angered over Harcourt's careful sabotaging of the Conference. They had deemed the meeting to be so important that they had even set up a Liberal committee to watch the progress of events. George Howell of Bethnal Green, R. L. Everett of Suffolk and Samuel Smith of Flintshire all protested vehemently to Harcourt upon implicitly foreclosing the possibility of an international agreement.[76] Smith warned Harcourt: 'I quite dread that the first result of the failure of the conference will be the stoppage of the silver coinage in America – if it happens silver could go down with a run – & the rupee might fall to 11-.'[77]

The Brussels Conference, attended by 20 countries, lasted from 22 November until 17 December 1892. There was a great deal of debate but precious little progress. Harcourt kept in the closest of touch with all the delegates; he had no cause for alarm and was delighted when early on there were signs that progress for international bimetallism had been frustrated.

> The Conference cannot be said to have been entirely a failure for it has demonstrated two things:
> 1. That the Bi-metallist theory is generally repudiated.
> 2. That there is no material for an agreement upon subsidiary measures for the support of a silver currency. As Bimetallism is admitted to rest upon a universal or at least general international agreement this result may be regarded as a *settler* for Bi-metallism.[78]

Moreover, Gladstone was also pleased with the proceedings. He wrote to his friend and secretary for the British delegation, Bertram Currie, thanking him for his speech at the Monetary Conference: 'it was indeed refreshing, and must have astonished a good deal the weak minds of some among them.'[79] As the Conference drew to a close, Harcourt pressed for a full adjournment rather than a temporary one as the bimetallist countries wished. 'If the reunion of the Conference is held in suspense we shall lead a dog's life in Parliament being badgered every day by wild bimetallists.'[80] Yet Harcourt lost in two respects. The delegates decided to reconvene six months later on 30 May 1893, and Harcourt was indeed 'badgered' by bimetallists.

Despite the actions and speeches of important political and economic leaders in favor of international bimetallism, the monometallists maintained their ascendency in the first half of 1893. In the winter of 1892–93, both Balfour and Chaplin made strong public calls for currency reforms through international agreements.[81] The secretary of the Bimetallic League, W. H. Grenfell, and the prominent London University economist, H. S. Foxwell, popularized international bimetallism.[82] Two highly respected Americans, the economist and President of the Massachusetts Institute of Technology, Francis Amasa Walker, and politician and author of the influential *Silver Pound*, Samuel Dana Horton, were frequently in London in the 1890s. They were both international bimetallists. Harcourt studied Horton's works and L. D. MacKay told his American friend Charles Norton in 1893: 'I am very much interested in your currency affairs and discuss them with Dana Horton, who is always here and kind of general referee on bimetallism.'[83]

The most important bimetallic convert was Leonard Courtney, a Liberal Unionist Member of Parliament from the Bodmin division of Cornwall and a former member of the Gold and Silver Commission of 1887. Disturbed that gold and silver prices continued to fluctuate and fearful of unilateral monetary action, Courtney came to the conclusion that international bimetallism 'could be accomplished with the minimum of change and with great advantage to the empire and the world…'[84] Leading bimetallists hailed Courtney's conversion as an event of great significance,[85] while E. L. Godkin was alarmed at his good acquaintance's volte-face.[86] These events explained why Harcourt and other monometallic financial experts took international bimetallism seriously, not to be viewed merely as a fad. Harcourt carefully tried to curb the anger of bimetallists like William Houldsworth who thought the Exchequer had not been courteous or fair towards the Americans at the Brussels Conference.[87] In a lengthy interview with Senator Jones, a member of the American delegation in Brussels, Harcourt assured himself that the Americans had no hard feelings towards the Liberal government: 'Senator Jones admitted that he saw no possibility of the Bimetallic system being proposed with any advantage and that in his view there was no alternative which the U.S.A. were likely to put forward.'[88]

The greatest victory for the monometallists came on 28 February. In a full day's Commons debate, a combination of Liberals and London financial leaders defeated a motion for the reconvention of the International Monetary Conference. They prepared their case with some care. Thus, for instance, Lubbock and T. H. Farrer exchanged views and literature in the days preceding the debate.[89] On the day, Gladstone,

Harcourt, and Lubbock were among those who argued against Chaplin and Balfour. Gladstone's peroration was particularly moving, filled with doctrine upon the power and stability of gold.[90] It gained great praise from Carnegie.[91] Harcourt demanded that the United States 'propose a scheme, then, of course, the Government of this country will be ready in the fairest and frankest way to discuss it.'[92] As the day approached in May for the reconvening of the conference, Harcourt worked busily to prevent the reopening. Through Henry White, as usual, he kept in touch with the attitudes of the Cleveland administration.[93] In the end, it was not so much Harcourt as American internal conflicts between silver men, international bimetallists, and hard money men that forced Cleveland to abandon the May reconvention. The American financier J. Pierpont Morgan tried one last meeting with Harcourt to argue for international bimetallism.[94] It was pointless. While bimetallists had been vociferous and made some progress, monometallists still held the upper hand. They were aided by the facts that the plans of the bimetallists were often vague and complicated, and by general transatlantic opposition to international legislation limiting individual financial freedoms. Liberal doctrines of state non-interference still retained their edge over the collectivist principles of the modern welfare state.

In 1893–94, silver developments in the United States assumed increasing importance and significance for British financial authorities. In the midst of the panic of 1893, President Cleveland turned away from international remedies towards unilateral action and the repeal of the Sherman Silver Purchase Act. It precipitated American politics into a seething confusion, as Republicans and Democrats broke party ranks to align themselves on the issue of silver. The Republican Carnegie told Cleveland that if forced to choose between a sound money Democrat and a tariff Republican, he would unequivocally endorse the former.[95]

Englishmen also hailed the American events. Moreton Frewen, married to Jennie Jerome Churchill's sister and intimately connected with silver lobbyists in America,[96] called the currency problem in America in June 1893 a crisis of immense concern to the British. 'If the United States repealed the Sherman Silver Purchase Act it would precipitate that panic which seems to be impending everywhere over the world of finance.'[97] A year later, after the repeal of the Silver Act had not noticeably failed to calm the fervid animosities of the American currency questions, Spring Rice warned Rosebery's private secretary, Munro-Ferguson:

I don't know whether you are interested in this question, which is all-absorbing here and which certainly, if the Republican policy in discriminating against gold-using countries is carried out, will intimately affect England. But it is a question that must soon become the most important for us, and it might be worth while for you to take it up seriously.[98]

Most Liberals were incapable of understanding the intricacies of the American silver question, let alone the various mysterious bimetallic theories abroad in Great Britain. In September 1893, former Liberal Chancellor of the Exchequer and Home Secretary Hugh Childers told his American friend, Yale professor Ellis Yarnell, that 'the Silver question, like many other American questions, beats me.' Furthermore,

> ... the notion of outraging all good sense and every economic law to the bidding of a few silver kings or rings is inexplicable to me. It seems so very absurd that I feel sometimes I must have missed something on the other side, in that a great and very sagacious nation couldn't act as I see very fairly the great American nation *is* acting.[99]

Even Bryce was greatly mystified by the American silver question, which significantly he largely ignored in his *American Commonwealth*, in both the 1888 and 1893–95 editions. In February 1895, Bryce admitted to Godkin:

> Your currency problem and the incapacity of Congress to deal with it have passed out of my range of knowledge; one needs probably to give close attention to those things to be able to follow them, but obviously from what you say Congress is just as helpless as it was to deal with the Slavery question from 1850 to 1860.[100]

Against this background of Liberal confusion over American currency, the views of a handful of liberally inclined Anglo-Americans took on more significance. Sir John Lubbock and T. H. Farrer in England, and Edward Atkinson and Andrew Carnegie in America were devout students of each other's finance and currency. The problem was an Anglo-American one, and these were the authorities to whom others looked for guidance.

In the summer of 1893, Lubbock, Atkinson and Carnegie all cautioned Britons and Americans to act calmly and deliberately in the midst of the repeal agitation over the Sherman Silver Purchase Act. Atkinson urged that Cleveland's administration was doing everything it could to stop Anglo-American distrust of American financial institutions: 'It must be supported by banks, bankers and people alike, else the disaster will come.'[101] Carnegie and Lubbock made a joint appeal for calm deliberation in the pages of the *North American Review*. Carnegie believed that the remedy lay in 'the restoration of confidence' and that America 'must stand as free from a suspicion of a desire to debase the currency and as resolute to prevent its debasement as the governments of Great Britain and Germany stand.'[102] Lubbock thought that the United States and India were equally responsible for the economic stability of the world. There was little likelihood that the United States, Great Britain, or any other nation would introduce general bimetallism. 'The United States Government has always, I think, attached too much importance to our action in the matter.'[103] Bimetallists, he suggested, would do better to consider more practical plans, such as perhaps 'to make the legal tender in the last resort half gold and half silver.'[104] However, in the end, Lubbock underlined the magnitude of the crisis: the American Treasury had lost an enormous amount of gold from its reserves between 1890 and 1893 – $64 300 000 to $37 700 000. Like Carnegie, he called for caution: 'investors will do well to sit quietly and wait for better times.'[105] Most orthodox Anglo-American monometallists certainly greeted the repeal of the Sherman Purchase Bill with relief. Bimetallists prepared themselves for the worst.[106]

In 1894, Carnegie, Atkinson, and Farrer all participated actively in the Anglo-American currency agitation. Carnegie republished in pamphlet form an article he had written on money earlier in the 1890s.[107] It was one of the best articles on the importance of gold for the stability of national economies and was widely circulated throughout the British Isles. Henry Fowler, President of the Local Government Board from 1892 to 1894 and Secretary for India from 1894 to 1895, declared that it was 'the best thing' written on the silver crisis in the United States.[108] Carnegie tried particularly hard to persuade Balfour to change his position. He argued that 'There is no doubt but our position in the United States is weakened by your advocacy of bimetallism.'[109] Carnegie saw two main reasons why Balfour should change his mind: because gold production had increased worldwide and therefore silver values would continue to fall and because it was virtually impossible to reach a stable ratio between gold and silver.[110] But Balfour held firmly to his bimetallism.

When you look forward, however, to silver becoming practically worthless for the purpose of coinage, have you reflected what a revolution this means in the monetary affairs of India, China and South America? I confess I find it difficult to contemplate this result with perfect equanimity![111]

Throughout the year, the Royal Commission of Agriculture, headed by G. J. Shaw-Lefevre, studied the causes of the continued agricultural depression.[112] A great deal of the testimony centered on bimetallic versus monometallic arguments. The star witness, certainly on the American aspects of the crisis, was none other than Edward Atkinson (President of the Boston Manufacturers Mutual Fire Insurance Company) who was in England during much of the year. In two days of testimony, Atkinson sought to assure the Commission of American common sense as well as of the danger of silver schemes and bimetallic currency reform.[113] Meanwhile, T. H. Farrer participated in an acrimonious debate in the Liberal *Fortnightly Review*. He berated for their stupidity the views of John Reed, a prominent Republican from Maine and also Speaker of the House as well as a presidential nomination candidate in 1892. In an interview, Reed had suggested 'a Tariff Reunion' of all the nations friendly to bimetallism, where reciprocity would be 'the reward of free coinage of silver.'[114] Farrer could not believe that such ideas had been genuinely fostered by Americans. He concluded that they were concocted by fanatical Englishmen:

> I have heard that there are Englishmen at Washington so fanatical on the subject of bi-metallism, so deeply imbued with the hatred of a gold standard, possibly infected also with some virus of Protection, that they are urging on American statesmen any measure however hostile and injurious, which they may think may drive England into the abandonment of her gold standard of value. Can it be from the quiver of such men rather than from that of a genuine American statesman that the above arrow has been drawn?[115]

Moreton Frewen, the Englishman that Farrer obviously had in mind since he had been in Washington lobbying during the Silver Purchase repeal, retorted vehemently to Farrer's accusations. Prominent British economists, such as J. S. Nicholson, supported Frewen's remarks.[116] Farrer, like Carnegie and Atkinson, was not afraid to attack certain bimetallists while maintaining the virtues of considered and careful thought. There was only one thing in the mid-1890s that Farrer, Carnegie, Atkinson, and their antagonists would have agreed upon: that the American election of 1896 would be one of critical importance to the world.

Bimetallic and monometallic arguments continued to circulate in the United States and Great Britain in the first half of 1895. In both countries there were active bimetallic leagues. Much of what was said on both sides was redundant, contradictory, and muddled, yet there was no doubt that support in both camps grew consistently. American and British politics were thoroughly linked in this debate. In January 1895, the British Bimetallic League founded a monthly journal, *The Bimetallist*. In February, they introduced another motion in the Commons to adopt international monetary negotiations as a remedy to end the agricultural depression. This time Harcourt could no longer stand in opposition. He was forced to accede and the motion was passed unanimously.[117] By June, the orthodox and London financial leaders realized the seriousness of their situation and thus banded together in the Gold Standard Defense Association.[118] There could be no doubt that, during the Liberal ministries of Gladstone and Rosebery in the 1890s, American financial and currency matters had been interlocked with British affairs more than at any other time in the late nineteenth century.

Liberal attitudes towards American labor, society, and democracy

While most Liberals viewed the United States between 1892 and 1895 more often than not in terms of diplomatic incidents, imperialism, constitutional aspects of Irish Home Rule, and currency/tariff measures, some were increasingly conscious of a range of American social, political, and municipal developments. Gladstonian Liberals were often slow to consider their own social policies or the condition of the working classes. Gladstone and Morley only reluctantly considered eight-hour-day proposals, minimum wage plans, and the claims of labor.[119] It would have been surprising had they become absorbed in studies of similar American themes. On the other hand, it would be unfair to suggest that the Liberals totally ignored the social condition of the working class in Britain or the United States. In Britain some Liberals had concerned themselves with social questions in the later 1880s and early 1890s,[120] while Gladstone had led the way in the study of American wages, capitalism, and various social movements. However, the purpose of this section is not to answer questions about fundamental conflicts within the weakened Liberal party of the 1890s. Rather it is to underline the fact that labor, municipal politics, and temperance movements in

Britain and the United States were closely related during the 1890s. Some Liberals studied these issues, and a few even went on to examine civil service reform, black issues, and woman's suffrage.

Although the American Federation of Labor had been founded by Terrence Powderly in 1869, it was not until the later 1880s that the American labor movement began to excite any real interest in Great Britain.[121] The Haymarket riots in Chicago in 1886 had greatly stirred British socialists and radicals. During the next ten years they took repeated encouragement from the American workers' movement. Henry Hyndman, Keir Hardie, John Burns, and Edward and Eleanor Marx Aveling all studied the career of labor in the United States.[122] As Pelling has observed, 'These years at the end of the eighteen-eighties constitute one of the few periods when the state of political organization of the working class as such in America could be regarded as more complete than that of the British workers.'[123] Subsequently, the contacts between British and American labor, symbolized most directly by the activities of the Knights of Labour in Britain, increased significantly, though 'there were few relics of the movement as such after 1892.'[124] In 1895, Keir Hardie journeyed to the United States where he befriended such American socialist or labor leaders as Henry Demarest Lloyd, Daniel de Leon, Eugene Debs, and Samuel Gompers.[125] But despite British labor and radical interest in the American labor movement in the 1880s, the major Liberals have left scant record of their concern. Thus, for instance, Bryce says very little about labor topics in *The American Commonwealth*.[126] Nor is there any evidence that Gladstone, Morley, Rosebery, and Harcourt thought American labor in the 1880s or 1890s particularly important. In the summer of 1889, the London dock strike directed Liberal attention to the seriousness of labor and trade unionism in Britain. The strike set off a wave of union agitation, stoppages, and working-class activities.

In 1892, the Homestead strike triggered casual Liberal attention in the causes of American labor. An army of Pinkerton detectives fired upon strikers at Carnegie's steel company plant at Homestead, Pennsylvania, killing and wounding several strikers. Since Gladstone, Morley, Rosebery, William Storey, and W. T. Stead were associated with Carnegie at the time, they could not but be disturbed by these events. Both Rosebery and Gladstone sent Carnegie letters in which they completely sided with management and their American friend. Gladstone wrote:

> ... how sure I am that no one who knows you will be prompted by the unfortunate occurrences across the water (of which we cannot

know the exact merits) to qualify in the slightest degree either his confidence in your generous views or his admiration of the good and great works you have already done.[127]

Rosebery professed:

I know nothing of the rights and wrongs of the Homestead case, but I cannot believe that you would ever be illiberal or unjust. And even had you been taken with a sudden fit of those complaints all the more necessity for your friends to stand by you.[128]

While Carnegie's acquaintance, Stead, pressed the American industrialist for information on Homestead, little to none was forthcoming.[129] In April 1893, Carnegie was able to reminisce about the Homestead incident with Morley, but all along he kept in strict confidence his private feelings and views. 'I [Carnegie] went to Homestead & shook hands with the old men, tears in their eyes & in mine. Oh, that Homestead Blunder, but its fading as all events do & we are at work selling steel one pound for a half penny.'[130] Homestead had sparked a Liberal awareness of the violence inherent in American labor activities, but it had not led them to any true understanding of labor problems. Their innate trust in Carnegie's philanthropic and Anglo-Saxon causes made it impossible for them to arrive at an unbiased assessment of Homestead.

In 1892, there was some slight increase in Liberal attention to labor across the Atlantic. The Royal Commission on Labour devoted a special report to American developments,[131] in addition to reports on labor progress in other foreign countries. A. J. Mundella, the new President of the Board of Trade, declared at the time that he 'owed much to American and Fabian influences' in the reorganization of the Board's labor information acts.[132] Various Liberal periodicals printed important articles about American labor movements.[133] At the same time, however, certain leaders of the radical wing of the Liberal party ignored the American implications. Chamberlain gave no attention to American developments in a lengthy article on labor in 1892, nor did Charles Dilke a year later.[134] Nor is there any real evidence in Carnegie's correspondence with a myriad of British leaders concerning events affecting the working class in the United States. In 1894, there was an upsurge of labor violence as the product of a year of financial depression and unemployment in the United States. Most spectacularly the Pullman Railway strike occurred and Coxey's army of the unemployed marched on

Washington, DC. Among the various Liberal leaders, only two, Bryce and Stead, gave these American issues any study.

Stead traveled widely in the United States in 1892–93 and gave the American working class fairly detailed study. In 1893, at the Chicago World Exhibition, he was a guiding light in the foundation of the Civic Federation for the discussion, and hopefully solution, of issues between representatives of capital and labor. In an article on Coxey's 1894 march, Stead deplored the increase of violence in America. 'Labor, on its part, relies more upon violence than upon organization, and when a strike occurs, slaughter, on one side or the other, is regarded as an ordinary and unavoidable incident.'[135] If something were not done soon, Stead believed, 'Coxeyism will in the future assume much more menacing dimensions.'[136] As he saw it, there were essentially three main faults with the American labor movement – a lack of 'honest and capable leaders,' a lack of a 'definite practical programme,' and a need to elect honest men to political office.[137]

Bryce's views were similar to those of Stead and were also influenced in part by the various warnings he received from his American correspondents. The President of Columbia University, Seth Low, informed Bryce in 1894: 'The great strike at Chicago seemed to me, in its first aspect, the most disturbing incident that had ever taken place in this country – at least in my day.'[138] Bryce did not need convincing. Throughout the period from 1892 to 1895, he maintained that violence and lawlessness in America was one of the new abiding evils in the country. More often than not, Bryce associated this violence with labor unrest.

> I am beginning to be rather painfully impressed by the tendency to lawlessness in the American population, recollecting no one year in which there have occurred five such instances as the N.Y. Central R.R. riots, the Homestead riots, the Idaho mining war, the Rustler's and Cattleman's war in Wyoming, and the Tennessee Convict War.[139]

In 1895, Bryce assured his intimate friend Godkin that the upsurge of labor activities proved no 'real danger' in Britain.[140] Surely this was wishful thinking. Most Liberals underestimated the importance of American labor developments, even as they did their own. 'As defenders of individualism, liberal reformers insisted that artificial interference in the labour problem demoralized workers and destroyed their self-confidence and self-respect.'[141] Such clearly old-fashioned notions underlined why Liberals were unable to redress major problems of the transatlantic world and why their party ultimately proved obsolete.[142]

In the 1890s, American municipal corruption was deplored by English observers as perhaps the most fundamental weakness of the American democracy. This was nothing new. The Conservative use of the word 'Americanization' as an evil expletive associated with caucus politics had been popularized in the 1860s and 1870s. Liberals usually chose not to deplore such tactics, but rather to treat the British caucus and American city politics independently. They were cautiously optimistic about the prospects of both. However, by the 1890s, urbanization in Britain and the United States had progressed by seemingly uncontrollable leaps and bounds. In England, the London City Council was created in 1888 in an attempt to establish local administrative control over growth in the greater London area. Other large urban areas such as Birmingham, Glasgow, and Manchester also pioneered in wrestling with local government. American municipal reformers, Albert Shaw and Frank Goodnow, studied the experiments of British municipal government in great detail. They believed that the British were ahead of the Americans and urged emulation of such plans as those of Chamberlain in Birmingham.[143] Liberals, Lib-Labs, Liberal Unionists, and London progressives usually saw little to emulate in American city management, although they gave some close examination to cities like New York, Chicago, Boston, and Philadelphia; as a result a shift took place during the 1890s in the nature of their optimism regarding municipal government. From among these political groups, the views of Bryce, Stead, and Chamberlain were the most interesting and well-formulated.[144]

In *The American Commonwealth*, Bryce devoted large portions of the second volume to a specific discussion of city bosses, 'spoils,' and urban electoral and financial graft.[145] He made an effort to enlist the expert contributions of two municipal reformers, Seth Low, formerly the mayor of Brooklyn, and Frank Goodnow.[146] The corruption of New York was legendary, but Bryce found municipal government in such cities as Philadelphia just as difficult. He told Professor Lea, an American academic correspondent, that municipal problems in Philadelphia surprised him more than New York 'because your population seems so much better in quality; fewer ignorant immigrants, working class better off, owning its houses and paying taxes.'[147] When Bryce returned to the United States in 1890 after an absence of seven years, it was the influence of urban corruption and the social conditions of the cities that most distressed him about the country.

He engaged in a transatlantic correspondence with another American authority, Goldwin Smith. The two men argued whether or not municipal corruption was worse in Canada, the United States, or Great Britain. Smith asserted:

> You are mistaken in thinking that corruption in Canada is not as bad as in the U.S. We have no Tammany or Philadelphia Ring, because we have no such large cities. But corruption with us is more universal, more shameless and more hopeless.[148]

Bryce earnestly disagreed:

> Dark as is the picture you draw to Canadian politics, what I saw last autumn in the United States made me doubt if things were not even more discouraging there; and while admitting that the stream of events is carrying Canada towards annexation, one feels apprehensive lest public morality and wisdom in legislation may not experience a further decline after that has happened.[149]

A year later, Bryce still found that 'in spite of the corruption of ministers & the bribery in constituencies, it seems to me that Canadian politics have not fallen quite so low as those of New York State or, Pennsylvania or Washington.'[150] Bryce's frequent discussions of municipal corruption were later referred to as evidence of the broader social and political weakness of the United States.

Joseph Chamberlain, the conspicuous reformer of Birmingham in the late 1870s, was the foremost late Victorian statesman seriously interested in the municipal problems of the United States. On his two trips to the United States, in 1887–88 and 1890, city government was the one American topic that genuinely excited him. In the midst of his official responsibilities in 1887–88, Chamberlain took time out to examine New York. Thus, for instance, he interviewed Abraham Hewitt, the newly elected mayor who had just defeated Theodore Roosevelt and Henry George. He recorded: 'Mr. Hewitt said there had been very little municipal corruption in New York since exposure of the Tweed business & now there was none. There were splendid free libraries, art museums, teaching institutes & all provided by private munificence.'[151] When Chamberlain gave Boston detailed study in the early 1890s, he did not discover out-and-out corruption but certainly saw there little to excite pride. In the fall of 1892, he prepared an article for the American *Forum* on the comparative virtues of Boston and

Birmingham. 'One would expect that in the land of Triumphant Democracy – the home of the most numerous portion of the Anglo-Saxon race – these institutions would have their most striking and most satisfactory development.'[152] The facts demonstrated unfortunately quite the contrary, that 'the municipal administration of the vast populations of towns and cities is lamentably ineffective and unsatisfactory.'[153] This failure had to do both with the nature of city government as well as with problems inherent in democracies. Chamberlain demonstrated that Birmingham was more progressive than Boston in every respect. The urban resident paid between 15 and 30 percent of his net income for services in Boston while a Birmingham resident paid only $2\frac{1}{2}$ to 5 percent. In concluding his article, Chamberlain implied that American progress had been retarded by 'deliberate dishonesty and corruption practised on a gigantic scale.'[154] Chamberlain's antipathy to American cities was further shaped by his pride in Birmingham's reforming innovations and by his general disdain for American political and social institutions.

In 1892, W. T. Stead made a detailed and remarkable study of Chicago which ranked as one of the finest pieces of muckraking literature in the 1890s. *If Christ Came to Chicago!* compared well with the sensational exposures of Jacob Riis's *How the Other Half Lives* and Henry Demarest Lloyd's *Wealth Against Commonwealth*.[155] While Stead's work was thoroughly colored by religious metaphors and fanatical moralistic adages, language which tended to weaken the effect of his work, it nonetheless established for the author a firm place in the transatlantic progressive mind. According to Richard Hofstadter:

> It is hardly an exaggeration to say that the Progressive mind was characteristically a journalistic mind and that its characteristic contribution was that of the socially responsible reporter-reformer. The muckraker was a central figure. Before there could be action, there must be information and exhortation. Grievances had to be given specific objects, and these the muckrakers supplied. It was muckraking that brought the diffuse malaise of the public into focus.[156]

Stead had examined the life of the street and described accurately the conditions of drunks, prostitutes, political bosses, gamblers, paupers, and the destitutes. Thus, for example, Stead recounted his conversation with a drunken worker from a Chicago ward:

> To most people, possibly to every one who reads this chapter, such an inside glimpse of the practical working of the Democratic

machine in Chicago would fill them with a feeling of despair. This, they will say, is the outcome of Democracy, the latest triumph which Republican institutions have achieved in the New World! What a picture! Bribery, intimidation, bull-dozing of every kind, knifing, shooting, and the whole swimming in whiskey![157]

The Nineteenth Precinct of the First Ward was particularly alarming. Stead, like Bryce and other Anglo-American liberals, found the main problem lay in the lack of inspired and educated leadership.[158] However, Stead also found some signs that American reformers were stirring. Hazen S. Pingree, mayor of Detroit, and John Hopkins, Chicago's young mayor, were hard-working, optimistic reformers of municipal conditions. Pingree had 'arisen to do battle in the popular cause against the tyranny of the corporations and the scandalous corruption which honeycombs civil life in America.'[159] The problem of the reformers was even more complicated by the vast rise of plutocracies in America which threatened to fling their 'all-devouring tentacles round almost every institution in the United States.'[160] Perhaps the most practical and exemplary development was that offered by Jane Addams' Hull House in Chicago: 'one of the best illustrations of what can be done by intelligent and sustained efforts in this direction.'[161] While Stead's personal philosophy or his strange campaign against Dilke made him a dangerous companion in Liberal circles, Bryce and the Liberal Unionst Goldwin Smith valued his studies of Chicago. In 1894, Bryce looked forward anxiously to his book on Chicago ('an extraordinary phenomenon') and Smith, taking a note from Stead, acknowledged the depravity of municipal corruption in that city.[162]

As the 1890s progressed, Liberal condemnation of civic corruption in the United States became more outspoken and unanimous. The Conservative or Liberal Unionist analysis was little different.[163] Cecil Spring-Rice took time off from his official reports to describe the abject scandals in New York in June 1894. He wrote: 'The New York authorities are being examined, with the results that it is proved that for the years past the brothel keepers have been taxed for the benefit of Tammany Hall, which instructs the police to protect them in return for the money paid.'[164]

Bryce was caught in a lingering lawsuit. Oakley Hall, a former mayor of New York, accused Bryce of personal attacks against himself in *The American Commonwealth*. In 1894–95, a New York party politician, David Bennett Hill, won a patronage battle with Cleveland, and two of the President's nominees for the Supreme Court were defeated. British Liberals no longer found reason for the sort of optimism in Cleveland which they had felt in the mid-1880s or in 1892–93. As Bryce wrote to Godkin:

> Cleveland's failure seems to me [Bryce] regrettable not only in respect of his own reputation and the loss to reform, but even more because it spoils the moral which we thought he was setting of what a man may effect in America by courage and indifference to wire-pullers and spoilsmongering bosses.[165]

By 1898, even Stead's sentimental and religious optimism concerning American city leaders had hardened and become more sardonic. New York city was described by him as *'Satan's Invisible World Displayed'; or Despairing Democracy.*[166]

Civil service reform was a leading topic for American genteel reformers in the late nineteenth century. 'Increasingly in the post-war period, liberal reformers turned to civil service reform as a panacea for all the ills of the nation – economic, social, moral as well as political.'[167] Carl Schurz, E. L. Godkin, and George William Curtis were the leaders of the movement, which looked to the experience of Great Britain from the Northcote-Trevelyan report onwards. In 1878, Dorman Eaton made a visit to Great Britain to study civil service reform and its results and others were at work in the framing of the Pendleton Act of 1883.[168] In the 1890s, Theodore Roosevelt, then Commissioner of Civil Service Reform in New York, also turned occasionally to cast a glance at British practices.[169] Transatlantic interest in civil service reform was almost totally a one-way affair.

British Liberals rarely turned to examine American developments on civil service reform. T. H. Farrer demonstrated some interest when, in 1886, he wrote to Godkin that James Blaine and Randolph Churchill had both made erroneous statements about the subject. He further suggested that all was not perfect with the British example, but underlined that certainly nothing would be done to redress it:

> But I have always thought our plan tentative & experimental, and entirely agree that the time has come for examining its working and revising it where necessary. But any general reflection on the Civil Service, or any intimation that its moral is bad, never for a moment entered into the head of Lord R. [Rosebery] or any one else on this side of the water.

But we cannot help being interested in what you are doing; and I think you are interested in us.[170]

In 1892, shortly after Cleveland's election, the third Earl Grey from Northumberland maintained to an American correspondent that the United States should embark on cleaning up its civil service.[171] But only Bryce among Liberals demonstrated more than a passing interest in the matter. In the late 1880s and early 1890s, he kept in touch with American progress through his friendship with Godkin, the Bostonian Thomas Wentworth Higginson, and finally Theodore Roosevelt.[172] He gave consideration to civil service reform in *The American Commonwealth* but it was not a large American interest of his in the 1890s. The growth of municipal corruption, the silver and the tariff questions meant that even for American reformers, civil service reform no longer held the dominant place it had owned in the 1870s and 1880s.

Bryce had two strong American interests during the early 1890s which only interested a few other Liberals – the condition of the American blacks and women's suffrage. Much of the fascination with the blacks was a by-product of continued interest in Civil War history, but also some saw a connection between protection of the blacks and Irish minority rights.[173] Others still looked upon the American blacks as a product of their expanding interest in Africa, imperialism, and the race question.[174] While Christine Bolt has underlined the falling away of effort by British reformers on the part of the American blacks after Reconstruction,[175] that should not be interpreted simply as a lack of British, especially Liberal, interest in the question of the blacks.

Englishmen appear to have been much more interested in the blacks than even some Americans themselves. Godkin thought that an article by Bryce on the blacks was valuable mainly because it 'excites interest in England. Here it excites none whatever – absolutely none.'[176] In 1891, Bryce underlined how much interest had been excited in Britain by a series of letters on the black problem published in *The Times*.[177] Liberal periodicals also had important articles on the South and the blacks.[178] Gladstone and Playfair each turned at times to study the economic conditions of the South and the blacks. Mrs Mahlon Sands, wife of the American reformer, frequently supplied Gladstone with information relevant to such matters – evidently at his request.[179] Playfair attended black gatherings on occasion when in the United States, and in 1895, Spring-Rice reported privately in great detail about such assemblies.[180] Most Englishmen continued to see the blacks as inferior but were concerned that they be fairly integrated into American economic, political, and social life. Bryce, alone among Liberals in understanding the deeper aspects of the black problem, asserted that 'Compared with [the black question], those tariff questions and currency questions and railway questions with which politicians busy themselves sink almost to insignificance.'[181] He was deeply perplexed by the racial antagonisms and the continued economic deprivation of their class. He was concerned that they threatened the stability of the United States. Solutions were hard to come by, but Bryce tended to place the responsibility for some meaningful effort on their behalf upon the States:

> If an educational or a property qualification, or a combination of both kinds of qualification, were honestly and fairly put in force at the South, both the sense of wrong among the negroes and the sense of danger among the whites would be removed, while the bad habit of tampering with the ballot-box would disappear.[182]

In the end, Bryce advocated a literacy test, and called upon the mysterious beneficial forces within the democracy of the United States to heal the great social malaise.[183] In his 1893–95 edition of *The American Commonwealth*, Bryce turned to write two new chapters on the South and the blacks, underlining what he foresaw as a major problem of the twentieth century.[184]

The progress of women's suffrage in the United States also periodically excited British attention in the 1890s, notably with Bryce and Goldwin Smith. The fact that Liberals turned their heads away from women's suffrage was not surprising, since Gladstone, Morley, Rosebery, and Godkin invariably denounced the notion of giving the vote to women. It was enough of a problem to energize men to educate themselves properly about voting responsibilities without having to worry about women. Many late-nineteenth-century Liberals were active anti-suffragettes.[185] Bryce, however, gave surprisingly more attention to the women's suffrage movement in the United States than he did to either civil service or to temperance reform – even though both of the latter were much more important American issues. Bryce pointed out the significant lack of leaders for the suffrage movement in the United States, more so even than in Great Britain. He believed that 'very few of the Reformers advocate women's suffrage, apparently because they are opposed to "sentimentalism," and think that "politics" as now practised would do more harm to women than women could possibly do good to politics.'[186] Despite this, Bryce was joined by Smith and also the future Unionist MP Horace Plunkett who had spent several years in Wyoming, in emphasizing the progress made in various States for the provision of voting for women.[187]

Of all the social reform movements in Britain in the late nineteenth century, perhaps the one with the largest number of American associations was the temperance movement.[188] Many of the most prominent Liberal leaders considered temperance reform a possible leading issue for the Liberal party in the 1890s. Harcourt thought that licensing should be 'made the backbone of the Liberal party.'[189] Many of the leaders of the movement in Britain were nonconformist Liberals like Sir Wilfrid Lawson, W. S. Caine, William Rathbone, and Samuel Smith, and the powerful pressure group, the United Kingdom Alliance. In November 1894, Caine reminded Rosebery that various Newcastle issues must be considered. If not, 'the discontent which is smouldering will break out into revolt, and the more fiery spirits in the Temperance ranks will follow the example of America, and form an independent prohibition party.'[190]

The activities of the American Prohibitionist Party were the focus of international attention and directly inspired British temperance reformers. Neal Dow, the foremost American temperance leader, visited Great Britain many times. In April 1894, he acknowledged that he had always received a great deal of information from British temperance sources and thought their movement had been 'well organized and persistent.'[191] Furthermore, William Rathbone thought the experience of American prohibition and temperance so important that he specially commissioned a London barrister, E. L. Fanshawe, to journey to the United States and Canada in order to make an unbiased report of his findings.[192] Fanshawe's report appeared in book form in 1893 and it included detailed studies of prohibition, local options and licensing systems in various states. It contained over four hundred pages of evidence.[193] Rathbone considered Fanshawe's discoveries 'absolutely impartial' and his facts 'absolutely fatal to prohibition.'[194] In 1895, he sent Gladstone a copy as well as a copy of a letter he had written the Lord Mayor of London and Chester on American temperance:

> Will they [British temperance leaders] never learn by their own experience, and by the still more extensive and elaborate experience of America, that the passage of laws, – of which the public will is not prepared to enforce the execution, – is to give impunity to the promotion of drunkenness, and to demoralise the police and the whole machinery of law?[195]

There was a great deal which Rathbone thought could be learned from the American temperance reformers, but which should not be repeated in Great Britain. What he had most in mind was the proposal of measures which it was impossible to enforce:

> At the present moment, the whole political life of America seems in danger of falling back into the extreme corruption from which its best men were trying with some success to purify it, because the Temperance Party there were insisting upon laws which it was impossible to enforce, in the state of opinion among the German population of New York.[196]

Rathbone called upon Britain to adopt a dual policy: to establish laws for minors (a paramount aim of American prohibitionists) and to strengthen law enforcement. Other British temperance reformers, such as Arthur Sherwell and Joseph Rowntree, also gave extensive attention to American facts and precedents.[197] While the British reformers received some support from Harcourt, Gladstone's opposition to altering the open and free licensing laws put an end to any great discussion of temperance by the Liberal party. Nonetheless, the transatlantic character of the temperance reform movement was everywhere evident in the 1890s.

Andrew Carnegie: a transatlantic liberal

Andrew Carnegie had become by the early 1890s absorbed in the issues of British Liberalism as has been testified by his active debates in the tariff and bimetallism controversies, and his friendships with John Morley and William Gladstone had consolidated into some of the most mature and important of his life. Carnegie was an ardent Republican, protectionist, an advocate of big business, in the 1880s a supporter of James Blaine, and by no means a whole-hearted proponent of urban and municipal reform. In some ways, it would have seemed odd that he established such close associations with British Liberals, and yet perhaps more than any other prominent American, he did align himself with British Liberalism. As one biographer has declared:

> There was so much to reform in Britain that Carnegie was often at a loss in deciding which crusade was in the most urgent need of his backing: Home Rule for Ireland, the dissolution of the British Empire, the abolition of the monarchy and the House of Lords, the

disestablishment of the Church of England, land reform, or a new public educational system.[198]

Moreover, Carnegie contributed to Liberal causes. He sent money to assist Keir Hardie in West Ham in 1892, and he even considered running for Parliament himself. He spent a portion of most years during the 1880s in the British Isles. For each of the ten years after his marriage in 1887, only in 1892 did he fail to spend some time in England, and from 1888 to 1898, the Carnegies leased Cluny Castle near Kinguisse in Scotland. Under this roof the Carnegies mingled with most of the leading British Liberals and Carnegie's coaching trips throughout the British Isles became legendary.[199]

In time, Carnegie became John Morley's closest American friend. They first met sometime in the spring of 1881 at a garden party in Southern England, introduced by Matthew Arnold.[200] Shortly thereafter, Morley accepted Carnegie's first article to be published in a British periodical, an account of a coaching trip through England. Their acquaintanceship steadily ripened. While Carnegie had many friends in the political, industrial and social worlds on both sides of the Atlantic, he declared in 1908 that Morley was 'the most intimate friend of my mature years.'[201] Morley, on his part, acknowledged to Carnegie in 1903 that 'men like you and Mr. G. are of the right and only healthy sort.' Morley's friendship with Carnegie was like that with Gladstone, a 'complementary kind of relationship that Morley always seemed particularly anxious to find.'[202]

Carnegie's reverence for Great Britain and liberalism is no better captured than in his grand peroration on the United States, *Triumphant Democracy*, which he published in 1886. He sent a copy to Morley and underlined the mission of the work: 'The lamentable ignorance concerning the new land which I have found even in the highest political circles of the old.'[203] It was a panegyric upon the greatness of the United States, with pithy quotations emblazoned on the front red cover of the book, that from Gladstone being: 'The American Constitution is, as far as I can see, the most wonderful work ever struck off at a given time by the breath and purpose of man.' Salisbury was also cited on the greatness of the American Senate. In listing the achievements of the American republic, there were few blemishes, 'except international copyright and the alleged corruption of local politics.'[204] He praised Englishmen for their contributions to Anglo-American progress and these men were almost exclusively liberals: 'the really able Britons like Morley, Huxley, Froude, Freeman, Farrar, Irving, Rosebery, Bell,

Richards, Pidgeon, Salt, Rogers, Seeley, Bryce, Spencer, Arnold and others.[205] Throughout he cited the highly favorable views towards America of Freeman, Froude, and Henry Maine.[206] In conclusion, Carnegie asserted that 'The assimilation of the political institutions of the two countries proceeds apace, by the action of the older in the direction of the newer land. Year after year some difference is obliterated.'[207]

Morley warmly praised the American industrialist's work. While he found it 'a trifle too republican for a middle-aged monarchist,' he regarded it as 'a solid contribution on the right side. And it is written in high spirits which give it an attractive literary vivacity.' Most importantly, Morley reiterated that 'there is no difference between us as to the roots of things.'[208] The closeness of the Morley and Carnegie relationship deepened in the 1890s, and in April 1892, as evidence, Morley was writing 'my dear Carnegie' asking for information on Carnegie's recent trip to San Francisco.[209] Both men were committed to democracy, Anglo-American progress, and the reform of liberal institutions.

While biographer Joseph Wall has indicated that Carnegie was 'quite willing to ride along on Gladstone's back and serve as his gadfly, even if Gladstone did not appreciate those services,' a closer examination of the Gladstone and Carnegie relationship also underlines a deeper common intellectual and reciprocal relationship.[210] John Morley and George Armistead were common friends, and Carnegie and Gladstone saw each other frequently, as testified to by references in the *Gladstone Diaries*; and in 1884, several of Gladstone's children went on one of Carnegie's coaching trips.[211] Carnegie supported the Liberal party with his philanthropy. When he sent a contribution of $25 000 in 1887, he enclosed a note to Gladstone:

> I send my contribution to you direct. It is so largely a personal admiration for your own self that prompts me to contribute at this time (I mean when a general election is not on) that I wish you to have the disposal of the enclosed. Certainly your own £700 must first be deducted & the remainder turned over to Mr. Morley [Arnold].[212]

In 1889, Carnegie came to the rescue of Gladstone's close friend, Lord Acton, the great historian who had been forced to sell his library because of debts. In the 1890s, Gladstone tried to encourage Carnegie to contribute substantially to the Bodleian Library. However, the lengthy appeals did not move Carnegie, who was at that moment in the midst of endowing a large library in his home city of Pittsburgh.

The quality of the Gladstone and Carnegie relationship was never too excessive but genuine and based on common admiration. The quality of that friendship was perhaps best underlined in 1892, when Gladstone wrote to Carnegie upon the occasion of the Homestead incident when workers and police clashed violently at one of Carnegie's steel plants:

> But I do not forget that you have been suffering from anxieties, and have been exposed to imputations in connection with your gallant efforts to direct rich men into a course of action more enlightened than that which they usually follow. I wish I could relieve you from these imputations of journalists, too often rash, concerted or censorious, sometimes ill-natured. I wish to do the little, the very little that is in my power, which is simply to say how sure I am that no one who knows you will be prompted by the unfortunate occurrences across the water (of which mercifully we cannot know the exact merits) to qualify in the slightest degree either his confidence in your generous views or his admiration of the good and great works you have already done.
>
> Wealth is at present like a monster threatening to swallow up the moral life of man: you by precept and by example have been teaching him to disgorge. I for one thank you.[213]

Carnegie responded warmly to Gladstone, exposing more of his private thoughts over the disastrous riots to him than to almost any other person. 'I write this to you freely, no one else have I written so.'[214]

During the 1890s, Carnegie, the ardent Republican and protectionist, moved increasingly towards a fuller Liberal program with respect to politics, thus solidifying the ideological common ground he shared with Morley and Gladstone. The American supported President Cleveland's sound money policy, isolationist stances in foreign policy, and swung round to support a tariff for revenue only. With regard to Britain, he engaged in frequent debates in liberal journals such as the *North American Review* or the *Nineteenth Century*, participating actively, and was an enthusiastic supporter for Gladstonian Home Rule. As old age crept up on Gladstone, he had somewhat fewer friendships, but the genuine comradeship between Morley, Carnegie, and Gladstone was sustained; and as has been pointed out, it was not insignificant that in 1903, Morley told Carnegie, 'men like you and Mr. G are of the right and only healthy sort.'[215]

Conclusion

One historian has declared that British Liberals were still essentially favorable to the United States in the late 1880s and early 1890s. 'There still existed, of course, the mass of moderate Liberal opinion under Gladstone's leadership which, while critical of aspects of American life, was yet willing to regard the Republic with favour rather than disfavour.'[216] While this holds true in a fashion, it is important to be more precise.

Between 1892 and 1895, Liberals like Conservatives and Radicals found the majority of events in the United States disturbing if not alarming. Liberal optimism over Cleveland's low tariff, anti-annexationist, civil service reform and sound money programs was continually shattered as spoilsmen and silvermen got the upper hand of the Democratic President. The rhetoric of the Western silver states and William Jennings Bryan was more than a little disquieting to the mass of monometallic Liberals. Harcourt and Gladstone had stemmed the international bimetallist movement in 1893, but they were unable to do so in 1895. There was no telling to what extreme Britain's own bimetallists and silvermen would go. With the failure of Irish Home Rule in 1893, Liberals were no longer certain to extol the virtues of American federalism and its Constitution. Municipal corruption, labor riots, the failure of civil service reform, and the inability to generate solutions for the black or temperance issues pointed to deep social and political weaknesses in the American democracy. Despite all this, most Liberals were pragmatic enough to realize how important and intertwined were the futures of the United States and Great Britain. In the period from 1892 to 1895, Liberals were aware of a swirling mass of Anglo-American issues which had hardly existed in the 1870s or 1880s. Thus it was that, along with their American friends, they began to work privately on behalf of an Anglo-American arbitration and rapprochement in the years of Salisbury's ministry. Whatever the limitations of Ian Bradley's characterization of the Victorian Liberals as 'The Optimists,'[217] it was a mark of some Liberals' optimism that they strove to cement Anglo-American understandings in the face of volatile and distressing conditions in the United States.

Notes

1. P. Stansky, *Ambitions and Strategies: The Struggle for the Leadership of the Liberal Party in the 1890s* (Oxford, 1964), pp. 99–134 and H. V. Emy, *Liberals, Radicals and Social Politics 1892–1914* (Cambridge, 1973), pp. 38–63.

2. C. S. Campbell, 'The Dismissal of Lord Sackville,' *MVHR*, vol. xliv (1958), pp. 635–48; 'The Anglo-American Crisis in the Bering Sea, 1890–1891,' *MVHR*, vol. xlviii (1961–2), pp. 393–414; and 'The Bering Sea Settlements of 1892,' *PHR*, vol. xxxii (1963), pp. 347–67.

3. R. Hofstadter, 'Racism and Imperialism,' *Social Darwinism in American Thought*, 2nd edn (New York, 1969), pp. 170–200.

4. C. S. Campbell, *The Transformation of American Foreign Relations, 1865–1900* (New York, 1976), p. 148.

5. N. E. Johnson, 'The Role of the Cabinet in the Making of Foreign Policy 1885–95, with Special Reference to Lord Salisbury's Second Administration' (Oxford Univ. DPhil thesis, 1971), p. 312.

6. Library of Congress, Washington, DC (Henry White Papers): Box 1, Diary of 1892–93, 22 Mar. 1893.

7. There are some scattered references to Irish-American activities in FO material, such as FO 5/2359.

8. WP, Box 14, White to J. Foster, 13 Dec. 1892.

9. A sample of White's private and unofficial activities are demonstrated in a report to his superior, the Secretary of State John Foster. 'I need not say that I assured Mr. Asquith that anything he might say to me would be strictly confidential and that it was only on that understanding that I obtained the information contained herein, which is consequently not really official.' Ibid.

10. Johnson, 'The Role of the Cabinet in the Making of Foreign Policy 1885–95,' p. 350.

11. BP, USA 4, W. Garrison to Bryce, 12 Dec. 1893, ff. 226–7.

12. God.P, Bryce to E. Godkin, 24 Mar. 1893 (133).

13. J. Smith, 'Anglo-American Rivalries in Latin America 1865–1895' (Univ. of London PhD thesis, 1970), pp. 252 and 370.

14. P. M. Kennedy, *The Samoan Triangle: A Study in Anglo-German-American Relations, 1878–1900* (Dublin, 1974), p. 111.

15. RP, 10068, Kimberley to Rosebery, 9 May 1894, ff. 136–7.

16. Car.P, Vol. 28, Carnegie to Morley, Oct. 1894 (5411).

17. Campbell, *The Transformation of American Foreign Relations*, p. 203.

18. Stansky, *Ambitions and Strategies: The Struggle for the Leadership of the Liberal Party in the 1890s*, p. 125.

19. Cabinet Papers, 41/23/24, 21 Nov. 1894.

20. RP, 10070, Rosebery to Kimberley, 6 Apr. 1895, ff. 21–2; 7 Apr. 1895, f. 33; and 16 Apr. 1895, f. 60. Also see RP, 10243, Rosebery to Kimberley, 2 Apr. 1895, f. 183; 14 Apr. 1895, f. 210; and 17 Apr. 1895, ff. 212–13.

21. RP, 10070, Kimberley to Harcourt, 16 Apr. 1895, ff. 64–5.

22. HP, Box 52, Harcourt to Kimberley, 13 Apr. 1895, ff. 137–8.

23. The fact that Rosebery and Kimberley had committed themselves originally to a Cabinet meeting over changes in policy is borne out by a Kimberley letter. RP, 10242, Kimberley to Rosebery, 17 Apr. 1895, f. 168.

24. HP, Box 52, Harcourt to Kimberley, 18 Apr. 1895, f. 164.

25. The letter is important, especially for American history. It demonstrates that Gresham and Cleveland had turned to informal and private diplomacy with British leaders and that they were very earnest about cordial Anglo-American relations. Gresham died shortly thereafter. See Appendix III for a copy of the letter.

26. D. A. Hamer, *Liberal Politics in the Age of Gladstone and Rosebery. A Study in Leadership and Policy* (Oxford, 1972), pp. 174–84.
27. See Chapter 4, pp. 127–8.
28. John Kendle, *Ireland and the Federal Solution. The Debate over the United Kingdom Constitution, 1870–1921* (Kingston and Montreal, 1989), pp. 74–85.
29. Argyll, 'English Elections and Home Rule,' *NAR*, vol. clv (Aug. 1892), p. 129.
30. Ibid., pp. 130–1.
31. Ibid., pp. 131–5.
32. Gladstone, 'A Vindication of Home Rule. A Reply to the Duke of Argyll,' *NAR*, vol. clx (Oct. 1892), p. 386.
33. Ibid., pp. 391–2.
34. Ibid., p. 394 and *The Times*, 29 Dec. 1885.
35. *The Times*, 20 Oct. 1892 ('Mr. Gladstone in the *North American Review*'); 31 Oct. 1892 ('The American View of Home Rule'); 11 Nov. 1892 ('The Federal Fallacy Once More'); and 31 Dec. 1892 ('Canada, the United States, and Home Rule').
36. A. Shaw, 'An American View of Home Rule and Federation,' *CR*, vol. lxii (Sept. 1892), p. 307.
37. Ibid., pp. 314–18.
38. New York Public Library, New York (Albert Shaw Papers): Box 177, Stead to Shaw, 28 Sept. 1892.
39. T. Raleigh, 'Lessons of American History: A Reply,' *CR*, vol. lxii (Aug. 1892), p. 532.
40. Stead, 'The General Election and After,' *CR*, vol. lxii (Aug. 1892), pp. 303–4. W. T. Stead also argued that the British should 'Americanise its constitution' and include Ireland in a British federation in 'To All English-Speaking Folk' in his *Review of Reviews*, vol. i (Jan. 1890), p. 16.
41. Raleigh, 'Lessons of American History: A Reply,' p. 533.
42. 15 Apr. 1893, pp. 476–7.
43. 13 Feb. 1893. Carnegie readily acknowledged that Gladstone's second Home Rule Bill was much more 'federalist' than his first. *Mr. Carnegie on Socialism, Labour, and Home Rule: An Interview* (Aberdeen, 1892), pp. 28–9.
44. *Hansard*, 4th series, vol. viii, 31 Jan. 1893, 23.
45. Ibid., 14 Feb. 1893, 1420–1.
46. Ibid., 1424.
47. Ibid., vol viii: 16 Feb. 1893, 1661–2 (Labouchere) and 17 Feb. 1893, 1772–3 (Courtney); vol. xi, 17 Apr. 1893, 487–8 (Rathbone); and vol. xvi: 15 Aug. 1893, 333–4 (Courtney) and 25 Aug. 1893, 1150–1 (Bryce).
48. Ibid., vol. xi, 21 Apr. 1893, 969.
49. The articles in the *Pall Mall Gazette*, entitled 'The Case Against Home Rule,' ran from 10 July through 22 August 1893. There were contributions by Salisbury, M. E. Grant Duff, W. E. Lecky, Chamberlain, Marquis Lorne, John Lubbock, and others.
50. Ibid., 20 July 1893.
51. Ibid.
52. Ibid.
53. WP, Box 14, Chamberlain to White, 21 Feb. 1893.

54. Chamberlain, 'A Bill for the Weakening of Great Britain,' *NCR*, vol. xxxiii (Apr. 1893), pp. 545–8 and 'The Home Rule Campaign,' *Nat.R*, vol. xxiii (May 1894), pp. 305–18.
55. *The Times*, 20 Feb. 1892 and 22 Feb. 1892 and Hansard, 4th series, vol. xvi, 15 Aug. 1893, 337.
56. Salisbury, 'Constitutional Revision,' *Nat.R*, vol. xx (Nov. 1892), p. 293.
57. Ibid., p. 298.
58. Hansard, 4th series, vol. xv, 21 July 1893, 173.
59. Ibid., pp. 178–83.
60. The best discussion of Anglo-American comparative constitutional practices in the decade after 1894 were W. E. H. Lecky's *Democracy and Liberty*, 2 vols (London, 1896) and M. Ostrogorski's *Democracy and the Organization of Political Parties*, 2 vols (London, 1902).
61. J. Clapham, *An Economic History of Modern Britain. Machines and National Rivalries (1887–1914)* (Cambridge, 1951), p. 14.
62. See L. Goodwyn's *Democratic Promise. The Populist Moment in America* (New York, 1976) for a good solid account of the Populist and silver agitation in the United States in the 1890s.
63. R. Hofstadter, 'Free Silver and the Mind of "Coin Harvey,"' *The Paranoid Style in American Politics 'and Other Essays'* (New York, 1965), p. 240.
64. *Proceedings of the Bimetallic Conference, December 13th, 1888.*
65. H. S. Foxwell, 'The International Monetary Conference,' *CR*, vol. lxii (Dec. 1892), p. 808.
66. W. M. Springer, 'An International Monetary Conference,' *NAR*, vol. cliv (Mar. 1892), p. 341.
67. See J. J. Green, 'Rentiers versus Producers? The Political Economy of the Bimetallic Controversy c. 1880–1898,' *EHR*, vol. ciii (July 1988), for Balfour's support for bimetallism, p. 589 and B. Dugdale, *Arthur James Balfour*, 2 vols (London, 1936). i, pp. 175–81.
68. HP, Box 166, G. Goschen to R. Welby, 14 Aug. 1892, f. 7.
69. J. P. Nichols, 'Silver Diplomacy,' *Political Science Quarterly*, vol. xliv (1933), pp. 565–88.
70. C. L. Currie (ed.), *Bertram Wodehouse Currie, 1827–1896: Recollections, Letters and Journals*, 2 vols (Roehampton, 1901).
71. HP, Box 166, Gladstone to R. Welby, 21 Aug. 1893, f. 43.
72. Ibid., 'Memorandum of Instructions for the British Delegates appointed by Her Majesty's Government to attend the International Monetary Conference at Brussels,' dated 17 Nov. 1892. Also see the plethora of correspondence between Harcourt and the delegates and various financial authorities.
73. Ibid., Harcourt to Freemantle, 19 Nov. 1892, f. 222.
74. WP, Box 14, Harcourt to White, 12 Nov. 1892.
75. Ibid., Box 1, Diary. 1892–93, 18 Nov. 1892. See Appendix II.
76. HP, Box 166, R. L. Everett to Harcourt, 14 Oct. 1892, ff. 101–2; G. Howell to Harcourt, 12 Oct. 1892, ff. 98–9; and S. Smith to Harcourt, 15 Oct. 1892, ff. 109–12. Also see Harcourt's responses: Harcourt to Everett, 16 Oct. 1892, ff. 124–32 and Harcourt to Smith, 18 Oct. 1892, ff. 113–20.
77. Ibid., S. Smith to Harcourt, 15 Oct. 1892, f. 111.
78. Ibid., Box 167, Harcourt to A. Rothschild, 6 Dec. 1892, f. 11.

79. W. Gladstone to B. Currie, 19 Dec. 1892, cited in B. W. Currie, *Recollections, Letters and Journals*, 2 vols (Roehampton, 1901), ii, p. 253.
80. HP, Box 167, Harcourt to R. Wilson, 14 Dec. 1892, f. 96.
81. Balfour speech on 'Bimetallism' at Manchester Town Hall, 27 Oct. 1892, reported in *The Times*, 28 Oct. 1892 and Chaplin speech on 'Land and Bimetallism' at the Surveyors' Institution in London, 23 Jan. 1893, reported in *The Times*, 24 Jan. 1893.
82. W. H. Grenfell, 'Mr. Gladstone and the Currency,' *FR*, vol. liv (Sept. 1893), pp. 297–316 and H. S. Foxwell, 'The International Monetary Conference' and 'Lord Farrer on the Monetary Standard,' *Nat.R*, vol. xxiv (Jan. 1895), pp. 637–60.
83. NP, L. D. MacKay to Norton, 27 Dec. 1893 (5718). Also see HP, Box 221, H. H. Gibbs to Harcourt, 15 Oct. 1892, f. 77.
84. L. Courtney, 'Bimetallism Once More,' *NC*, vol. xxxiii (Apr. 1893), p. 630.
85. W. H. Grenfell, 'Mr. Gladstone and the Currency' and M. Frewen, 'The Currency Crisis in the United States,' *FR*, vol. liii (June 1893), pp. 772–3.
86. God.P, L. Courtney to Godkin, 2 May 1893 (219).
87. HP, Box 167, W. Houldsworth to Harcourt, 23 Dec. 1892, f. 139.
88. Ibid., Box 168, 'Harcourt memorandum of a meeting with Senator Jones,' 17 Jan. 1893, ff. 42–3.
89. Brit. Mus., Addit. MSS 49659 (Avebury Papers): Farrer to J. Lubbock, 22 and 26 Feb. 1893, ff. 38–40.
90. Hansard, 4th series, vol. ix, 28 Feb. 1893, 606–19.
91. Car.P, Vol. 20, Carnegie to Morley, 16 Apr. 1893 (3706).
92. Hansard, 4th series, vol. ix, 28 Feb. 1893, 683.
93. WP, Box 14, Harcourt to White, 10 and 11 May 1893, and HP, Box 168, White to Harcourt, 13 May 1893, ff. 104–5.
94. WP, Box 14, Harcourt to White, 16 May 1893.
95. Car.P, vol. 20, Carnegie to G. Cleveland, 22 Apr. 1893 (3746).
96. A. Leslie, *Mr. Frewen of England. A Victorian Adventurer* (London, 1968) pp. 143–50 and M. Frewen, *The Economic Crisis* (London, 1888).
97. M. Frewen, 'The Currency Crisis in the United States,' p. 762.
98. Spring-Rice to R. Munro Ferguson, 9 June 1894, cited in S. Gwynn (ed.), *The Letters and Friendships of Sir Cecil Spring-Rice: A Record*, 2 vols (Boston, 1929), i, p. 157.
99. H. Childers to E. Yarnell, Sept. 1893, cited in E. Childers, *The Life and Correspondence of the Right Hon. Hugh C. E. Childers, 1827–1896*, 2 vols (London, 1901), ii, p. 337.
100. God.P, Bryce to Godkin, 17 Feb. 1895 (142).
101. E. Atkinson, 'How Distrust Stops Trade,' *NAR*, vol. clvii (July 1893), p. 29.
102. Carnegie, 'The Silver Problem. I. A Word to Wage-Earners,' *NAR*, vol. clvii (Sept. 1893), pp. 364–5.
103. J. Lubbock, 'The Silver Problem. II. The Present Crisis,' *NAR*, vol. clvii (Sept. 1893), p. 371.
104. Ibid., p. 375.
105. Ibid., p. 378.
106. M. Frewen, 'Silver in the Fifty-Third Congress,' *Nat.R*, vol. xxii (Dec. 1893), pp. 542–57.

107. Carnegie, 'The ABC of Money,' *NAR*, vol. clii (June 1891), pp. 723–50.
108. Car.P, Vol. 24, T. Bantock to Carnegie, 18 May 1894 (4749).
109. Ibid., Carnegie to A. Balfour, 14 May 1894 (4731).
110. Ibid. (4732).
111. Ibid., A. Balfour to Carnegie, 16 May 1894 (4742).
112. PP, *Reports, minutes and evidence of the Royal Commission on Agricultural Depression*, Part I (1894) XVI, C. 7400; Part II (1894) XVI, C. 7400-II; Part III (1894) XVI, C. 7400-III; and Part IV (1894) XVI, C. 7400-IV.
113. PP, Part II (1894) XVI, C. 7400-II, 26 and 27 July 1894, pp. 559–94. Another interesting American participant in the Commission's proceedings was John Clay, a partner in a Chicago cattle firm and also cattle rancher in the Western States. Clay was appointed a member of the Commission and also testified. PP, Part I (1894) XVI, C. 1894, C. 7400, pp. 248–58.
114. 'Silver and the Tariff at Washington,' *FR*, vol. lv (June 1894), pp. 837–8.
115. Farrer, 'Silver and the Tariff at Washington,' *FR*, vol. lvi (July 1894), p. 118.
116. Frewen, J. S. Nicholson and J. Faraday, 'Silver and the Tariff at Washington,' *FR*, vol. lvi (July 1894), pp. 119–31.
117. Hansard, 4th series, vol. xxx, 26 Feb. 1895, 1573–1655.
118. See Chapter 6, pp. 236–7.
119. H. V. Emy, *Liberals, Radicals and Social Politics, 1892–1914* (Cambridge, 1973), pp. 38–63 and D. A. Hamer, *John Morley: Liberal Intellectual in Politics* (Oxford, 1968), pp. 255–70. American liberals also were reluctant to champion the causes of 'dangerous classes.' See J. Sproat, *'The Best Men': Liberal Reformers in the Gilded Age* (London, 1968), pp. 205–42.
120. Thompson, *Socialists, Liberals and Labour. The Struggle for London 1885–1914* (London 1967), pp. 90–111. Also see the biographies of A. J. Mundella, G. J. Shaw-Lefevre, Joseph Arch, William Caine, Jesse Collings, George Howell, and William Rathbone.
121. American labor problems had attracted some British interest in 1877 over a series of railway strikes. PP, *Reports respecting the late Industrial conflicts in the United States* (1877) LXXXIV, C. 1853 and G. Smith, 'The Labour War in the United States,' *CR*, vol. xxx (Sept. 1877), pp. 529–41.
122. H. Hyndman, *The Chicago Riots and the Class War in the United States* (London, 1886); Kenneth O. Morgan, *Keir Hardie, Radical and Socialist* (London, 1975), pp. 85–7; E. Marx Aveling, *Working Class Movement in America* (London, 1887); and E. Aveling, *The Chicago Anarchists* (London, 1888).
123. Pelling, *America and the British Left*, p. 63.
124. H. Pelling, 'The Knights of Labor in Britain, 1880–1901,' *Econ.HR*, vol. ix, no ii (1956), p. 328.
125. Kenneth O. Morgan, *Keir Hardie*, pp. 85–7 and 185–8, and 'The Future at Work,' eds H. C. Allen and R. Thompson, *Contrast and Connection: Bicentennial Essays in Anglo-American History* (London, 1976), pp. 250–1.
126. *The American Commonwealth* (London, 1888), ii, pp. 369–71 and iii, pp. 69–71.
127. Car.P, Vol. 17, Gladstone to Carnegie, 19 Sept. 1892 (3149–50).
128. Ibid., Rosebery to Carnegie, 10 Oct. 1892 (3212–13).

129. Ibid., Carnegie to Stead, 6 Aug. 1892 (3132–3); Stead to Carnegie, 9 Aug. 1892 (3137); and Carnegie to Stead, 11 Aug. 1892 (3138–9).
130. Ibid., Vol. 20, Carnegie to Morley, 16 Apr. 1893 (3703–4).
131. PP, *Report of the Royal Commission on Labour, foreign reports. United States,* Part V (1892) XXXVI, C. 6795-X, pp. 1–59.
132. W. H. G. Armytage, *A. J. Mundella 1825–1897. The Liberal Background to the Labour Movement* (London, 1951), p. 293.
133. E. R. L. Gould, 'The Social Condition of Labour,' *CR*, vol. lxiii (Jan. 1893), pp. 125–52; Stead, 'Incidents of Labour War in America,' *CR*, vol. lxvi (July 1894), pp, 65–76; and J. S. Jeans, 'The Labour War in the United States,' *NC*, vol. xxxvi (Aug. 1894), pp. 259–67.
134. Chamberlain, 'The Labour Question,' *NC*, vol. xxxii (Nov. 1892), pp. 677–710 and Dilke, 'The Labour Problem,' *Ne.R*, vol. viii (Mar. 1893), pp. 313–27.
135. '"Coxeyism:"' A Character Sketch,' *RR* (New York edn), vol. x (July 1894), p. 47.
136. Ibid., p. 56.
137. Stead, *If Christ Came to Chicago!* (London, 1894), pp. 388–9.
138. BP, USA 7, S. Low to Bryce, 6 Aug. 1894, f. 233.
139. God.P, Bryce to Godkin, 20 Sept. 1892 (130).
140. Ibid., 1 Jan. 1895 (140).
141. Sproat, 'The Best Men,' p. 207.
142. The whole question of Liberal attitudes towards American trusts, combinations, and industry does not enter into focus in this study. Henry Pelling identified 1897 as the year in which British labor leaders suddenly turned to analyze the problems of American industry. 'The American Economy and the Foundation of the British Labour Party,' *Econ.HR*, vol. viii, no. i (1955), pp. 1–17.
143. A. Shaw, *Municipal Government in Great Britain* (London, 1895); F. Goodnow, *Municipal Home Rule. A Study in Administration* (New York, 1895), pp. 233–66; and also D. Eaton, *The Government of Municipalities* (New York, 1899), pp. 309–36. The whole topic of Ango-American municipal reform and the contacts between the reformers is very much in need of additional study.
144. David Cannadine notes that it was in the 1880s that 'the attack on the aristocratic monopoly of land in England shifted its emphasis from the rural to the urban context' and that consequently 'the transatlantic arguments and analogies were deployed even more.' 'Urban Development in England and America in the 19th Century: Comparisons and Contrasts,' *Econ.HR*, vol. xxxiii, no iii (Aug. 1980), p. 309.
145. ii, pp. 262–320 and 429–536. Also see, Bryce's first impressions of American cities, Chapter 1, pp. 27–8.
146. Low, 'An American View of Municipal Government in the United States,' ii, pp. 296–317, and Goodnow, 'The Tweed Ring in New York City,' iii, pp. 173–98.
147. BP, USA 22, Bryce to H. Lea, 10 Dec. 1887, f. 23.
148. Ibid., 16, Smith to Bryce, 16 Apr. 1892, f. 75.
149. Ibid., 17, Bryce to Smith, 24 Apr. 1892, f. 179.
150. Ibid., 22 Mar. 1892, f. 180.

151. Ch.P, Diary 1887–88, 9 Nov. 1887, JC 3/13/4.
152. Chamberlain, 'Municipal Institutions in America and England,' *The Forum*, vol. xiv (Nov. 1892), p. 268.
153. Ibid.
154. Ibid., p. 279.
155. *How the Other Half Lives* (New York, 1890) and *Wealth Against Commonwealth* (New York, 1894).
156. R. Hofstadter, *The Age of Reform* (New York, 1955), p. 185.
157. *If Christ Came to Chicago!*, p. 54.
158. Ibid., p. 273 and Bryce, *The American Commonwealth*, i, pp. 100–10.
159. *If Christ Came to Chicago!*, p. 274.
160. Ibid., p. 351.
161. Ibid., pp. 399–400.
162. Bryce to Stead, 17 Mar. 1894, cited in R. Whyte, *The Life of W. T. Stead*, 2 vols (London, 1925), ii, p. 39 and Smith, '"If Christ Came to Chicago,"' *CR*, vol. lxvi (Sept. 1894), pp. 389–98.
163. G. C. S. Churchill, 'Virginia Mines and American Rails,' *FR*, vol. lxix (Apr. and May 1891), pp. 570–83 and 780–97; Lady Grey-Egerton and Lady Sykes, 'Two Englishwomen in America,' *NAR*, vol. clvi (Apr. 1893), pp. 449–60; and A. S. Northcote, 'American Life Through English Spectacles,' *NC*, vol. xxxiv (Sept. 1893), pp. 476–88 and 'The Utter Corruption in American Politics,' *NC*, vol. xxxv (Apr. 1894), pp. 692–700.
164. Spring-Rice to Munro-Ferguson, 9 June 1894, cited in Gwynn (ed.), *Letters of Spring-Rice*, i, p. 157.
165. God.P, Bryce to Godkin, 17 Feb. 1894 (137).
166. (New York, 1898). Bryce is only a bit more optimistic about New York politics. 'The Mayorality Election in New York,' *CR*, vol. lxxii (Nov. 1897), pp. 751–60.
167. Sproat, 'The Best Men,' p. 257.
168. D. Eaton, *The Civil Service in Great Britain. A History of Abuses and Reforms and their bearing upon American Politics* (London, 1880) and R. Titlow, *American Import Merit: Origins of the United States' Civil Service and the Influence of the British Model* (Washington, 1979).
169. Roosevelt made no mention of British practices in an article, 'An Object Lesson in Civil Service Reform,' *AM*, vol. lxvii (Feb. 1891), pp. 252–7.
170. God.P, Farrer to Godkin, 30 Dec. 1886 (272).
171. Earl Grey to M. Trumbull, 18 Nov. 1893, cited in M. Trumbull, *22 Pamphlets on Free Trade* (Chicago, 1893) (Bodleian Library, Oxford), p. 19.
172. See in particular the Bryce–Roosevelt material. Roosevelt Papers, Bryce to Roosevelt, 23 Feb. 1891 (275–6); 12 Dec. 1891 (290–1); 15 June 1892 (306–7); 22 Feb. 1895 (409–10); and 10 Apr. 1895 (417–8), Reel 1, Series 1 (1889–1898). Roosevelt letters are in BP, USA 10.
173. Argyll, 'The English Elections and Home Rule,' pp. 300–2 and W. Gladstone, 'A Vindication of Home Rule,' pp. 392–4.
174. C. Dilke, *The Problems of Greater Britain*, 2 vols (London, 1890), i, pp. 173–80.
175. C. Bolt, 'The Growth of Racial Consciousness,' *The Anti-Slavery Movement and Reconstruction: A Study in Anglo-American Co-operation, 1833–77* (1969), pp. 141–70.

176. BP, USA 5, Godkin to Bryce, 19 Feb. 1892, f. 88. Bryce, 'Thoughts on the Negro Problem,' *NAR*, vol cliii (Dec. 1891), pp. 641–60.
177. God.P, Bryce to Godkin, 18 Mar. 1891 (121).
178. G. Cable, 'The Negro Question in the United States,' *CR*, vol. liii (Mar. 1888), pp. 443–68 and C. F. Aked, 'The Race Problem in America,' *CR*, vol. lxv (June 1894), pp. 818–27.
179. GP, Mrs Sands to Gladstone: 44509, 28 Jan. 1890, ff. 90–1; 44511, 20 Sept. 1890, ff. 28–9; and 44518, ff. 255–6. Gladstone condemns slavery in a book review '"Memorials of a Southern Planter,"' *NC*, vol. xxvi (Dec. 1889), pp. 984–6.
180. W. Reid, *Memoirs and Correspondence of Lyon Playfair* (London, 1899), ii, pp. 186–9 and Spring-Rice to 'Agnes,' 1 Apr. 1895, cited in Gwynn (ed.), *Letters of Spring-Rice*, pp. 168–72.
181. Bryce, 'Thoughts on the Negro Problem,' p. 641.
182. Ibid., p. 657.
183. Bryce, *The American Commonwealth* (New York, 1893–95), ii, pp. 518–20.
184. Ibid., 'Present and Future of the Negro' and 'The South Since the War,' ii, pp. 469–520.
185. B. Harrison, *Separate Spheres. The Opposition to Women's Suffrage in Britain* (London, 1978), pp. 27–105.
186. Bryce, *The American Commonwealth* (1888), iii, p. 303.
187. Smith, 'Woman Suffrage,' *Essays on Questions of the Day. Political and Social* (New York, 1893), pp. 183–200 and H. Plunkett, 'The Working of Woman Suffrage in Wyoming,' *FR*, vol. xlvii (May 1890), pp. 656–69.
188. Two other groups, the secularists and proportional representation members, had a wide variety of late-nineteenth-century contacts with America. See E. Royle's *Radicals, Secularists and Republicans: Popular Freethought in Britain, 1866–1915* (Manchester, 1980) and F. D. Parsons, 'Thomas Hare and the Victorian Proportional Representation Movement, 1857–1888' (Cambridge Univ. PhD thesis, 1990).
189. M. Barker, *Gladstone and Radicalism. The Reconstruction of Liberal Policy in Britain 1885–94* (London, 1975), p. 209.
190. W. Caine to Rosebery, 11 Nov. 1894, cited in Hamer, *Liberal Politics in the Age of Gladstone*, p. 188. Also, W. Caine, 'The Attitude of the Advanced Temperance Party,' *CR*, vol. lxiii (Jan. 1893), pp. 48–52.
191. N. Dow to W. Caine, 16 Apr. 1894, cited in J. Newton, *W. S. Caine, M.P. A Biography* (London, 1907), p. 268. For Dow's activities in England, see N. Dow, *The Reminiscences of Neal Dow. Recollections of Eighty Years* (Portland, ME, 1898), pp. 570–617, and for Anglo-American temperance contacts before 1870, see B. Harrison, *Drink and the Victorians* (London, 1976), pp. 196–7.
192. Goldwin Smith had urged Britons to study the rise of prohibition movements in the New World in 1889. 'Prohibition in Canada and the United States,' *MM*, vol. lix (Nov. 1889), pp. 338–49.
193. E. L. Fanshawe, *Liquor Legislation in the United States and Canada …* (London, 1893).
194. GP, 44521, Rathbone to Gladstone, 26 Oct. 1895, f. 100.
195. Ibid., Rathbone to Lord Bishop, 26 Oct. 1895, f. 101.
196. Ibid., p. 102.

197. A. Sherwell and J. Rowntree, *The Temperance Problem and Social Reform* (London, 1898), pp. 121–257.
198. J. Wall, *Andrew Carnegie* (New York, 1970), p. 424.
199. For instances of Carnegie's associations with British Liberals in the 1880s – he took regular coaching trips through England with his friends (i.e. 1884, with Mr and Mrs Matthew Arnold, novelist William Black, Edwin Arnold, and Samuel Storey); ran *The Echo* (a chain of Midland newspapers from 1883 to 1885; entertained Englishmen who visited the United States (E. Arnold, Mr. Arnold, Rosebery, and W. Storey); wrote many articles for British Liberal periodicals; and praised Liberalism highly in his *Triumphant Democracy* (London, 1886) – see especially, *An American Four-in-Hand in Britain* (New York, 1884), and *Our Coaching Trip: Brighton to Inverness* (New York, 1882).
200. Car.P, Box 258, 'Carnegie's notes on Morley's friendship' (1908).
201. Ibid.
202. Morley to Carnegie, 28 Dec. 1903, cited in Hamer, *Morley*, p. 181.
203. *Triumphant Democracy*, p. v.
204. Ibid., p. 480. In a section of his work, Carnegie lists the 17 major accomplishments of the United States (pp. 489–91).
205. Ibid., p. 496.
206. Ibid., pp. 501–6.
207. Ibid., p. 508.
208. Car.P, Vol. 9, Morley to Carnegie, 17 May 1886 (1534–5).
209. Ibid., Vol. 15, Morley to Carnegie, 18 Apr. 1892 (2832). Also see ibid., Vol. 16, Morley to Carnegie, 18 May and 25 May 1892 (2895 and 2925) and 8 June 1892 (2977).
210. Wall, *Carnegie*, p. 439.
211. Car.P, Vol. 6, 'Extracts from Mr. Gladstone's diary' (985). Also see Carnegie's contributions to Mrs Gladstone's charity and orphanage projects in London; New York Public Library, New York (Gladstone Collection): Mrs Gladstone to Carnegie, 4 July 1883, 27 Feb. 1884, 24 June 1887, and 3 July 1888.
212. GP, 44501, Carnegie to Gladstone, 21 July 1887, f. 199. See B. Hendricks, *The Life of Andrew Carnegie*, 2 vols (New York, 1932), i, p. 320.
213. Car.P, Vol. 17, 19 Aug. 1892 (3149–50), cited in Hendricks, *Andrew Carnegie*, i, p. 420.
214. GP, 44516, 24 Sept. 1892, f. 61.
215. See Hamer, *Morley*, p. 181.
216. Pelling, *America and the British Left*, pp. 53–4.
217. I. Bradley, *The Optimists: Themes and Personalities in Victorian Liberalism* (London, 1980).

6
Venezuela, Silver, and Rapprochement, 1895–1898

Introduction

The general election of June 1895 produced devastating results for the Liberal party. In 1892 they had held a respectable 270 seats; in 1895 they were down to 177. The Liberal Unionist group had prospered, rising from 47 to 70. The Unionists had added almost eighty to their 1892 total to number 341 at the time of the formation of the third Salisbury ministry. Nor had individual leaders survived the debacle. Morley had lost his seat at Newcastle, and some members of the Radical and Labour left, like W. Cremer and Keir Hardie, were similarly defeated. Internal party weakness and the inability of the Liberals to handle the major imperial and social problems of the day were primary causes for the defeat. Rosebery was hardly on speaking terms with either Morley or Harcourt, and their feud continued to fracture the party from 1895 to 1900. Each Liberal leader had his favorite view of the reasons for the party's collapse: sectionalism, faddism, programs, or Irish Home Rule. Many of the leaders turned, frustrated, away from active roles in politics, to travel, journalism, or historical and biographical pursuits. Gladstone's immense surplus of energy was running out and he sought peace among family and friends at Hawarden. On the other hand, there were some Liberals whose political philosophies and activities moved with the times. A body of younger men trained in Gladstonian Liberalism, such as Asquith, Edward Grey, and Richard Haldane, 'focused increasingly on foreign and imperial affairs.'[1] Moreover, another young group who composed the 'Rainbow Circle' founded the *Progressive Review* in 1890. L. T. Hobhouse, J. A. Hobson, Graham Wallas, and J. L. Hammond evolved a 'new' liberalism which advocated a larger national roll for the state in social and economic policy.[2] The term 'progressive' gained in acceptance on both sides of the Atlantic. Thus while older Liberal leaders struggled to maintain their faith in liberalism and their positions within the Liberal party leadership, younger men pressed forward with new ideas and vigorous policies.[3]

The major issues during the Salisbury ministry were foreign and imperial. A series of crises arose with alarming regularity: the Jameson raid, German–British relations, South Africa, Sudan and the Nile Valley, and Fashoda. In each case, there was little unity or consensus among the Liberal party. In addition, for the first time since the early 1870s, American issues attracted great national attention. The Venezuelan boundary question, bimetallism and silver, Anglo-Saxon racism, the titanic 1896 American presidential election, and finally the Spanish–American war, all, in different ways had profound consequences in Great Britain. At the same time, there were many positive influences at work which helped to shape what historians have defined as 'The Great Rapprochement' between Great Britain and the United States.[4]

Many studies have been made of the Anglo-Americans most responsible for the forging of the rapprochement of the late 1890s. Importance has been attached to the diplomatic contributions of Salisbury and Chamberlain on one side, and of Cleveland and Olney on the other, or to the Ambassadors Julian Pauncefote and Thomas Bayard.[5] Emphasis has been placed on the large contributions of major American imperialists and Anglo-Saxon racists Theodore Roosevelt, John Hay, and Henry Cabot Lodge, who realized the strategic necessity of the special English-speaking relationship.[6] Informal diplomacy has also been identified as an important contributing factor to Anglo-American settlements, notably over Venezuela.[7] None would deny the impact of these men upon Anglo-American rapprochement, or the impact of racism and economic forces.[8] On the other hand, British Liberals have received very little attention from historians.[9] Nor have the activities of their American counterparts been particularly evaluated. Gladstone, Harcourt, Morley, Bryce, and Playfair headed a body of Liberal activists on one side of the Atlantic while Carnegie, Atkinson, and Godkin led those on the other in the reaffirmation of a transatlantic understanding. For them, the various crises in Anglo-American relations between 1895 and 1898 never seriously threatened war, or were new departures. Instead, they constituted a fresh opportunity to cement the great moral and Anglo-Saxon cause which they had always believed in and worked for.

Anglo-Americans and international arbitration

When President Cleveland declared in his famous message on 17 December 1895 that the United States had the right to intervene on the basis of the Monroe Doctrine in a boundary dispute between British Guiana and Venezuela, Britons reacted with alarm and shock. For the first time since the 1860s, there was serious talk of a fratricidal Anglo-American war, and simultaneously, there was a sudden burst of interest in schemes of Anglo-American arbitration. These concerns were not new for Liberal leaders. Throughout the 1880s and 1890s, Liberals had been prominent advocates of a mixture of general and specific proposals to bring about the union of the English-speaking peoples. Some of these were the by-product of British plans for imperial federation; others were the result of the various British and American arbitration movements. They were important forerunners of the plans that gained great popularity between 1895 and 1898, and hence they deserve some treatment.

British Liberals had been associated with international arbitration ever since the Geneva settlement of the *Alabama* claims in 1871–72.[10] As the prime mover behind the Anglo-American understanding, Gladstone's name had become associated with harmonious Anglo-American relations. However, somewhat ironically, it was Gladstone who defeated a motion in the House of Commons in July 1873 to petition the American government on behalf of a permanent international arbitration treaty.[11] Gladstone's reason combined a two-fold argument that the time was not ripe and that artificial interference in the two countries' natural relations was wrong in principal.[12] The movement for Anglo-American arbitration went into hibernation for over a decade before it surfaced with renewed vigor in the mid-1880s.

In Great Britain, international and Anglo-American arbitration causes gained new strength under the leadership of British radicals and Liberals. Its guiding lights were William Randal Cremer, the 'Lib-Lab' MP for Haggerston from 1885 to 1895, and Hodgson Pratt, the President of the Working Men's Club from 1885 to 1902. Pratt had founded the International Arbitration and Peace Association of Great Britain in 1880. Its activities expanded conspicuously throughout Europe, especially in France, Belgium, and Austria.[13] Its journal, *Concord*, gained some popularity. The Association in 1888 included such varied members as Derby, Ripon, Cardinal Manning, John Bright, Sir John Lubbock, Justin McCarthy, Henry Broadhurst, Thomas Burt, Samuel Smith, Joseph Arch, William Rathbone, Samuel Storey, and

Andrew Carnegie.[14] It had significant ties with arbitration movements in the United States. The other major British peace organization, The Workmen's Peace Association, had been started by Cremer as far back as 1871, but in the 1880s, it gained momentum. In 1886 and 1887, Cremer organized a petition drive in the House of Commons which called for a bilaterial Anglo-American arbitration treaty. With the substantial aid of men like Burt and Carnegie, 233 members signed the petition. In the autumn of 1887, a delegation of Liberals and Labour leaders traveled to the United States and personally delivered the petition to President Cleveland. Cremer and Lyon Playfair headed the group of 13 MPs. 'All were Gladstonian Liberals.'[15] Playfair, who had only just finished with a panegyric on Anglo-American relations at the American centennial in Independence Hall in Philadelphia a month before, addressed the President on behalf of the delegation on 31 October.

> Even if it does not effect an immediate or proximate treaty of arbitration, you will, Mr. President, recognize that the memorial is a remarkable expression of the brotherly feelings which our working classes entertain for their kinsmen in the United States. International arbitration, if established, would only be one step further in the history of civilization. When individuals quarrel, society does not permit them to settle the dispute by violence, but it refers them to courts of equity or law, in order that the differences may be composed. Why should not this principle be extended to nations, especially when, as in the case of the United Kingdom and the United States, they are allied by blood and knit together by love? We are both the common inheritors of the traditions and glories of the Anglo-Saxon race from which we have obtained the spirit of conciliation, a spirit that has so aided the national development of both countries.[16]

While President Cleveland was sympathetic towards the petition, he was unable to take any specific action. His hands were tied by the coming elections, and he did not want to alienate Irish voters by being overly friendly with Britain. On the other hand, the petition did have 'a tonic effect on peace and arbitration advocates in America, Britain, and France.'[17] In Great Britain, many prominent Liberals pushed hard for Anglo-American arbitration in the late 1880s and early 1890s, but their success was checked by opposition from Conservative and Liberal party leaders. Bryce and Playfair lavishly endorsed the movement in public.[18] Morley and Harcourt argued that 'We Liberals are the party of arbitration' during a controversy with Salisbury over British policy with France over the colony of Newfoundland.[19] But Salisbury, Rosebery, and even Gladstone were cool towards the movement. Clearly, Salisbury opposed such a policy which would encumber an active and even aggressive imperial foreign policy. Rosebery too believed that international arbitration 'was sublime but not practical.'[20] Gladstone, while friendly to the concept of Anglo-American understandings, neither openly disapproved nor denigrated arbitration. Yet he refused to attend the conference of the International Arbitration League or to send a letter of endorsement, this despite the urgent appeals of Cremer.[21] That Gladstone, the prime mover of the Geneva Treaty, had not endorsed Anglo-American arbitration was a major stumbling block in the efforts of the arbitrationists to garner wider public support for their schemes.

The real catalyst for a British position on Anglo-American arbitration appears to have emerged in the person of Andrew Carnegie. In 1892–93, an arbitration treaty became the Scottish-American industrialist's overriding passion. His almost utopian aims and his personal appeal to many Liberals did have an impact upon Liberals' views of arbitration. Carnegie's views were first spelled out in coherent form in an article in the *Nineteenth Century* in September 1891. He called for a 'Race Alliance' with a supreme court to adjudicate any differences between members of English-speaking nations.[22] The article gained the attention of many British enthusiasts for similar schemes. J. Ashley Cooper, a Liberal Unionist journalist, asked Carnegie if his *Greater-Britain* might not become 'the organ of those who supported the idea of re-union of the Anglo-Saxon Race.'[23] A. J. Balfour also was most advanced in regard to the 'federation of the race.'[24] Nobody was more excited than W. T. Stead, who himself had propounded ideas similar to Carnegie's a decade earlier in his *Review of Reviews*.[25] Stead met with the South African adventurer, Cecil Rhodes, whose ideas he reported to Carnegie to be 'almost identical' with the latter's.[26] Inspired by these important responses of leading figures, Carnegie moved ahead to publish a more detailed plan.

'A Look Ahead' in the *North American Review* in June 1893 outlined a scheme that fell just short of the total reunification of Great Britain and the United States. He called for 'The Re-united States' or 'The British-American Union': 'the future is certainly to see a re-union of the separated parts and once again a common citizenship.'[27] While Carnegie admitted the utopian nature of the plan, he argued that this new state would profit enormously from the chance to join American and British economic and political merits. Public and private reactions were excited and far-ranging. Salisbury thanked Carnegie for a copy of the article, while Chamberlain underlined his approval of the Anglo-American themes of unity and race but not the practical plan.[28] Goldwin Smith likewise thought the plan impractical, but lauded Carnegie's campaign on behalf of Anglo-American union.[29] In fact, the Canadian Unionist movement, which advocated union between the United States and Canada, was greatly impressed by Carnegie's plan.[30] In retrospect, very few individuals found much substance in 'The British-American Union,' but Carnegie had succeeded in firing up a large transatlantic discussion on the general question of Anglo-American union.'[31]

In the midst of British disputations over Carnegie's schemes in the summer of 1893, there were significant warming of attitudes in British public circles to Anglo-American arbitration. On 16 June 1893, the Liberal government supported a unanimous resolution in the House of Commons for an arbitration treaty with the United States. The resolution, introduced by Cremer and seconded by Sir John Lubbock, finally induced Gladstone to break his silence. In turning to support the measure, the Prime Minister cited the many American moves towards arbitration as a major factor in his endorsement. He also called for a tribunal to adjudicate European differences, in addition to an Anglo-American tribunal.[32] While almost all of the leading Gladstonian Liberals – Harcourt, Morley, Bryce, and Playfair – enthusiastically championed the Anglo-American arbitration cause following the passage of the resolution, Rosebery withheld his support. Not until Cremer circulated another arbitration petition in the House of Commons in 1894 did Rosebery apparently finally come around.[33] Even then Rosebery was anxious to keep his new views hidden. Cremer, who had focused a great deal of energy on winning Rosebery over to the cause in 1893–94, reported excitedly to Carnegie: 'what a change has been affected in his views upon the subject since I had a similar meeting with him eighteen months ago.'[34] With Rosebery's support, now the Prime Minister, the prospects of an Anglo-American arbitration treaty noticeably improved. W. Evans Darby, the Secretary of the International Arbitration and Peace Association, urged Rosebery not to 'fail to take any opportunity which may present itself of furthering the principle of International Arbitration.'[35] In fact, as it will be recalled, Rosebery did exactly the opposite. When the opportunity arose to arbitrate with the United States over the Nicaraguan incident in the winter of 1894–95, Rosebery and Kimberley urged force. Harcourt in vain urged arbitration. The fact that Rosebery had moved against arbitration in the face of the majority of the Liberal leaders' steady adoption of arbitration in theory and practice did not augur well for Liberal party consensus.

Silver and bimetallism: final reconsiderations

From June to December 1895, or the period immediately prior to the Venezuelan crisis, many British Liberals were alive to critical developments in the United States. While President Cleveland's address surprised the vast majority of Englishmen in December, a few keen observers feared such an international incident. There were two fundamental American issues of potential danger in the eyes of these few Liberals: silver and aggressive overseas imperialism.

American silver dominated the attention of most British experts on the United States in the summer and fall of 1895. While T. H. Farrer had passed on the views of Edward Atkinson to Harcourt 'that the Silver danger is really over in America,' Liberal economists were not convinced.[36] The mushrooming American support for the 'silver fanaticism' of William Jennings Bryan and Anglo-American support for international bimetallism were conspicuous dangers to orthodox Liberals. In July, a body of bankers and politicians countered this growing silver menace. 'The agitation on behalf of silver, both abroad and at home, has assumed such proportions that it is thought desirable to form an *Association to oppose the policy known as Bimetallism and to unite in defense of the Gold Standard.*'[37] Their organization, the Gold Standard Defense Association, was a predominantly Liberal body. It had the open and active support of Gladstone, Harcourt, Playfair, Farrer, and Shaw-Lefevre, in addition to such Liberal Unionists as Lubbock and Sir M. E. Grant-Duff.[38] The fact that the Conservative government included several bimetallists in its Cabinet, Balfour and Henry Chaplin, made the gold–silver debate something approaching a party issue.

In the spring of 1895, Balfour had been in close touch with his intimate Republican friend and former American Secretary at the London Legation, Henry White. He was anxious to discover support for international bimetallism among Republicans, who seemed likely to defeat the weakened President Cleveland in the following election year. White likewise was interested in possible official British sympathy for bimetallism. Both men calculated that any move towards international bimetallism would have to come simultaneously from both British and American leaders. Both also were relatively optimistic, but concluded that any common British–American moves would have to await the presidential election.[39] British and American monometallists also cooperated. Farrer, Shaw-Lefevre, Playfair, and others were closely in touch with Edward Atkinson, guiding light of the Boston Sound Money and liberal-reform clubs.[40] There was something of an informal alliance between British Conservatives and American Republicans over international bimetallism, and between Liberals and Democrats over monometallism. This endured until the Democrats chose Bryan as their candidate and the Republicans selected McKinley.

T. H. Farrer and Lyon Playfair took the lead among prominent Liberals in arguing against the dangers of both international bimetallism and American silver. Farrer, who wrote more pamphlets for the Gold Standard Defense Association than anybody else, argued strongly against international bimetallism. It was pure 'folly' to push for international conferences for silver parity because there were gigantic inequalities between the British and American financial systems. Moreover, while the Western States of America were silver rich, Britain had no stock of silver and could not mine any.[41] Playfair, in response to the Association's belief that American bimetallism was a critical issue in Great Britain, published a pamphlet on that topic in November.

Playfair demonstrated that the silver system had been long tried in the United States earlier in the nineteenth century. Unable to produce stable prices and wages, it had failed. In the 1890s, there was more than ever a lack of faith in silver, with investors, creditors, and debtors preferring gold to silver. Everyone preferred to trade in gold rather than silver. Because of the threat of silver, people were withholding their gold from transactions. Thus for instance, in 1889, 90 percent of the tariff duties were paid in gold. By the end of 1893, no tariff duties were paid in gold. In conclusion, a dual monetary system just did not work.

> This short history of Bimetallism in the United States conclusively shows that no ratios between silver and gold have been able to maintain a parity of value between silver and gold, or to lessen the operation of the Gresham law, that undervalued and overvalued money cannot remain in concurrent circulation – at least, in parity.[42]

Gold had been drained from the United States because of her partially bimetallic system. Liberals feared that that should happen in Britain: that London should be drained of all her vast financial and commercial credit.

The second American topic that excited some Liberal interest in the United States between June and December 1895 was the new imperialistic and aggressive foreign spirit of America. For a small corps of Liberal authorities on American expansion in South America, Hawaii, Samoa, and the Far East, the Venezuela crisis did not catch them by surprise. W. T. Stead, in an article in the *Contemporary Review* and another in the *Westminster Gazette,* warned Englishmen 'not to belittle the significance of the ebullition of American sentiment on the question of the Venezuelan frontier.'[43] In November, the American Edward Atkinson and Lady Henry Somerset, leader of the Women's Temperance and International Arbitration movements, both warned against the rise of American jingoism.[44] Leo Maxse's jingoistic Unionist periodical, the *National Review*, which led all British periodicals in the regular coverage of American events from 1895 to 1898, drew attention to Venezuela: 'Venezuela has resorted to the device of endeavouring to excite the jealousy of the United States in this dispute with Great Britain.'[45] Finally, from across the Atlantic came Goldwin Smith's warnings about the dangers of the bellicose Joseph Chamberlain. 'Chamberlain's Jingoism is stirring up the tail-twisters at Washington, and I should not wonder if, in the end, he stirred them up to some purpose.'[46] Close observers of American politics and finance, men like Playfair, Stead, Farrer, and Goldwin Smith, were worried about either 'silver' or 'Venezuela.' They could not gauge the extent of the crisis, or its form, but they were apprehensive of the United States.[47]

Liberalism and informal diplomacy over Venezuela

On 17 December 1895, Cleveland delivered a message to Congress. In it, the President appointed an American commission with powers to collect facts and make recommendations on a solution to the boundary conflict between Venezuela and British Guiana. He based his interference upon the Monroe Doctrine.[48] British reactions expressed shock and amazement. The London dailies for 18 December bristled with rage.[49] The official British response was stiff. Chamberlain, the Colonial Secretary, believed that Cleveland's address represented typical American opportunistic electioneering tactics which underlined the inglorious traits of American politics.

> At bottom, I believe it is due to the extreme sensitiveness and vanity of Americans as a nation ...
>
> I have very little confidence in the Senate as it is constituted at present. The majority are not received even in Washington Society. They are local lawyers, speculators & professional politicians.

> Cleveland is a coarse-grained man, with, I think, a good deal of the bully in his composition. He has yielded to the Jingoes but not altogether without sympathy with their views.[50]

Chamberlain and Salisbury adhered firmly to the full British position which refused to acknowledge any American rights to act as a party in the South American dispute. They followed a policy of temporization, with protection of all British interests in British Guiana, and only a limited arbitration. Other more crucial issues suddenly exploded on the scene, such as the failure of the Jameson raid in South Africa. Yet, official British attitudes towards the United States were decidedly cool. Most Liberal leaders, on the other hand, reacted much differently.

While British Liberals were as stunned by Cleveland's address as anyone, most leaders took an active part from the start in issuing calming and conciliatory exhortations to the Americans.[51] Many of the latter turned anxiously to Liberals, as the party in opposition, in the hope that they could help stem the tide of war talk. On 20 December, Joseph Pulitzer, the editor of the *New York World*, telegraphed Gladstone for his view. Pulitzer saw his words as carrying immense importance, as an influence on both British and American opinion:

> American sentiment is at the turning point, once turned the wrong way no power on earth can hold it back. In the American mind you [Gladstone] more than any score of other men, and more than the government, epitomize the British people. A word of peace and fellowship from you today will aid to check clamor, to soothe passion, to encourage sober thought, and may avert a calamity.[52]

Gladstone responded quickly, eager, for once, his private secretary noted, to please an enthusiastic American journalist.[53] 'I dare not interfere. Only common sense is required. I cannot say more with advantage.'[54] While Gladstone had apparently said little, 'common sense' was adopted in both the United States and Great Britain as a rallying call by arbitrationists and conciliators. Pulitzer also sought out Rosebery's response. 'I can only reply that I absolutely disbelieve in the possibility of war between the United States and Great Britain on such an issue as this, for it would be the greatest crime on record.'[55] Other Liberal voices responded warningly. L. Atherley-Jones, a radical Liberal MP, called upon the British to acknowledge the Monroe Doctrine.[56] Playfair urged that 'common sense' must prevail.[57] Finally, a leading Liberal daily, the *Westminster Gazette*, pushed for well thought out, calm consideration, and zaccused the Conservative government of agitating the crisis.[58] The response of Liberal leaders to the outbreak of the Venezuelan crisis was much more than an emotive appeal to 'common sense' and Anglo-American understanding. From the start, they sought to publicize practical remedies, which constituted compromises between American and British positions. Gladstone was one of the first who thought the Liberal party should have a policy regarding Venezuela. On his way to vacation in Biarritz, he wrote Ripon that the 'party ought to have its opinion and its line upon [Venezuela].'[59] While Gladstone acknowledged Cleveland's 'astounding folly,' he firmly believed there should be a detailed study of who had title to the disputed land and of the full real and implicit nature of the Monroe Doctrine. He listed the most pressing problem as:

1. The American Monroe Doctrine
2. The Schomb[urgk] line[60]
3. Any prescriptive title from occupation
4. The question whether that occupation has been under protest from Venezuela.[61]

Gladstone was cautiously optimistic about Anglo-American relations. They were 'rosy enough,' if given proper attention. His letter was passed among Liberal leaders, from Ripon to Kimberley to Rosebery. All three imperialists believed that a policy indeed needed framing, but they were not sure that Gladstone had his priorities right. Rosebery thought Gladstone's points were not the central ones, rather it was 'Cleveland's attitude' that was 'the first problem & the main difficulty.' In this respect, Rosebery supported the hard-line approach of Salisbury. 'He [Cleveland] cannot recede, & we cannot give away to his menace.'[62] Kimberley fully concurred: 'We cannot submit to be bullied by the United States.'[63] However, as leader of the Liberals, Rosebery was concerned that the party adopt some sort of unified policy before the opening of parliament in February. Yet before the meeting at Mentmore, the anti-imperialist or Cobdenite wing of the party had gone a long way in associating British Liberals with the twin policy of a formal Anglo-American arbitration treaty and compromise on the boundary dispute in Venezuela. Between Christmas 1895 and February 1896, the Liberals divided into two camps over Venezuela – those led by Rosebery, Kimberley, and Ripon who urged a stance not much different from the government's, and those led by Harcourt,

Morley, and Playfair who called for the policy of conciliation and arbitration.

Harcourt was the distinct leader of the arbitration-minded body of Liberals. His reaction to this major Anglo-American crisis was similar to that of 1863 to 1871, when 'Historicus' had calmed Anglo-American sensibilities over the *Alabama* raiders. Even after the Jameson raid emerged in January as an equally or more threatening crisis for the Salisbury ministry, Harcourt believed that Venezuela was more important. He was not alone in his views. On 10 January, Edward Hamilton admitted: 'Far more serious however than the Transvaal business is the American difficulty, towards which there is apparently no solution at present forthcoming.'[64] Harcourt's initial reaction represented the stances of many Liberals:

> I cannot understand the grounds on which arbitration as a mere question of boundary has been refused by us. It is above all the sort of question to which arbitration is most appropriate ... A war with America *must be avoided at all* costs and irrespective of all Party considerations.[65]

Other prominent Liberals thought the situation serious, but were sure that if the British offered arbitration or conciliatory stances on Venezuela, there would be no danger of war.

A flurry of schemes appeared in letters to *The Times*: from Cremer; Playfair; Carnegie; the Dean of Canterbury, F. W. Farrer; the Methodist Reverend Hugh Price Hughes; Atherley-Jones; the Cambridge economist Alfred Marshall; the legal authority, James Westlake; and Samuel Smith MP.[66] In the *Westminster Gazette*, a series of interviews of leaders was prominently displayed. Sir John Lubbock urged the British 'to keep cool and firm,' suggesting that they should not forget Cobden's famous emphasis upon the importance of harmonious economic and political Anglo-American links.[67] Henry Fowler reiterated his own faith in arbitration. It had been the policy of many Americans and Englishmen for years.[68] Finally, the *Daily Chronicle* also published crucial views of Liberals. Playfair stressed that the working classes on both sides of the Atlantic, as well as the 'best classes,' wanted a permanent system of arbitration.[69] Gladstone himself gave his support for arbitration. He remarked that his views were unchanged since his Commons address in 1893.[70] Harcourt could easily feel inspired to take a hard-line stand on permanent arbitration, backed as he was by this vast public expression of conciliatory views by leading non-interventionist Liberals.

In January 1896, in a series of private moves, Harcourt sought to put pressure on the Salisbury government to act. While Salisbury and Chamberlain waited for the Americans to clarify their position, Harcourt became impatient. On 9 January, he confronted Chamberlain in a long and difficult meeting. Both men left unhappy accounts. Chamberlain was convinced that Harcourt was 'the greatest enemy of peace' in part because the latter wanted to reject the Schomburgk line (the Salisbury's government's minimum demand) in favor of arbitration:

> He [Harcourt] was sure that the people were on his side, and the fate of the Govt. if it did not settle the question, would be that of the Govt. of Lord North. I asked whether he meant to suggest that the Govt. which had always declined to submit to arbitration, the impossible claims of Venezuela the territory which had been for 100 years in British possession, were now to yield absolutely, and without conditions, to their demand because it was supported by the menace of Cleveland's message. He said that he would not go into that, but he had come to tell me that he would have nothing to do with war with America. I told him that if he spoke as he seemed inclined to do, he would be the greatest enemy of peace, for he would harden the hearts of Americans against any reasonable compromise or argument which might be suggested to settle the matter without dishonour to either nation.[71]

On his part, Harcourt lamented to his son that the Colonial Secretary had not been 'friendly to arbitration,' and to Edward Hamilton that the government's policy 'was not a good one.'[72] After testing each other's position, both Chamberlain and Harcourt changed tack. With Salisbury's full support, Chamberlain opened up informal negotiations with the United States. For these, he turned to a leading arbitration-minded friend of the Americans, Lyon Playfair. The contents of Playfair's talks with the thoroughly Anglophile American Ambassador, Thomas Bayard, were dutifully relayed back to Chamberlain. The early optimism of the private and secret meetings waned little by little. Playfair and Bayard were apt to find greater agreement than either of their chiefs, Chamberlain and Olney. By the end of January, these talks had ground to a halt.[73]

Meanwhile, Harcourt sought ways in which he could bring pressure to bear upon the intransigent Chamberlain. Other Liberals thought that the culprit was not the jingo Cleveland but the jingo Chamberlain. Bryce admitted to Godkin: 'Chamberlain has already begun to do mischief here – one thinks naturally of him as our typical unscrupulous demagogue. He advertises himself daily in the newspapers, and makes speeches of offensive character to the rest of the world.'[74] While Harcourt received supporting letters from many quarters, including Bryce, Henry Fowler, Tom Ellis, Shaw-Lefevre, and the social imperialist Alfred Milner,[75] his concern remained the government. He did find a large degree of sympathy for 'Conciliation with America' on the parts of Balfour and Hartington at a meeting at Chatsworth,[76] but neither Conservative Cabinet member desired to publicly support arbitration or oppose Salisbury and Chamberlain.[77] Harcourt's sense of frustration increased as January proceeded. He was not alone. Morley and Playfair, and the Americans Bayard, Carnegie, and Atkinson, joined him.[78]

Two celebrated Americans gave significant encouragement to the arbitration-minded wing of the Liberal party. Both Atkinson and Carnegie took individual initiatives in pressuring the British Unionist government to adopt arbitration, and throughout they cooperated closely with their Liberal friends. When Atkinson first heard Cleveland's message, he immediately cabled urgently to Goschen, the first Lord of the Admiralty with whom he had had contact on currency matters. Salisbury should propose 'to arbitrate and define the Monroe Doctrine on behalf of England and States, with whom it jointly originated, thus laying down conditions for permanent peace among English speaking peoples.'[79] Goschen thought Atkinson's plan 'certainly ingenious' but refused to push Salisbury.[80] Unable to influence the course of things in that manner, Atkinson turned to Playfair. Moreover, he was convinced that the Liberals had far 'the greatest role to play' in the crisis.[81]

Playfair, though doubtful that the government would consider the Monroe Doctrine as it stood in 1896 as opposed to what it was in the 1820s, approached Henry Buckle on Atkinson's behalf.[82] The editor of *The Times* was 'favourably inclined to consider the question.'[83] Playfair himself argued for Atkinson's plan in the *Daily Chronicle*.

> That doctrine [Monroe Doctrine], which means America for Americans, at least as regards the preponderating influence, is an idea that originated with the English rather than with the Americans, and it has never been opposed by any leading statesman of this country. If you recollect, it was England that drove foreigners out of America.[84]

Playfair was actively engaged in circulating arbitration and conciliatory schemes among British leaders even before he became the Salisbury government's informal negotiator.

Carnegie as the most famous progenitor of arbitration plans also directed his influence upon British leaders. On 26 December, he wrote to the Duke of Devonshire, like Goschen a former Liberal and considered perhaps as more favorable to arbitration. It was vital that a speedy solution be found by 'statesmen desirous of cementing the bonds of peace and goodwill between the two nations which comprise our race,' and before the beginning of the presidential campaign in 1896.[85] But Carnegie also placed his faith in the Liberals. He saw the cause of arbitration as a great moral cause capable of reinvigorating the fortunes of the party. Increasingly, he directed these views towards his good friend Morley.

> If Mr. Gladstone were only your age, we should have the Liberal Party back to power on the issue, Arbitration. If I were in your place, I should demand a day to discuss Lord Salisbury's refusal to arbitrate; denounce it; offer a resolution that this house disapproves Lord Salisbury's refusal to carry out the agreement to arbitrate made in 1885. Here is a moral question worth all your other questions put together, petty Home Rule included. If you ever mean to be leader of the Liberal Party, here is your chance. You will never probably have so grand an issue.[86]

Atkinson's and Carnegie's exhortations did not fall on unsympathetic ears. By the summer of 1896, Morley was very near to making arbitration his first issue.[87]

On the eve of Parliament's opening on 11 February, it was necessary for Liberals to agree on a common policy towards Venezuela. While Harcourt, Morley, Playfair, Fowler, and Shaw-Lefevre had argued for arbitration and conciliation, Rosebery, Kimberley, and Ripon had maintained silence. The latter essentially supported the government. Cooperation between the two Liberal bodies was bound to be difficult. Personal relations between Morley and Harcourt, and Rosebery had also deteriorated. Hamilton, who quite remarkably managed to remain friendly with all three, noted the impasse: 'R continues to feel the estrangement of John Morley much more than that of Harcourt.'[88] In addition, Hamilton described the wide divergence in Harcourt's and Rosebery's approaches to Venezuela:

> The Venezuelan business is evidently what is occupying his [Harcourt's] mind most; and I expect, that no matter what line Rosebery may take, Harcourt will go in strongly for arbitration – that

the American case and our case should be submitted to some third party, unless the matter can be arranged with Venezuela herself. He is convinced that the United States people are not going to 'climb down' at all – the feeling which Cleveland has roused is too strong except in places like New York & Washington.

R. [Rosebery] is observing a discreet silence; and I expect he will keep his counsels entirely to himself. ... Today he had his interview with Chamberlain.[89]

It would be unfair to say that Rosebery was any less seriously concerned over Venezuela than Harcourt, or that he accepted the full government position. In fact, he had lamented, the 'angular, bragging, tactless words of Salisbury and Chamberlain are largely responsible for our present difficulties.'[90] Yet he was also unimpressed with formal arbitration treaties and found it very difficult to co-operate with the activities of Harcourt or the political figures more openly supportive of arbitration.

Rosebery held an important meeting of Liberals at Mentmore on 8 February.[91] It was attended by Asquith, Bryce, Campbell-Bannerman, Ellis, Fowler, Herschell, Kimberley, Ripon, Tweedmouth, and Grey. Harcourt and Morley were not invited. Those present took a middle-line position. They neither wanted to embarrass the government, nor to alienate the arbitrationist Liberals, Asquith, Fowler, Ellis, and Bryce, who had demonstrated some such sympathies. There seems to be good evidence that the Mentmore meeting turned to Bryce, the unquestioned authority on America, for advice. Bryce, who had been on his way home from South Africa when the crisis exploded, originally had not followed the details closely. He had sought advice from Godkin.[92] Godkin had warned that Cleveland's message was political. It had been motivated by his wish to capture Republican jingoes and to promote another major issue other than the perilous ones of tariffs and currency. Godkin's advice was that Britain stand firm. 'If Salisbury is weak, & gives ground, we shall be covered with ridicule, & contempt.'[93] Bryce had been greatly impressed by these views as evidenced by the fact that he forwarded them to both Gladstone and Harcourt.[94] At the Mentmore meeting, it was Godkin's or Bryce's view that emerged and prevailed. Asquith reported the decision to present a strong front towards American demands to Harcourt.

> In the meantime, he [Lord Rosebery] and others think that it is very important to avoid saying anything that can stiffen the backs of the American jingoes – as e.g. anything that would seem to admit that a

case had actually arisen in Venezuela affecting the interests of the U.S. and so coming within the Monroe doctrine; or anything that would exclude the question of the character and extent of the actual occupation on both sides from the proposed arbitration.[95]

Despite the warning of the Mentmore group, Harcourt proceeded with a mild denunciation of Salisbury's Venezuelan policy on the opening day of Parliament, on 11 February. Rosebery made some remarks, praising the efforts of both Americans and British officials. Perhaps feeling that it was important to conciliate the arbitrationists, he welcomed 'in the most ungrudging spirit of delight' the arbitration movement to set up a Permanent Court. However, he said nothing of the difficult issues of the Monroe Doctrine or whether settled or unsettled districts should be excluded from negotiations.[96] On the other hand, Harcourt continued to press the government. He called for acceptance of the Monroe Doctrine, and for British cooperation with the American Commission that was investigating the Venezuelan crisis. He also attacked the government's approach towards arbitration:

> It is the question of the limitation of arbitration, but in the matter of limitation of arbitration you ought not to be too stiff or too arbitrary. It is not for one party in a dispute to define what is the dispute. It is quite plain that both parties to the dispute will have different opinions upon the subject. ... But mark this, if you choose to lay down a definite line which is to exclude the extreme claims of one party, do you think it reasonable that on the other side of the line your extreme claims should be left open, so that you may gain what you can in the arbitration and they can gain nothing?[97]

While Harcourt's criticisms of Salisbury were stiff, he did not want to handicap their ability to come to a successful solution. Five days later, Harcourt helped to crush a move by Atherley-Jones which called upon the government to formally accept arbitration. Yet, he did use the occasion to attack the government's dangerous delay.[98]

The Venezuelan Settlement and Anglo-American arbitration

By the end of February 1896, there was no longer any danger that the Venezuelan crisis would erupt into an Anglo-American war. Hamilton, who had been so mindful of the implications of the affair, noted on

16 February that Playfair thought that 'anything like hostilities between the two countries is out of all question.'[99] Thereafter, Hamilton hardly mentioned Venezuela in his diary during the remainder of 1896.[100] Nonetheless, British and American leaders, both jingoes and pacifists, Liberals and Unionists, Democrats and Republicans, diplomats and private citizens, journalists and editors, all searched for solutions.

The problems were two-fold: first, where the line should be drawn between British Guiana and Venezuela coupled with whether or not 'settled' districts should be included in an arbitration; and second, whether or not an Anglo-American Arbitration Tribunal should be established. By March, the British government had given up on informal diplomacy – through Playfair and Bayard, and Smalley, Olney, and Buckle – and resorted to formal negotiations through British Minister Pauncefote and Secretary of State Olney in Washington. Salisbury and Chamberlain stuck adamantly to their position. Arbitration was acceptable, but only of the unsettled areas and an arbitration treaty depended upon the outcome of the Venezuelan negotiations, and upon what specific issues would be arbitrable.

In July, Secretary of State Olney shifted ground. Threatened by an impending presidential election, it was deemed more profitable to have solved Venezuela than to twist the lion's tail. The Americans were now willing to accept arbitration excluding settled districts in lieu of full arbitration. The one remaining major problem was what constituted 'settled districts.' In the summer, Chamberlain took advantage of a visit to his wife's family in Massachusetts to try personal diplomacy himself with the vacationing Olney. Both men stuck obstinantly to their respective positions.[101] There was some softening up just prior to Chamberlain's departure. Anglo-American cooperation seemed much more possible over protestation on the Turkish massacres in Armenia than on the Venezuelan issue.[102] At long last, the final breakthrough came in the winter of 1896–97.

In November, Olney and Pauncefote signed an agreement which outlined 'settled' districts: fifty years' residence became the test of 'settled.' On the other problem of an arbitration treaty, a solution was reached on 11 January 1897, when Olney and Pauncefote signed another agreement. The Anglo-American tribunal would have jurisdiction over a specified number of issues. While the treaty on arbitration needed the approval of the Senate, both countries hailed with great relief the magnificent accord. In retrospect, the Venezuelan crisis had passed by relatively calmly in the winter. Anglo-American attention was now riveted on another matter, the 'battle of the standards.'

During this period, Liberal leaders were arguably the moving spirits behind both the actual Venezuelan settlement and the Anglo-American arbitration accord. Gladstone, with his failing health, and Rosebery, with his difficulties with various Liberals and his stance on Venezuela, took little part in these activities. Rosebery officially resigned from the leadership of the party in October 1896. Meanwhile, Harcourt and Morley led a corps of Liberals, both inside and outside Parliament, who improved Anglo-American relations.

We can only account for Lord Salisbury's action in negotiating with the United States a treaty to set up machinery for a permanent and obligatory system of arbitration, by examining the gradual influence of current ideas on the government, and by noting how they were absorbed and transformed by political necessity.[103]

Certainly, one of the most prominent voices for arbitration at this time became the extra-parliamentary organization inspired by W. T. Stead. On 14 January, all the various peace organizations and advocates met in London to establish a movement on behalf of an Anglo-American Permanent Court of Arbitration. Its guiding lights, in addition to Stead, were Lubbock, who chaired the meeting, the Dean of Canterbury, the Rev. Hugh Price Hughes, Lady Henry Somerset, and W. E. Darby. The aim of the meeting was to organize ways by which members could successfully popularize arbitration:

> But mere signatures, although valuable and indispensable, as laying the foundation for the Anglo-American Social Union for Arbitration and other purposes, are not enough. We want a public national expression of the universal opinion of all the best amongst us in favour of the establishment of some peace-making nexus between the Empire and the Republic. The press, the platform, and the pulpit, the three methods by which our Democracy expresses itself, must all be used.[104]

Following the meeting, Stead drew up a lengthy pamphlet, *Always Arbitrate Before You Fight*, which underlined the wide support for the movement. It included warm letters from Gladstone, President Cleveland, A. J. Balfour, and Playfair, as well as copies of resolutions passed in the Commons, Congress, and the New York Chamber of Commerce (15 January 1896). 'Arbitration is regarded in America as an American principle as national as the Monroe Doctrine.'[105] Moreover, favorable views of Lubbock, Fowler, James Stansfeld, Sir George Grey, James Bryce, and John Burns were also cited.[106] In the end a five-pronged attack was devised. Enthusiasts were urged to procure signatures for a memorial, to hold public meetings, to induce clergymen to bring it before their congregations, to secure resolutions from public bodies, and to influence the press.[107] As a start, Stead issued a clarion call in *The Times* and his *Review of Reviews*.[108]

The Anglo-American movement gained momentum. On 3 March, a second large meeting was held in London. The majority of the participants, as one historian has noted, were Liberals.[109] James Stansfeld, the leader of the repeal of the Contagious Diseases Acts, was the chairman. Many followers were unable to attend, but they sent their letters of support. Gladstone referred to his earlier positions. 'I am not fond of declarations in the abstract from men who are or have been responsible in public affairs, and I should wish my views of arbitration in lieu of war to be gathered from the part I took in the matter of *Alabama*.'[110] Even now Rosebery declared openly for arbitration, though it is difficult to figure how enthusiastically. He called for 'some court, or rather machinery for arbitration, to which the differences between ourselves and our kinsmen of the United States may be referred.'[111] Bryce, Asquith, Leonard Courtney, Labouchere, and Herbert Spencer also wrote in favorable fashions.[112] In addition to calling for a step up in public agitation, the meeting passed an important resolution, proposed by A. J. Mundella and the Baptist leader, John Clifford, to form an Anglo-American Union with a General Council.[113] The Council was dominated by Liberals but its various members included the Liberal-imperialist Asquith, the radical Labouchere, the Liberal Unionists Courtney and Chamberlain, and the Unionist Balfour.[114] There is no doubt that this large meeting did have its effect on the government. Two days later, Salisbury decided to negotiate a treaty of arbitration with the United States.[115] Across the Atlantic, the New York Bar Association mobilized its prominent members. On 22 and 23 April, it held a conference in Washington on behalf of the plan, 'The International Court of Arbitration.'[116]

Many prominent arbitration-minded Liberals became increasingly angry at the almost intentional delays on the part of the Salisbury ministry in solving the Venezuelan issue. It was one thing to put up a strong front to Cleveland's address in December 1895. It was a totally different matter to do so in March 1896. Harcourt, Morley, and Campbell-Bannerman all remonstrated over the delays.[117] Nor were the complaints from those who had participated in the informal diplomacy any less forceful. Smalley asserted that had Rosebery been in power Venezuela 'would have been practically settled before this.'[118] More and more the pressure fell upon Balfour, in part because he was the one member of the Cabinet who had asserted the need for conciliatory settlements and the vitality of Anglo-Saxon unity.[119] In mid-February, Harcourt urged Balfour that 'the necessity of coming to some arrangement at once is *very urgent*... We ought to assure at once the *principle* of arbitration.'[120]

In April, Harcourt was much more impatient, and an 'alarmist communication' by Smalley in *The Times* set off his wrath.[121] He told Balfour that he had 'remained tranquil' while the government had negotiated, but he no longer could hold his peace. He demanded some assurances that the British government were acting, otherwise he would have to force 'an official declaration of the present situation.'[122] Two days later, he informed Balfour that he would ask a question in the House. He also sent him a copy of the question he would ask.[123] Balfour gave his response in the House on 27 April. He was amiable but evasive.[124] If he had wished to act more directly, he was bound by an official diplomatic stalemate. Salisbury and Chamberlain insisted that settled districts be excluded from arbitration, while Olney still demanded full arbitration. In June, Olney admitted this situation to Henry White: 'You thus perceive that there is almost a dead-lock as respects both the Venezuelan boundary dispute and the general arbitration scheme – it perhaps being more pronounced in the former case than in the latter.'[125] Harcourt could no longer wait patiently. He undertook a new, more public offensive. In a speech at the National Liberal Club on 5 May, he attacked the government in his strongest language yet. He insisted that 'no personal pride, that no diplomatic obstinacy should be allowed to interpose to prevent a settlement of that nature.'[126]

In June and July, a number of prominent Americans lent their support to the Liberal agitation on behalf of the Venezuelan settlement and Anglo-American arbitration. For Carnegie, arbitration continued to be his central political interest. However, another American also appeared on the British scene. In April, the Permanent Committee of the American International Arbitration Movement chose William Dodge to journey to Britain to determine support for arbitration. His instructions were to try 'to secure... a cooperative Committee in England, made up of leading men in both parties.'[127] While Dodge only personally knew a few British leaders, Carnegie supplied him with a batch of lengthy introductions: to Balfour, the Attorney-General Richard Webster, Chamberlain, Gladstone, and Rosebery.[128] The two key figures in the eyes of American arbitrationists were Salisbury, particularly because he had not supported arbitration, and of course Gladstone. In Carnegie's ever adulatory view: 'a word from you [Gladstone] could carry great weight on both sides of the Atlantic – greater than that of any other human being.'[129]

Once in England, Dodge's attempts to gain support from the government were far from satisfactory. His suspicions that the British arbitration movement was composed essentially of 'extreme liberal or radical views' and lacked support from members of the 'governing classes' were confirmed.[130] In July, Dodge had productive meetings with Harcourt (whom he had met in 1895), Bryce, Morley, and Richard Webster (a close friend of Carnegie); from Gladstone he had a warm letter. The enthusiasm did come all from Liberals. Balfour was too ill to see him, and Salisbury apparently was unapproachable. Chamberlain was too 'overpressed' with work for even a short meeting.[131] Unquestionably, the most sympathetic and friendliest to Dodge turned out to be John Morley. Morley reported to Carnegie about his full cooperation with and respect for Dodge:

> We agree not only about the matter at hand, but what is more important – about the general tone and temper in which such matters should be handled ... He is quite at one with me in seeing the importance of getting the business away from the excitable, hysterical, and sentimental preaching people.[132]

In other words, the arbitrationist movement should be taken out of the hands of clergymen like Rev. Hughes and fanatical evangelistic journalists like Stead and turned over to responsible politicians. Moreover, Dodge was very appreciative that Morley had talked fully with all the important Liberal leaders about the American's mission.[133] When Dodge left England he left without having found any one in 'the right position to take the initiative & form the Committee.' Yet he was confident that the groundwork had been laid.[134] Dodge's visit had made it plain that arbitrationist enthusiasm in Britain did not lay with the Conservative government. It was predominantly a Liberal movement, as has been demonstrated, and its greatest enthusiasts were Harcourt and Morley.

In the summer of 1896, arbitration became a vital issue for Morley. Dodge's visit, Carnegie's exhortations, and finally the release by Salisbury of the parliamentary papers on Venezuela all inspired Morley to write.[135] In an article in the *Nineteenth Century* in August, he gave his views both on the Venezuelan negotiations and on the general arbitration treaty. On the first issue, Morley underlined the closeness to American and British positions as to make accommodation 'inevitable,' unless the Foreign Office continued to loiter. On the second, and to Morley more crucial issue, he denounced Salisbury's lack of purpose:

> On the other hand, Lord Salisbury, though he shows abundance of incidental acuteness and sagacity, hardly conducts the controversy with the vigorous grasp of a man who has energetically thought the thing out as a whole, or with the resolute faith of a man who means to drive lions from the path, and to bring the business strenuously through.[136]

The fact that the Venezuelan boundary line had been difficult to define for arbitration, should not prevent Anglo-American cooperation over a permanent arbitrational tribunal: 'The truth is that the creation of a permanent tribunal would be the best way of improving the rules of what is called international law.'[137]

Morley's article evidently made a strong impression. Carnegie thought it had done 'infinite good' and Morley himself thought it had 'made a strong impression.'[138] Balfour had been forwarded a copy of the article by Harcourt a few days before the former's important speech in the House on 14 August.[139] The article probably influenced Balfour. After Balfour's speech, Morley exclaimed jubilantly: 'The *whole* claim is to be submitted to arbitration.' For Morley there can be no doubt that the Venezuela arbitration causes genuinely excited his fullest political interests. 'Now we must see what can be done to promote the larger issue of a permanent tribunal. I am not sure that I can do better with myself than take up that mighty question, and forward it in the public mind.'[140] Had not Morley turned soon thereafter to write his majestic life of Gladstone, he might well have made arbitration his most important 'single cause.'

In the meantime, Harcourt continued with his private pressure upon British and American leaders. From Henry White and John Hay, he gained much information which he could not obtain from the British government. He kept both White and Hay closely advised of his activities. To White, he wrote:

> As you know my object has been all throughout without entangling our Govt. by any Party attacks to get them to retire from the various fake positions to which they had committed themselves and I know *that this could be done a good deal better by private actions than by publication.*[141]

Harcourt came to believe that the Unionist government had delayed for a specific reason: that a likely new Republican administration in 1897 would prove more flexible to British demands. Hay assured Harcourt that he was mistaken. McKinley would not 'yield an inch of the position taken by Cleveland.'[142] Despite Harcourt's continued upset with the Salisbury government, he continued to work with them. In the end, they turned to him for advice. Harcourt prepared a detailed memorandum, in which he underlined two points.

1. That it is in the highest degree expedient that the Venezuelan question should be *settled by the present Administration* in America, who I believe are sincerely anxious for a settlement.
2. That it is of the last importance that the question of arbitration should be *arranged before the present Commission in the U.S. reports.*[143]

The emphasis was upon quick action. Moreover, Harcourt believed that Olney had been much more friendly and flexible during the negotiations than either Salisbury or Chamberlain. The British government could not reasonably claim the expanded boundary line – or Schomburgk line.

The Schomburgk line, therefore, being hopelessly disabled and discredited, there remains nothing but to leave the Arbitration to define the true line, either without limitations or with Mr. Olney's proviso as to settled districts which must be regarded as a very handsome concession.[144]

The memorandum was sent to Balfour and evidently impressed even Salisbury. When Julian Pauncefote arrived in London to discuss arbitration, the Prime Minister immediately sent him to see Harcourt. When Pauncefote called upon Harcourt, the latter sat down and dictated a 'plan' while the Ambassador waited. This was conveyed back to Salisbury.[145] Harcourt also wrote to Balfour on 12 August.[146] In the end it is quite evident that the Salisbury government had turned to Harcourt and to Morley.[147] When Balfour made his major speech on 14 August in the House, he accepted, more than ever, the Harcourt tone and line on the long-delayed Venezuelan crisis. Harcourt, like Morley, was filled with exuberance.[148] 'Historicus' had made another vital, but hidden, contribution to Anglo-American relations.

Between September and November, the Venezuelan and arbitration issues both came to conclusions. While Harcourt and Morley were no longer particularly anxious, several other Liberals played moderate roles which should be identified: Playfair, the Chief Justice Lord Russell, and the former Liberal Solicitor-General Frank Lockwood were all in the United States. In their private and public capacities, they agitated for arbitration.[149] Playfair spent most of the summer on Cape Cod, meeting with Olney, helping Chamberlain with his Olney introduction, and reporting back upon his progress to Rosebery.[150] Lord Russell made a strong address on arbitration and the union of the English-speaking peoples at the meeting of the American Bar Association in Saratoga, New York. He also met with Olney and President Cleveland on Cape Cod, and reported back to Liberal leaders, Rosebery, Gladstone, and Harcourt.[151] He told Harcourt that the latter, the Queen, and the Prince of Wales were regarded by Americans 'as the most friendly to the U.S.' and 'Salisbury & the Press generally are not popular here.'[152] Sir Frank Lockwood also made conciliatory speeches to the American Bar Association.[153] Nor should one minimize the efforts of James Bryce, who reported on the nature of American politics to Balfour in July.[154] Many Liberals played parts in conciliating Anglo-American sensibilities in the summer of 1896.

On 12 November 1896, Pauncefote and Olney signed the arbitration agreement, which was negotiated in a convention of general arbitration signed on 11 January 1897. In the autumn of 1896, a vast array of prominent American and British leaders who had worked so arduously for Anglo-American friendship congratulated each other on their contributions. Liberals in Britain were convinced that they had had a leading hand in the final settlements. Nor did their government look lightly on Liberal efforts. There were many expressions of happiness. Harcourt rejoiced to Morley: 'Olney has behaved very well & let Salisbury down easily; that when you come to compare the arrangement agreed to with the rash & foolish despatches of last Nov., we may well exclaim *quantula sapienta*.'[155]

Silver and the Presidential election of 1896

In the beginning of 1896, Venezuela was undeniably the most critical American issue in the minds of Liberals. By summer, it appealed only to those who had some personal interests at stake. By Christmas, it had passed altogether. Its place was taken by the dramatic presidential campaign and election of 1896, 'the battle of standards.' When President Cleveland determined not to run for a third term, the Democratic standard was swept up by William Jennings Bryan, the idol of the Western free-silver advocates. When the Republicans selected William McKinley, the Ohio champion of the Eastern establishment, it became very much a sectional and even a class conflict. The Eastern professional and business classes aligned themselves against the agrarian, Western, and debtor classes. Bryan's oratorical feats such as the 'Cross of Gold' address, stamped him as a thorough 'free-silver' man. His fanaticism in part drove McKinley, who originally had been a bimetallist, to campaign as an orthodox monometallist and solid money man. The presidential election and 'silver' gripped the Liberal attention in 1896 and 1897.

Britain's own currency problems continued to mount. In the year 1896, many prominent British currency experts believed currency to be the most critical issue facing Great Britain.[156] The battle continued to be most conspicuously drawn between the international bimetallists and the monometallists, between the Bimetallic League and the Gold Standard Defense Association. Support for international bimetallism came primarily from the cotton industry areas of Lancashire and Manchester, but one article in the *National Review* in September, claimed that there was 'only one avowed Monometallist in the present Cabinet.' All other members either supported or leaned towards bimetallism.[157] Adherents of bimetallism mainly favored international bimetallism. Yet such a position rested upon the assumption that the United States would join simultaneously with Great Britain in the use of both gold and silver as legal tender.

Britain's attention to the United States mounted as the American silver movement gained momentum in 1896. The *National Review* took the lead among British periodicals in covering the American currency crisis. Articles by the noted American economist Francis Amasa Walker and the Conservative Moreton Frewen stood out.[158] *The Bimetallist* declared in July: 'Recent events have given an exceptional interest to the attitude of the United States on the Silver Question.'[159] The *National Review* compared the battles between gold and silver, and Republicans and Democrats, to those between the Bimetallic League and the Gold Standard Defense Association. Furthermore, it warned: 'It is worth trying to understand the two bimetallisms now fighting it out in the United States, as before long both terms will appear in Europe if we continue to allow Lombard Street to dictate our financial policy.'[160] As the election approached in the United States, the British press reacted with greater concern. In its first issue in October 1896, the *Progressive Review* spoke at length about the crucial relationship between English and American silver politics.

Amid all the growing complications of our time, no feature is more marked than what may be called the international contingencies arisen out of a purely national policy…If Mr. Bryan is elected, to put it quite plainly, the actual income of not a few people in England will be altered in value. Whatever may be the outcome of the Free Silver movement, there can be no doubt that it will profoundly affect the fortunes of all those dependent on the valuations of the money market, and hence persons who are absolutely ignorant of the American financial controversy, who know nothing whatever of the combatants on either side, who have never set foot on the American soil, find themselves whirling in the vortex of this great contest.[161]

In October, the *National Review* sent a special correspondent to America who wrote regular monthly American columns. It was a mark of the importance of American issues in British politics that following the election the columns continued.

Liberal leaders were caught up in heated disputations about the American silver crisis. Playfair's article for the Gold Standard Defense Association upon American bimetallism came under vicious attack. Francis Walker vehemently disagreed with Playfair's view that bimetallism had been fairly tried in America. A Chicago lawyer, Wharton Barker, berated Playfair for 'gross and inexcusable errors.' Finally, the Bimetallic League published a special pamphlet to rebut Playfair's contentions. Playfair was made out to be illogical and unreasonable. The fact that so many people in the United States were silver enthusiasts was a typical citation that seemed to prove Playfair wrong.[162] Other Liberals, Shaw-Lefevre, the former Liberals Lubbock and Labouchere, and Playfair defended monometallism and the dangers of American silver.[163] Edward Atkinson continued to work closely with his British compatriots and reported American activities.[164] Labouchere wrote that the silver movement was a conspiracy between American silver mine owners and British landowners. 'The first want to sell their silver for more than it is worth; the second want to pay off their mortgages for less than what they received. The whole thing Bimetallism is pernicious nonsense.'[165] When Democrats chose Bryan as their standard-bearer, Shaw-Lefevre reacted with surprised alarm. 'It is obvious that the Silver interest is much stronger than we thought…It is difficult for us to suppose that the majority of people of the U.S. could agree to such a policy.'[166]

The Gold Standard Defense Association decided it needed a stronger line against the evil lessons of American silver. For a new pamphlet, they turned to Horace White, former writer for Morley's *Fortnightly*,

Mugwump, free trader, and editor of the *New York Evening Post*. White tried his best to urge Britain not to follow in the silver path of the United States:

> That England should abandon the gold standard, either alone or in conjunction with others, while this preference of the commercial world for gold exists, is unimaginable. Much of the uncertainty and prolonged agony that have afflicted us has arisen from concessions indiscreetly made by the friends of sound money, that the decline in the price of silver is a world-wide evil. An evil it is undoubtedly to those who have silver, but not to others. We had none of it, but we took some, to our infinite harm. If our example is worth anything to England, she will continue to shun it.[167]

The British political, financial, and governing classes waited with bated breath for the results of the November election. Since McKinley had certain sympathies for international bimetallism, Conservatives, Liberals, Unionists, and Labour leaders united in their support for the Republican candidate. The Liberals had been forced to abandon the Democratic party, which, since Cleveland's first victory in 1880, they had unofficially but strongly endorsed.

Studies of democracy

While a combination of American and British liberals viewed the rise of American silver with varying degrees of horror, others were concerned with the condition of American democracy. During 1896, two excellent works appeared on the strengths and weaknesses of American democratic institutions. W. E. Lecky, the Irish historian and newly elected Liberal Unionist MP from Dublin University, published his two-volume work, *Democracy and Liberty*. E. L. Godkin came out with his *The Problems of Modern Democracy* in the fall.[168] Both books evoked a Liberal reaction which indicated fear that the American state of politics was in danger.

Godkin's book consisted of eleven articles which he had previously published between 1865 and 1896. All but three of them were written in the 1890s. The main thrust of these was contained in two chapters: 'The Political Situation in 1896' and 'The Real Problems of Democracy.'[169] His view of American politics, a thoroughly pessimistic one, involved the necessity of the growth of an educated, reformist, governing elite as being of critical importance for the continuance of progress in democratic countries. His position was encapsulated in a letter to Bryce:

> We are in an astounding position politically. The sad point of it is, that both parties have been for twenty years preparing for this state of things. Nearly all the public men have flattered, cajoled, or gone half way with the *silverites*, and legislate to please them. There is not a single *sincere* gold man in the field, though many now frightened ones.[170]

Godkin was first and foremost a critic. He had few precise remedies for America, except that something should be done to reform it. As the historian John Sproat has put it: 'A carping, pedantic, often sniveling quality permeated their [liberal-reformers] remarks on political reform.'[171]

The Problems of Modern Democracy stirred many of Godkin's British Liberal friends to whom he had sent copies. One of Bryce's first reactions was that 'the same vague sentimentalism' infected social politics in both the United States and Great Britain. He thought that 'few people connected with politics have the courage to tell these sentimentalists that they are running their heads against the natural laws of society & human character.'[172] A. V. Dicey, the former MP Albert Pell, and T. H. Farrer, all reacted with pleasure to the book. Dicey believed that democracy was inevitable to Britain, but not necessarily composed of the best elements.[173]

In many ways, Farrer's remarks were the most interesting. Almost an octogenarian in 1896, he had led a most active career as an essayist and lobbyist for a myriad of social and political causes. While Farrer never became a member of Parliament, he was an important, often ignored, part of the official Liberal mind. He was the British counterpart of an American genteel reformer. He was glad to find in Godkin a genteel reformer who believed that disputation was the core of political progress. Yet, whereas Godkin's optimism over democratic progress was cautious at best, Farrer's, like the American Atkinson's, was convincingly positive. Farrer admitted 'that the struggle between truth and falsehood – good and evil – will not be settled by modern democracy – any more than it has been settled by Monarchs and Oligarchics.'[174] Yet he could not doubt 'that the mass of mankind are better & better off than when I was young. It is in and by struggle that we live – and if struggle onwards were to cease there would be no life.'[175] Farrer saw two main threats to democracy, whether in America or England. First was the danger of labor coupled together with 'practical socialism.' Secondly, there was the rise of a class of 'monopolizing, wealthy, vile capitalist[s].'[176]

Like Godkin's work, Lecky's *Democracy and Liberty* made a strong impression on the British Liberal mind. The critical attitudes towards democracies throughout the Western world which permeated Lecky's work had been anticipated by Bryce. In January 1896, he had deplored the rebirth of the Tammany machine in New York and saw it as evidence of deep-rooted evils in many democracies. 'We shall soon be beginning to have essays on the failure of democracy all over the world. France in one way and Australia in another are little better than New York.'[177] Bryce was an aristocratic democrat, upset at the worsening conditions of American democracy. Lecky was never a democrat, thoroughly convinced that democracies constrained rather than protected liberties. In this approach, Lecky fell into line with Sir Henry Maine as another major voice in the late Victorian age for aristocratic and conservative political institutions.[178]

In his two-volume work, Lecky analyzed democratic institutions throughout history and in many countries. A great deal of attention was given to Italy, France, and even India, but the sharpest commentary was reserved for the United States.[179] After briefly praising the conservative strengths of the Constitution,[180] Lecky devoted the majority of his American comments to criticisms of corruption in cities, parties, the judiciary, and Congress. The word 'corruption' rumbles through the pages:

> There is one thing which is worse than corruption. It is acquiescence in corruption. No feature of American life strikes a stranger so powerfully as the extraordinary indifference, party cynicism and partly good nature, with which notorious frauds and notorious corruption in the sphere of politics are viewed by American public opinion. There is nothing, I think, altogether like this to be found in any other great country.[181]

Lecky frequently quoted Bryce on America. The latter found Lecky's work 'honest' but thought it gave a 'distorted impression' of the United States. 'He [Lecky] did not seem to me even to have understood the passages he quotes from my book, because he omits all the qualifications and allowances which in other places I had stated fully.' In short, Lecky had pictured the United States 'altogether with English eyes, and has no idea of what your [American] politics really are like.'[182] However, the most condemning attacks came from Morley. In an article for the *Nineteenth Century*, Morley severely criticized Lecky's historical method, inaccuracies, 'digressions,' and 'platitudes.' Morley did not deny that democracy was experiencing major difficulties. However, he felt that its weaknesses were not the result of the 'mere form of government, and must have its roots in the hidden and complex working of those religious and scientific ideas which at all times have exercised a preponderating influence upon human institutions and their working.'[183]

Bryce, Morley, Godkin, Farrer, and Lecky all agreed that democracy in the United States in 1896 was under severe strain. On the other hand, what the Liberals saw as temporary aberrations, the conservative-tempered Lecky (and Conservative Unionists in general) attributed to the whole structure of American democracy. While Liberals were distraught over the depths to which the character of politics in America had plunged – jingoism, silver, Tammany, and demagogues – they were equally disturbed by parallel concerns in Britain. In Chamberlain, they had their demagogue and jingo ('typical unscrupulous demagogue'),[184] in bimetallism they had their 'ill conceived silver,' and in urban socialism and labor they had their 'Tammany.'[185]

Silver and bimetallism defeated, 1896–97

On 3 November 1896, William McKinley defeated William Jennings Bryan by 271 electoral votes to 176 and seven million popular votes to six-and-a-half million. There was no doubt that this was a shattering blow to the cause of silver, and, it seemed equally at the time, to the career of Bryan. Silver never would recover; yet Bryan was to try for the presidency twice again and to become Secretary of State. In Britain, the results were welcomed with immeasurable relief. There was no divergence in British opinion. Liberals and Unionists rejoiced together. The results were analyzed closely by British periodicals and many of the contributions were by men who had had some previous sympathies with silver; Frewen and Courtney were two.[186]

There had been some British Liberal rejoicing after the election of Cleveland in 1884, and again in 1892, but it did not match that in 1896. At the same time the victory was more one for sound money than it was for McKinley. Harcourt wrote to Morley: 'I am so pleased with the U.S. outcome of the Election and Venezuela that I care for little else.'[187] A week before, he had written: 'I must confess relief at the defeat of Bryan. It would have been a great disaster if he had won. But it is not pleasant to think that 5 millions of ' "free & enlightened" should have voted for such a programme.'[188] T. H. Farrer exclaimed: 'It is a great victory for common sense and justice throughout the world and we feel it here very sensibly.'[189] At the same time, Liberal leaders also were not that sure that the evil had finally been trampled. Bryce asked Godkin 'has it [Bryanism] really been killed for the time, or may it not revive as soon as the attempt to pass a high tariff bill divides the party which carried McKinley by uniting on sound money?'[190] Farrer also was not convinced. 'Before I heard of Bryan I thought McKinley the worst possible candidate the US could produce – and I shall see his success with mixed feelings.'[191] While it seemed logical that Liberal leaders would be most disturbed over McKinley's imperialism and protectionism, it was his silver tendencies – ironical since McKinley had won on a sound money platform – which concerned them most. Farrer observed to Atkinson: 'Your unsettled currency is perhaps the greatest danger of all – to you – & through you to us.'[192] Balfour also had sensed the direction of things. Hamilton recorded in his diary the day after the American results were known in Britain that Balfour saw McKinley's election first and foremost 'between American bimetallism and international bimetallism, and that it was only the former that had been defeated.'[193]

On 4 March 1897, President McKinley declared his commitment to international bimetallism in his inaugural address:

> The question of international bimetallism will have early and earnest attention. It will be my constant endeavor to secure it by cooperation with the other great commercial powers of the world. Until that condition is realized when the parity between our gold and silver money springs from and is supported by the relative value of the two metals, the value of the silver already coined and of that which may hereafter be coined, must be kept constantly at par with gold by every resource at our command.[194]

McKinley had inside information on the stands of European nations, for during the election he had sent Senator Wolcott, a free silver advocate from Colorado,[195] to make studies of sympathy for international bimetallism. It was on the basis of this report that he had committed himself in his inaugural address, and it was on this basis that he promptly appointed a commission to visit Europe to officially negotiate an international monetary agreement. The appointments were made. Senator Wolcott headed the three-man group. President Cleveland's former Vice-President, Adlai Stevenson, and General C. J. Paine were the other two members. The Bimetallic League reacted with great excitement to the turn of events, somewhat unexpectedly because of the defeat of silver in the American election. 'In the United States 6,500,000 voted for National Bimetallism, 7,000,000 for International Bimetallism, and every one of the voters in the United States voted for Bimetallism in some form or other.'[196] At the same time, Godkin urged Farrer to do all he could to stop this recrudescence of silver: 'I trust you will use your influence to prevent any serious attention being paid, or encouragement given to Senator Wolcott who has gone over to talk about another international conference about silver.'[197] Nor should this last wave of international silver in the nineteenth century be seen in the same light as those of the 1880s or even 1893. In June 1897, the new Ambassador to Great Britain, John Hay, considered 'some settlement of the silver question' as his 'primary work' in Great Britain.[198]

In June and July, Senator Wolcott met with various appropriate bodies in London and presented his schemes before the Unionist government.[199] While the activities of France and Germany were important, British determinations were still the key. Also of critical importance was the position of India. Since 1893, after the closure of her mints, India had been on the gold standard. If she now supported a return to a bimetallic currency, it would put enormous pressure on the British to follow suit. The Americans recognized the position of India in presenting their plans. Their proposal consisted of four parts: first, that the Indian mints be reopened; second, that one-eighth of the reserves of the Bank of England be kept in silver; third, that the gold half-sovereign be withdrawn and replaced by a silver half-sovereign; and finally, that the legal tender of silver be raised from £2 to £5.[200] Had these proposals been presented by the United States a year earlier, their chances for adoption by Britain would have been greater. In June 1897, economic prospects were considerably brighter in both Europe and the United States than they had been for any part of the 1890s. During a Cabinet meeting on 2 August, only two landowners, Henry Chaplin and Walter Long (the President of the Agricultural Board), stood in favor of the American proposals. Edward Hamilton, who was consulted in detail about the American propositions, found that for all the talk (of Balfour, in particular), nobody in the Cabinet was willing to move from the realm of theory to practice. 'Bimetallists like Lord Salisbury & Arthur Balfour know that their theories cannot be translated into practice: and the bulk of the other ministers, ... do not profess to understand the question.'[201]

Farrer took the lead in denouncing the American proposals and presenting the Liberal case. In a series of letters to *The Times*, he focused on the commercial position of India. Should she stick to her new monometallist policy, there was no possible chance that international bimetallism would be accepted.[202] Harcourt was not as anxious as Farrer. He was completely convinced of the defeat of the American mission. 'I have some knowledge of what is going on under the cards. Monometallism is in no danger here. The Govt. is disposed to soothe the American Govt. by *appearing* to be willing to "do something for silver."'[203] Nonetheless, Farrer continued his pressure. In this, he relied upon the help of Charles Francis Adams, Mugwump and reformer.[204]

Adams had been a convinced bimetallist in the 1890s, but had made a 'melodramatic return to his earlier conviction' for gold in 1896.[205] His close political friendship with Ambassador Hay was fortunate, for Adams was able to pass inside assurances along to Farrer. It was Adams' belief that American business classes were prospering more widely than they had for a long time – 'so why should we interfere with the natural courses which are making for recuperation.'[206] Adams assured Farrer that all bimetallist talk would pass harmlessly.[207] Shaw-Lefevre thought that international bimetallism would never have any long-term beneficial impacts upon the Anglo-American financial world. 'International bimetallism would almost certainly fail to have any substantial effect in raising the value of silver – apart from temporary speculations.'[208] On 16 October, the Cabinet was informed that India rejected any alteration of her currency system. Without debate, the Cabinet decided to reject the American proposals.[209] The rejection of international bimetallism was in part a victory for Liberals such as Farrer, Harcourt, Playfair, and Shaw-Lefevre who had for a number of years fought against American silver schemes in Britain. In November 1896, the radical ideas of Bryan had been defeated in the United States. In the summer of 1897, the international bimetallic silver movement had received its death blow. International bimetallism had been primarily an American movement, but it had been aided by a band of Conservative, Unionist and economic leaders in Britain. On 6 December 1897, President McKinley publicly acknowledged the futility and inexpediency of international bimetallism.[210]

Conclusion

On 2 February 1897, the United States and Britain signed a treaty which provided for a tribunal to decide on a boundary line between Venezuela and British Guiana. Earlier in the year, on 11 January, Pauncefote and Olney had settled the other entangling diplomatic issue – the Anglo-American arbitration problem. Henceforth all disputes would be submitted to arbitration with minor issues settled by a majority and larger territorial or other issues settled by a more lengthy process.

On both sides of the Atlantic, peace advocates and leaders of opinion hailed the agreements. On 19 February in reply to the Queen's address, Harcourt and Balfour praised the great steps that had been made in Anglo-American relations. The two countries were united in much more than language, race, and traditions in a hard-fought-for diplomatic union.[211]

While the Treaty was accepted by Parliament, in May the euphoria was deflated when the Senate rejected the arbitration treaty by a narrow vote.[212] The American imperialists and Republicans who defeated the treaty tried to make amends to English friends. They described in great detail the distressing nuances of American politics. Thus Henry White sent Balfour a letter from Olney. The latter emphasized the new self-assertiveness of the Senate over foreign policy, the silver elements hostile towards monometallic Britain for the defeat of their cause, and, more irrationally, the former Ambassador Bayard's 'Anglo-phil effusiveness.'[213] Some English arbitrationists continued to fight for their cause. William Randal Cremer, no longer in Parliament after his defeat in 1895, circulated a petition among the working classes. In the autumn of 1897, Cremer was again in the United States, this time with a memorial signed by 7432 English trade officials which he claimed represented 8 750 000 workmen.[214] He saw McKinley, but the latter vacillated. On 15 February 1898, everything changed. In Havana harbor, the *Maine* was blown up, the most sensational incident in a series of revolutionary affairs that had boiled up in Cuba since 1895. The American yellow press seized upon 'the Maine' to inflame American patriotism. With the formal outbreak of the Spanish–American War on 25 April, the possibility of an arbitration treaty perished. The fervid American imperialist spirit found outlet in a new more aggressive foreign policy. The movement for Anglo-American arbitration, a foremost cause of transatlantic liberals, ceased to exist. On the other hand, it is more accurate to see their efforts as producing the foundation of the modern strategic and military alliance between the two Anglo-Saxon powers. Many of the Anglo-American arbitrationists were also influential in the first Hague Peace Conference held in 1899. The true Cobden-Gladstone liberal did not like war or military aggression except on behalf of the most righteous cause. The blowing up of the *Maine* by 'Spanish Catholic barbarians' was just such a war. In the spring of 1898, British opinion, whatever its political leanings, more than ever acclaimed the greatness of the United States and the closeness of the Anglo-American relationship.[215]

The year proved to be a watershed in the political relationship of the United States and Great Britain. It marked the end of an essentially isolationist period in American foreign policy and the beginning of a new imperialism. It signaled the emergence of the United States on the world scene as a great power. In Britain, it was the end of the Gladstonian age and a particular brand of British Liberalism. His passing away in his eighty-ninth year on 19 May symbolized the end of a pacific, individualistic, and partially non-interventionist Liberal era. Gladstone had been a man of great moral causes, and one of his most important had been that of Anglo-American understanding. In 1898, other British leaders who had been or were Gladstonian Liberals also celebrated the special American relationship: Harcourt, Chamberlain, Morley, Bryce, Playfair, Dilke, Stead, and many others. Their themes included Anglo-Saxon racial unity, kinship, political and economic interdependency, military alliance, and a common destiny.[216] Most of these themes had been voiced by the same leaders throughout the 1880s and 1890s. In the future, there would be no monopoly of Anglo-American preoccupations by Liberals. Unionists, Labour, and Liberal leaders all joined in, in equal strengths, the broad movement on behalf of Anglo-American rapprochement. Thus, when Jennie Churchill formed the *Anglo-Saxon Review*, all parties were represented equally on the new Anglo-American Committee, established in London in 1896.[217]

Notes

1. H. C. G. Matthew, *The Liberal Imperialists. The Ideas and Politics of a Post-Gladstonian Elite* (Oxford, 1972), p. 19.
2. P. F. Clarke, *Liberals and Social Democrats* (Cambridge, 1978) and M. Freeden, *The New Liberalism. An Ideology of Social Reform* (Oxford, 1979).
3. Some of these 'new liberals' were very enamoured with the Progressive movement in the United States. See P. F. Clarke, 'The Progressive Movement in England,' *TRHS*, 5th series, vol. xxiv (1974), pp. 159–81; Kenneth O. Morgan, 'The Future at Work: Anglo-American Progressivism, 1890–1917,' in H. C. Allen and Roger Thompson (eds), *Contrast and Connection: Bicentennial Essays on Anglo-American History* (London, 1976); and Stokes, 'The Origins of the Progressive Mind in the United States: The Social Thoughts of Twelve Progressive Publicists in the Period up to 1910' (Oxford University DPhil. thesis, 1977).
4. B. Perkins, *The Great Rapprochement: England and the United States, 1895–1914* (New York, 1969); A. E. Campbell, *Great Britain and the United States, 1895–1903* (London, 1960); and C. S. Campbell, *Anglo-American Understanding, 1898–1903* (Baltimore, MD, 1957).
5. J. A. S. Grenville, *Lord Salisbury and Foreign Policy, the Close of the Nineteenth Century* (London, 1964). C. Tansill, *The Foreign Policy of Thomas F. Bayard, 1885–1897* (New York, 1940); and R. Mowat, *The Life of Lord Pauncefote: First Ambassador to the United States* (London, 1929).

6. J. Garraty, *Henry Lodge: A Biography* (New York, 1965); W. Thayer, *The Life and Letters of John Hay*, 2 vols (New York, 1915); H. K. Beale, *Theodore Roosevelt and the Rise of America to World Power* (New York, 1963); D. H. Burton, 'Theodore Roosevelt and His English Correspondents: The Intellectual Roots of the Anglo-American Alliance,' *Mid-America*, vol. liii (1971), pp. 12–34, and *Theodore Roosevelt and His English Correspondents: A Special Relationship of Friends* (Philadelphia, 1973).

7. J. J. Matthews, 'Informal Diplomacy in the Venezuelan Crisis of 1896,' *MVHR*, vol. 1 (1963), pp. 195–212 and *George Smalley, Forty Years a Foreign Correspondent* (Chapel Hill, NC, 1973), pp. 115–30.

8. S. L. Anderson, 'Race and Rapprochement, Anglo-Saxonism and Anglo-American Relations, 1895–1904' (Claremont Graduate School PhD thesis, 1978) and W. LaFeber, *The New Empire: An Interpretation of American Expansion, 1860–1898* (Ithaca, NY, 1963).

9. T. Boyle, 'The Venezuela Crisis and the Liberal Opposition, 1895–96,' *Journal of Modern History*, vol. 1, no. iii (Sept. 1978), pp. D1185–D1212.

10. For earlier British efforts on behalf of Anglo-American peace, see K. Phelps, *The Anglo-American Peace Movement in the Mid-Nineteenth Century (1835–54)* (New York, 1930).

11. Hansard, 3rd series, vol. ccxvii, 8 July 1873, pp. 52–3.

12. M. M. Robson, 'Liberals and Vital Interests: The Debate on International Arbitration, 1815–72,' *IHRB*, vol. xxxii (1959), pp. 52–3.

13. For the extent of the international cooperation among arbitration societies, see *International Arbitration and Peace Association Monthly Journal*, vol. i (July 1884), pp. 1–11.

14. *Seventh Annual Report of the International Arbitration Association* (1888), pp. 6–9.

15. D. S. Patterson, *Towards a Warless World: The Travail of the American Peace Movement 1887–1914* (Bloomington, IN, 1976), p. 20.

16. W. Reid, *Memoirs and Correspondence of Lyon Playfair* (London, 1899), pp. 365–6.

17. C. D. Davis, *The United States and the First Hague Peace Conference* (Ithaca, NY, 1962), p. 18. For a list of the most active British and American peace and arbitration societies in 1888, see *List of Societies in Europe and America founded for the Promotion of International Concord* (1888). For the progress of the American Arbitration and Peace Movements, see Patterson, *Towards a Warless World*, pp. 1–47 and Car.P, Box 249, 'Memorial to Congress in Favor of Arbitration for the Settlement of International Disputes,' 10 Jan. 1888.

18. BP, USA 22, Bryce to T. Stanton, 13 Oct. 1887, ff. 21–2 and Playfair, 'A Topic for Christmas,' *NAR*, vol. cli (Dec. 1890), pp. 676–87.

19. HP, Box 22, Morley to Harcourt, 22 Mar. 1891, f. 140. Also see, Harcourt to Morley, 26 Mar. 1891, ff. 142–4, both letters cited in K. Gardiner, *The Life of Sir William Harcourt*, 2 vols (London, 1923), ii, pp. 125–6. For other Liberal positions on arbitration, see PP, *Correspondence with regard to the Commercial Treaty between Great Britain and Venezuela, 1825 to 1886* (1886), LXXIII, C. 4911, pp. 489–571 and HP, Box 230, E. Fitzmaurice to Harcourt, 4 Feb. 1896, ff. 18–22.

20. RP, 10017, Rosebery to M. Ferguson, 7 Nov. 1887, f. 121. See Salisbury's response in Imperial College Science and Technology Library, London (Lyon Playfair Papers): Salisbury to Playfair, 10 Jan. 1891 (870).

21. GP, 44510, Cremer to Gladstone, 25 June 1890, f. 116.
22. A. Carnegie, 'Imperial Federation. II. An American View,' pp. 498–512.
23. Car.P, Vol. 15, J. A. Cooper to Carnegie, 17 Mar. 1892 (2677–8). Also see J. A. Cooper, 'An Anglo-Saxon Olympiad,' *NC*, vol. xxxii (Sept. 1892), pp. 380–8, and 'Americans and the Pan-Britannic Movement,' vol. xxxviii (Sept. 1895), pp. 426–41.
24. Car.P, Vol. 16, Carnegie to Stead, 16 May 1892 (2892).
25. See Chapter 3, pp. 79–80.
26. Car.P, Vol. 16, 17 May 1892 (2893). For Gladstone's views on English-speaking unions, see Chapter 4, p. 132.
27. vol. clvi, p. 690. This article was the concluding chapter in the second edition of *Triumphant Democracy* (London, 1894).
28. Car.P, Vol. 21, Chamberlain to Carnegie, 17 July 1893 (3982) and Salisbury to Carnegie, 25 July 1893 (4018). Carnegie sent copies of his important articles to leaders of both the Conservative and Liberal parties.
29. Smith, 'Anglo-Saxon Union: A Response to Mr. Carnegie's,' *NAR*, vol. clvii (Aug. 1893), pp. 170–85 and Car.P, Vol. 21, Smith to Carnegie, 8 June 1893 (3902–3).
30. J. Wall, *Andrew Carnegie* (New York, 1970), p. 677.
31. G. S. Clarke, 'A Naval Union with Great Britain. A Reply to Mr. Andrew Carnegie,' *NAR*, vol. clviii (Mar. 1894), pp. 353–65; A. S. White, 'An Anglo-American Alliance,' *NAR*, vol. clviii (Apr. 1894), pp. 484–93; and A. T. Mahan, 'Possibilities of an Anglo-American Reunion,' *NAR*, vol. clix (Nov. 1894), pp. 551–63.
32. Hansard, 4th series, vol. xiii, 16 June 1893, 1240–73, *passim*.
33. The petition was signed by 354 members, in contradistinction to 233 in 1887. Cremer delivered the petition to the United States in 1895. See Patterson, *Towards a Warless World*, pp. 28–31.
34. Car.P, Vol. 26, Cremer to Carnegie, 11 Aug. 1894 (5074). Also see ibid., Cremer to Carnegie, 29 Aug. 1894 (5117–18).
35. RP, 10097, E. Evans Darby to Rosebery, 18 Aug. 1894, f. 88. For the progress of the International Arbitration Society, see W. E. Darby, *The Continuing Progress of International Arbitration* (London, 1893).
36. HP, Box 170, Farrer to Harcourt, 1 Mar. 1895, f. 38. For additional Liberal concern about American silver in the spring of 1895, see Massachusetts Historical Society, Boston, MA (Edward Atkinson Papers): Shaw-Lefevre to Atkinson, 9 Apr. 1895, and *Report of the Annual Meeting of the Cobden Club, 1895* (London, 1895).
37. *Gold Standard Defense Association* (pamphlets) (1895–98), p. 1. The Bimetallist League contained 68 MP's in January 1895. *The Bimetallist*, vol. i (Jan. 1895), pp. 26–7.
38. For Gladstone's support, see *The Times*, 13 Sept. 1895. The others were Vice-Presidents of the Association.
39. Brit. Mus., Addit. MSS 49742 (Balfour Papers): White to Balfour, 28 Feb. and 6 May 1895, ff. 34–44.
40. The Atkinson Papers are excellent on the associations between American and British monometallist liberals in the 1890s. See especially containers 16–18.
41. Farrer, 'The Weakness of Bimetallism, and the Folly of a Conference,' *Gold Standard Defense Association* (pamphlet no. 2) (n.d.), p. 6.

42. Playfair, 'The Working of Bimetallism in the United States,' *Gold Standard Defense Association* (pamphlet no. 13) (Nov. 1895), p. 6.
43. *Westminster Gazette*, 24 Oct. 1895 ('The Monroe Doctrine and Venezuela'). Also see Stead, 'Jingoism in America,' *CR*, vol. lxviii (Sept. 1895), pp. 343–7.
44. Atkinson, 'Jingoes and Silverites,' *NAR*, vol. clxi (Nov. 1895), pp. 554–60 and Somerset, 'Great Britain, Venezuela and the United States,' *NC*, vol. xxxviii (Nov. 1895), pp. 758–68. Also see, G. H. D. Gossip, 'England in Nicaragua and Venezuela: from an American point of view,' *FR*, vol. lviii (Dec. 1895), pp. 829–42.
45. *Nat.R*, vol. xxvi (Nov. 1895), p. 298.
46. Smith Papers, Smith to Farrer, 4 Dec. 1895, Reel 6, cited in A. Haultain (ed.), *A Selection from Goldwin Smith's Correspondence* (New York, 1913), p. 288.
47. The International Arbitration and Peace Association was also concerned over the lagging Anglo-American diplomacy upon Venezuela. See *Concord*, vol. x (Jan. 1895), pp. 7–8. Other important articles that warned British Liberals of American 'jingoism' included: E. L. Godkin, 'Diplomacy and the Newspaper,' *NAR*, vol. clx (May 1895), pp. 570–9 and H. C. Lodge, 'England, Venezuela, and the Monroe Doctrine,' *NAR*, vol. clx (June 1895), pp. 651–8.
48. The literature on the Venezuelan crisis is large. See notes 4–7 and P. R. Fossum, 'The Anglo-Venezuelan Boundary Controversy,' *Hispanic American Historical Review*, vol. viii (1928), pp. 299–329; N. Blake, 'Background of Cleveland's Venezuelan Policy,' *AHR*, vol. xlvii (1942), pp. 259–78 and W. LaFeber, 'The Background of Cleveland's Venezuelan Policy: A Reinterpretation?' *AHR*, vol. lxvi (1961), pp. 947–67.
49. *The Times* and the *Daily News*, 18 Dec. 1895.
50. Ch.P, Chamberlain to Selborne, 20 Dec. 1895, JC 7/5/1B/4, cited in part in D. Judd, *Radical Joe: A Life of Joseph Chamberlain* (London, 1977), pp. 202–3.
51. Bryce was on a trip in South Africa at the outbreak of the Venezuelan crisis so that his surprise over the issue was quite extreme. He had not followed American events particularly closely in the autumn of 1895. God.P, Bryce to Godkin, 1 Jan. 1896 (143).
52. GP, 44521, Pulitzer to Gladstone, 20 Dec. 1895, ff. 231–2.
53. Hamilton Diary, 48668, 24 Dec. 1895, f. 51. Hamilton's daily comments and reactions to Venezuela are fascinating, especially from 19 to 24 Dec. 1895, ff. 44–51.
54. *New York World*, 21 Dec. 1895. George Smalley reported that Gladstone's message had had a large impact upon conciliating Americans. *The Times*, 23 Dec. 1895. 'Every hour brings some fresh expression of rational, peaceful, and conciliatory views.'
55. *New York World*, 24 Dec. 1895. Also see RP, 10106, Pulitzer to Rosebery, 23 Dec. 1895 (8 a.m.), ff. 138–40.
56. *The Times*, 21 Dec. 1895.
57. Ibid., 25 Dec. 1895. Also see, Edward Dicey, 'Common Sense and Venezuela,' *NC*, vol. xli (Feb. 1896), pp. 7–15.
58. *Westminster Gazette*, 18, 19, 21, 23, and 24 Dec. 1895.
59. RP, 10089, Gladstone to Ripon, 27 Dec. 1895, f. 275.
60. A boundary line drawn up by a British commissioner Robert Schomburgk in 1840, to the west of which Britain claimed as her territory and to the east of which Venezuela claimed.

61. RP, 10059, Gladstone to Ripon, 27 Dec. 1895, f. 275.
62. Brit. Mus., Addit. MSS 43516 (Ripon Papers): Rosebery to Ripon, 5 Jan. 1896, f. 228.
63. Ibid., 43527, Kimberley to Ripon, 31 Dec. 1895, f. 77. 'What posh the gush about the friendship of our American cousins is! I never saw any practical proof of their friendship.'
64. Hamilton Diary, 48668, 10 Jan. 1896, f. 75.
65. Harcourt to Shaw-Lefevre, 18 Dec. 1895, cited in Boyle, 'The Venezuela Crisis and the Liberal Opposition,' p. D1197.
66. *The Times*, 19, 21, 23, 24, 25, and 28 Dec. 1895 and 2, 6, 10, and 11 Jan. 1896.
67. *Westminster Gazette*, 9 Jan. 1896.
68. Ibid., 11 Jan. 1896.
69. *Daily Chronicle*, 11 Jan. 1896.
70. Ibid., 13 Jan. 1896.
71. Ch.P, 'Memo of interview with Harcourt, the Cabinet, Ld. Playfair, re. Venezuela & U.S.A.,' 9 Jan. 1896, JC 7/5/1B/14.
72. W. Harcourt to L. V. Harcourt, 10 Jan. 1896, cited in Gardiner, *Life of Harcourt*, ii, p. 397, and Hamilton Diary, 48668, 10 Jan. 1896, f. 75.
73. The informal talks between Salisbury's emissary, George Buckle, the editor of *The Times*, and Olney's, George Smalley, also proved unproductive. One reason that the talks broke down, yet not fully explored, was on account of Olney's personal antagonism towards Smalley and particularly the former Secrertary of State Bayard. For informal negotiations, see Playfair Papers; Chamberlain Papers (JC 7/5/1B/-); Bayard Papers (vols 163–4); Hatfield House, Hatfield (Salisbury Papers): Class E, Box 38; Library of Congress, Washington, DC (Olney Papers): Containers 43–6; and New Printing House Square, London, *The Times* Archives (Smalley Papers).
74. God.P, Bryce to Godkin, 24 Jan. 1896 (144).
75. HP, Box 82, Fowler to Harcourt, 22 Jan. 1896, ff. 144–5; Box 230, Ellis to Harcourt, 23 Jan. 1896, f. 7 and Bryce to Harcourt, 24 Jan. 1896, ff. 9–13; Box 91, Shaw-Lefevre to Harcourt, 10 Feb. 1896, f. 141; and Box 73, Milner to Harcourt, 17 Jan. 1896, ff. 185–6.
76. Ibid., Box 28, Harcourt to Morley, 18 Jan. 1896, ff. 4–5 and Box 230, Harcourt to Bryce, 22 Jan. 1896, ff. 3–5.
77. The Cabinet member most disposed to favor arbitration and conciliation was Balfour. Speech at Manchester,' 15 Jan. 1896, reported in *The Times*, 16 Jan. 1896.
78. Playfair Papers, Morley to Playfair, 24 Jan. 1896; Car.P, vol. 36, Carnegie to Morley, 27 Jan. 1896 (7047–9); Bayard Papers, Vol. 206, Bayard to Morley, 24 Jan. 1896 (385–6); HP, Box 28, Harcourt to Morley, 21 Jan. 1896, ff. 8–9 and Morley to Harcourt, 25 Jan. 1896, ff. 12–3; and Atkinson Papers, 17, Playfair to Atkinson, 8 Jan. 1896.
79. Atkinson Papers, 16, Atkinson to Farrer, 20 Dec. 1895 (telegram).
80. Ibid., 17, Goschen to Atkinson, 27 Jan. 1896.
81. Ibid., 16, Atkinson to Farrer, 20 Dec. 1895.
82. Ibid., 17, Playfair to Atkinson, 8 Jan. 1896.
83. Ibid.
84. *Daily Chronicle*, 11 Jan. 1896. For further British Liberal appreciation of Atkinson's efforts for arbitration, see Atkinson Papers, 17, Shaw-Lefevre to

Atkinson, 11 Jan. 1896; J. Lubbock to Atkinson, 12 Feb. 1896; and Farrer to Atkinson, 19 Feb. 1896.

85. Car.P, Vol. 35, Carnegie to Devonshire, 26 Dec. 1895 (6862).
86. Ibid., Vol. 36, Carnegie to Morley, 27 Jan. 1896 (7047–8). Also see Carnegie, 'The Venezuelan Question,' *NAR*, vol. clxii (Feb. 1896), pp. 129–44.
87. For other American liberal support for arbitration-minded British Liberals, see D. A. Wells, 'Great Britain and the United States: Their True Relations,' *NAR*, vol. clxii (Apr. 1896), pp. 384–405 and Carl Schurz, 'The Anglo-American Friendship,' *AM*, vol. lxxxii (1896), p. 433.
88. Hamilton Diary, 48668, 4 Jan. 1896, f. 62.
89. Ibid., 5 and 6 Feb. 1896, f. 103.
90. BP, U.B. 27, Rosebery to Bryce, 28 Jan. 1896.
91. Boyle, 'The Venezuela Crisis and the Liberal Opposition,' p. D1202; P. Stansky, *Ambitions and Strategies: The Struggle for the Leadership of the Liberal Party in the 1890s* (Oxford, 1964), p. 200; and R. James, *Rosebery* (London, 1963), p. 388.
92. God.P, Bryce to Godkin, 1 Jan. 1896 (143). Also see Roosevelt Papers, Bryce to Roosevelt, 1 Jan. 1896 (519–22), and Bryce, 'British Feeling on the Venezuelan Question,' *NAR*, vol. clxii (Feb. 1896), p. 145.
93. BP, USA 5, Godkin to Bryce, 3 Feb. 1896, f. 132. Also see ibid., 9 Jan. 1896, ff. 128–31.
94. HP, Box 230, Bryce to Harcourt, 24 Jan. 1896, ff. 9–13 and BP, 12, Bryce to Gladstone, 30 Jan. 1896, ff. 187–9.
95. Asquith to Harcourt, 10 Feb. 1896, cited in Gardiner, *Life of Harcourt*, ii, p. 400.
96. Hansard, 4th series, xxxvii, 11 Feb. 1896, 39–42.
97. Ibid., 89.
98. Ibid., 16 Feb. 1896, 511–15. Also see Balfour's remarks. He accepted the Monroe Doctrine, but defended the government's right to set limits on arbitration. 11 Feb. 1896, 107–10.
99. Hamilton Diary, 48668, 16 Feb. 1896, f. 115.
100. Ibid., 48669, 5 Aug. 1896, ff. 114–15 and 43670, 29 Sept. 1896, ff. 11–12.
101. Ch.P, Olney to Chamberlain, 28 Sept. 1896, JC 7/5/1A/23 and Olney–Chamberlain correspondence, Sept.–Aug. 1898 JC 7/5/1B/49–53. Also see Salisbury Papers, Class E, Box 38.
102. Ibid., Chamberlain to Olney, 28 Sept. 1896, JC 7/5/1B/53.
103. O. Gollancz, 'Anglo-American Arbitration Policies, 1890–1914' (Cambridge Univ. PhD thesis, 1939), p. 27.
104. *Always Arbitrate Before You Fight* (1896), p. 5.
105. Ibid., p. 46.
106. Ibid., pp. 55–64.
107. Ibid., p. 71.
108. *The Times*, 20 Feb. 1896 and 'To All English-Speaking Folk,' *RR*, vol. xiii (Feb. 1896), pp. 99–101.
109. Boyle, 'The Venezuela Crisis and the Liberal Opposition,' pp. D1204–5.
110. 'International Response to the Appeal for Arbitration,' *RR*, vol. xiii (Mar. 1896), p. 260.
111. Ibid.

112. Ibid., pp. 260–1.
113. See Mundella's resolution, ibid., p. 265. By the time the *Review of Reviews'* report of the 3 March meeting was published, 136 MPs had signed the memorial in favor of Anglo-American arbitration.
114. 'The Anglo-American Union,' *RR*, vol. xiii (Apr. 1896), p. 365.
115. Davis, *The United States and the First Hague Peace Conference*, p. 30.
116. *The American Conference on International Arbitration held in Washington D.C., April 22 and 23, 1896* (New York, 1896).
117. Hansard, 4th series, xxxvii, 17 Feb. 1896 (Harcourt), 511–15; Car.P, Vol. 36, Morley to Carnegie, 28 Feb. 1896 (7147); and Campbell-Bannerman speech at Southwark on 5 Mar. 1896, cited in *The Times*, 6 Mar. 1896.
118. RP, 10061, Smalley to Rosbery, 10 May 1896, f. 120.
119. Balfour's speech at Manchester on 15 Jan. 1896, cited in *The Times*, 16 Jan. 1896. Almost alone among the Cabinet, Balfour was in communication with leading private American opinion. See Balfour Papers, 49742, H. C. Lodge to Balfour, 1 Feb. 1896, ff. 156–61 and 49851, C. Kellogg to Balfour, 19 Jan. 1896, ff. 5–6.
120. Ibid., 49696, Harcourt to Balfour, 17 Feb. 1896, f. 225.
121. *The Times*, 22 Apr. 1896 ('the proposal for arbitration made by the United States Govt. was rejected by Lord Salisbury and all negotiations relating to Venezuela thereupon came to an end and none are now pending').
122. Balfour Papers, 49696, Harcourt to Balfour, 18 Apr. 1896, ff. 229–30.
123. Ibid., Harcourt to Balfour, 24 and 26 Apr. 1896, ff. 231–9.
124. Hansard, 4th series, xxxix, 27 Apr. 1896, 1736.
125. WP, Box 15, Olney to White, 30 June 1896.
126. Cited in *The Times*, 6 May 1896.
127. Car.P, vol. 38, W. Dodge to Carnegie, 5 June 1896 (7380–1).
128. Ibid., Carnegie to Balfour, 26 June 1896 (7394–5); Carnegie to Webster, 26 June 1896 (7396–7); Carnegie to Chamberlain, 27 June 1896 (7398–9); Carnegie to Gladstone, 27 June 1896 (7402–3); and Carnegie to Rosebery, 27 June 1896 (7406–7).
129. Ibid., Carnegie to Gladstone, 27 June 1896 (7402).
130. Ibid., W. Dodge to Carnegie, July 1896 (7421).
131. Ibid., W. Dodge to Carnegie, 15 July 1896 (7493) and Gladstone to Carnegie, 15 July 1896 (7494).
132. Ibid., Morley to Carnegie, 8 July 1896 (7468–9).
133. Ibid., W. Dodge to Carnegie, 15 July 1896 (7492).
134. Ibid., (7493).
135. PP, *Documents and Correspondence relating to the Question of the Boundary between British Guiana and Venezuela* (1896), XCVII, C. 7972.
136. Morley, 'Arbitration with America,' *NC*, vol. xl (Aug. 1896), p. 329.
137. Ibid., p. 336.
138. Car.P, vol. 38, Carnegie to Morley, 1 Aug. 1896 (7531) and Morley to Carnegie, 4 Aug. 1896 (7536).
139. Balfour Papers, 49696, Harcourt to Balfour, 2 Aug. 1896, f. 248. See Hansard, 4th series, xliv, 14 Aug. 1896, 851–2.
140. Car.P, vol. 39, Morley to Carnegie, 17 Aug. 1896 (7576). See ibid., Carnegie to Morley, 19 Aug. 1896 (7578).

141. WP, Box 15, Harcourt to White, 27 Nov. 1896 (my italics).
142. Ibid., Hay to White, 5 Aug. 1896. Also see Hay to his wife, 7 June 1896, cited in W. Thayer, *The Life and Letters of John Hay*, 2 vols (New York, 1915), ii, pp. 143–5 and Hay to his wife, 31 July 1896, cited in ibid., ii, p. 147.
143. Balfour Papers, 49696, Harcourt to Balfour, 2 Aug. 1896, f. 244.
144. Ibid., f. 248.
145. Loulou Harcourt memo, n.d., cited in Gardiner, *Life of Harcourt*, ii, p. 402.
146. Balfour Papers, 49696, Harcourt to Balfour, 12 Aug. 1896, ff. 249–50.
147. American authorities also continued to seek advice from Harcourt. Thus, for instance, White wrote to Harcourt: 'If you are able to impart to me in confidence any information on the subject, I shall be very glad to hear from you and if there be any suggestions which you can make as to what might be done on this side to facilitate a settlement I am in a position to get them at once to the proper quarter.' HP, Box 231, 21 Aug. 1896, f. 68.
148. Ibid., Harcourt to White, 6 Sept. 1896, ff. 91–3.
149. Matthews argues that Playfair, Russell, and Lockwood did have an impact upon American opinion in 1896. 'Informal Diplomacy,' p. 210. Boyle believes they did not. 'The Venezuela Crisis and the Liberal Opposition,' p. D1209.
150. Playfair Papers, Chamberlain to Playfair, 14 Aug. 1896 (163); Atkinson Papers, 18, Playfair to Atkinson, 6 July 1896; and RP, 10109, Playfair to Rosebery, 11 Oct. 1896, ff. 19–20.
151. 'The Lord Chief Justice on Arbitration,' *RR*, vol. xiv (Sept. 1896), pp. 318–20; C. Russell, 'International Law and Arbitration,' *The Forum*, vol. xxii (1896), pp. 192–216; R. B. O'Brien, *The Life of Lord Russell of Killowen* (New York, 1901), pp. 305-13; RP, 10107, Russell to Rosebery, 23 Aug. 1896, ff. 215–18; 24 Aug. 1896, ff. 221–2; and 31 Aug. 1896, ff. 238–41; and GP, 44523, Russell to Gladstone, 4 Sept. 1896, ff. 221–6; and HP, Box 231, Russell to Harcourt, 24 Sept. 1896, ff. 102–9.
152. HP, Box 231, Russell to Harcourt, 24 Sept. 1896, f. 107.
153. A. Birrell, *Sir Frank Lockwood*, 2nd edn (London, 1898), pp. 165–87 and RP, 10107, Russell to Rosebery, 23 Aug. 1896, f. 213.
154. Balfour Papers, 49851, Bryce to Balfour, 23 and 26 July 1896, ff. 88–95.
155. HP, Box 28, Harcourt to Morley, 13 Nov. 1896, ff. 71–2. Also see: Ch.P, Chamberlain to Harcourt, 17 Nov. 1896, JC 5/38/112; Playfair Papers, Bayard to Playfair, 29 Nov. 1896 (23); Atkinson Papers, 18, T. Farrer to Atkinson, 6 Dec. 1896; WP, Box 15, Harcourt to White, 27 Nov. 1896; HP, Box 232, Pauncefote to Harcourt, 20 Nov. 1896, ff. 55–8 and Box 61, Harcourt to Chamberlain, 19 Nov. 1896, ff. 100–1. For Salisbury, see speech at Guildhall, 9 Nov. 1896, cited in *The Times*, 10 Nov. 1896.
156. See Michael Hicks Beach, Hansard, 4th series, xxxviii, 17 Mar. 1896, 1194, and God.P, T. Farrer to Godkin, 10 Dec. 1896 (277).
157. *Nat.R*, vol. xxviii (Sept. 1896), pp. 17–18. Balfour, Chaplin, Lord James of Hereford, and Sir M. Ridley were listed as 'convinced bimetallists,' while Salisbury, Lansdowne, George Hamilton, Goschen, Cross, and Akers Douglas were 'benevolent towards bimetallism.' Others were uncommitted.

158. *Nat.R*: A. Higgins and M. Frewen, 'Correspondence: The American "sound money" problem and its solution,' vol. xxvi (Nov. 1895), pp. 422–42; M. Frewen, 'American Politics,' vol. xxvi (Jan. 1896), pp. 595–608; F. A. Walker, 'The Monetary Situation and the United States,' vol. xxvii (Aug. 1896), pp. 783–92; T. Lloyd, A. Peel, and J. Tritton, 'The American Crisis,' vol. xxviii (Sept. 1896), pp. 59–74; and A. Powell, A. Hepburn, and H. Schmidt, 'The Bimetallic Side of the American Crisis,' vol. xxviii (Oct. 1896), pp. 269–84. Also for Frewen, see *The Economist*, 2 Apr. 1896 and 8 Aug. 1896.

159. *The Bimetallist*, vol. iii (July 1896), p. 140.

160. *Nat.R*, vol. xxvii (July 1896), p. 609.

161. *PR*, vol. i, no. i (Oct. 1896), p. 82.

162. F. A. Walker, 'Bimetallism in the United States,' *The Bimetallist*, vol. ii (Feb. 1896), pp. 38–44; W. Barker, 'Bimetallism in the United States,' ibid. (Mar. 1896), pp. 61–2; and H. Schmidt, 'The Working of Bimetallism in the United States,' *The Bimetallic League*, pamphlet no. 13 (Manchester, 1896).

163. All wrote pamphlets for the Gold Standard Defense Association in 1896. *The Gold Standard Defense Association (1895–98)*, passim.

164. George Peel, the Secretary of the Gold Standard Defense Association, asked Atkinson to report 'any move made by Bimetallists on your side for an International agreement.' Atkinson Papers, 18, G. Peel to Atkinson, 30 Dec. 1896. Atkinson complied with Peel's request. See   ibid., for letters from Peel, T. Farrer, Thring, Shaw-Lefevre, Playfair, and William Fowler.

165. H. Labouchere, 'What I Think of Bimetallism,' *The Gold Standard Defense Association (1895–98)*, pamphlet no. 21 (Nov. 1896), p. 6.

166. Atkinson Papers, 18, Shaw-Lefevre to Atkinson, 20 July 1896.

167. Horace White, 'The Monetary Issue in the United States,' *The Gold Standard Defense Association, 1895–98* (Oct. 1896), p. 206.

168. W. Lecky, *Democracy and Liberty*, 2 vols (London, 1896), and E. L. Godkin, *The Problems of Modern Democracy* (New York, 1896).

169. Godkin, *Problems of Democracy*, pp. 249–310.

170. BP, USA 5, Godkin to Bryce, 28 July 1896, f. 135.

171. J. Sproat, *'The Best Men': Liberal Reformers in the Gilded Age* (London, 1968), p. 271.

172. God.P, Bryce to Godkin, 3 Dec. 1896 (146).

173. Ibid., A. V. Dicey to Godkin, 5 Nov. 1896 (247).

174. Ibid., Farrer to Godkin, 20 May 1896 (276).

175. Ibid., 10 Dec. 1896 (277).

176. Ibid.

177. Ibid., Bryce to Godkin, 1 Jan. 1896 (143).

178. N. Pilling, 'The Conservatism of Sir Henry Maine,' *Political Studies*, vol. xviii (1970), pp. 107–20 and B. E. Lippincott, *Victorian Critics of Democracy* (New York edn, 1964), pp. 207–43. See also Jon Roper, *Democracy and Its Critics*: *Anglo-American Democratic Thought in the Nineteenth Century* (London, 1988). Also on Lecky, see Donal McCartney, *W. E. H. Lecky: Historian and Politician, 1838–1903* (London, 1994), especially 'Liberty or Democracy?' (pp. 151–61), and on Maine, see Alan Diamond (ed.) *The Victorian Achievement of Sir Henry Maine: A Centennial Reappraisal* (Cambridge, 1991), especially Stefan Collini, 'Democracy and Excitement: Maine's Political Pessimism' (pp. 88–95), and S. Collini,

P. Winch, and J. Burrow, *That Noble Science of Politics: A Study in Nineteenth-Century Intellectual History* (Cambridge, 1983).

179. *Democracy and Liberty*, i, pp. 75–136, in addition to many other passages.
180. Ibid., pp. 63–73. Also see, W. E. Lecky, 'The Conservatism of the British Democracy,' *NAR*, vol. clxiv (Feb. 1897), p. 227.
181. *Democracy and Liberty*, i, p. 113.
182. God.P, Bryce to Godkin, 3 Dec. 1896 (146).
183. Morley, 'Mr. Lecky on Democracy,' *NC*, vol. xxxix (May 1896), p. 719. For another Liberal defense of American democracy in the face of Lecky's attack, see *RR*, vol. xiii (Apr. 1896), pp. 366–73.
184. God.P, Bryce to Godkin, 3 Dec. 1896 (146).
185. For further Liberal views that British democracy was at least in as poor a condition as American, probably worse, see Bryce, 'Political Organization in the United States and England,' *NAR*, vol. clvi (Jan. 1893), pp. 105–18 and G. W. Smalley, 'Checks on Democracy in America,' *NC*, vol. xxxv (June 1894), pp. 873–89.
186. W. Alden and W. Dillon, 'The Battle for Standards in America,' *NC*, vol. xl (Aug. 1896), pp. 199–210; M. Frewen, 'The American Elections of 1896,' *Nat.R*, vol. xxviii (Nov. 1896), pp. 400–5; F. Browne and Sen. Chandler, 'The Presidential Contest,' *Nat.R*, vol. xxviii (Dec. 1896), pp. 452–76; F. H. Hardy, 'Lessons from the American Election,' *FR*, vol. lx (Dec. 1896), pp. 894–903; and L. Courtney, 'The Recent Presidential Election,' *NC*, vol. xli (Jan. 1897), pp. 1–16.
187. HP, Box 28, Harcourt to Morley, 13 Nov. 1896, f. 71.
188. Ibid., 7 Nov. 1896, f. 67.
189. Atkinson Papers, 18, Farrer to Atkinson, 6 Dec. 1896.
190. God.P, 3 Dec. 1896 (146).
191. Atkinson Papers, 18, Farrer to Atkinson, 27 Oct. 1896.
192. Ibid., 3 Dec. 1896.
193. Hamilton Diaries, 48670, 5 Nov. 1896, f. 48.
194. J. D. Richardson (ed.), *A Compilation of the Messages and Papers of the Presidents, 1789–1897*, 20 vols (Washington, 1897), xiv, p. 6237.
195. Senator Wolcott was extremely popular in Britain, especially with Liberals and arbitrationists, because of his early condemnation of Cleveland's message of 17 Dec. 1895. E. H. H. Green discusses Senator Wolcott's visit to England in 1897 in 'Rentiers versus Producers?' *EHR*, vol. ciii (July 1988), pp. 604–7. Green believes that while the British and US governments were not serious about the mission, the bimetallic proponents certainly were. Also see T. F. Dawson, *The Life and Character of Edward Oliver Wolcott*, 2 vols (New York, 1909), i, pp. 623–95.
196. *The Bimetallist*, vol. iii, no. vi (June 1897), p. 94.
197. London School of Economics Library, London (Farrer Collection): vol. i R(S.R.) 1018: Godkin to Farrer, 6 Jan. 1897 (155), ff. 140–1.
198. Hamilton Diaires, 48671, 6 June 1897, f. 74.
199. The Cabinet occasionally discussed bimetallism. On 4 Mar. 1896, there had been 'a division on Bimetallism.' Cabinet Papers, 41/23/48, 5 Mar. 1896.
200. Farrer Collection, vol. iii (18), Peel to Farrer, 16 Aug. 1897, f. 70.
201. Hamilton Diaries, 48671, 3 Aug. 1897, f. 117.

202. *The Times*, 17 and 24 Sept. 1897. Also see, the *Manchester Guardian*, 27 Sept. 1897.
203. Farrer Collection, vol. i, Harcourt to Farrer, 28 Sept. 1897, f. 169.
204. C. F. Adams spent several days at Farrer's. For reports upon the men's views of international bimetallism, see Balfour Papers, 49742, J. Hay to H. White, 29 Sept. 1897, ff. 55–6.
205. E. C. Kirkland, *Charles Francis Adams, Jr. 1835–1915. The Patrician at Bay* (Cambridge, MA, 1965), p. 179.
206. Balfour Papers, 49696, Hay to White, 29 Sept. 1897, f. 65. Several such letters were passed on to Balfour by White.
207. Farrer Collection, vol. i, C. F. Adams to Farrer, 28 Sept. and 9 Oct. 1897 (1–2), ff. 1–4.
208. Ibid., vol. iii, Shaw-Lefevre to Farrer, 1 Oct. 1897 (54), f. 161.
209. Cabinet Papers, 41/24/20, 17 Oct. 1897.
210. Richardson, *Messages of the Presidents*, vol. xiv, pp. 6265–6.
211. Hansard, 4th series, xlv, 19 Jan. 1897, 49–51 (Harcourt) and 71–2 (Balfour).
212. H. C. Allen, *Great Britain and the United States: A History of Anglo-American Relations (1783–1952)* (London, 1954), pp. 541–2.
213. Balfour Papers, 49742, R. Olney to White, 14 May 1897, f. 53.
214. FO 96/200 and Patterson, *Towards a Warless World*, p. 46.
215. G. Seed, 'British Reactions to American Imperialism Reflected in Journals of Opinion, 1898–1900,' *Political Science Quarterly*, vol. lxxiii (1958), pp. 254–72.
216. Harcourt, cited in *The Times*, 9 May 1898; Chamberlain, 'Recent Developments of Policy in the United States,' *Scribner's Magazine*, vol. xxiv (Dec. 1898), pp. 674–82, and cited in *The Times*, 14 May 1898; C. Dilke, 'The Future Relations of Great Britain and the United States,' *The Forum*, vol. xxvi (Jan. 1899), pp. 521–8; Bryce, 'The Essential Unity of Britain and America,' *AM*, vol. lxxxii (July 1898), pp. 22–9; Stead, 'Why Not a British Celebration of the Fourth of July,' *RR*, vol. xvii (May 1898), pp. 599–613; and A. V. Dicey, 'A Common Citizenship for the English Race,' *CR*, vol. lxxi (Apr. 1897), pp. 457–76.
217. T. Boyle, 'The Liberal Party and Foreign Affairs, 1895–1905' (Univ. of London MPhil thesis, 1974), pp. 75–89.

Conclusion

In the 1860s, Americans and Englishmen were separated by more than just the Atlantic Ocean. The previous decade had brought them to the edge of actual conflict, especially at sea, during the Civil War and there were divisive and strong feelings held by Englishmen about the bitter conflict between the Union and the Confederacy. A sense of Anglo-American confrontation and animosity existed which had not been lessened by such struggles as those over Fenianism and the *Alabama* claims settlements, and the violence injected into British politics by radical Irish-Americans bent on freeing and liberating kinsmen from British jails.

At the turn of the twentieth century and the end of the Victorian age, by contrast, Americans and Englishmen stood shoulder to shoulder supporting each other against the belligerent activities of old European states, especially Spain and Germany. In between the 1860s and the late 1890s, a transition had occurred in Anglo-American relations. During that transition, and playing an important role in it, were the tenets and leaders of British Liberalism. Gladstone, Morley, Harcourt, Bryce, and many others, but also Americans like E. L. Godkin, Edward Atkinson, Henry George, and Andrew Carnegie, helped to define how Britain and the United States evolved into a modern cordial twentieth-century partnership and to delineate how individuals could make an impact upon the diplomatic relations between two major powers.

At the outset, four questions were posed as central to this study. The first was how attentively did Liberal leaders follow developments in the United States? Any response to this question must necessarily be qualified, for the problem of quantification looms very large. Certainly, it may be said that most Liberal leaders were marginally interested in a range of American issues in the 1860s, but were profusely concerned with the United States in 1898, the year of Gladstone's death and on the eve of the passing of the Victorian age. But how to measure the degree of this interest or to judge how keenly Liberal leaders followed which American developments is difficult to assess with any precision. Yet some measurements may be made. Hansard rarely mentions American events or issues in the 1870s, but does so often by the end of the 1880s and 1890s. American articles are not common in major

British periodicals in the 1870s, or at least not so frequent as by the end of the nineteenth century. There is an almost three-fold increase in such articles in the *Nineteenth Century* and the *Fortnightly Review* from 1886 to 1892 as compared with the period 1874 to 1880. Few Liberal leaders had visited the United States by the mid-1860s; almost every one had done so by the end of the Victorian age.

Noticeably, Gladstone and Harcourt never made the transatlantic journey. Few had American friends earlier; every one had them by the end of the century. Through visits and friendships Liberals learned both much more and more accurately about the United States. Over the last several decades of the nineteenth century, Liberals' American interests evolved from being largely biased, general, and usually second-hand understandings to more often than not fair, detailed, and first-hand understandings of a range of specific issues.

Secondly, there is the question of which American issues were most seriously examined and why. Liberals examined those issues which had some direct relationship to events in Great Britain, and by the 1880s there had been a great proliferation of such issues. Irish-American revolutionary activities, Irish Home Rule and federalism, protectionism, and bimetallism were vital issues, questions Liberals, in guiding the government from 1880 to 1885, and from 1892 to 1895, had to derive something about from related lessons, parallels, and events across the Atlantic. The fact that Great Britain quelled the Irish-American agitations and rejected protectionism, Irish Home Rule, and bimetallism should not obscure that they thought seriously about the American experience. There were many American issues in addition to the obvious though often minor diplomatic ones between 1874 and 1895.

The serious way in which Liberal leaders approached the United States in the Gilded Age can be seen by the volume of their exceptionally close studies. Certainly, Bryce's *The American Commonwealth* stood out. Yet, it was not the only important American analysis, nor did it have the immediate impact upon the broad Anglo-American public enjoyed by other Liberal publications. Moreover, nor was *The American Commonwealth* the unbiased political tract that many generations have assumed it to be. Rather, it was a Mugwump critique, keenly perceptive but muckraking, at least in dealing with the political decay found primarily in the big Eastern cities.

Among the many other notable pieces by British Liberals on the United States, one would have to include Gladstone's articles for the *North American Review* on divorce, protectionism, and Christianity, or for the *Youth's Companion* on the English-speaking races, on the life of

John Motley, or the industrialist Sydney Gilchrest Thomas; Dilke's *Greater Britain* and *The Problems of Greater Britain*; Morley's professional responsibilities for the *Pall Mall Gazette*, the *Fortnightly Review*, *Macmillan's Magazine*, and the English Men of Letters series; Bryce's many articles on such American topics as education, law, and the blacks; Chamberlain's studies upon American municipalities and caucuses; Playfair's on American protectionism and bimetallism; and Thomas Farrer's and William Stead's many American analyses.

The impact of these various Liberal opinions was often immediate and controversial: Dilke's *Greater Britain*; Gladstone's 'Kin Beyond Sea' or call to 'common sense' during the Venezuelan crisis; and Chamberlain's views on American caucuses became important Anglo-American events. Morley's editorial positions on American affairs for his various publications arguably affected the American views of more British readers than Bryce's *The American Commonwealth*. Whereas the range of Liberal American interests in the 1870s was fairly limited to national politics (especially presidential elections), diplomacy, and Irish-American affairs; it included in the 1880s, concern with copyright, arbitration, federalism, bimetallism, protectionism, divorce, religion, and urban politics.

One primary measure of the increasing Liberal interest in the United States can be found in their attention to American presidential elections. The elections of 1884, 1888, 1892, and finally, most dramatically, that of 1896, were watched with expanding British fascination. As the *Progressive Review* remarked in 1896: 'At the present moment thousands of persons in England are directly interested in the issue of the presidential election. No political contest has taken place in the United States that has so closely affected persons outside the direct and ostensible sphere of American law and political action.'[1] By the mid-1890s, British and American political, social, and economic activities were so intertwined, even dependent, that only the most blind and ignorant or chauvinistic patriot might have refused to admit the crucial importance of the Anglo-American relationship for the individual prosperity of each nation.

Did British leaders form sympathies for the people and institutions of the United States similar to those by James Bryce, astute student of American politics and the author of the seminal study, *The American Commonwealth*? In, fact, Liberal leaders did form a basically favorable affection for both the American people and the country's institutions. Bryce's American proclivities, while notably profuse, were not unique. Much of the Liberal regard for the United States was based on an idealized conception of American democracy: that fabric of government founded upon education, freedom of religion, equality of opportunity, federalism, and a written Bill of Rights. In the midst of an expanding British Empire and particular dissension in Ireland, Liberal leaders quite naturally saw themselves as the British equivalents of the American founding fathers, Gladstone and Morley among others idolizing the life of George Washington. In addition, Liberals formed collectively and independently a number of instrumental and important personal attachments to Americans. Those that stood out were Rosebery's friendship with Samuel Ward and other Americans in the 1870s, Bryce's with Edwin L. Godkin, Morley's with Charles Norton and Andrew Carnegie, Playfair's with his wife's family (similar to those of Harcourt and Chamberlain), and Gladstone's warm relations with a wide representation of leaders from all sections of American professional life.

A general idolization of the United States and specific friendships were constant denominators in the Liberal relationship with the United States during the late Victorian age. In fact, both sorts of international sympathies deepened as the century developed. On the other hand, Liberal leaders grew increasingly disturbed with a series of worsening conditions in the United States. In the 1890s, these involved the issues of protectionism, bimetallism, urban corruption, and political bossism. This evident Liberal despair with the United States was personified by Stead's 1898 book on New York: *'Satan's Invisible World Displayed'; or Despairing Democracy*.

Nonetheless, Liberals still retained their admiration and optimism for the American experience. They did so most conspicuously by placing their faith in the politics of Cleveland's Democratic party and the Mugwumps. Liberal support for the Democrats was significant. It represented, historically, a shift. From the time of Lincoln until the early 1880s, Liberals were fully sympathetic to the Republican party. Dilke and Bryce praised Republicanism in the period 1868–70. Morley supported Hayes in the election of 1876. Gladstone and Harcourt deplored the Democratic Congress's defeat of their friend Richard Henry Dana Jr's nomination to be American Minister in Great Britain. Between 1884 and 1896, this Liberal sympathy changed in party affiliation. Liberal causes and Cleveland's were unquestionably interlocked, directed toward a non-entangling foreign policy, more moderate protectionist policies, monometallism, and certain governmental reforms. In addition, many personal friends of Liberals were Mugwumps and Democrats: Godkin, Ward, Lowell, Norton, Atkinson, and even, in a manner, Carnegie (though a Republican, he drew closer to Cleveland in the 1890s).

Liberal and Democratic-Mugwump intercourse was no better displayed than in the pages of the *North American Review* and the *Nineteenth Century* where American and British writers debated common issues. When, in 1896, Liberals returned to support the Republican cause, and William McKinley, they did so not out of any great respect for the party but because of their unilateral opposition to the noxious silver fanaticism of Bryan. As Thomas Farrer reported to Edward Atkinson: 'Before I heard of Bryan I thought McKinley the worst possible candidate the US could produce – and I shall see his success with mixed feelings.'[2] But any real notion of British antagonism towards the United States had pretty well disappeared, for integral Anglo-American issues had emerged which made the simple idea of antipathy to the United States irrational and impractical.

Lastly, it must be considered whether American friendships, methods of government, or modes of behavior had any influence on the actions and political philosophies of Liberal leaders or the British government. It is clear that they did. Liberals turned towards American ideals, and simultaneously attempted to prevent the growth of American abuses within their own social and political communities. In this, they could be seen as following the same path trodden by Mugwump reformers. William Stead in his studies of Chicago and New York; Playfair and Farrer in their examinations of American currency and trade; Harcourt in his advocacy of gold, and Gladstone in his of free trade; Bryce in his attitudes towards blacks and political reform were ever as bold as 'American-type genteel reformers' like Godkin, Atkinson, and Norton. They were all activists and used public speeches and popular journals to promote their causes.

But one Anglo-American cause, however, emerged that dominated all others: that of Anglo-Saxon unity. Liberals had bound their own emotions and interests to many American private associations for two or so decades by the mid-1880s. In the 1890s, they moved forward to strengthen British and American ties. Under the umbrella of better Anglo-American relations, they worked specifically for Anglo-American copyright, arbitration, free trade, monometallism, and finally for a solution of the Venezuelan problem. Liberals had founded the Anglo-American Association in 1870. They had presented the idea of 'real' Anglo-American union in the *Pall Mall Gazette* in 1881. Harcourt, who as 'Historicus' had struggled for Anglo-American amity in the 1860s, fought even more strenuously in the 1890s. It had been the

Liberals who had delivered the arbitration petititon to President Cleveland in 1887. Morley considered making international arbitration his single most important political issue in 1896. Bryce worked hard to educate Americans and Englishmen about similar problems and perspectives. Bryce, Chamberlain, Morley, Harcourt, Playfair, Dilke, Farrer, Stead, McCarthy, Rosebery, and many other Liberals were 'Anglo-Americanists.'

Yet, no man, whether on the American or the British side, was more important to the warming of Anglo-American relations than Gladstone. Gladstone had made such a catastrophic blunder in 1862 when he had proclaimed that the Confederates 'had made a nation,' which he lamented all his life. The great Liberal Prime Minister became bent on eradicating any memory of Anglo-American animosity associated with his name. With the publication of 'Kin Beyond Sea' in 1878, most Americans were moved to see Gladstone as a champion of American destiny. Gladstone did not stop his campaign. His policies towards the Irish over Home Rule and his article on the union of the English-speaking peoples were further dramatic attempts to incorporate his name with the cause of Anglo-American understanding (this despite the fact that on certain issues such as copyright and arbitration he was hesitant to declare some shortcomings). It was a grand, moral, overriding issue for him and one in which he, personally, sought to symbolize the aspirations of millions of people on two continents. Gladstone now stood out as a model leader in the United States, Great Britain, and Anglo-American relations.

Great Britain had often isolated herself from allies during the 1880s and 1890s, as she fought for an empire and European hegemony with Germany, Russia, and France. The United States, equally, maintained an isolationist stand and showed relatively little interest in territorial expansion or European affairs. For most Gladstonian Liberals, an alliance with the United States was an alternative to European alliances. Anglo-Saxon culture, racism, and the respective international positions of Britain and the United States conspired to make greater Anglo-American rapprochement in the late 1890s almost a certainty.

In conclusion, it must be emphasized that the 'great Anglo-American rapprochement'[3] of 1895–98 was not produced, as historians usually claim, by a diplomatic settlement of the Venezuelan crisis or a sudden realization of Anglo-American amity. Rather, there were many positive forces at work. As Charles Campbell has noted:

> The common heritage, the close economic relations, the absence of clashing vital interests, the rise of British democracy and of admiration for American institutions, the dwindling of Irish and

free-silver fanaticism, and Anglo-Saxon race patriotism – these were positive forces moulding the British–American relationship.[4]

In the 1860s, there had existed genuine hostility between the countries – which revolved more around differences (though obviously there was language, heredity, etc.) than around similarities or common concerns. In the 1880s, a transition occurred – aided enormously by the transportation and communication revolutions – from a diverse Anglo-American world to a common Anglo-American world based upon the increased frequency of exchange and upon similar developments in both countries. Interchange of views and the growth of knowledge are historical facts. In the 1880s, these worked, in the absence of any critical diplomatic incidents, to inspire the so-called Anglo-American rapprochement. The Venezuelan incident never threatened to disrupt this already existing relationship. A close analysis of the events in 1895–6 has indicated that the actual dangers were averted, not by the leaders of the American and British governments, but by the private intervention on both sides of prominent political leaders and businessmen, who had had extensive contacts and Anglo-American interests in the previous decade. Importance has been given to the efforts of Theodore Roosevelt, John Hay, Richard Olney, Cleveland, Salisbury, and Chamberlain in this situation, and their recognition of the British–American special relationship. But equally as important were the efforts of British Liberal leaders, men such as Gladstone, Bryce, Harcourt, Morley, and Playfair.

Most importantly, the final legacy of the Gladstonian Liberals was that of both British and Americans as promoters of understanding between countries, of their moral leadership, and of the view of an Anglo-American responsibility to the world. Their influence upon Anglo-American relations could not have been more profound. On 28 June 1919, two men sat in the great Hall of Mirrors in the Versailles Palace ready to sign a treaty for world peace. Both were Gladstonians and to some degree Anglo-Americans – the one an American Presbyterian and the other a Welsh Baptist.[5] David Lloyd George and President Woodrow Wilson provided a commentary, in their way, on the evolution of Anglo-American relations of a generation earlier, between the end of the American Civil War in 1865 and the waning of the Victorian age in the 1890s.

Notes

1. Vol. i, no. i (Oct. 1896), p. 82.
2. Atkinson Papers, 18, Farrer to Atkinson, 27 Oct. 1896.

3. B. Perkins, *The Great Rapprochement: England and the United States, 1895–1914* (New York, 1968).
4. *From Revolution to Rapprochement: The United States and Britain, 1783–1900* (New York, 1974), p. 204.
5. Michael Fry discusses the Anglo-American entourage surrounding Lloyd George's Prime Ministership in *Illusion of Security. North Atlantic Diplomacy 1918–22* (Toronto, 1972).

Appendix I: Biographical and American Notes

Liberal leaders

Bright, John (1811–89): MP 1843–89; President of the Board of Trade, 1868–70; Chancellor of the Duchy of Lancaster, 1873–74 and 1880–82; supported the North during the Civil War. Primary American interest: free trade vs. protection. American friends: C. Sumner, Emerson, J. Motley, and J. Lowell.

Bryce, James (1838–1922): MP 1880–1906; Chancellor of the Duchy of Lancaster, 1892–94; President of the Board of Trade, 1894–95; Chief Secretary for Ireland, 1905–06; Ambassador to US, 1907–13; *The American Commonwealth* (1888); regular contributions to the *Nation*; many other American articles, diaries of American visits, 1870, 1881, 1883 (Papers). Visited US 1870, 1881, 1883, 1889–90, 1891, 1901, 1904, and 1907–13. Many American friends.

Chamberlain, Joseph (1836–1914): Birmingham municipal leader; Liberal MP 1876–86; Unionist MP 1886–1914; President of the Board of Trade, 1880–85; President of the Local Government Board, 1886; Colonial Secretary, 1895–1903; second wife, the American Miss Endicott (1888); articles on American politics and cities; diary of American visit, 1887–88 (Papers). Visited US 1887–88, 1888, 1890, and 1896. American friends: Henry White, Endicott family, and various others.

Childers, H. C. E. (1827–96): MP 1860–92; First Lord of the Admiralty, 1868–71; Chancellor of the Duchy of Lancaster, 1872–73; Secretary of State for War, 1880–82; Chancellor of the Exchequer, 1882–85; Home Secretary, 1886; American business interests. Visited US 1859, 1874, 1875, 1876, and 1877.

Dilke, Sir Charles W. (1843–1911): MP 1868–86, 1892–1911; Under-Secretary of the Foreign Office, 1880–82; President of the Local Government Board, 1882–85; *Greater Britain* (1868); *Problems of Greater Britain* (1890); expert on imperial affairs. Visited US 1866–67, 1875, & 1904. American friends: K. Field, M. Twain, H. James, J. Lowell, and G. Smalley.

Forster, William E. (1818–86): MP 1861–86; Vice-President of the Council, 1868–74; Chief Secretary for Ireland, 1880–82; supported North in the Civil War. Visited US 1874. American friends: E. Yarnell, C. Adams, and C. Sumner.

Fowler, Henry H. (1830–1911): MP 1880–1908; President of the Local Government Board, 1892–94; Secretary of State for India, 1894–95; Chancellor of the Duchy of Lancaster, 1905–08; Lord President of the Council, 1908–10. Primary American interests: bimetallism and protectionism.

Gladstone, William E. (1809–98): MP 1833–45 and 1847–95; Prime Minister, 1868–74, 1880–85, 1886, 1892–94; American articles for *NAR* and *YC*, 1878–98. Primary American interests: protectionism and social questions. Wide range of contacts with American leaders of politics, society, religion, and literature.

Granville, Earl (2nd) (1815–91): Foreign Secretary, 1851–52, 1870–74, 1880–85; Colonial Secretary; 1868–70, 1886. American interests confined to diplomatic questions. American friends: J. Motley and J. Lowell.

Harcourt, William Vernon (1827–1904): MP 1868–1904; Solicitor General 1873–74; Home Secretary, 1880–85; Chancellor of the Exchequer, 1886, 1892–95; wrote 'Historicus' articles for *The Times*, 1863–71; American wife, Miss Motley (1877); authority on American legal and diplomatic matters. American friends: Motley family, J. Lowell, Smalley, Dana family, and H. White.

Hartington, Marquess of (1833–1908): Postmaster-General, 1868–70; Chief Secretary for Ireland, 1870–74; Secretary of State for India, 1880–82; Secretary of State for War, 1882–85; favored South in Civil War. Few American interests. Visited US 1862.

Herschell, Lord (1837–99): MP 1874–85; Solicitor-General, 1880–85; Lord Chancellor, 1886, 1892–95. Visited US 1887 (lecture tour) and 1899 (died in Washington at work on Anglo-American commission).

Kimberley, Lord (1826–1902): Lord Privy Seal, 1868–70; Colonial Secretary, 1870–74, 1880–82; Secretary of State for India, 1882–85, 1886, 1892–94; Foreign Secretary, 1894–95. Few American interests.

Morley, John (1838–1923): MP 1883–1908; Chief Secretary for Ireland, 1886, 1892–95; Secretary for India, 1905–10; editor of the *FR* 1867–82, *PMG* 1880–83. Primary American interest in Irish-American affairs. Visited US 1867 and 1904. American friends: A. Carnegie, C. Norton, E. L. Godkin, M. Conway, J. Lowell, and writers.

Mundella, A. J. (1825–97): MP 1868–97; Vice-President of Committee of Privy Council for Education, 1880–85; President of the Board of Trade, 1886, 1892–94. Visited US 1870 (studied education). American friends: R. H. Dana Jr, J. Lowell, and H. James.

Ripon, Marquess of (1827–1909): Lord President of the Council, 1868–73; Governor-General of India, 1880–84; First Lord of the Admiralty, 1886; Colonial Secretary, 1892–95; Lord Privy Seal, 1905–08. Visited US 1871 (Chairman of British Commission to Washington).

Rosebery, Earl (1847–1929): Foreign Secretary, 1886, 1892–94; Prime Minister, 1894–95; Liberal imperialist; diaries of American visits – 1873 and 1874–75 (Papers). Visited US 1873, 1874–75, 1876, and 1883. American friends: S. Ward, Hurlbert, G. Smalley, J. Lowell, H. James, and many others.

Selborne, Earl (1812–95): MP as Roundell Palmer, 1861–72; Lord Chancellor, 1872–74, 1880–85; knowledgeable on Anglo-American diplomatic issues. American friends: J. Lowell and G. Smalley.

Shaw-Lefevre, G. J. (1831–1928): MP 1863–95; Secretary to the Board of Trade, 1868–70; Secretary for the Admiralty, 1871–74; First Commissioner of Works, 1880–83, 1892–94; Postmaster-General, 1883–85; President of the Local Government Board, 1894–95. Primary American interests were economic and social issues. American friends: J. Lowell, G. Smalley, and E. Atkinson.

Spencer, Earl (1835–1910): Lord-Lieutenant of Ireland, 1868–74, 1882–85; President of the Council, 1880–82, 1886; First Lord of the Admiralty, 1892–95. Primary American interests in Irish–American affairs. Visited US 1857.

Trevelyan, George O. (1838–1928): MP 1865–97; Civil Lord of the Admiralty, 1868–70; Parliamentary Secretary for the Admiralty, 1881; Chief Secretary for Ireland, 1882–84; Chancellor of the Duchy of Lancaster, 1884–85; Secretary for Scotland, 1886, 1892–95; *History of the American Revolution*, 6 vols (1899–1914). American friends: T. Roosevelt, A. Carnegie, H. Lodge, J. Hay, E. Root, and Adams family.

Other Liberals

Asquith, Herbert H. (1852–1928): MP 1886–1918; Home Secretary, 1892–95; Liberal imperialist; Chancellor of Exchequer, 1905–08; Prime Minister, 1908–16. Primary American interest before 1898, Irish–American affairs.

Bradlaugh, Charles (1833–91): MP 1880–91; free-thinker and secularist; letters on American trips published in *National Reformer*. Visited US 1873, 1874, and 1875 (three separate lecture tours). American friends: R. G. Ingersoll, W. Garrison, and M. Conway.

Caine, William S. (1842–1903): MP 1880–90, 1892–95, 1900–03; Baptist and temperance reformer. Visited US 1875, 1876, 1887–88, 1891, and 1894 (Temperance Congress), 1898. American friends: Neal Dow and other temperance leaders.

Campbell, George (1824–92): MP 1875–92; authority on the American South and Home Rule. Wrote *White and Black. The Outcome of a Visit to the United States* (1879). Visited US 1878 and 1887.

Courtney, Leonard (1832–1918): MP 1875; Secretary of Treasury, 1882–84; Deputy Speaker, 1886–92; authority on bimetallism; proportional representation movement leader; wrote articles on American finance and politics. Visited US 1866 and 1873. American friends: J. Lowell and A. Carnegie.

Cremer, William Randal (1838–1908): Radical MP 1885–95, 1900–08; formed Workmen's Peace Association, 1871, and Anglo-American arbitration leader; edited the *Arbitrator* (1889–1908). Visited US 1887, 1895, 1896, and 1904.

Goschen, George (1831–1907): MP 1863–85; First Lord of the Admiralty, 1871–74; joined Conservatives in 1887; economic authority; studied American finance; worked in family business in South America, 1854–56. American friends: J. P. Morgan and E. Atkinson.

Grey, Sir Edward (1862–1933): MP 1885–1916; Under-Secretary at the Foreign Office, 1894–95; authority on Anglo-American relations (1898–1916). American friends: T. Roosevelt and others.

Labouchere, Henry (1831–1912): MP 1880–1906; supporter of radical causes; journalist; editor of the weekly *Truth*; letters to *Daily News* on America, 1870–71; wanted to become British Ambassador to America. Visited US 1852–55 (especially the West). American friends: S. Ward, W. Hurlbert, and J. Whistler.

Morley, Arnold (1849–1916): MP 1880–95; Chief Whip, 1886–92; Postmaster-General, 1892–95. Visited US 1872 and 1881.

Munro-Ferguson, Ronald (1860–1934): MP 1884–1914; Liberal imperialist; private secretary to Rosebery at the Foreign Office, 1886, 1892–94; stayed closely in touch on American events through Spring-Rice. Visited US 1887.

Playfair, Sir Lyon (1819–98): MP 1868–92; Postmaster-General, 1873–74; Vice-President of the Council, 1886; distinguished scientist; American wife, Miss Russell (1878); many articles on American protectionism, finance, and politics; visited US almost every year after his marriage. Visited US 1877, 1818, 1879–86, 1887 (British representative at the Philadelphia Centennial), and 1888–98. American friends: mostly Bostonian literary personalities, J. Lowell, H. Longfellow, W. Holmes, and R. W. Emerson.

Rathbone, William (1819–1902): MP 1868–95; member of a great Liverpool mercantile family; philanthropist; interested in educational and social issues; first wife American, Miss Wainwright (d. 1851). Visited US 1841–42, 1843, and 1848–49. American friends: J. M. Forbes, J. R. Bush, and E. Burnett.

Russell, Sir Charles (1832–1900): MP 1880–85, 1886, 1892; Lord Chief Justice, 1894–1900; Visited US 1883 and 1896 (lecture tour). American friends: E. Godkin, H. Villard, and W. Evarts.

Smith, Samuel (1836–1906): MP 1882–1905; Liverpool businessman and philanthropist; bimetallist. Visited US 1860, 1866, 1896, and 1899 (Pan-Presbyterian Congress in Washington). American friends: H. George, C. Moody, and I. Sankey.

Watkin, Edward (1819–1901): MP 1864–68, 1874–95; railway promoter and authority; Manchester businessman. Visited US 1851, 1861, 1875, 1886, etc. (wrote that his 1886 trip was his 30th crossing of the Atlantic).

Politicians, Journalists, Intellectuals, and Radicals

Acton, Lord (1834–1902): famous historian and close friend of Gladstone; 'Lord Acton's American Diaries', *FR* (Dec. 1921–Jan. 1922). Visited US 1853 and 1855. American friends: Andrew D. White, J. Lowell and C. Norton.

Arnold, Matthew (1822–88): poet and critic; inspector of schools, 1851; daughter married an American; *Discourses on America* (1885) and *Civilization in the*

United States (1888). Visited US 1883–84 & 1886 (gave lectures). American friends: A. Carnegie, C. Norton, G. Smalley, H. James and J. Lowell.

Balfour, Arthur J. (1848–1930): Conservative MP 1874–1922; Prime Minister 1902–05; member of Anglo-American social group the 'Souls'; primary American interest prior to 1898, bimetallism. Visited US 1874 and 1917. American friends: A. Carnegie, H. White, J. Hay, and Norton family.

Churchill, Randolph (1849–94): Conservative MP 1874–94; member of the 'Fourth Party'; Chancellor of the Exchequer, 1816; American wife, Miss Jennie Jerome (1874). Visited US 1876.

Curzon, Lord (1859–1925): Conservative MP 1886–92; Parliamentary Under-Secretary for Foreign Affairs, 1895–98; world traveler; member of the 'Souls'; American wife, Mary Leiter (1895). Visited US 1887 and 1892–95 (diaries of these trips in his Papers).

Davitt, Michael (1846–1906): Irish revolutionary and labor agitator; Irish MP 1882–99; particularly interested in Irish-American and American labor issues; American wife, Mary Yore (1886). Visited US 1878 (lecture tour), 1880 (organized American Land League), 1882 (lecture tour), 1886, 1897 (lecture tour), and 1901 (United Irish Societies meeting in Chicago). American friends: H. George, P. Ford, A. Carnegie, and C. Depew.

Dicey, Albert Venn (1835–1922): jurist and Vinerian Professor of English Law and Fellow of All Souls, Oxford, 1882–1909; authority on American federalism. Visited US 1870 and 1898. American friends: H. James, E. Godkin, C. Eliot, O. Holmes, J. Lowell, and C. Norton.

Farrer, Thomas H. (1819–99): civil servant; Permanent-Secretary to the Board of Trade, 1865–86; authority on economic affairs. Primary American interests were protectionism and bimetallism. Visited America in 1886. American friends: E. Godkin and E. Atkinson.

Freeman, Edward A. (1823–92): historian; Regius Professor of Modern History, Oxford, 1884–92; authority on American federalism; *Some Impressions of America* (1883) and *Lectures to American Audiences* (1882). Visited US 1881–82 (lecture tour). American friends: J. Lowell and E. Godkin.

Frewen, Moreton (1853–1924): Irish-Nationalist MP 1910–1; American wife, Clara Jerome, 1880 (sister of Jennie Churchill); extensive knowledge of the United States, especially the West. Primary American interests in silver and protectionism; wrote many articles on America. Visited US 1878–88 (cattle business) and 1892. American friends: Jerome family, W. D. Duncan, Western free silver men, and many others.

Froude, James A. (1818–94): historian and man of letters; traveled extensively in the empire; *Oceana* (1886). Visited US 1872 (lecture tour) and 1885. American friends: G. Smalley, M. Conway, G. Peabody, B. Harte, J. Motley, J. Lowell, A. Carnegie, and J. P. Morgan.

Hardie, James Keir (1856–1915): miner, journalist, and Socialist leader; Labour MP 1892–95, 1900–15; 'My American Diary,' *The Labour Leader*, 14 Sept. 1895;

authority on American labor movement. Visited US 1895, 1908, and 1912. American friends: H. Lloyd and S. Gompers.

Holyoake, George (1817–1906): cooperator and secularist; studied American history and economic conditions; wrote fairly extensively upon America; *Among the Americans* (1881). Visited US 1879 and 1882. American friends: H. George, and R. G. Ingersoll.

Hughes, Thomas (1822–96): Liberal MP 1865, 1868–74; author of *Tom Brown's School Days*, founded Rugby, model community in Tennessee, in 1879; letters on America to *London Spectator* in 1880–1, signed 'Vacuus Viator.' Visited US 1870, 1880–81 and 1885. American friends: J. Lowell, C. Eliot, C. Norton, O. Holmes Jr and others.

Hyndman, Henry (1842–1921): socialist leader and journalist; on staff of the *PMG* 1871–80; very knowledgeable of American labor issues and politics; lived and worked in America through much of the 1870s. American friends: H. George, B. Harte, Dr Vaughn, W. Hurlbert, and others.

Jennings, Louis (1836–93): Conservative MP 1885–93; edited the *New York Times*, 1868–76; American wife, Miss Herriques, 1868; *Eighty Years of Republican Government in the United States* (1868); wrote various articles on American politics. Visited US 1865–67 (correspondent of *The Times*), 1868–76. American friends: J. Gould, S. Ward, and many others.

Landsdowne, Marquess of (1845–1927): Under-Secretary for War, 1872–74; inherited liberal traditions but moved to Conservatives over opposition to Gladstone's Irish policies; Governor-General of Canada, 1883–88; Viceroy of India, 1888–94; Secretary of State for War, 1895–1900. Visited US periodically between 1883 and 1888. American friends: J. Lowell and others.

Lawley, Francis C. (1825–1901): sportsman and journalist; Liberal MP 1852; private secretary to Gladstone; close friend of Rosebery; settled in America, 1854–65; correspondent to *The Times* during the Civil War; edited the *Anglo-American Times* (London) in the 1890s. Many American acquaintances.

Lecky, William E. (1838–1903): historian and essayist; Unionist MP 1845–1902; wrote various articles on American-related topics. American friends: Henry Lee, T. Bayard, Phelps, A. D. White, and Lowell.

Lubbock, Sir John (1834–1913): banker, scientist, and author; Liberal MP 1870–1900; Unionist after 1886; authority on American bimetallism and financial issues. American friend: E. Atkinson.

McCarthy, Justin (1830–1912): Irish politician, historian, and novelist; MP 1879–1900; chairman of the anti-Parnellite nationalist party, 1890–96; wrote various articles on America; part-time correspondent for the *New York Tribune* (1880s). Visited US 1867–70; 1870s, and 1886–87 (lecture tour). American friends: C. Sumner, J. Lowell, C. Field, W. Whitman, M. Conway, and others.

Maine, Sir Henry (1822–88): jurist and author; studied American federalism and the Constitution; critic of democracy; *Popular Government* (1885).

Milnes, Richard M. (1809–85): Conservative and then Liberal MP; literary figure and prominent host; supported the North during the Civil War; ardent friend of Americans. Visited US 1875 (lecture tour). American friends: S. Ward, H. Adams, J. Lowell, W. Hurlbert, C. Sumner, H. James, and many others.

Plunkett, Horace (1854–1932): Irish statesman; cattle-rancher in Wyoming, 1879–89; cooperative leader; Unionist MP 1892–1900; wrote upon American politics and agriculture; *The Rural Problem in America* (1910). Visited US 1879–90s (usually took annual trips through the nineteenth century). American friends: A. Carnegie, T. Roosevelt, and others.

Sackville-West, Lionel (1827–1908): diplomatist, envoy in Washington, 1881–88; recalled from Washington because of alleged intervention in American presidential election, Oct. 1888.

Salisbury, Marquess of (1830–1903): Prime Minister, 1885–86, 1887–92, 1895–1900; few American interests outside diplomatic matters. American friends: J. Lowell, Henry White, and J. Hay.

Smith, Goldwin (1823–1910): controversialist; author; Regius Professor of Modern History, Oxford, 1858–66; supported the North during the Civil War; married a North American in 1875; moved and resided permanently in Toronto, 1871–1910; wrote extensively upon American politics and society; vehemently opposed Gladstone's Irish policies. Visited US 1864, 1868–70 (taught at Cornell University, Ithaca, NY), 1871–1910 (many times). American friends: C. Norton; E. Godkin, A. D. White, J. Lowell, and others.

Spencer, Herbert (1820–1903): philosopher; advocated individualism and evolution; wrote on America; E. L. Youmans, *Herbert Spencer on Americans* (1883). Visited US 1882 (lecture tour). American friends: E. L. Youmans, A. Carnegie and J. Lowell.

Spring-Rice, Cecil (1859–1918): diplomatist; Secretary to British Legation in Washington, 1886–92; large correspondence with British friends, such as Rosebery. Visited US 1886–92 and 1894–95. American friends: T. Roosevelt, J. Hay, Henry White, C. Lodge, C. F. and Henry Adams, and many others.

Stead, William (1849–1912): journalist and author; assistant editor of the *PMG*, 1880–83, and editor, 1883–90; staunch liberal; started *RR*, 1890; took up psychical research and became extreme religious enthusiast, wrote many articles on American social, historical, and political topics. Visited US 1893–94, periodically in 1890s and 1900s.

Stephen, Sir Leslie (1832–1904): man of letters, philosopher and editor of the *DNB*; supported emancipation of slaves and the North during the Civil War; very friendly with Americans; *The Times and the American War* (1865). Visited US 1863, 1868, and 1890. American friends: J. Lowell, H. James, C. Norton, E. Godkin, and C. F. Adams.

Appendix II: Dinner Engagements of William Hoppin and Henry White, 1870s–1890s

The Secretaries to the American Legation in London kept records for periods of time of their dinner engagements. These give outstanding evidence of the close social associations of British politicians and prominent Americans. Primary British Liberal hosts of Americans in the late-nineteenth century included William Harcourt, James Bryce, Lyon Playfair, Lord Rosebery, Edward Dicey, and Joseph Chamberlain. Americans who gave similar private parties included the diplomats John Welsh, James Lowell, Edward Phelps, and Henry White, the journalist George Smalley, and Andrew Carnegie.

Dinner at Edward Dicey's on 9 February 1878 [Hoppin Diaries, MS Am 986, iii (1878), p. 12].

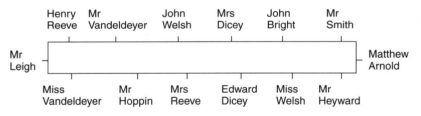

Dinner at George Smalley's on 18 February 1878 [Hoppin Diaries, MS Am 986, iii (1878), p. 13].

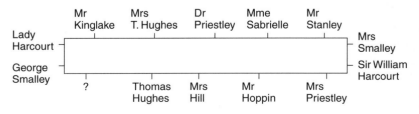

Dinner at John Welsh's on 23 March 1879 [Hoppin Diaries, MS Am 986, iv (1879), p. 1].

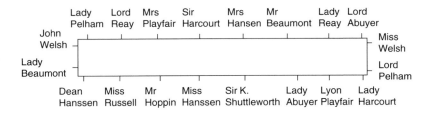

Dinner at the Savoy Club given by Henry White on 18 November 1892 [WP, Box 1 (Diary), 18 Nov. 1892].

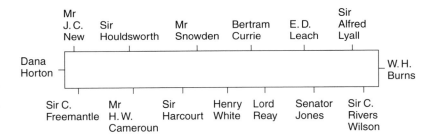

Dinner at Henry White's on 16 March 1893 [WP, Box 1 (Diary), 16 Mar. 1893].

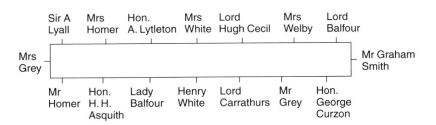

Dinner at Henry White's on 22 March 1893 [WP, Box 1 (Diary), 22 Mar. 1893].

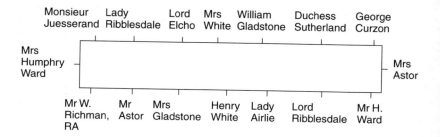

Appendix III: Letter from Gresham to Rosebery, 1895

Letter from the Secretary of State W. L. Gresham to Prime Minister Rosebery, 12 April 1895, on Anglo-American cooperation over British and American interests in South America. Churchill College, Cambridge (Cecil Spring-Rice Papers): 1/57 Rosebery.

> Department of State
> Washington D.C.
> 12 April 1895

I will write this to assure you of the thorough friendship of the American people and government and to deprecate the wrath of your government against us. We are perfectly willing for you to do what you please with all South American republics as even if we wished to resist you, we have not the necessary fighting force at command. Of course this is all a strictly private matter between us two. I write this with the full consent, nay by direction of the president and cabinet, but of course in affairs of this kind no publicity is possible.

The movements of British ships have seemed to us so alarmingly belligerent of late that it has been deemed proper by this government in its solicitude for the country to take such steps as will avoid all risks to us, the people of the United States, and the best way to accomplish this purpose is no doubt by a private note, such as I now write, addressed directly to those in power in London. You understand of course that a display of vessels of war such as we have, is a necessary part of the equipment of every government, but our demonstrations in the various parts of the world, such as those of Hawaii, Central America and Brazil is only to inspire a certain sense of our national dignity but not to incur any danger or risk to ourselves. Of course mistakes and collisions occasionally take place which lead to misunderstandings with foreign governments, but we would not like to have them construct as evidence of hostile intentions on our part. The presence of our ships in West Indian waters at the present moment is no indication of a hostile attitude and they are not likely to interfere with the plans of the British government having received no orders to that effect.

You no doubt recognize the awkwardness involved in the writing of a secret note like this, and will pardon any hasty or inaccurate statements, although I think I have made my meaning quite clearly that you have nothing to fear from American war vessels.

I am Dear Sir,

> [Yours Respectfully]

Bibliography

Overview

Private papers
  In Great Britain
  In the United States
  Public records in Great Britain
Official printed sources
Newspapers, periodicals, and pamphlets
  Newspapers
  Periodicals
  Selected contemporary articles by Liberal leaders
  Further selected contemporary articles
  Contemporary pamphlets and reports
Biographies, letters, and diaries
Books published before 1920
Some selected secondary works
Learned articles and theses

All printed matter is published in London unless otherwise indicated.

Private papers

In Great Britain

In the British Museum:
  Avebury Papers
  Balfour Papers
  Bright Papers
  Dilke Papers
  Gladstone Papers
  Edward Hamilton Diary
  Macmillan Company Papers
  Ripon Papers

In the Bodleian Library, Oxford:
  Bryce Papers
  Harcourt Papers
  Morley–Carnegie Correspondence (microfilm)
  Goldwin Smith Papers (microfilm)

In the National Library of Scotland:
  Rosebery Papers

In the Birmingham University Library:
  Chamberlain Papers

In the London School of Economics Library:
T. H. Farrer Collection

In the Imperial College Science and Technology Library:
Playfair Papers

In the Public Records Office, London:
Granville Papers

In Churchill College Library, Cambridge:
Spring-Rice Papers

In *The Times* Archives, New Printing House Square, London:
George Smalley Papers

In private possession:
Salisbury Papers, in the possession of Lord Salisbury, Hatfield House, Hatfield

In the United States

In the Library of Congress, Washington, D.C.:
Bayard Papers
Blaine Papers
Carnegie Papers
John Hay Papers
Manton Marble Papers
Olney Papers
Whitelaw Reid Papers
Theodore Roosevelt Papers
David Wells Papers
Henry White Papers

In the New York Public Library:
Carnegie Collection
Henry George Papers
Gladstone Collection
Albert Shaw Papers
Samuel Ward Papers

In the Houghton Library, Cambridge, MA:
Edwin L. Godkin Papers
Gladstone Autograph Collection
Higginson Papers
O. W. Holmes Papers
Hoppin Diaries
Henry James Papers
Longfellow Papers
James R. Lowell Papers
C. E. Norton Papers

In the Harvard Law School Library, Cambridge, MA:
  O. W. Holmes Jr Papers

In the Massachusetts Historical Society, Boston, MA:
  Atkinson Papers
  Bancroft Papers
  R. H. Dana Jr Papers
  Norcross Papers
  Winthrop Papers

In the Boston Public Library, Boston, MA:
  Kate Field Papers

In the Columbia University Library, New York:
  Moncure Conway Papers

In the Huntington Library, San Marino, CA:
  George Smalley Papers

Public records in Great Britain

Cabinet:
  CAB 37 (Cabinet Papers)
  CAB 41 (Cabinet Papers)

Foreign Office:
  FO 5
  FO 96
  FO 97

Official printed sources

Hansard, *Parliamentary Debates*, 1874–1898, 3rd and 4th Series.
Report of the Select Committee on Parliamentary and Municipal Elections, PP (1868–69), VIII, 352.
Report on the Philadelphia International Exhibition of 1876, PP (1877), XXXIV, C. 1774.
Reports respecting the late Industrial conflicts in the United States, PP (1877), LXXXIV, C. 1853.
Reports, minutes, and evidence of the Royal Commission on laws regulating home, colonial and international copyrights, PP (1878), XXIV, C. 2036.
Report of the Royal Commission on Extradition, PP (1878), XXIV, C. 2039.
Report of the Committee at the International Monetary, Conference (Paris), PP (1878–79), XXI, C. 2196.
Reports and minutes of the Royal Commission on depressed condition of Agriculture, PP (1881) XV, C. 2778, 2778-I and (1881), XVI, C. 2778-II.
Report of the Committee at the International Monetary Conference (Paris), PP (1881), LXXV, 409.
Correspondence respecting the imprisonment in Ireland under the Protection of Person and Property (Ireland) Act 1881 of Naturalized Citizens of the United States, PP, United States, No. 2 (1882), C. 3193.

Correspondence respecting the Publication in the United States of Incitements to Outrages in England in 1882, PP, United States, No. 3 (1882), C. 3194.

Correspondence with the United States respecting the sentence passed upon the Convict O'Donnell, PP, United States, No. 2 (1884), LXXXVII, C. 3835.

Reports, minutes and evidence of the Royal Commission into the Depression of Trade and Industry, PP (1886), XXI, C. 4621 and C. 4715; (1886), XXII, C. 4715-I; (1886), XXIII, C. 4797 and C. 4893.

Reports of the Royal Commission appointed to inquire into the recent changes of the relative value of the precious metals, PP (1887), XXII, C. 5099 and (1888), XLV, C. 5248, C. 5512, and C. 5512-I.

Correspondence relating to copyright convention between the United States and Great Britain, PP (1890–91), LXXXIII (671).

Report of the Royal Commission on Labour, foreign reports. United States, PP (1892), XXXVI, C. 6795-X.

Reports, minutes and evidence of the Royal Commission on Agricultural Depression, PP (1894), XVI, C. 7400-I, -II, and -III; (1896), XVI, C. 7981; (1896), XVII, C. 8021 and C. 8146; and (1897), XV, C. 8540, C. 8541, and C. 8300.

Documents and Correspondence relating to the Question of the Boundary between British Guiana and Venezuela, PP (1896), XCVII, C. 7972.

Newspapers, periodicals, and pamphlets

Newspapers

Anglo-American Times
Birmingham Daily Gazette
Birmingham Daily Post
Daily Chronicle
Daily News
Irish World
Manchester Guardian
New York Times
New York Tribune
New York World
Pall Mall Gazette
The Times
United Irishman
Westminister Gazette

Periodicals

Atlantic Monthly
The Bimetallist
Board of Trade Journal
Century Magazine
The Concord
Contemporary Review
Cornhill Magazine
Fortnightly Review

The Forum
Greater Britain
Harper's New Monthly Review
International Arbitration and Peace Association Monthly Journal
Liberal Magazine
Macmillan's Magazine
The Nation
National Review
New Review
Nineteenth Century
North American Review
Princeton Review
Progressive Review
Review of Reviews
Scribner's Magazine
Speaker
Spectator
Transatlantic Review
Youth's Companion (Boston)

Selected contemporary articles by Liberal leaders

Bryce, James

'American Experience in the Relief of the Poor,' *Macmillan's Magazine*, vol. xxv (Nov. 1871)
'The Legal Profession in America,' *Macmillan's Magazine*, vol. xxv (Jan. 1872)
'American Judges,' *Macmillan's Magazine*, vol. xxv (Feb. 1872)
'On Some Peculiarities of Society in America,' *Cornhill Magazine*, vol. xxvi (Dec. 1872)
'A Glimpse of the United States,' *Cornhill Magazine*, vol. xlvi (Oct. 1882)
'Some Aspects of American Public Life,' *Fortnightly Review*, vol. xxxii, n.s. (Nov. 1882)
'Do We Need a Second Chamber?,' *Contemporary Review*, vol. xlvi (Nov. 1884)
'A Word as to the Speakership,' *North American Review*, vol. cli (Oct. 1890)
'Legal and Constitutional Aspects of the Lynching at New Orleans,' *New Review*, vol. iv (May 1891)
'Thoughts on the Negro Problem,' *North American Review*, vol. cliii (Dec. 1891)
'Political Organizations in the United States and England,' *North American Review*, vol. clvi (Jan. 1893)
'British Feeling on the Venezuelan Question,' *North American Review*, vol. clxii (Feb. 1896)
'The Mayoralty Election in New York,' *Contemporary Review*, vol. lxxii (Nov. 1897)
'The Essential Unity of Britain and America,' *Atlantic Monthly*, vol. lxxxii (July 1898)
(Bryce also wrote approximately two hundred articles for *The Nation* between 1865 and 1898. Most of these were upon British domestic and foreign issues.)

Chamberlain, Joseph.

'Free Schools,' *Fortnightly Review*, vol. xxi, n.s. (Jan. 1877)
'The Caucus,' *Fortnightly Review*, vol. xxiv (Nov. 1878)
'Labourers' and Artisans' Dwellings,' *Fortnightly Review*, vol. xxxiv (Dec. 1883)
'A Radical View of the Irish Crisis,' *Fortnightly Review*, vol. xxxix (Feb. 1886)
'Shall We Americanise our Institutions?' *Nineteenth Century*, vol. xxviii (Dec. 1890)
'Favorable Aspects of State Socialism,' *North American Review*, vol. clii (May 1891)
'The Labour Question,' *Nineteenth Century*, vol. xxxii (Nov. 1892)
'Municipal Institutions in America and England,' *The Forum*, vol. xiv (Nov. 1892)
'A Bill for the Weakening of Great Britain,' *Nineteenth Century*, vol. xxxiii (Apr. 1893)
'The Home Rule Campaign,' *National Review*, vol. xxiii (May 1894)
'Recent Developments of Policy in the United States,' *Scribner's Magazine*, vol. xxiv (Dec. 1898)

Gladstone, William E.

'Last Words on the County Franchise,' *Nineteenth Century*, vol. iii (Jan. 1878)
'Kin Beyond Sea,' *North American Review*, vol. cxxvii (Sept.–Oct. 1878)
'Free Trade, Railways, and the Growth of Commerce,' *Nineteenth Century*, vol. vii (Feb. 1880)
'An Olive Branch from America,' *Nineteenth Century*, vol. xxii (Nov. 1887)
'Further Notes and Queries on the Irish Demand,' *Contemporary Review*, vol. liii (Mar. 1888)
'Colonel Ingersoll on Christianity,' *North American Review*, vol. cxlvi (May 1888)
'The Future of the English-Speaking Races,' *Youth's Companion*, vol. lx (Nov. 1888)
'Divorce – A Novel,' *Nineteenth Century*, vol. xxv (Feb. 1889)
'Memorials of a Southern Planter,' *Nineteenth Century*, vol. xxvi (Dec. 1889)
'The Question of Divorce,' *North American Review*, vol. cxlix (Dec. 1889)
'Free Trade,' *North American Review*, vol. cl (Jan. 1890)
'Correspondence of John Lothrop Motley,' *Youth's Companion*, vol. lxiii (24 July 1890)
'Mr. Carnegie's "Gospel of Wealth": A review and a recommendation,' *Nineteenth Century* , vol. xxviii (Nov. 1890)
'A Rare Young Man [Sydney Gilchrest Thomas],' *Youth's Companion*, vol. lxv (11 Aug. 1892)
'A Vindication of Home Rule. A Reply to the Duke of Argyll,' *North American Review*, vol. clv (Oct. 1892)
'The Future Life and the Condition of Men Therein,' *North American Review*, vol. clxii (Jan.–June 1896)
'Arthur Henry Hallam,' *Youth's Companion*, vol. lxxii (6 Jan. 1898)

Morley, John

'The Liberal Eclipse,' *Fortnightly Review*, vol. xvii (Feb. 1875)
'England and Ireland,' *Fortnightly Review*, vol. xxix (Apr. 1881)

'Cobden's First Pamphlets,' *Fortnightly Review*, vol. xxix (May 1881)
'Conciliation with Ireland,' *Fortnightly Review*, vol. xxx (July 1881)
'Some Irish Realities: An Historical Chapter,' *Fortnightly Review*, vol. xxxi (Mar. 1882)
'Irish Revolution and English Liberalism,' *Nineteenth Century*, vol. xii (Nov. 1882)
'Review of the Month,' *Macmillan's Magazine*, vol. xlviii (Oct. 1883) to vol. lii (July 1885)
'The Expansion of England,' *Macmillan's Magazine*, vol. xlix (Feb.1884)
'Sir H. Maine on Popular Government,' *Fortnightly Review*, vol. xxxix (Feb. 1886)
'The Government of Ireland,' *Nineteenth Century*, vol. xxi (Jan. and Feb. 1887)
'Mr. Balfour's Answer to Mr. Parnell,' *North American Review*, vol. cli (Oct. 1890)
'Mr. Lecky on Democracy,' *Nineteenth Century*, vol. xxxix (May 1896)
'Arbitration with America,' *Nineteenth Century*, vol. xl (Aug. 1896)

Playfair, Lyon

'The Industries of the United States in Relation to the Tariff,' *Macmillan's Magazine*, vol. xlv (Feb. 1882)
'The Progress of Applied Science in its Effects upon Trade,' *Contemporary Review*, vol. liv (Mar. 1888).
'The Presidential Election in the United States,' *Nineteenth Century*, vol. xxiv (Dec. 1888)
'A Topic for Christmas [Arbitration],' *North American Review*, vol. cli (Dec. 1890)
'The Demas Invitation to Abandon Gold for Silver in the United States,' *New Review*, vol. iv (Feb. 1891)
'A New Departure in English Taxation,' *North American Review*, vol. clx (Mar. 1895)

Smith, Goldwin

'A Word More About the Presidential Election,' *Macmillan's Magazine*, vol. xxxv (Mar. 1877)
'The Labour War in the United States,' *Contemporary Review*, vol. xxx (Sept. 1877)
'The Organization of Democracy,' *Contemporary Review*, vol. xlvii (Mar. 1885)
'The Moral of the Late Crisis,' *Nineteenth Century*, vol. xx (Sept. 1886)
'Why Send More Irish to America?,' *Nineteenth Century*, vol. xxx (Sept. 1887)
'American Statesmen,' *Nineteenth Century*, vols. xxiii and xxiv (1888)
'The American Commonwealth,' *Macmillan's Magazine*, vol. lix (Feb. 1889)
'Prohibitionism in Canada and the United States,' *Macmillan's Magazine*, vol. lix (Mar. 1889)
'The Hatred of England,' *North American Review*, vol. cl (May 1890)
'The American Tariff,' *Macmillan's Magazine*, vol. lxii (Sept. 1890)
'Exit McKinley,' *Macmillan's Magazine*, vol. lxiii (Jan. 1891)
'The Contest for the Presidency,' *Nineteenth Century*, vol. xxxii (Sept. 1892)
'England and America,' *Atlantic Monthly*, vol. xiv (1892)

'Anglo-Saxon Union: A Response to Mr. Carnegie,' *North American Review*, vol. clvii (Aug. 1893)

'The Situation at Washington,' *Nineteenth Century*, vol. xxxiv (Nov. 1893)

'"If Christ Came to Chicago,"' *Contemporary Review*, vol. lxvi (Sept. 1894)

'Our Situation Viewed from Without,' *North American Review*, vol. clx (May 1895)

Stead, William T.

'Review of the Month,' *Macmillan's Magazine*, vol. xlviii (May–Sept. 1883)

'To All English-Speaking Folk,' *Review of Reviews*, vol. i (Jan. 1890)

'The General Election and After,' *Contemporary Review*, vol. lxii (Aug. 1892)

'The Uncrowned Queen of American Democracy,' *Review of Reviews*, vol. iv (Nov. 1892)

'The Two Babylons: London & Chicago,' *New Review*, vol. x (May 1894)

'"Coxeyism:" A Character Sketch,' *Review of Reviews*, vol. x (July 1894)

'Incidents of Labour War in America,' *Contemporary Review*, vol. lxvi (July 1894)

'Jingoism in America,' *Contemporary Review*, vol. lxviii (Sept. 1895)

'To All English-Speaking Folk,' *Review of Reviews*, vol. xiii (Feb. 1896)

'International Response to the Appeal for Arbitration,' *Review of Reviews*, vol. xiii (Mar. 1896)

'The Anglo-American Union,' *Review of Reviews*, vol. xiii (Apr. 1896)

'Why Not a British Celebration of the Fourth of July,' *Review of Reviews*, vol. xvii (May 1898)

Further selected contemporary articles

Contemporary Review

Herbert Spencer, 'The Americans,' vol. xlii (Jan. 1883)

Marquis of Lorne, 'Transatlantic Lessons on Home Rule,' vol. l (July 1886)

Albert Shaw, 'The American State and the American Man,' vol. li (May 1887)

D. A. Wells, 'The Great Depression of Trade,' vol. lii (Aug.–Sept. 1887)

George Cable, 'The Negro Question in the United States,' vol. liii (Mar. 1888)

Albert Shaw, 'The American Tariff,' vol. liv (Nov. 1888)

Albert Shaw, 'The American State Legislatures,' vol. lvi (Oct. 1889)

Frederick Pollock, 'Anglo-American Copyright,' vol. lix (Apr. 1891)

James Kitson, 'The Iron and Steel Industries of America,' vol. lix (May 1891)

Albert Shaw, 'An American View of Home Rule and Federation,' vol. lxii (Sept. 1892)

Robert Donald, 'McKinleyism and the Presidential Election,' vol. lxii (Oct. 1892)

T. Raleigh, 'Lessons of American History: A Reply,' vol. lxii (Oct. 1892)

H. S. Foxwell, 'The International Monetary Conference,' vol. lxii (Dec. 1892)

W. Caine, 'The Attitude of the Advanced Temperance Party,' vol. lxiii (Jan. 1893)

E. R. L. Gould, 'The Social Condition of Labour,' vol. lxiii (Jan. 1893)

Samuel Dike, 'The Problem of Family in the United States,' vol. lxiv (Nov. 1893)

C. F. Aked, 'The Race Problem in America,' vol. lxv (June 1894)

A. Carnegie, 'Britain and the United States: Cost of Living,' vol. lxvi (Sept. 1894)

W. R. Lawson, 'American Currency Cranks,' vol. lxx (Sept. 1896)

A. V. Dicey, 'A Common Citizenship for the English Race,' vol. lxxi (Apr. 1897)

A. Carnegie, 'Does America Hate England?' vol. lxxii (Nov. 1897)

Fortnightly Review

Charles Norton, 'On Emigration,' vol. vi, n.s. (Aug. 1869)

Justin McCarthy, 'Prohibitory Legislation in the United States,' vol. x (Aug. 1871)

Charles Dilke, 'Free Schools,' vol. xiv (Dec. 1873)

Horace White, 'An American's Impressions of England,' vol. xviii (Sept. 1875)

Francis Abbott, 'The Catholic Peril in the United States,' vol. xix (Mar. 1876)

Horace White, 'The Financial Crisis in America,' vol. xix (June 1876)

Louis Jennings, 'Unsettled Problems of American Politics,' vol. xx (Aug. 1876)

Horace White, 'The American Centenary,' vol. xx (Oct. 1876)

R. Lowe, 'A New Reform Bill,' vol. xxii (Oct. 1877)

Henry Fawcett, 'The Recent Development of Socialism in Germany and the United States,' vol. xxiv (Nov. 1878)

George Campbell, 'Black and White in the Southern States,' vol. xxv (Mar.–Apr. 1879)

Horace White, 'Parliamentary Government in America,' vol. xxvi (Oct. 1879)

Edward Atkinson, 'An American View of Competition,' vol. xxvi (Dec. 1879)

Matthew Arnold, 'Copyright,' vol. xxvii (Mar. 1880)

George Campbell, 'Home Rule in Several Countries,' vol. xxvii (May 1880)

Henry Hyndman, 'Lights and Shades of American Politics,' vol. xxix (Mar. 1881)

Edward Atkinson, 'The Railroads of the United States: Their Effects on Farming and Production in that Country and in Great Britain,' vol. xxix (May 1881)

A. Carnegie, 'As Others See Us,' vol. xxxi (Feb. 1882)

Henry George, 'England and Ireland: An American View,' vol. xxxi (June 1882)

Edward Freeman, 'Some Impressions of the United States,' vol. xxxii (Aug.–Sept. 1882)

C. R. Lowell, 'English and American Federalism,' vol. xliii (Feb. 1888)

Horace Plunkett, 'The Working of Woman Suffrage in Wyoming,' vol. xlvii (May 1890)

Edmund Gosse, 'The Protection of American Literature,' vol. xlviii (July 1890)

Moreton Frewen, 'The National Policy of the United States,' vol. xlviii (Nov. 1890)

Earl Meath, 'Anglo-Saxon Unity,' vol. xlix (Apr. 1891)

G. C. S. Churchill, 'Virginia Mines and American Rails,' vol. xlix (Apr.–May 1891)

J. S. Jeans, 'The American Tariff: Its Past and Its Future,' vol. lii (Dec. 1892)

T. W. Russell, 'American Side-lights on Home Rule,' vol. liii (Mar. 1893)

Moreton Frewen, 'The Currency Crisis in the United States,' vol. liii (June 1893)

W. H. Grenfell, 'Mr. Gladstone and the Currency,' vol. liv (Sept. 1893)

Dana Horton, 'Current Arguments for the Outlawry of Silver,' vol. liv (Oct. 1893)

T. H. Farrer, 'Silver and the Tariff at Washington,' vol. lvi (July 1894)

M. Frewen, J. S. Nicholson, and J. Faraday, 'Silver and the Tariff at Washington,' vol. lvi (July 1894)

G. H. D. Gossip, 'England in Nicaragua and Venezuela: From an American Point of View,' vol. lviii (Dec. 1895)

Edward Dicey, 'The Isolation of England,' vol. lix (Feb. 1896)

F. H. Hardy, 'Lessons from the American Election,' vol. lx (Dec. 1896)

Lucien Wolf, 'Is There an Anglo-American Understanding?' vol. lxiv (July 1898)

National Review

Lord Salisbury, 'Constitutional Revision,' vol. xx (Nov. 1892)

Moreton Frewen, 'Silver in the Fifty-Third Congress,' vol. xxii (Dec. 1893)

T. H. Farrer, 'Shall We Degrade Our Standard of Value?' vol. xxiii (June 1894)

H. S. Foxwell, 'Lord Farrer on the Monetary Standard,' vol. xxiv (Jan. 1895)

A. Higgins and M. Frewen, 'Correspondence: The American "Sound Money" Problem and Its Solution,' vol. xxvi (Nov. 1895)

Moreton Frewen, 'American Politics,' vol. xxvi (Jan. 1896)

Francis A. Walker, 'The Monetary Situation and the United States,' vol. xxvii (Aug. 1896)

T. Lloyd, A. Peel, and J. Tritton, 'The American Crisis,' vol. xxvii (Sept. 1896)

A. Powell, A. Hepburn, and H. Schmidt, 'The Bimetallic Side of the American Crisis,' vol. xxvii (Oct. 1896)

Moreton Frewen, 'The American Elections of 1896,' vol. xxviii (Nov. 1896)

F. Browne and Senator Chandler, 'The Presidential Contest,' vol. xxviii (Dec. 1896)

Nineteenth Century

E. D. J. Wilson, 'The Political Crisis in the United States,' vol. i (Apr. 1877)

W. F. Rae, 'Political Clubs and Party Organization,' vol. iii (May 1878)

George Holyoake, 'A Stranger in America,' vol. viii (Mar. 1880)

Earl Airlie, 'The United States as a Field for Agricultural Settlers,' vol. ix (Jan. 1881)

Matthew Arnold, 'A Word About America,' vol. xi (May 1882)

Lord Blandford and Justin McCarthy, 'Home Rule,' vol. xi (June 1882)

E. L. Godkin, 'An American View of Ireland,' vol. xii (Aug. 1882)

George Holyoake, 'American and Canadian Notes,' vol. xiv (Sept. 1883)

Duke Argyll, 'The Prophet of San Francisco,' vol. xv (Apr. 1884)

Matthew Arnold, 'A Word More About America,' vol. xvii (Feb. 1885)

E. L. Godkin, 'American Home Rule,' vol. xix (Jan. 1886)

E. L. Godkin, 'An American View of Popular Government,' vol. xix (Feb. 1886)

Thomas Brassey, 'A Flying Visit to the United States,' vol. xx (Mar. 1886)

Henry Maine, 'Mr. Godkin on Popular Government,' vol. xx (Mar. 1886)

E. L. Godkin, 'American Opinion on the Irish Question,' vol. xxii (Oct. 1887)

George Smalley, 'Notes on New York,' vol. xxi (Oct. 1887)

Edward J. Phelps, 'The Constitution of the United States,' vol. xxiii (Mar. 1888)

Frederic Harrison, 'Mr. Bryce's American Commonwealth,' vol. xxv (Jan. 1889)

Henry C. Lodge, 'Parliamentary Obstruction in the United States,' vol. xxix (Feb. 1891)

A. Carnegie, 'The McKinley Bill,' vol. xxix (June 1891)

A. Carnegie, 'Imperial Federation: An American View,' vol. xxx (Sept. 1891)

A. Carnegie, 'The Impending Elections in England and America,' vol. xxxii (July 1892)

J. A. Cooper, 'An Anglo-Saxon Olympiad,' vol. xxxii (Sept. 1892)

Leonard Courtney, 'Bimetallism Once More,' vol. xxxiii (Apr. 1893)

A. S. Northcote, 'American Life Through English Spectacles,' vol. xxxiv (Sept. 1893)

Chauncey Depew, 'Prospects of Free Trade in the United States,' vol. xxxv (Feb. 1894)

A. S. Northcote, 'The Utter Corruption in American Politics,' vol. xxxv (Apr. 1894)

George Smalley, 'Checks on Democracy in America,' vol. xxxv (June 1894)

J. S. Jeans, 'The Labour War in the United States,' vol. xxxvi (Aug. 1894)

J. A. Cooper, 'Americans and the Pan-Britannic Movement,' vol. xxxvii (Jan. 1895)

Lady Somerset, 'Great Britain, Venezuela, and the United States,' vol. xxxviii (Nov. 1895)

Edward Dicey, 'Common Sense and Venezuela,' vol. xli (Feb. 1896)

W. Alden and W. Dillon, 'The Battle for Standards in America,' vol. xl (Nov. 1896)

Sidney Low, 'The Olney Doctrine and American's New Foreign Policy,' vol. xl (Nov. 1896)

Leonard Courtney, 'The Recent Presidential Election,' vol. xli (Jan. 1897)

North American Review

O. P. Aldis, 'Louis Napoleon and the Southern Confederacy,' vol. cxxix (Oct. 1879)

James A. Froude, 'Romanism and the Irish Race in the United States,' vol. cxxx (Jan. 1880)

Charles Parnell, 'The Irish Land Question,' vol. cxxx (Apr. 1880)

Henry Hyndman, 'The Coming Revolution in England,' vol. cxxxv (Oct. 1882)

John Welsh, 'English Views of Free Trade,' vol. cxxxv (Nov. 1882)

A. V. Dicey, 'Some Aspects of Democracy in England,' vol. cxxxvii (Oct. 1883)

Henry George, 'England and Ireland,' vol. cxlii (Feb. 1886)

Henry George, 'More about American Landlordism,' vol. cxlii (Apr. 1886)

Charles Bradlaugh, 'Socialism: Its Fallacies and Dangers,' vol. cxliv (Jan. 1887)

Henry M. Field, 'An Open Letter to Robert G. Ingersoll,' vol. cxlv (Aug. 1887)

Robert Ingersoll, 'A Reply to the Rev. Henry M. Field, D.D.,' vol. cxlv (Nov. 1887)

Henry M. Field, 'A Last Word to Rogert G. Ingersoll,' vol. cxlv (Dec. 1887)

Robert Ingersoll, 'Letter to Dr. Field,' vol. cxlvi (Jan. 1888)

Robert Ingersoll, 'Col. Ingersoll to Mr. Gladstone,' vol. cxlvi (June 1888)

Various authors, 'The Combat for the Faith: The Field–Ingersoll–Gladstone Controversy,' vol. cxlvii (July 1888)

Robert Ingersoll, 'The Divided Households of Faith,' vol. cxlvii (Aug. 1888)

Archbishop of Westminister and others, 'The Gladstone–Ingersoll Controversy,' vol. cxlvii (Sept. 1888)

Robert Ingersoll, 'Rome or Reason? A Reply to Cardinal Manning,' vol. cxlvii (Oct.–Nov. 1888)

A. Carnegie, 'The Bugaboo of Trusts,' vol. cxlviii (Feb. 1889)

Charles Bradlaugh, 'Humanity's Gain from Unbelief,' vol. cxlviii (Mar. 1889)

Lloyd S. Bryce, 'Errors in Prof. Bryce's "Commonwealth,"' vol. cxlviii (Mar. 1889)

Robert Ingersoll, 'Professor Huxley and Agnosticism,' vol. cxlviii (Apr. 1889)

A. Carnegie, 'Wealth,' vol. cxlviii (June 1889)

H. Clews, 'Great Britain and the Confederacy,' vol. cxlix (Aug. 1889)

S. W. Dike, 'Is Divorce Wrong?' vol. cxlix (Nov. 1889)

A. Carnegie, 'The Best Fields for Philanthropy,' vol. cxlix (Dec. 1889)

James G. Blaine, 'Protection,' vol. cl (Jan. 1890)

Margaret Lee and others, 'Final Words on Divorce,' vol. cl (Feb. 1890)

Roger Mills, 'The Gladstone–Blaine Controversy,' vol. cl (Feb. 1890)

Senator Morrill and others, 'Free Trade or Protection. A Continuation of the Gladstone–Blaine Controversy,' vol. cl (Mar. 1890)

F. W. Farrer, 'A Few Words on Colonel Ingersoll,' vol. cl (May 1890)

A. Carnegie and others, 'Do Americans Hate England?' vol. cl (June 1890)

Marquis of Lorne, 'Sir Charles Dilke's New Book,' vol. cl (June 1890)

William McKinley, 'The Value of Protection,' vol. cl (June 1890)

Charles Parnell, 'Mr. Balfour's Land Bill,' vol. cl (June 1890)

Arthur J. Balfour, 'Mr. Parnell Answered,' vol. cli (July 1890)

A. Carnegie, 'Summing Up the Tariff Discussion,' vol. cli (July 1890)

Charles Dilke, 'Critics of "Problems of Greater Britain,"' vol. cli (July 1890)

Michael Davitt, 'Labor Tendencies in Great Britain,' vol. cli (Oct. 1890)

W. E. H. Lecky, 'Why Home Rule is Undesirable,' vol. clii (Mar. 1891)

Cardinal Gibbons, 'Wealth and Its Obligations,' vol. clii (Apr. 1891)

Marquis of Lorne, 'Canada and the United States,' vol. clii (May 1891)

Edward Phelps, 'Irresponsible Wealth,' vol. clii (May 1891)

Henry C. Potter, 'The Gospel of Wealth,' vol. clii (May 1891)

A. Carnegie, 'The ABC of Money,' vol. clii (June 1891)

Robert Ingersoll, 'Is Avarice Triumphant?' vol. clii (June 1891)

E. L. Godkin, 'The Economic Man,' vol. cliii (Oct. 1891)

Robert Ingersoll, 'Three Philanthropists,' vol. cliii (Dec. 1891)

William M. Springer, 'An International Monetary Conference,' vol. cliv (Mar. 1892)

Duke of Argyll, 'English Elections and Home Rule,' vol. clv (Aug. 1892)

Henry W. Lucy, 'Electioneering Methods in England,' vol. clv (Sept. 1892)

James G. Blaine, 'The Presidential Election of 1892,' vol. clv (Nov. 1892)

Lady Grey-Egerton and Lady Sykes, 'Two Englishwomen in America,' vol. clvi (Apr. 1893)

A. Carnegie, 'A Look Ahead,' vol. clvi (June 1893)

Edward Atkinson, 'How Distrust Stops Trade,' vol. clvii (July 1893)

A. Carnegie and John Lubbock, 'The Silver Problem,' vol. clvii (Sept. 1893)

John Lubbock, 'The Income Tax in England,' vol. clviii (Feb. 1894)

G. S. Clarke, 'A Naval Union with Great Britain. A Reply to Mr. Andrew Carnegie,' vol. clviii (Mar. 1894)

Arthur S. White, 'An Anglo-American Alliance,' vol. clviii (Apr. 1894)

J. Henniker Heaton, 'The Transatlantic Mails,' vol. clix (Oct. 1894)

Captain Mahan and Captain Beresford, 'Possibilities of an Anglo-American Reunion,' vol. clix (Nov. 1894)

E L. Godkin, 'Diplomacy and the Newspaper,' vol. clx (May 1895)

Henry C. Lodge, 'England, Venezuela, and the Monroe Doctrine,' vol. clx (June 1895)

Edward Atkinson, 'Jingoes and Silverites,' vol. clxi (Nov. 1895)

Reginald Palgrave, 'The House of Representatives and the House of Commons,' vol. clxi (Dec. 1895)

A. Carnegie, 'The Venezuela Question,' vol. clxii (Feb. 1896)

D. A. Wells, 'Great Britain and the United States: Their True Relations,' vol. clxii (Apr. 1896)

Mayo Hazeltine, 'The United States and Great Britain,' vol. cxlii (May 1896)

A. Carnegie, 'The Ship of State Adrift,' vol. clxii (June 1896)

Walter Besant, 'The Future of the Anglo-Saxon Race,' vol. clxiii (Aug. 1896)

A. Carnegie, 'The Ship of State Adrift. II,' vol. clxiii (Oct. 1896)

W. E. H. Lecky, 'The Conservatism of the British Democracy,' vol. clxiv (Feb. 1897)

Lyman Abbott, 'The Basis of an Anglo-American Understanding,' vol. clxvi (May 1898)

Other periodicals

Leslie Stephen, 'Some Remarks on Travelling in America,' *Cornhill Magazine*, vol. xix (Mar. 1869)

Leslie Stephen, 'Thoughts on an Outsider: International Prejudices,' *Cornhill Magazine*, vol. xxxiv (July 1876)

Walter H. Pollock, 'An American View of England,' *Macmillan's Magazine*, vol. xxxix (Feb. 1879)

Leonard Courtney, 'International Copyright,' *Macmillan's Magazine*, vol. xl (June 1879)

Thomas Hughes, 'Rugby Tennessee,' *Macmillan's Magazine*, vol. xliii (Feb. 1881)

Matthew Arnold, 'Emerson,' *Macmillan's Magazine*, vol. l (May 1884)

Louis J. Jennings, 'General Grant,' *Macmillan's Magazine*, vol. liii (Jan. 1886)

Edward Freeman, 'International Copyright,' *The Nation*, vol. viii (1889)

Henry Labouchere, 'Democracy in England,' *The Forum*, vol. viii (1889)

John Lubbock, 'On Bimetallism,' *New Review*, vol. x (July 1890)

Richard H. Dana Jr, 'American View of the Irish Question,' *The Forum*, vol. xiii (1891)

Theodore Roosevelt, 'An Object Lesson in Civil Service Reform,' *Atlantic Monthly*, vol. lxvii (Feb. 1891)

T. H. Farrer, 'English Views of the McKinley Tariff,' *The Forum*, vol. xiv (1892)
Edward Freeman, 'Debt of the Old World to the New,' *The Forum*, vol. xiv (1892)
Charles Dilke, 'The Labour Problem,' *New Review*, vol. viii (Mar. 1893)
Albert Shaw, 'Mr. Bryce's New Chapters on Current American Questions,' *Review of Reviews*, vol. xi (1895)
A. V. Dicey, 'England and America,' *Atlantic Monthly*, vol. lxxxii (1896)
Albert Shaw, 'The Anglo-American Union,' *Review of Reviews*, vol. xiii (Apr. 1896)
Charles Russell, 'International Law and Arbitration,' *The Forum*, vol. xxii (1896)
Carl Schurz, 'The Anglo-American Friendship,' *Atlantic Monthly*, vol. lxxxii (1896)
Albert Shaw, 'The Lord Chief Justice on Arbitration,' *Review of Reviews*, vol. xiv (Sept. 1896)
Lady W. Harcourt, 'Recollections of John Motley,' *Youth's Companion*, vol. lxxi (Apr. 1897)

Contemporary pamphlets and reports

The American Conference on International Arbitration held in Washington D.C., April 22 and 23, 1896 (New York, 1896)
The American Testimonial Banquet to Henry M. Stanley, 30 May 1890 (1890)
Arnold, Matthew, *General Grant: An Estimate* (Boston, 1887)
Atkinson, Edward, *Report Made by Edward Atkinson of Boston, Mass., to the President of the United States, upon the present state of Bimetallism in Europe* (Washington, DC, 1887)
Baxter, W. E., *United States Protection v. British Free Trade* (Cobden Club Pamphlet, 1882?)
Bimetallic League Pamphlets (1895–6)
Carnegie, A., *Mr. Carnegie on Socialism, Labour, and Home Rule: An Interview* (Aberdeen, 1892)
——, *Home Rule in America* (Glasgow, 1888)
The Case of the United States to be Laid Before the Tribunal of Arbitration to be Convened at Geneva (Washington, DC, 1871)
Celebration of the Fourth of July in London. Mr. Cyrus W. Field's Banquet for his, Excellency Hon. Edward J. Phelps at the Buckingham Palace Hotel, 4th July 1885 (1885)
Darby, W. E., *The Continuing Progress of International Arbitration* (1893)
Farrer, T. H., *Free Trade versus Fair Trade* (Cobden Club Pamphlet, 1882, 1885, and 1886)
——, *Retaliation and Commercial Federation* (Cobden Club Pamphlet, 1891)
——, *Shall We Retaliate on Sugar Bounties?* (Cobden Club Pamphlet, 1888)
——, *Sugar Convention* (Cobden Club Pamphlet, 1889)
——, *The Sugar Convention and Bill. Letters to 'The Daily News'* (Cobden Club Pamphlet, 1889)
——, *The State and Its Relation to Trade* (Cobden Club Pamphlet, 1881)
Forwood, William, *The Effects of Protection in America* (Cobden Club Pamphlet, 1884)
Freeman, Edward A., *Greater Greece and Greater Britain, and George Washington the Expander of England* (1886)
Gladstone, W. E., *The Bulgarian Horrors and the Question of the East* (1876)

Gold Standard Defense Association (pamphlets) (1895–98)
Industrial Remuneration Conference. The Report of the Proceedings and the Papers (1885)
List of Societies in Europe and America Founded for the Promotion of International Concord (1888)
Lowell, James R., *On Democracy* (Birmingham, 1884)
Playfair, Lyon, *The Tariffs of the United States in Relation to Free Trade* (Leeds, 1890)
The Proceedings of the Bimetallic Conference held at the Westminster Palace Hotel, December 13th 1888 (Manchester, 1889)
Report of the Annual Meeting of the Cobden Club, 1895 (1895)
Report of the Imperial Federation Conference held at the Westminister, 29 July 1884, London (1884)
Seventh Annual Report of the International Arbitration Association (1888)
Special Report of the Cobden Club Dinner held at the Ship Hotel, Greenwich on the 13th day of June 1885 (1885)
Stead, William T., *Always Arbitrate Before You Fight* (1896)
——, *James Russell Lowell, His Message and How it Helped Me* (1892)

Biographies, letters, and diaries

Acton, Lord, *Lord Acton. A Study in Conscience and Politics*, G. Himmelfarb (Chicago, 1952)
Adams, Charles Francis Jr, *Charles Francis Adams, Jr. 1815–1915. The Patrician at Bay*, E. C. Kirkland (Cambridge, MA, 1965)
Adams, Henry, *Letters of Henry Adams, 1858–1892*, ed. W. C. Ford (New York, 1930)
Arch, Joseph, *Story of his Life, told by himself* (1898)
Argyll, Duke of (8th), *Eighth Duke of Argyll … 1823–1900. Autobiography and Memoirs* , ed. Dowager Duchess of Argyll, 2 vols (1906)
Arnold, Matthew, *Letters of Matthew Arnold 1848–88*, ed. G. Russell, 2 vols (1901)
Atkinson, Edward, *Edward Atkinson. The Biography of an American Liberal 1827–1905*, H. Williamson, 2nd edn (New York, 1972)
Balfour, James A., *Arthur James Balfour*, B. Dugdale, 2 vols (1936)
Bancroft, George, *The Life and Letters of George Bancroft*, ed. M. A. Howe, 2 vols (New York, 1908)
Beecher, Henry W., *A Preacher's Life. An Autobiography and an Album*, J. Parker (1899)
Blaine, James G., *James G. Blaine. A Political Idol of Other Days*, D. Muzzey (New York, 1935)
——, *Twenty Years of Congress*, 2 vols (Norwich, CT, 1886)
Bradlaugh, Charles, *Charles Bradlaugh: A Record of His Life and Work*, H. Bonner and J. Robertson, 2 vols (1895)
Bright, John, *The Diaries of John Bright*, ed. R. Walling (1930)
——, *John Bright*, K. Robbins (1979)
——, *The Public Letters of the Right Hon. John Bright, M.P.*, ed. H. J. Leech (1885)
Bryce, James, *James Bryce and American Democracy, 1870–1922*, E. Ions (1968)
——, *Jame Bryce (Viscount Bryce of Delmont, O.M.)*, H. Fisher, 2 vols (1927)
Caine, William S., *W. S. Caine, M. P., A Biography*, J. Newton (1907)

Carnegie, Andrew, *Andrew Carnegie*, J. Wall (New York, 1970)
——, *Autobiography of Andrew Carnegie* (1920)
——, *The Life of Andrew Carnegie*, B. Hendricks, 2 vols (New York, 1932)
Carpenter, Edward, *My Days and Dreams. Being Autobiographical Notes*, 3rd edn (1918)
Chamberlain, Joseph, *The Life of Joseph Chamberlain*, J. Garvin, 3 vols (1932–34)
——, *A Political Memoir 1880–92 by Joseph Chamberlain*, ed. C. Howard (1953)
——, *Radical Joe: A Life of Joseph Chamberlain*, D. Judd (1977)
——, *Speeches of the Right Hon. Joseph Chamberlain, M.P.*, ed. H. Lucy (1885)
——, *With Mr. Chamberlain in the United States and Canada, 1887–8*, W. Maycock (1914)
Chaplin, Henry, *Henry Chaplin. A Memoir*, Marchioness of Londonderry (1926)
Childers, Hugh C. E., *The Life and Correspondence of the Right Hon. Hugh C. E. Childers 1827–1896*, E. Childers, 2 vols (1901)
Cleveland, Grover, *Grover Cleveland, A Study in Courage*, A. Nevins (New York, 1932)
Coleridge, John, *Forty Years of Friendship as Recorded in the Correspondence of John Duke Lord Coleridge and Ellis Yarnell during the Years 1856 to 1895*, ed. C. Yarnell (1911)
——, *Life and Correspondence of Lord Coleridge*, E. Coleridge, 2 vols (1904)
Conway, Moncure D., *Autobiographical Memories and Experiences of Moncure Daniel Conway*, 2 vols (Boston, 1904)
Courtney, Leonard, *Life of Lord Courtney*, G. Gooch (1920)
Cremer, Randal, *Sir Randal Cremer: His Life and Work*, H. Evans (1909)
Currie, Bertram W., *Recollections, Letters and Journals*, 2 vols (Roehamptom, 1901)
Curzon, Lord, *The Life of Lord Curzon, Earl Ronaldshay*, 3 vols (1928)
Dana, Richard H., *Hospitable England in the Seventies: The Diary of a Young American 1875–76* (Boston, 1921)
Davitt, Michael, *Michael Davitt. Revolutionary, Agitator and Labour Leader*, F. Sheehy-Skeffington (1908)
Depew, Chauncey, *My Memories of Eighty Years* (New York, 1922)
Dicey, Albert Venn, *Memorials of Albert Venn Dicey*, R. Rait, 2 vols (1925)
Dilke, Charles W., *The Life of the Rt. Hon. Sir Charles W. Dilke, Bart., M.P.*, S. Gwynn and G. Tuckwell, 2 vols (1917)
——, *Sir Charles Dilke. A Victorian Tragedy*, R. Jenkins (1958)
Dow, Neal, *The Reminiscences of Neal Dow. Recollections of Eighty Years* (Portland, ME, 1898)
Dunraven, Earl, *Past Times and Pastimes*, 2 vols (1922)
Eliot, Charles W., *Charles V Eliot*, H. James, 2 vols (Boston, 1930)
Field, Kate, *Kate Field. A Record*, L. Whiting (New York, 1899)
Forster, William E., *Life of the Right Honourable William Edward Forster*, 2 vols (1888)
Fowler, Henry H., *The Life of Henry Hartley Fowler, First Viscount Wolverhampton, G.C.S.I.*, E. Fowler (1912)
Freeman, Edward A., *The Life and Letters of Edward A. Freeman*, W. Stephens, 2 vols (1895)
Frewen, Moreton, *Mr. Frewen of England. A Victorian Adventurer*, A. Leslie (1968)
Froude, James, *James Anthony Froude. A Biography*, W. Dunn, 2 vols (Oxford, 1961–63)
George, Henry, *Henry George*, C. Barker (New York, 1955)

George, *Henry George in the British Isles*, E. Lawrence (East Lansing, MI, 1957)
——, *The Life of Henry George*, H. George Jr (New York, 1900)
Gladstone, William E., *Gladstone*, E. Feuchtwanger (1975)
——, *Gladstone. A Biography*, R. Jenkins (New York, 1995)
——, *Gladstone I: 1809–1865*, R. Shannon (1982)
——, *Gladstone: Heroic Minister, 1865–1898*, R. Shannon (1998)
——, *Gladstone 1809–1874*, H. C. G. Matthew (1986)
——, *Gladstone 1875–1898*, H. C. G. Matthew (1995)
——, *Gladstone and the Irish Nation*, J. Hammond, 2nd edn (1964)
——, *Gladstone. A Progress in Politics*, P. Stansky (New York, 1979)
——, *Gladstone, William, The Prime Minister's Papers: W. E. Gladstone*, J. Brooke and M. Sorensen, 4 vols (1971–81).
——, *The Gladstone Diaries (1825–54)*, eds M. Foot and H. C. G. Matthew, 4 vols (Oxford, 1968–75)
——, *The Gladstone Diaries (1855–98)*, ed. H. C. G. Matthew, vols 5–14 (Oxford, 1978–1994)
——, *Life of William Ewart Gladstone*, J. Morley, 3 vols (1903)
——, *The Political Correspondence of Mr. Gladstone and Lord Granville 1868–1876*, ed. A. Ramm, 2 vols (1952)
——, *The Political Correspondence of Mr. Gladstone and Lord Granville 1876–1886*, ed. A. Ramm, 2 vols (Oxford, 1962)
——, *Speeches of Gladstone*, ed. H. Lucy (1885)
——, *The Speeches and Public Addresses of the Right Hon. W.E. Gladstone M.P.*, eds A. Hutton and H. Cohen, vols ix–x (1892–94)
Godkin, Edwin L., *The Gilded Age Letters of E. L. Godkin*, ed. W. Armstrong (Albany, NY, 1974)
——, *Life and Letters of E. L. Godkin*, ed. A. Ogden, 2 vols (New York, 1907)
——, *E. L. Godkin and American Foreign Policy, 1865–1900*, W. Armstrong (New York, 1969)
Goschen, George, *The Life of George Joachim Goschen*, A. Elliott, 2 vols (1911)
Granville, Earl, *The Life of Granville George Leveson Gower Second Lord Granville K.G. 1815–1891*, E. Fitzmaurice, 2 vols (1905)
Hamilton, Edward, *The Diary of Sir Edward Hamilton 1880–1885*, ed. D. Bahlman, 2 vols (Oxford, 1972)
Harcourt, William Vernon, *The Life of Sir William Harcourt*, K. Gardiner, 2 vols (1923)
——, *Letters by 'Historicus' on Some Question of International Law; reprinted from 'The Times', with additions* (1863)
Hardie, James Keir, *Keir Hardie, Radical and Socialist*, K. O. Morgan (1975)
Hartington, Lord, *The Life of Spencer Compton, Eighth Duke of Devonshire*, B. Holland, 2 vols (1911)
Hay, John, *John Hay: From Poetry to Politics*, T. Dennett (New York, 1933)
——, *Letters of John Hay and Extracts from a Diary*, ed. Mrs Hay, 3 vols (New York, 1969)
——, *The Life and Letters of John Hay*, W. Thayer, 2 vols (New York, 1915)
Holmes, Oliver W. Jr, *Justice Holmes: The Shaping Years, 1841–1870*, M. Howe (Cambridge, MA, 1957)
Holyoake, George, *Bygones Worth Remembering*, 2 vols (1905)
——, *Life and Letters of George Jacob Holyoake*, J. MacCabe, 2 vols (1908)

Houghton, Lord, *The Life, Letters, and Friendships of Richard Monckton Milnes, First Lord Houghton*, T. W. Reid, 2 vols (1890)

Howell, George, *Respectable Radical: George Howell and Victorian Working Class Politics*, P. Leventhal (1971)

Hughes, Thomas, *Thomas Hughes: A Life of the Author of Tom Brown's Schooldays*, E. Mack and W. Armytage (1952)

Hurlbert, William H., *Ireland under Coercion. The Diary of an American*, 2 vols (Edinburgh, 1888)

Hyndman, Henry, *H. M. Hyndman and British Socialism*, C. Tsuzuki (1961)

Ingersoll, Robert, *Letters of Robert G. Ingersoll*, ed. E. I. Wakefield (New York, 1951)

——, *Royal Bob: Robert G. Ingersoll*, C. H. Cramer (New York, 1952)

——, *The Works of Robert G. Ingersoll*, 12 vols (New York, 1902)

James, Henry, *Henry James and John Hay. The Record of a Friendship*, G. Monteiro (Providence, RI, 1965)

——, *The Life of Henry James*, L. Edel, 3 vols (1953)

Johnson, Reverdy, *Life of Reverdy Johnson*, B. Steiner (Baltimore, MD, 1914)

Knaplund, P. and Clewes, C. (eds), 'Private Letters from the British Embassy in Washington to the Foreign Secretary, Lord Granville, 1880–1885,' *Annual Report of the American Historical Association*, vol. i (1941)

Labouchere, Henry, *The Life of Henry Labouchere*, A. Thorold (1913)

Lansdowne, Lord, *Lord Lansdowne: A Biography*, Lord Newton (1929)

Lecky, William, *A Memoir of the Right Hon. William Edward Hartpole Lecky*, E. Lecky (1909)

Lincoln, Robert T., *Robert Todd Lincoln: A Man in His Own Right*, J. Goff (Norman, OK, 1968)

Lockwood, Frank, *Sir Frank Lockwood*, A. Birrell, 2nd edn (1898)

Lodge, Henry C., *Henry Lodge: A Biography*, J. Garraty (New York, 1965)

Lowell, James Russell, *James Russell Lowell*, M. Duberman (Boston, 1966)

——, *James Russell Lowell. A Biography*, H. Scudder, 2 vols (New York, 1901)

——, *Letters of James Russell Lowell*, ed. C. Norton, 2 vols (1894)

——, *New Letters of James Russell Lowell*, ed. M. Howe (New York, 1932)

Lucy, Henry, *Sixty Years in the Wilderness* (1909)

McCarthy, Justin, *An Irishman's Story* (1904)

——, *Reminiscences*, 2 vols (1899)

Macmillan, Alexander, *Letters of Alexander Macmillan*, G. Macmillan (1908)

Marble, Manton, *Genteel Partisan: Manton Marble, 1834–1917*, G. McJinsey (Iowa State, 1971)

Mill, John S., *Autobiography* (1876)

Morley, John, *Early Life Letters of John Morley*, F. Hirst, 2 vols (1927)

——, *Free Minds John Morley and His Friends*, F. Knickerbocker (Cambridge, Mass., 1943)

——, *John Morley: Liberal Intellectual in Politics*, D. A. Hamer (Oxford, 1968)

——, *Recollections*, 2 vols (1917)

Motley, John L., *The Correspondence of John Lothrop Motley*, ed. G. I. Curtis, 2 vols (1889)

Mundella, A. J., *A. J. Mundella 1825–1897. The Liberal Background to the Labour Movement*, W. H. G. Armytage (1951)

Norton, Charles E., *Letters of Charles Eliot Norton*, eds S. Norton and M. Howe, 2 vols (Boston, 1913)

Olney, Richard, *Richard Olney and His Public Service*, H. James (Boston, 1923)

Parnell, Charles, *Charles Stewart Parnell*, F. S. L. Lyons (1977)

——, *Life of Charles Stewart Parnell*, R. O'Brien, 2 vols, 3rd edn (1899)

——, *Parnell and His Party, 1880–90*, C. O'Brien (Oxford, 1964)

Pauncefote, Julian, *The Life of Lord Pauncefote: First Ambassador to the United States*, R. Mowat (1929)

Playfair, Lyon, *Memoirs and Correspondence of Lyon Playfair*, W. Reid (1899)

Plunkett, Horace, *Horace Plunkett: An Anglo-American Irishman*, M. Digby (Oxford, 1949)

Rathbone, William, *William Rathbone, a Memoir*, E. Rathbone (1905)

Reid, Whitelaw, *The Life of Whitelaw Reid*, R. Cortissoz, 2 vols (New York, 1921)

Richardson, J. D. (ed.), *A Compilation of the Messages and Papers of the President, 1789–1897*, 20 vols (Washington, DC, 1899)

Ripon, Marquess, *Life of the First Marquess of Ripon, K.G., P.C., G.C.S.K, D.C.L.*, L. Wolf, 2 vols (1921)

Roosevelt, Theodore, *An Autobiography* (1913)

——, *The Letters of Theodore Roosevelt*, eds E. Morrison and J. Blum, 8 vols (Cambridge, MA, 1951–54)

Rosebery, Lord, *Lord Rosebery*, Marquess of Crewe, 2 vols (1931)

——, *Lord Rosebery's North American Journal – 1873*, eds A. Grant and C. Combe (1967)

——, *Rosebery*, R. James (1963)

Russell, Charles, *Diary of a Visit to the United States of America in the Year 1883* (1910)

——, *The Life of Lord Russell of Killowen*, R. O'Brien (New York, 1901)

Sala, George, *The Life and Adventures of George Augustus Sala, written by himself* (New York, 1895)

Salisbury, Lord, *Life of Robert, Marquis of Salisbury*, Lady Cecil, 3 vols (1922–32)

Schurz, Carl, *Speeches, Correspondence and Political Papers of Carl Schurz*, ed. F. Bancroft (1913)

Seeley, John, *Sir John Seeley and the Uses of History*, Deborah Wormell (Cambridge, 1980)

Smalley, George W., *Anglo-American Memories* (New York, 1912)

——, *George W. Smalley: Forty Years a Foreign Correspondent*, J. Matthews (Chapel Hill, NC, 1973)

——, *London Letters and Some Others*, 2 vols (New York, 1891)

Smith, Goldwin, *Goldwin Smith, Victorian Liberal*, E. Wallace (Toronto, 1957)

——, *Goldwin Smith: His Life and Opinions*, A. Haultain (New York, 1913)

——, *A Selection from Goldwin Smith's Correspondence, Comprising letters chiefly to and from his English friends, written between the years 1846 and 1910*, ed. A. Haultain (New York, 1913)

——, *Reminiscences*, ed. A. Haultain (New York, 1911)

Smith, Samuel, *My Life-Work* (1902)

Smith, William, *Life and Times of the Right Honourable William Henry Smith, M.P.*, H. Maxwell, 2 vols (1893)

Spencer, Herbert, *An Autobiography*, 2 vols (1904)

——, *Life and Letters of Herbert Spencer*, D. Duncan, 2 vols (1908)

——, *The Social and Political Thought of Herbert Spencer*, D. Wiltshire (Oxford, 1978)

Spring-Rice, Cecil, *The Letters and Friendships of Sir Cecil Spring-Rice: A Record*, ed. S. Gwynn, 2 vols (Boston, 1929)

Stead, William T., *The Life of W. T. Stead*, R. Whyte, 2 vols (1925)

Stephen, Leslie, *Leslie Stephen*, N. Annan (1951)

——, *The Life and Letters of Leslie Stephen*, F. Maitland (1906)

Sumner, Charles, *Memoirs and Letters of Charles Sumner*, E. Pierce, 4 vols (Boston, 1881–93)

Vincent, Howard, *Life of Sir Howard Vincent*, S. Jeyes and F. How, 2 vols (1885)

Wallace, Alfred R, *Letters and Reminiscences*, ed. J. Marchant, 2 vols (1916)

——, *My Life, A Record of Events and Opinions*, 2 vols (New York, 1905)

Ward, Samuel, *Sam Ward, 'King of the Lobby'*, L. Thomas (Boston, 1965)

——, *Uncle Sam Ward and His Circle*, M. Elliott (New York, 1938)

Watkin, Edward W., *Canada and the States: Recollections 1851 to 1886* (1887)

Webb, Beatrice, *Beatrice Webb's American Diary 1898*, ed. D. Shannon (Madison, WI, 1963)

——, *Beatrice Webb: A Life, 1858–1943*, K. Muggeridge and R. Adams (1967)

Welsh, John, *Letters of John Welsh, Envoy Extraordinary and Minister Plenipotentiary to the Court of St. James*, ed. E. Stokes (New York, 1937)

White, Henry, *Henry White. Thirty Years of American Diplomacy*, A. Nevins (New York, 1930)

White, Horace, *Horace White, Nineteenth Century Liberal*, J. Logsdon (Westport, CT, 1971)

Wolcott, Edward Oliver, *The Life and Character of Edward Oliver Wolcott*, J. Dawson, 2 vols (New York, 1909)

Books published before 1920

Arnold, Matthew, *Civilization in the United States* (1888)

——, *Discourses in America* (1885)

Aveling, Edward, *The Chicago Anarchists* (1888)

——, *The Working Class Movement in America* (1887)

Bancroft, George, *History of the Formation of the Constitution of the United States of America* (New York, 1882)

Bell, Isaac L., *Notes of a Visit to the Coal and Iron Mines of the United States* (1886)

Bright, John, *Speeches of John Bright, M.P. on the American Question* (1865)

Bryce, James, *The American Commonwealth*, 3 vols (New York, 1888 edn and 1893–95 edn)

——, *Handbook of Home Rule* (1887)

——, *Social Institutions of the United States* (1891)

—— and other authors, *Essays on Reform* (1867)

—— and other authors, *Questions for a Reformed Parliament* (1867)

Caine, William S., *A Trip Around the World in 1887–8* (1888)

Campbell, George, *White and Black. The Outcome of a Visit to the United States* (1879)

Carnegie, Andrew, *An American Four-in-Hand in Britain* (New York, 1884)

——, *Our Coaching Trip: Brighton to Inverness* (New York, 1882)

——, *Triumphant Democracy or Fifty Years March of the Republic* (1886)

Carpenter, Edward, *Civilization: Its Cause and Cure, and Other Essays* (1889)

——, *Towards Democracy* (1905)

Chamberlain, Joseph, *The Radical Programme*, ed. D. A. Hamer (1971)

Cleveland, Grover, *The Venezuelan Boundary Controversy* (New York, 1913)

Collings, Jesse, *An Outline of the American School System* (Birmingham, 1868)

Dale, Robert W., *Impressions of America* (New York, 1878)

Davitt, Michael, *The Fall of Feudalism in Ireland, or the Story of the Land League Revolution* (1904)

Dicey, A. V., *The Law and Working of the Constitution* (1885)

——, *Introduction to the Study of the Law of the Constitution*, 9th edn (1914)

——, *England's Case Against Home Rule* (1886)

Dilke, Charles W., *Greater Britain: A Record of Travel in English-Speaking Countries during 1866 and 1867*, 2 vols (1868)

——, *Problems of Greater Britain*, 2 vols (1890)

Dunraven, Earl, *The Great Divide: Travels in the Upper Yellowstone in the Summer of 1874* (1876)

Eaton, Dorman, *The Civil Service in Great Britain, a History of Abuses and Reforms and their Bearing upon American Politics* (1880)

——, *The Government of Municipalities* (New York, 1899)

Fanshawe, E. L., *Liquor Legislation in the United States and Canada* (1893)

Farrer, T. H., *Studies in Currency, 1898, or Inquiries into Certain Modern Problems Connected with the Standard of Value and the Media of Exchange* (1898)

Freeman, Edward, *Introduction to American Institutional History* (Baltimore, MD, 1882)

——, *Lectures to American Audiences* (1882)

——, *Some Impressions of the United States* (1883)

Frewen, Moreton, *The Economic Crisis* (1888)

Froude, James A., *Oceana, or, England and Her Colonies* (1886)

George, Henry, *The Irish Land Question* (New York, 1881)

——, *Progress and Poverty* (1881)

——, *Protection or Free Trade* (1887)

——, *Social Problems* (1884)

Godkin, Edwin L., *The Problems of Modern Democracy* (New York, 1896)

Goodnow, Frank, *Municipal Home Rule. A Study in Administration* (New York, 1895)

Hatton, Joseph, *To-day in America. Studies for the Old World and New*, 2 vols (1881)

Hatton, Joseph, *Journalistic London. Being a Series of Sketches of Famous Pens and Papers of the Day* (1882)

Holmes, Oliver Wendell, *One Hundred Days in Europe* (1887)

Holyoake, George, *Among the Americans, and a Stranger in America* (Chicago, 1881)

——, *Travels in Search A Settler's Guide Book of America and Canada* (1884)

Hughes, Thomas, *Rugby Tennessee* (1881)

Hurlbert, William, *England Under Coercion* (1893)

Huxley, Thomas, *American Addresses: With a Lecture on the Study of Biology* (1877)

Hyndman, Henry, The *Chicago Riots and the Class War in the States* (1868)

Jennings, Louis, *Eighty Years of Republican Government in the United States* (1868)

Lecky, William, *Democracy and Liberty*, 2 vols (1896)

Leng, John, *America in 1876: Pencillings during a Tour in the Centennial Year: With a Chapter on the Aspects of American Life* (Dundee, 1877)

Lester, Charles, *The Glory and Shame of England*, 2 vols (New York, 1866 edn)

Lloyd, Henry D., *Wealth Against Commonwealth* (New York, 1894)

Lowell, James R., *Literary and Political Addresses* (Boston, 1891)

Lucy, Henry M., *East by West: A Journey in the Recess*, 2 vols (1885)

Maine, Henry, *Popular Government* (1885)

Morley, John, *Burke* (1879)

——, *Critical Miscellanies*, 3 vols (1886)

——, *The Life of Richard Cobden*, 2 vols (1881)

——, *On Compromise* (1886)

Ostrogorski, M., *Democracy and the Organization of Political Parties*, 2 vols (1902)

Playfair, Lyon, *Subjects of Social Welfare* (1889)

Rideing, W. H., *At Hawarden with Mr. Gladstone and other Transatlantic Experiences* (New York, 1896)

Riis, Jacob, *How the Other Half Lives* (New York, 1890)

Rosebery, Lord, *Appreciations and Addresses* (1899)

Russell, Henry B., *International Monetary Conferences: Their Purposes, Character, and Results* (1898)

Sala, George, *America Revisited: From the Bay of New York to the Gulf of Mexico, and from Lake Michigan to the Pacific*, 2 vols (New York, 1880)

Saunders, William, *Through the Light Continent, or, the United States in 1877–8* (1879)

Seeley, J. R., *The Expansion of England. Two Courses of Lectures* (1883)

Shaw, Albert, *Municipal Government in Great Britain* (1895)

Sherwood, A. and Rowntree, J., *The Temperance Problem and Social Reform* (1898)

Smith, Goldwin, *Canada and the Canadian Question* (1891)

——, *Commercial Union in North America* (1897)

——, *Lectures and Essays* (New York, 1882)

——, *Handbook on Commerical Union* (1888)

——, *Essays on Questions of the Day, Political and Social*, 2nd edn (New York, 1894)

Stanley, Dean, *Inaugural on America* (Birmingham, 1878)

Stead, William, *The Americanization of the World, or the Trend of the Twentieth Century* (New York, 1902)

——, *Chicago Today or the Labour War in America* (1894)

——, *If Christ Came to Chicago!* (1894)

——, *'Satan's Invisible World Displayed'; or Despairing Democracy* (1898)

Stephen, Leslie, *Social Rights and Duties*, 2 vols (1896)

Storey, Samuel, *To the Golden Land: Sketches of a Trip to Southern California* (1889)

Swansea, H. V., *Notes of a Tour in America: From August 7th to November 17th 1877* (1878)

Toynbee, Arnold, *Progress and Poverty: A Criticism of Henry George* (1883)

Vincent, Mrs Howard, *Forty Thousand Miles Over Land and Water*, 2 vols (1885)

Vivian, A. P., *Wanderings in the Western Land* (1879)

Walker, Francis, *International Bimetallism* (1896)

Watkin, Edward W., *A Trip to the United States and Canada* (1852)

Wells, David A., *The Silver Question* (New York, 1887)

Youmans, E. L., *Herbert Spencer on the American and the Americans on Herbert Spencer* (New York, 1883)

Some selected secondary works

Adams, E. D., *Great Britain and the American Civil War*, 2 vols (New York, 1925)

Adler, D. R., *British Investment in American Railways, 1834–1898*, ed. M. Hiddy (Charlottesville, VA, 1970)

Allen, H. C., *Great Britain and the United States: A History of Anglo-American Relations (1783–1952)* (1954)

—— and Thompson, R. (eds), *Contrast and Connection: Bicentennial Essays in Anglo-American History* (1976)

Allen, W. E. (ed.), *Transatlantic Crossing: American Visitors to Britain and British Visitors to America in the Nineteenth Century* (1971)

Athearn, R. G., *Westward the Briton* (New York, 1954)

Bagwell, P. S. and Mingay, G. E., *Britain and America, 1850–1939; A study of Economic Change* (1970)

Barker, M., *Gladstone and Radicalism. The Reconstruction of Liberal Policy in Britain 1885–94* (Hassocks: 1975)

Beale, H. K., *Theodore Roosevelt and the rise of America to World Power* (New York, 1963)

Bentley, Michael, *The Climax of Liberal Politics. British Liberalism in Theory and Practice 1868–1918* (1987)

Biagini, E. F., *Liberty, Retrenchment and Reform. Popular Liberalism in the Age of Gladstone, 1860–1880* (Cambridge, 1992)

—— (ed.), *Citizenship and Community: Liberals, Radicals and Collective Identities in the British Isles, 1865–1931* (Cambridge, 1996)

——, *Gladstone* (2000)

Bogdanor, V., *Devolution* (Oxford, 1979)

Bolt, C., *The Anti-Slavery Movement and Reconstruction: A Study in Anglo-American Co-operation, 1833–77* (1969)

——, *Victorian Attitudes to Race* (1971)

Bourne, K., *Britain and the Balance of Power in North America, 1815–1908* (Berkeley, CA, 1967)

Bradley, I., *The Optimists: Themes and Personalities in Victorian Liberalism* (1980)

Brown, B., *The Tariff Reform Movement in Great Britain, 1880–1895* (New York, 1943)

Brown, T. N., *Irish-American Nationalism, 1870–1890* (Philadelphia, 1966)

Burton, D. H., *Theodore Roosevelt and His English Correspondents: A Special Relationship of Friends* (Philadelphia, 1973)

Campbell, A. E., *Great Britain and the United States, 1895–1903* (1960)

Campbell, C. S, *Anglo-American Understanding, 1898–1903*. (Baltimore, MD, 1957)

——, *From Revolution to Rapprochement: The United States and Britain, 1783–1900* (New York, 1974)

——, *The Transformation of American Foreign Relations, 1865–1900* (New York, 1976)

Clapham, J., *An Economic History of Modern Britain, Machines and National Rivalries (1887–1914)* (Cambridge, 1951)

Clark, A. J., *Movement for International Copyright in Nineteenth Century America* (1960)

Clarke, P., *Liberals and Social Democrats* (Cambridge, 1978)

Collini, S., *Liberalism and Sociology: L. T. Hobhouse and Political Argument in England, 1880–1914* (Cambridge, 1979)

Cook, A., *The Alabama Claims, American Politics and Anglo-American Relations, 1865–1872* (Ithaca, NY, 1975)

Curtis, L. P., *Anglo-Saxons and Celts: A Study of Anti-Irish Prejudice in Victorian England* (1968)

D'Arcy, W., *The Fenian Movement in the United States, 1858–1886* (Washington, DC, 1947)

Davis, C. D., *The United States and the First Hague Peace Conference* (Ithaca, NY, 1962)

Emy, H. V., *Liberals, Radicals and Social Politics 1892–1914* (Cambridge, 1973)

Farnie, D. A., *The English Cotton Industry and the World Market 1815–1896* (Oxford, 1979)

Faulkner, H., *Politics, Reform and Expansion, 1890–1900* (New York, 1963)

Field, J. A. Jr, *America and the Mediterranean World 1776–1882* (Princeton, NJ, 1969)

Fine, S., *Laissez Faire and the General-Welfare State: A Study of Conflict in American Thought, 1865–1901* (Ann Arbor, MI, 1956)

Freeden, M., *The New Liberalism. An Ideology of Social Reform* (Oxford, 1978)

Fry, M., *Illusion of Security. North Atlantic Diplomacy 1918–22* (Toronto, 1972)

Garraty, J. A., *The New Commonwealth, 1877–1890* (New York, 1968)

Gelber, L. M., *The Rise of Anglo-American Friendship: A Study in World Politics, 1898–1906* (1938)

Goodwyn, L., *Democratic Promise. The Populist Movement in America* (New York, 1976)

Grenville, J. A. S., *Lord Salisbury and Foreign Policy, the Close of the Nineteenth Century* (1964)

Grimes, A. P., *The Political Liberalism of the New York Nation* (Chapel Hill, SC, 1953)

Hamer, D. A., *Liberal Politics in the Age of Gladstone and Rosebery. A Study in Leadership and Policy* (Oxford, 1972)

Hanham, H. J., *Elections and Party Management, Politics in the Time of Disraeli and Gladstone*, 2nd edn (1978)

Harrison, B., *Drink and the Victorians* (1976)

——, *Separate Spheres. The Opposition to Women's Suffrage in Britain* (1978)

Hartz, L., *The Liberal Tradition in America: An Interpretation of American Political Thought since the Revolution* (New York, 1955)

Harvie, C., *The Lights of Liberalism. University Liberals and the Challenge of Democracy 1860–86* (1976)

Haskell, D., *Index of Contributors to The Nation*, 2 vols (New York, 1953)

Hawkins, Angus, *British Party Politics, 1852–1886* (1998)

Heindel, R. H., *The American Impact on Great Britain, 1898–1914: A Study of the United States in World History* (Philadelphia, 1940)

Heyck, T. W., *The Dimensions of British Radicalism. The Case of Ireland 1874–95* (Urbana, IL, 1974)

Hind, R. J., *Henry Labouchere and the Empire 1880–1905* (1972)

Hofstadter, R., *The Age of Reform* (New York, 1955)

——, *The Paranoid Style on American Politics and other Essays* (New York, 1965)

——, *Social Darwinism in American Thought*, 2nd edn (New York, 1969)

Howe, Anthony, *Free Trade and Liberal England 1846–1946* (Oxford, 1997)

Hurst, M., *Joseph Chamberlain and Liberal Reunion, the Round Table Conference of 1887* (1967)

Jenkins, B., *Fenians and Anglo-American Relations during the Reconstruction* (Ithaca, NY, 1969)

Jenkins, T. A., *Gladstone, Whiggery and the Liberal Party, 1874–1886* (Oxford, 1988)
——, *The Liberal Ascendancy, 1830–1886* (London, 1994)

Kelley, R. L., *The Transatlantic Persuasion: The Liberal-Democratic Mind in the Age of Gladstone* (New York, 1969)

Kendle, John, *Ireland and the Federal Solution. The Debate over the United Kingdom Constitution, 1870–1921* (Kingston and Montreal, 1989)
——, *Federal Britain, a History* (1997)

Kenin, R., *Return to Albion. Americans in England 1760–1940* (New York, 1979)

Kennedy, P. M., *The Samoan Triangle: A Study in Anglo-German-American Relations, 1878–1900* (Dublin, 1974)

LaFeber, W., *The New Empire: An Interpretation of American Expansion, 1860–1898* (Ithaca, NY, 1963)

Lillibridge, G. D., *Beacon of Freedom: The Impact of American Democracy upon Great Britain, 1830–1870* (Philadelphia, 1954)

Lippincott, B. E., *Victorian Critics of Democracy* (New York edn, 1964)

Lorimer, D. A., *Colour, Class and the Victorians. English Attitudes to the Negro in the Mid-Nineteenth Century* (Leicester and New York, 1978)

Loughlin, J., *Gladstone, Home Rule and the Ulster Question 1882–93* (Dublin, 1986)

Lyons, F. S. L., *Ireland Since the Famine (1971)*

Malchow, H. L., *Population Pressures: Emigration and Government in Late 19th Century Britain* (Palo Alto, CA, 1979)

Matthew, H. C. G., *The Liberal Imperialists. The Ideas and Politics of a Post-Gladstonian Elite* (Oxford, 1972)

May, E. R., *Imperial Democracy: The Emergence of America as a World Power* (New York, 1961)

Metcalf, P., *James Knowles. Victorian Editor and Architect* (Oxford, 1980)

Moore, J. R., *The Post-Darwinian Controversies: A Study of the Protestant Struggle to Come to Terms with Darwin in Great Britain and America 1870–1900* (Cambridge, 1979)

Moore, R. L., *European Socialists and the American Promised Land* (New York, 1970)

Morgan, K. O., *Wales in British Politics 1868–1922* (Cardiff, 1970)

Neale, R. G., *Great Britain and United States Expansion: 1898–1900* (East Lansing, MI, 1966)

Nevins, A. J., *America Through British Eyes* (New York, 1948)

O'Brien, L., *Fenian Fever: An Anglo-American Dilemma* (New York, 1971)

Pachter, M. (ed.), *Abroad in America* (Washington, DC, 1976)

Parry, Jonathan, *Democracy and Religion: Gladstone and the Liberal Party, 1865–1875* (Cambridge, 1986)
——, *The Rise and Fall of Liberal Government in Victorian Britain* (New Haven, CT, 1993)

Patterson, D. S., *Towards a Warless World: The Travail of the American Peace Movement 1887–1914* (Bloomington, IN, 1976)

Pelling, H., *America and the British Left: From Bright to Bevan* (New York, 1957)

Perkins, B., *The Great Rapprochement: England and the United States, 1895–1914* (New York, 1968)

Perkins, D., *The Monroe Doctrine, 1867–1907* (Baltimore, MD, 1937)

Phelps, K., *The Anglo-American Peace Movement in the Mid-Nineteenth Century (1835–54)* (New York, 1930)

Plesur, M., *America's Outward Thrust: Approaches to Foreign Affairs, 1865–1890* (Dekalb, IL, 1971)

Pletcher, D., *The Awkward Years: American Foreign Relations under Garfield and Arthur* (Columbia, MS, 1962)

Rapson, R. L., *Britons View America: Travel Commentary, 1860–1935* (Seattle, WA, 1970)

Robinson, R. and Gallagher, J., *Africa and the Victorians: The Official Mind of Imperialism* (1961)

Rodechko, & J. P., *Patrick Ford and his Search for America. A Case Study of Irish-American Journalism 1870–1913* (New York, 1976)

Rodgers, Daniel, *Atlantic Crossings. Social Politics in a Progressive Age* (Cambridge, MA, 1998)

Roper, Jon, *Democracy and its Critics: Anglo-American Democratic Thought in the Nineteenth Century* (1989)

Rossi, J. P., *The Transformation of the British Liberal Party: A Study of the Tactics of the Liberal Opposition, 1874–1880* (Philadelphia, 1978)

Royle, E., *Radicals, Secularists and Republicans: Popular Free Thought in Britain, 1866–1915* (Manchester, 1980)

Russett, C. E., *Darwin in America: The Intellectual Response 1865–1912* (San Francisco, 1976)

Saas, A. P., *Reluctant Icon: Gladstone, Bulgaria, and the Working Classes, 1856–1878* (Cambridge, MA, 1991)

Schrier, A., *Ireland and the American Migration, 1850–1890* (Minneapolis, MN, 1958)

Searle, G. R., *The Liberal Party. Triumph and Disintegration, 1886–1929*, 2nd edn (Basingstoke, 2001)

Short, K. R. M., *The Dynamite War: Irish-American Bombers in Victorian Britain* (1979)

Spence, C. C., *British Investments and the American Mining Frontier, 1860–1901* (1958)

Sproat, J., *'The Best Men': Liberal Reformers in the Gilded Age* (1968)

Stansky, Peter, *Ambitions and Strategies: The Struggle for the Leadership of the Liberal Party in the 1890s* (Oxford, 1964)

Sykes, Alan, *The Rise and Fall of British Liberalism 1776–1988* (1997)

Tansill, C. C., *The Foreign Policy of Thomas F. Bayard, 1885–1897* (New York, 1940)

Thompson, P., *Socialists, Liberals and Labour. The Struggle for London 1885–1914* (1967)

Titlow, R., *American Import Merit: Origins of the United States, Civil Service and the Influence of the British Model* (Washington, DC, 1979)

Tulloch, Hugh, *James Bryce's American Commonwealth: The Anglo-American Background* (Woodbridge, 1988)

Turner, James, *The Liberal Education of Charles Eliot Norton* (Baltimore, 1999)

Vincent, J. R., *The Formation of the Liberal Party, 1857–1868* (1966)

Weintraub, S., *London Yankees: Portraits of American Writers and Artists in England 1894–1914* (New York, 1979)

Welland, D., *Mark Twain in England* (1978)

Wilson, B., *America's Ambassadors to England (1785–1928)* (1928)

——, *Friendly Relations: A Narrative of Britain's Ministers and Ambassadors to America (1791–1930)* (1934)

Learned articles and theses

Anderson, S. L., 'Race and Rapprochement, Anglo-Saxonism and Anglo-American Relations, 1895–1904' (Claremont Graduate School PhD thesis, 1978)

Blake, N. M., 'The Background of Cleveland's Venezuelan Policy,' *American Historical Review*, vol. xlvii (1942)

——, 'The Olney–Pauncefote, Treaty of 1897,' *American Historical Review*, vol. 1 (1945)

Bolt, C. A., 'British Attitudes to Reconstruction in the United States, 1863–77' (London University College PhD thesis, 1966–67)

Boyle, T., 'The Liberal Party and Foreign Affairs, 1895–1905' (Univ. of London MPhil thesis, 1974)

——, 'The Venezuela Crisis and the Liberal Opposition 1895–1896,' *Journal of Modern History*, vol. 1, no. iii (Sept. 1978)

Brooks, D. C., 'Gladstone's Fourth Ministry, 1892–4: Policies and Personalities' (Cambridge University PhD thesis, 1975)

Bullen, M. M., 'British Policy towards Settlement with America, 1865–1872' (Univ. of London PhD thesis, 1955)

Burgess, M. D., 'Lord Rosebery and the Imperial Federation League, 1884–1893,' *The New Zealand Journal of History*, vol. xiii, no. ii (Oct. 1979)

Burton, D. H., 'Theodore Roosevelt and His English Correspondents: The Intellectual Roots of the Anglo-American Alliance,' *Mid-America*, vol. liii (1971)

Campbell, C. S., 'American Tariff Interests ... 1883–1888,' *Canadian Historical Review* , vol. xlv (1964)

——, 'The Anglo-American Crisis in the Behring Sea, 1890–1891,' *Mississippi Valley Historical Review*, vol. xlviii (1961–62)

——, 'The Behring Sea Settlements of 1892,' *Pacific Historical Review*, vol. xxxii (1963)

——, 'The Dismissal of Lord Sackville,' *Mississippi Valley Historical Review*, vol. xliv (1958)

Cannadine, D., 'Urban Development in England and America in the 19th Century: Comparisons and Contrasts,' *Economic History Review*, vol. xxxiii, no. iii (Aug. 1980)

Clarke, P., 'The Progressive Movement in England,' *Transactions of the Royal Historical Society*, 5th series, vol. xxiv (1974)

Collyer, C., 'Gladstone and the American Civil War,' *Proceedings of the Leeds Philosophical Society*, vol. vi (1951)

Crawford, M., 'British Travellers and the Anglo-Saxon Relationship in the 1850s,' *Journal of American Studies*, vol. xii (1978)

——, '*The Times* and America, 1850–1865: A study in the Anglo-American Friendship' (Oxford Univ. DPhil thesis, 1980)

Dunne, T. J., 'Ireland, England and Empire 1868–86: the Ideologies of British Political Leadership' (Cambridge Univ. PhD thesis, 1975)

Dusinberre, W., 'Henry Adams in England,' *Journal of American Studies*, vol. xi (1977)

Edwards, R. D., 'Parnell and the American Challenge to Irish Nationalism,' *University Review*, vol. ii (1958–61)

Finnie, H. M., 'Scottish Attitudes to American Reconstruction, 1865–1877' (Univ. of Edinburgh PhD thesis, 1974)

Gerlach, M., '*The Times* of London: Editorial Policy and the American News, 1850–1861' (San Diego State Univ. MA thesis, 1976)

Gollancz, O., 'Anglo-American Arbitration Policies, 1890–1914' (Cambridge Univ. PhD thesis, 1939–40)

Green, E. H. H., 'The Bimetallic Controversy: Empiricism Believed or the Case for the Issues,' *English Historical Review*, vol. cv (July 1990)

——, 'Rentiers versus Producers? The Political Economy of the Bimetallic Controversy c. 1880–1898,' *English Historical Review*, vol. ciii (July 1988)

Green, J. J., 'American Catholics and the Irish Land League, 1879–1882,' *Catholic Historical Review*, vol. xxv (1949–50)

Griffiths, P. C., 'The Carucus and the Liberal Party in 1886', *History*, vol. 61 (1976), pp. 183–97

Harvie, A., 'Ideology and Home Rule: J. Bryce, A. V. Dicey, Ireland, 1880–87,' *English Historical Review*, vol. xiii (Apr. 1976)

Herrick, F. H., 'Gladstone and the Concept of the "English-speaking Peoples,"' *Journal of British Studies*, vol. xii (1972)

Heyck, T. W., 'Home Rule, Radicalism and the Liberal Party, 1886–1895,' *Journal of British Studies*, vol. 13 (1974), pp. 66–91

Horsman, R., 'Origins of Racial Anglo-Saxonism in Great Britain Before 1850,' *Journal of the History of Ideas*, vol. xxxvii (July–Sept. 1976)

Howe, A. C., 'Bimetallism, c. 1880–1898: a Controversy Re-opened?' *English Historical Review*, vol. cv (Apr. 1990)

——, 'Towards the "hungry forties": free trade in Britain, c. 1880–1906,' in Biagini, E. F. (ed.), *Citizenship and Community: Liberals, Radicals and Collective Identities in the British Isles, 1865–1931* (Cambridge, 1996), pp. 193–218.

Jenkins, T. A., 'Gladstone, The Whigs, and the Leadership of the Liberal Party, 1879–1880,' *Historical Journal*, vol. 27 (1984), pp. 337–60.

Jensen, R. J., 'Eugene Schuyler and the Balkan Crisis,' *Diplomatic History*, vol. v, no. i (Winter 1981)

Johnson, N. E., 'The Role of the Cabinet in the Making of Foreign Policy 1895–95, with Special Reference to Lord Salisbury's Second Administration' (Oxford Univ. DPhil thesis, 1971)

LaFeber, W., 'The Background of Cleveland's Venezuelan Policy: A Reinterpretation?' *American Historical Review*, vol. xlvi (1960–61)

Lawrence, E. P., 'Henry George's British Mission,' *American Quarterly*, vol. iii (1951)

——, 'The Uneasy Alliance, the Reception of Henry George by British Socialists in the Eighties,' *American Journal of Economics and Sociology*, vol. xi (1951–52)

Mann, A., 'British Social Thought and American Reformers of the Progressive Era,' *Mississippi Valley Historical Review*, vol. xlii (1955–56)

Matthews, J. J., 'Informal Diplomacy in the Venezuelan Crisis of 1896,' *Mississippi Valley Historical Review*, vol. 1 (1963)

Nichols, J. P., 'Silver Diplomacy,' *Political Science Quarterly*, vol. xliv (1933)

Parry, J. P., 'Religion and the Collapse of Gladstone's First Government, 1870–1874,' *Historical Journal*, 25 (1982), pp. 71–101

Parsons, F. D., 'Thomas Hare and the Victorian Proportional Representation Movement, 1857–1888 (Cambridge University PhD thesis, 1990)

Pelling, H., 'The American Economy and the Foundation of the British Labour Party,' *Economic History Review*, vol. viii, no. i (1955)

——, 'The Knights of Labor in Britain, 1880–1901,' *Economic History Review*, vol. ix, no. ii (1956)

Pilling, N., 'The Conservatism of Sir Henry Maine,' *Political Studies*, vol. xviii (1970)

Robson, M. M., 'The Alabama Claims and the Anglo-American Reconciliation, 1865–71,' *Canadian Historical Review*, vol. xlii (1961)

——, 'Liberals and Vital Interest: The Debate on International Arbitration, 1815–72,' *Institute of Historical Research Bulletin*, vol. xxxii (1959)

Sandiford, K., 'Gladstone and Liberal-Nationalist Movements,' *Albion*, vol. xiii (Spring 1981)

Seed, G., 'British Reactions to American Imperialism Reflected in Journals of Opinion, 1898–1900,' *Political Science Quarterly*, vol. lxxiii (1958)

Smith, J., 'Anglo-American Rivalries in Latin America, 1865–1895' (Univ. of London PhD thesis, 1969–70)

Stokes, M. B., 'The Origins of the Progressive Mind in the United States: The Social Thoughts of Twelve Progressive Publicists in the Period up to 1910' (Oxford Univ. DPhil thesis, 1977)

Trainor, L., 'The British Government and Imperial Economic Unity, 1890–1895,' *Historical Journal*, vol. xiii, no. 1 (1970)

Trevail, J. J., 'British Opinion of the Afro-American with Special Reference to the Prominent Travellers, 1877–1932' (Univ. of Edinburgh MLitt thesis, 1975)

Tulloch, H. A., 'The Anglo-American Background of James Bryce's *American Commonwealth*' (Cambridge Univ. PhD thesis, 1974)

——, 'Changing British Attitudes towards the United States in the 1880s,' *Historical Journal*, vol. xx (1977)

Ward, J. B., 'Land Reform in England, 1880–1914' (Reading Univ. PhD thesis, 1976)

White, John, 'Andrew Carnegie and Herbert Spencer: A Special Relationship,' *Journal of American Studies*, vol. xiii (1979)

Whitridge, A., 'British Liberals and the American Civil War,' *History Today*, vol. xii (1962)

Index

Abbott, Francis, 58
Adams, Charles Francis, 7–8, 244
Alabama claims
  British attitudes, 80
  British relations, 11–13
Alden, H. M., 50
American caucuses, 61–3
American cities
  Boston, 190–1
  Chicago, 28, 189, 191–2
  municipal corruption, 189–93, 240
  New York, 23, 28, 43–4, 189–93, 240
  San Francisco, 19
American civil service reform, 192–3
American Civil War
  British attitudes, 5–11, 60, 170–1
  Confederate leaders, 46
American Constitution
  Liberals and their views, 101–10, 125–33, 171–6
American currency and bimetallism
  activities and debate, 1880s–1892, 139–42
  presidential election, 1896, 235–8, 241–2
  silver question, 1890s, 176–85, 217–19, 235–8, 241–4
American divorce, 149–51
American federalism
  British views, 101–8, 124–33, 170–6
American labor
  British attitudes towards, 185–9
American Land League (Irish), 83–6
American politics
  British attitudes, 28–9, 55–7, 104–10
  Liberal-Republicans, 24, 64
  Republican leaders, 60–1, 64
  Senate, 104–5, 125, 219
American protectionism and tariffs, 20, 76–8, 133–9

American religion, 43, 146–9
American schools
  colleges and universities, 19
  general systems, 21, 28, 62–3
American society
  Southern states, 45–6, 55
American temperance movement
  British attitudes, 196–7
American woman's suffrage
  British attitudes, 195–6
Anderson, Sir Robert, 87
Anglo-American arbitration
  international movement, 1890s, 213–17, 222–35
  Liberal support for, 169–70
  Venezuelan issue, 221–35
Anglo-American Association, 15
Anglo-American copyright, 142–5
Anglo-American Permanent Court of Arbitration, 229–30
Anglo-American rapprochement
  British views of, 172–3
  general movement, 1890s, 211–46, 257–63
Anglo-Saxonism
  British attitudes, general, 44–5, 165–6, 212
  unity of the race, 21, 54–7, 78–81, 130–3, 215–16, 261–3
Arch, Joseph, 16
Argyll, Duke of, 54, 95–6, 175–6
  Irish Home Rule and federalism, 169–70
Arnold, Matthew, 143, 198
  American federalism, 103
Arthur, President Chester, 72, 76
Asquith, Henry, 164–7, 211, 226–7
Atherley-Jones, L., 220
Atkinson, Edward, 58, 141, 257
  American silver question, 182–5, 217–19, 237
  Venezuelan issue and debates, 224

Balfour, Arthur J., 96, 121, 140, 174,
243
Anglo-Saxon race, 215
bimetallism, 180, 183–4, 217
Venezuela and arbitration, 229,
231, 233–5
Bayard, Thomas, 47, 92–3, 223–4
Bering fishery issues, 165–7
Bimetallic League, 140–2, 185, 236–8,
242–3
bimetallism, international
support for, 1890s, 176–85, 217–19
Birmingham
municipal reform, 190–1
political organizations, 61–3
blacks (African Americans)
British attitudes, 45–6, 55–6, 58
James Bryce's attitudes, 194–5
Blaine, James, 74–6, 91
Gladstone debate, 1890, 136–8
Blandford, Lord, 102
Bodleian Library, 199
Bradlaugh, Charles, 16
Bright, John, 97
British bimetallism
activities and debate, 1880s–1892,
139–42
activities and debate, 1890s,
176–85, 217–19
British protectionism, 133–9
British trade and industry
American impact, 1886–92, 133–9
depression, 1890s, 176–85
free trade advocacy in the 1880s,
76–8
Brussels Conference, 1892, 179–80
Bryan, William Jennings, 235–8,
241–2
Bryce, James
American cities, 189–90, 192–3
American Civil War, 8
American friendships, 128–30,
188–90, 257–62
American labor, 188–9
American silver question, 182
American trip, 1870, 26–9
American trip, 1881, 80–1
Anglo-American copyright, 143–5
democracy views, 239–41

federalism views, 125–30
general observations, 27–8
Irish Question and Home Rule, 84,
101, 104
mentioned, 39, 91, 126, 139, 167,
174
The American Commonwealth,
128–30, 134, 146, 186, 189–90,
195, 258–60
Venezuelan issue and debates,
223–4, 226–7
woman's suffrage, 195–6
Bryce, Lloyd, 136–7, 170
Buckle, Henry, 224
Bulgarian atrocities, 54
Burritt, Elihu, 53

Caine, W. S., 196
Campbell, George, 29, 58, 102
Carnegie, Andrew
American silver question, 182–5
Anglo-American arbitration, 224–5,
231–3
Anglo-Saxon and English-speaking
views, 131–2
friendship with Gladstone, 132,
151–2, 186–7, 197–200
Homestead strike, 186–7, 200
international arbitration, 213–16
Irish Home Rule, 103–5, 107–8
mentioned, 3, 48, 76, 103–4, 107–8,
132, 138, 165, 168, 171, 257,
260–1
Triumphant Democracy, 105,
198–9
views on philanthropy, 151–2
Cavendish, Frederick, 84
Chamberlain, Joseph
American cities, 190–1
American Civil War, 8
American federalism, 101–8
American imperialism and
jingoism, 219–20
American politics, 62–3
American protectionism, 78, 135
Anglo-Saxon race, 216
as Liberal leader, 3, 72, 97–101,
105–10, 175–6
Birmingham politics, 61–3, 190–1

Chamberlain, Joseph – *continued*
  Henry George and land reform,
    96–101
  Irish Home Rule, 75, 101–8
  mentioned, 38–40, 57, 60–4, 77, 90,
    140, 163, 172–3, 187
  Venezuelan issue and debates, 223,
    226, 228, 231, 234–5
Chaplin, Henry, 140, 180, 217, 243
Childers, Hugh, 16, 182
Clan na Gael, 84–94
Cleveland, President Grover, 177,
    192–3, 214, 230, 235, 260–1
  British views of, 91–4, 139, 142,
    167, 217
  Democractic administration, 72,
    101–5, 142, 166, 181
  Irish-Americans, 91–4
  response to international
    arbitration petition, 213–15
  Venezuelan policy, 219–21, 224–7
Cobden, Richard, 60, 78
Coleridge, Lord, 88–9
Collings, Jesse, 14
Conkling, Roscoe, 61
Conservative Party
  leadership issues, 38–40
Conway, Moncure, 22–3
Corinto incident, 168–9
Courtney, Leonard, 95, 107, 140, 174,
    180, 230
Coxe, Cleveland, 148
Cremer, William Randal
  American visit, 1897, 245
  international arbitration, 213–16
Currie, Bertram, 178–9

Dana Jr., Richard Henry, 51
  nomination as British minister,
    53–4
  praise for Harcourt, 8–9
Darby, W. Evans, 216
Davis, Jefferson, 46
Davitt, Michael, 82–3
democracy
  American and British views, 238–41
Democrats (American), 92–4, 101–5,
    138–9
Devonshire, Duke, 176, 225

Devoy, John, 84
Dewess, E. P., 86
Dicey, A. V., 103
  federalism views, 125–6
Dike, Samuel, 150–1
Dilke, Charles
  American Civil War, 8
  American interests, 57
  American trip, 1866, 17–21
  Greater Britain, 18–21
  mentioned, 71, 77–8, 106, 164
Disraeli
  American attitudes, 50–1, 61, 74
Dodge, William
  American International Arbitration
    Movement, 231–2
Dow, Neal, 196
Dunraven, Earl, 133

Eaton, Dorman, 193
Ecroyd, W. Farrer, 76
Eliot, Charles W., 27, 52
Evarts, William, 50, 52, 74

Fair Trade League, 76
Fanshawe, E. L., 196
Farrer, T. H., 143
  American protectionism, 134–6
  bimetallism and silver, 141, 178,
    182, 184, 217–19, 241–4
  civil service reform, 192–3
  democracy views, 239
Fawcett, Henry, 58
Fenianism
  British relations, 11–12, 81–94
Field, Cyrus, 7, 51–3
Field, Henry, 146–9
Field, Kate, 21, 57
Fish, Hamilton, 40
  Gladstone's American positions,
    48–51
Forster, William, 86
Fortnightly Review, 22–3, 57–9, 61–2,
    99
Fortune Bay, 74–5
Fowler, Henry, 183, 222
Fowler, William, 134
Freeman, Edward, 80, 103, 130
Freemantle, Charles, 178

Frelinghuysen, Sec. of State, 90
Frewen, Moreton, 181, 184, 236
Froude, J. A., 130–1

Garfield, President
  assassination, 72, 79–80
Garrison, William P., 167
Geneva Treaty
  general history, 13, 73
George, Henry, 83, 88, 190, 257
  British associations and land
    reform, 94–101
  British Liberal associations,
    95–101
  Progress and Poverty, 95–9
Gibbs, Henry H., 140
Gladstone, Herbert, 105
Gladstone, William Ewart
  'Kin Beyond Sea,' 50, 54–7
  American activities, 1880s and
    1890s, 145–52
  American Civil War, 6–7, 9, 48–51,
    170–1
  American federalism, 101–10,
    124–33
  American foreign policy, 73–6
  American friendships and
    associations, 96–7, 109–10,
    121–53, 145–53, 257–63
  American invitations, 51–3
  American opinion of, 48–57, 220
  American politics, 54–6, 137–9
  American protectionism, 134–9
  Anglo-American arbitration, 221–2,
    229–35
  Anglo-American copyright, 143–5
  Anglo-Saxonism and
    English-speaking views, 131–2
  as Liberal leader, 1–3, 73–6, 84–110,
    163–85, 211–38
  bimetallism, 140–2
  Carnegie friendship, 132, 151–2,
    186–7, 197–200
  clash with Argyll over federalism,
    169–70
  Fenians, 12
  Irish Question and Home Rule,
    101–10, 124–33, 170–6
  Irish-Americans, 84–94

mentioned, 25, 39, 59, 63–4, 77,
    80–1, 95–6, 122, 134, 185,
    194–5, 201
  North American Review, 54–6, 145–51
  temperance movement attitudes,
    196–7
  United States, destiny, 77–81
  Venezuelan issue, 220–2
Godkin, Edwin L., 21, 25, 27, 58, 91,
    104, 125–7, 134, 139, 167, 180,
    188, 194, 226
  democracy views, 238–41
Gold Standard Defense Association,
    185
  bimetallism opposition, 217–19,
    236–8
Goodnow, Frank, 189
Goschen, 177–8, 224
Grant, President, 11, 53–4, 60–1
Granville, Earl, 6, 12, 40, 56, 74–6
  American foreign policy, 73–6,
    84–94
  Irish-Americans, 84, 88–94
Gresham, Walter (Secretary of State),
    168–9

Hall, Oakley, 192
Hamilton, Edward, 76, 81, 222,
    225–6, 243
Harcourt, William Vernon
  American Civil War, 8–11
  American election of 1896, 241
  Anglo-American arbitration, 223–35
  as Liberal leader, 4, 84–94, 163–70,
    178–85, 211–12, 221–35, 241–4
  bimetallism, 142, 178–85, 243–4
  clash over foreign policy with
    Rosebery, 168–70, 222–35
  Irish-Americans, 1880s, 85–94
  mentioned, 38–40, 71, 107, 109,
    126–7, 257–8, 260, 263
  Venezuelan issue and debates,
    222–35
Hardie, Keir, 198
  American labor, 186
Harrison, Frederic, 128
Hartington, Lord, 6–7, 56, 72
Hawaiian Islands, 166–7
Hay, John, 233–4

Hewitt, Abraham, 190
Holmes Jr., Oliver Wendell, 27–8, 59
Homestead strike, 186–7, 200
Hoppin, William, 61, 74–5, 88
Horton, S. Dana, 140
Houghton, Lord, 14
Houldsworth, William, 140, 178, 180
Howell, George, 179
Hurlbert, William, 41–2, 44, 47
Hyndman, Henry, 16

Immigration
  Irish, American, 82–3
Imperial federation, British, 130–3
Ingersoll, Robert
  Gladstone debate, 1887–88, 146–9
International Arbitration and Peace
    Association of Great Britain,
    213–15
international bimetallism, 139–42,
    176–85, 217–19, 235–8, 242–4
International Monetary Conferences,
    139–42
Irish Home Rule
  British politics and the American
    experience, 101–10, 124–33,
    170–6
  Conservative attacks, 125–6
  Liberal policies, 101–10, 124–33,
    170–6
Irish National League, 84
Irish-Americans
  Anglo-American relations, 1880s,
    81–94
  assassination literature, 85–90
  violence, 84–94, 166–7

James, Henry, 41, 48, 59
Jenkinson, Edward, 87
Jennings, Louis, 16, 133
Johnson, Reverdy, 51–2
Johnson, Robert Underwood
  American Copyright League, 142–5

Kimberley, Lord
  American foreign policy, 166,
    168–9
  Venezuelan issue and debates, 221,
    226

Kitson, James, 109–10
Knowles, James, 130, 143

Labouchere, Henry, 95, 102, 106–7,
    174, 230, 237
Latin America
  Anglo-American rivalries, 166–70,
    219–35
Lawley, Francis, 46
Lecky, W. E.
  democracy views, 240–1
Lee, Margaret, 150
Lester, Charles, 9
liberal intellectuals
  British, 24–6
Liberal Party
  American foreign policy, 73–6,
    81–94, 165–70, 219–35
  American protectionism, 76–8
  foreign policy, 38–40, 73–8, 81–94,
    165–70, 219–35
  its position in the 1870s, 38–40
  its position in the 1880s, 71–94,
    121–4
  its position in the 1890s, 163–5,
    211–12
  leadership contests, 1–5, 71–3,
    163–5, 211–12, 225–35
Liberals
  American Constitution, federalism
    and Home Rule, 101–8, 124–33
  American interests, 13–17, 57–64,
    94–101, 258–63
  American silver issues, 139–42,
    176–85, 217–19, 235–8
  American travels, 15–29
  Anglo-American copyright, 142–5
  blacks (African Americans),
    general attitudes, 45–6, 55–6,
    194–5
  diplomacy over Venezuela, 219–35
  George Washington, views of,
    128–30
  Irish-Americans, 81–94
  party leadership, 1–5, 38–40, 71–94,
    101–10, 163–70, 211–35
  transatlantic community, 121–53
Lloyd George, David, 100
Lockwood, Frank, 235

Low, Seth, 188–9
Lowell, James Russell, 27, 59, 74–6, 79, 84, 88–9
Lubbock, Sir John, 140, 237
   American silver question, 180–3
   Anglo-American understanding, 222

Macmillan, Alexander, 15, 22, 59
Maguire, John, 23
Maine, Henry, 124–6
Manning, Henry, 149
Marble, Manton, 140–1
McCarthy, Justin
   American home rule, 102–3
McKinley Tariff, 1890, 135–9
McKinley, William, 137, 235–8, 241–2
Mentmore meeting, 226–7
Monroe Doctrine
   Liberal views of, 220–1, 224, 226–7, 229
Moore, J. S., 91–2
Morley, John
   American federalism, 125–7
   American interests, 57–64, 101–8, 130
   American trip, 1867, 21–4
   Andrew Carnegie friendship, 186–7, 197–200
   Anglo-American arbitration, 224–5, 232–5
   as Liberal leader, 2–3
   democracy views, 240–1
   editor, *Fortnightly Review,* 22–4, 57–9, 61
   friendship, Charles E. Norton, 24–6, 59–61
   Henry George and land reform, 96–101
   Homestead strike, 186–7
   Irish question, 101–4, 107
   mentioned, 38–40, 79, 91, 121, 185
Morrill, Justin, 137
Mundella, A. J., 187, 230

National Liberal Federation, 61–2
Nicaragua, 168–70
Nineteenth Century, 122–4
   American articles, 122–3, 143, 152
North American Review

British liberals and articles, 124, 136–7, 145–51, 170–2, 183, 215, 258
Northbrook, Lord, 74
Norton, Charles Eliot, 24–6, 57, 59–61

O'Connor, A., 133
O'Donnell, Patrick, 88–90
Olney, Secretary of State, 228, 231, 235

Pall Mall Gazette, 79–80, 98
Pan-American Conference, 1890, 177
Parnell, Charles Stewart
   American associations, 16, 82–3
   Irish politics and Home Rule, 84, 127–8
Pauncefote, Julian, 228, 234–5
Percy, George A., 47
Pierrepont, Edwards, 127
Pingree, Hazen S., 192
Playfair, Sir Lyon
   American associations, 16
   American protectionism, 77–8, 134–8
   American silver and bimetallism, 140–2, 218, 237
   Anglo-American and international arbitration, 214–16
   mentioned, 130, 194
   Venezuelan issue and debates, 223–6
Pomeroy, Henry Sterling, 149
Populist Party, 177
Pratt, Hodgson, 213
Presidential election, 1876, 59–60
Presidential election, 1896, 235–8
Pulitzer, Joseph, 220

Raleigh, T., 172
Rathbone, William, 108, 127, 174, 196–7
Reed, John, 184
Republicans (American), 136–9
Rhodes, Cecil, 215
Rice, Allen Thorndike
   North American Review editor, 53–6, 146
Roosevelt, Theodore, 190, 193–4

Rosebery, Lord
  American trip, 1873, 40–5
  American trip, 1874–5, 45–8
  Anglo-American and international
    arbitration, 215–16
  as Liberal leader, 1, 163–70, 211–35
  clash over foreign policy with
    Harcourt, 168–70, 221–35
  friendship, Samuel Ward, 41–2,
    46–8
  general observations, 43–8
  Homestead strike, 186–7
  Imperial federation, 130–3
  mentioned, 63–4, 175
  Venezuelan issue and debates,
    221–7
Rossa, Jeremiah O'Donovan, 83
Rothschild, Alfred de, 178
Rothschild, Hannah, 41
Russell, Lord, 235

Salisbury, Lord, 40, 74, 121
  American attitudes, 105, 215–16
  foreign policy, 1890s, 215–16,
    220
  Venezuelan issue and debates,
    220–35
Sands, Mary, 146, 194
Saunders, William, 100
Schenck, General, 48–9
Schulyer, Eugene, 53–4
Seeley, J. R., 130–1
Selborne, Earl, 88–9
Shaw, Albert, 189
  English-speaking races, 172
Shaw-Lefevre, G. J., 134, 184, 237
Sherman Silver Purchase Act, 181–2
Smalley, George, 48, 143
Smith, Goldwin, 103, 128
  American municipal issues, 189–90,
    192
  American views, 14, 16
  Irish Home Rule, 174–5
Smith, Samuel, 100, 179
Spanish–American War, 245
Spencer, Lord
  Irish-Americans, 86–90
Spring-Rice, Cecil, 181, 194
Stead, William T.

American attitudes, 79–80
American cities and Chicago,
  191–2, 260
American labor, 188
Anglo-American and international
  arbitration, 215–16
Anglo-American Permanent Court
  of Arbitration, 229–30
English-speaking race, 172–3
Venezuelan issue, 219
Stephen, Leslie, 14
Sullivan, Alexander, 87
Sumner, Charles, 7, 13, 21

The Times, 8, 10, 56, 61–2, 172–3
Tilden, Samuel, 61

United States
  British foreign policy, 11–13, 73–6,
    84–94, 165–70, 176–85,
    219–35
United States Supreme Court
  British views, 106

Venezuela
  Anglo-American issue and debates,
    1895–96, 219–35
  Liberals and informal diplomacy,
    219–27
  settlement, 227–35, 244–5
Vincent, Howard, 133
  Irish-Americans, 86–8

Walker, Francis A., 236–7
Ward, Samuel, 41–2, 48
Washington Fishery Treaty
  Conference, 164
Watkin, Edward, 16, 91
Wells, David A., 140
White, Henry, 175, 178–9, 181, 217,
  233
White, Horace, 58, 91, 237–8
Wilson, Charles Rivers, 178
Winthrop. Robert C., 81
Wolcott, Senator
  British visit to study bimetallism,
    242–3

Yarnell, Ellis, 53, 182